Jacobite Estates
of the Forty-Five

Jacobite Estates of the Forty-Five

ANNETTE M. SMITH

Department of Modern History,
University of Dundee

JOHN DONALD PUBLISHERS LTD

EDINBURGH

© Annette M. Smith, 1982

The publishers acknowledge the financial assistance of the Scottish Arts Council in the publication of this volume.

ISBN 0 85976 079 0

Filmset by R D Composition Ltd., Glasgow
Printed in Great Britain by Bell & Bain Ltd., Glasgow

Acknowledgements

The first debt owed by most research workers in Scottish history is to the unfailing courtesy and helpfulness of the staffs of the Scottish Record Office and the National Library of Scotland. I should like to record my gratitude for all the assistance I have received from them over many years. Noteworthy too is the speed with which books and manuscripts appear on one's desk in both these institutions. In the libraries of the Universities of St. Andrews and Dundee, I have also received all the help I could have wished for. The Royal Scottish Geographical Society allowed me access to early maps many years ago. Indeed, so many people have given me assistance over the years that I find it impossible to thank them all individually here and can only hope that they realise how much I have appreciated time and effort spent.

Some, however, must be mentioned. Over the years, I have had many thought-provoking and constructive conversations on the forfeitures with Mrs Virginia Wills and have benefited from her comprehensive knowledge of the contents of the collection of papers concerning the 1745 forfeitures. I have to thank Mrs Carolyn Bain of the Geography Department of Dundee University for preparing Map B in this volume. Mrs Helen Mulvey was responsible for typing my original thesis and Mrs Margaret Greatorex had to cope with the very considerable alterations and additions required to prepare it for publication. For their labour and patience, I am most grateful. My husband's forbearance has been considerable and his grammatical and syntactical help beyond measure.

But the person to whom I owe most is Dr. Ronald G. Cant. He first suggested the subject to me, a subject that has never lost its interest. He supervised my research from beginning to end and was a never-failing source of encouragement and wisdom.

Abbreviations and Spelling

APS   Acts of the Parliaments of Scotland

CHRB   Reports of the Parliamentary Commission for making roads and building bridges in the Highlands of Scotland

E   Exchequer – Prefaces all references to the current cataloguing of the Forfeited Estates Papers, 1745, lodged in the Scottish Record Office

NLS   National Library of Scotland
(Adv. Ms. Manuscripts from the Advocates' Library, obtainable in the NLS)

NSA   New Statistical Account of Scotland

OSA   First (or Old) Statistical Account of Scotland

PLA   Perthshire Local Authority Records – Perth County Justices of the Peace and Commissioners of Supply Records

RHP   Register House Plans (obtainable in the Scottish Record Office)

RSGS   Royal Scottish Geographical Society

SHR   Scottish Historical Review

SHS   Scottish History Society

SRO   Scottish Record Office

    The spelling adopted for families and estates in the Scottish Record Inventory of the Forfeited Estates Papers, 1745 is followed except in the cases of Monaltrie and Cromartie. In the latter case, the family title normally ends 'ie'. Ordnance Survey usage is followed for town names, but other place names and proper names are reproduced as they appear in the original sources, when direct reference is being made to these, even though they are not being quoted verbatim.

    Note on currency: by the eighteenth century, it is usually calculated that twelve Scots pounds equal £1 sterling. Readers are also reminded of pre-decimilisation equivalents, valid for both Scots money and sterling:

        12d. (pennies, pence) = 1s. or 1/- (shilling)
        20/-   = £1

Contents

1

Forfeitures and Management
by the Barons of the Exchequer

IT is not to be wondered at that, in the years immediately after 1745, government circles devoted much thought to the administration of Scotland. In thirty years, three rebellions or risings – as one prefers – had gained considerable military support for Stewart claims to the throne, particularly in the northern parts of the country. This was enough to make the least perceptive of rulers give some thought to possible causes, as well as to preventative and remedial action. Politicians and officials, both Scottish and English, determined that the northern inhabitants should be led to appreciate, as the greater part of the British Isles apparently did, to judge from their reaction to the rebellions, that life under the Hanoverians was infinitely preferable to what the Stewarts had to offer. Furthermore, whether this fact was appreciated or not, it was clearly necessary to ensure that it would be impossible in the future to take up arms to express the opposite conviction. The period after 1715 had seen a similar reaction, resulting in the execution of a few eminent Jacobites, the ostensible disarmament of the Highlands, and the forfeiture of rebels' estates in both England and Scotland. The events of 1745–46 seemed to demonstrate that the steps taken then had not been fully successful, even allowing for the fact that the presence of Prince Charles Edward from the beginning of the rising had roused only a small proportion of the population to military action. Now it was felt that more stringent and effective action must be taken to preserve Hanoverian peace from Stewart disturbance. 'Public opinion was in full accord with the Duke of Cumberland's intention to root out, once for all, any danger to the stability of the government'.[1]

Agreement on the ends desired was one thing, however; agreement on the means to the ends was more difficult to achieve.[2] In government circles it was possible to find advocacy of policies reflecting many shades of opinion, from the vindictiveness of the Duke of Cumberland to the realism of Archibald, third Duke of Argyll. Cumberland was moved by hate and fear of the Scots generally, and of the Highlanders particularly, declaring 'I tremble for fear that this vile spot may still be the ruin of this island and our family'.[3] Argyll, on the other hand, tacitly accepted the facts of Scottish life; he knew that many families totally loyal to Hanover had Jacobite connections, while many who had not openly supported the rebellion would not have been unhappy had Charles Edward reached London. Argyll therefore tried to temper the wind of repression so that the mistaken English belief that all Scots were rebels and Jacobites at heart would not become fact through resentment. Somewhere in between these two were the pragmatists who thought that the rebellion offered an opportunity that must be seized;

Scottish laws and institutions that in 1707 had been left intact, and indeed somewhat irrational in the views of eighteenth century 'enlightened' thinkers and improvers, could now legitimately be altered for the better or abolished. Those in power were faced with the dilemma of reconciling these views or of imposing their own, and the decisions of the years after 1745 reflect the shifting balance of power in Parliament at the time. Between 1746 and 1748, the Dukes of Newcastle and Cumberland had similar views on foreign policy and cooperated with some success in that field. Success in one area led to acceptance by the king of their ideas in others. Hence Cumberland's Scottish policy predominated, as Newcastle was not specially interested; therefore the restoration of law and order by punitive measures predominated.

An Act of Attainder was passed in June 1746,[4] and for the second time in thirty years heads were lost, some noble, some humble. Of the nobles captured, Lords Balmerino, Kilmarnock and Lovat were beheaded. About eighty others were executed at various places, but in June, 1747, an Act of Indemnity was passed.[5] Other measures, similar to but sterner than those put into effect after 1715, were expected to be more successful. The Disarming Act, passed in 1746,[6] stipulated heavier penalties and more certain methods of achieving the aims of the act. The Highlands were defined in the act as 'Dumbarton, such parts as lie upon the east, west and north side of Lochleven, to the northward of that part where the water of Leven runs from Lochleven, Stirling, north of the Forth, Perth, Kincardine, Aberdeen, Inverness, Nairn, Cromarty, Argyll, Forfar, Banff, Sutherland, Caithness, Elgin and Ross'. The use of Highland dress was forbidden in 1747 and wardholding as a system of tenure was abolished. This very ancient method of landholding – by which the vassal rendered military services to his superior – was one of the last remnants of the feudal system in Scotland. Henceforth, a fixed sum, a feu-duty, was to be paid to the superior, and if the Crown was the feudal superior, only blench was due, i.e. a nominal sum or token payment.

There was general approval in Scotland for that measure, but an easy passage through Parliament was secured largely by separating it from the act abolishing the heritable jurisdictions.[7] The suggestion that the long-established practice of private law-giving should be swept away roused widespread opposition among Scots of all political persuasions and in all parts of the country, but the necessary Act was passed nonetheless.[8] On the grounds that it was correcting a 'wrong and dangerous model of government', Lord Hardwicke, the Lord Chancellor, pushed the bill through, in the face of both the Court of Session's argument that the Treaty of Union had confirmed possesion of such heritable jurisdictions and Argyll's doubts about the political expediency of a step that would seem a punishment to all Scots. As Argyll's henchman, Lord Milton, pointed out, many of the jurisdictions were in the hands of the king's best friends and it did not seem a sensible time to disoblige them. Though the peers voted in favour, even Argyll's faction among Scottish M.P.'s in the House of Commons refused to support the bill, because of the certainty that so doing would cost them votes. Argyll did manage to secure the retention of the baron courts because of the use made of these by Lowland lairds. But had the only aim of this act been the curbing of the chiefs' powers, it could be criticised as misdirected. Far less tangible assets than legal rights had brought the clans out in 1745; MacDonald of Keppoch was only one among many who had no heritable jurisdiction. The measure has been described as an example of the growing tendency to expand the power of the central government, as well as the desire for rationalisation of the Scottish legal system.[9] Another modern historian considers that even an independent Scotland would have been forced to take some similar action.[10]

While Cumberland's ideas held sway, as they did in the immediate post-Culloden years, the heaviest penalty apart from loss of life was also imposed on many of the rebels. Their estates were forfeited to the Crown. Like disarmament, this had been tried after 1715 with indifferent results. Many of the estates forfeited then had found their way back into the hands of the forfeiting families. Settlement of the debts of lawful creditors, costs of management and payment of the commissioners appointed to value and sell the estates had absorbed almost all the profits, so that there was little material gain for the state. It is also doubtful if the shareholders of the York Buildings Company which bought many of the largest estates felt they had benefited.[11] Further, the 1715 and 1745 affairs seemed to give the lie to the belief that the fear of forfeiture totally restrained the disaffected. Memories of the ineffectiveness of the earlier proceedings led to the airing of various solutions of the problem posed. One question was whether the estates should be forfeited to the Crown or to their feudal superiors; another concerned the type of management needed. Should they be kept by the Crown or sold? Or should they be used to reward government supporters? There would have been nothing new in either of these solutions. What is interesting in the light of later events is that, as early as July, 1746, there were suggestions that forfeited estates should be held on a permanent basis as Crown land,[12] a suggestion that was realised in 1752, when legislation annexed fourteen of the estates 'unalienably' to the Crown,[13] only thirteen in fact being affected in the long run.

However, in the atmosphere of these post-rebellion years, anything but simple forfeiture could be interpreted by Cumberland and those who thought like him as being too kind and lenient to the Scots. So despite any doubts about the efficacy of the measure, in 1747 it was decreed by Parliament merely that 'all and every Lands, Heretages, Debts or Sums of Money, Goods or Chattels whatsoever' and generally the 'Estates, Goods and Effects Heretable and Moveable, Real and Personal, descendible to Heirs or Executors, Jurisdictions, Life-Rent Rights' belonging to any persons attainted for treason between the 24 June, 1745 and the same date in 1746 were to be 'discovered, known, described and ascertained, and that Rents, Issues and Profits be brought for the Use of His Majesty'.[14]

The administration of all estates affected was made the responsibility of the five Barons of the Exchequer Court in Scotland, despite the knowledge that the Lord Chief Baron and his name, Idle, were well-suited. His habit of spending as much time as he could furth of Scotland did not expedite business, but, as he was Hardwicke's man, this arrangement gave the Lord Chancellor opportunities to intervene in Scottish affairs, just as later, Henry Pelham corresponded secretly with Baron Edlin, another Englishman on the Exchequer Court, who became one of the first Commissioners for the Annexed Estates.[15] Nevertheless this was a logical allocation of duties, for the Scottish Court of Exchequer acted 'as a kind of subordinate Treasury for Scotland'.[16] Nor were the Barons strangers to the business of forfeitures. Since the dissolution of the Board of Trustees and Commissioners appointed to deal with the 1715 forfeitures, the Barons, now an 'ancient and unhealthy' group, had been trying, if somewhat lethargically, to complete the settlement of claims of creditors still outstanding from that time.

On this occasion, no special board was to be appointed with outrageous salaries, as happened earlier. The Exchequer Court, operating with a quorum of three, was given very clear instructions in the Vesting Act as to how the estates should be managed. The Barons were empowered to arrange for the states to be surveyed, to discover the whole extent of what was forfeited; to appoint the necessary surveyors, messengers and officers; to decide on their salaries and to ensure that these servants took oaths of loyalty to the king. Rents once obtained from the tenants were to be paid to the Receiver-General of His Majesty's Land Rents and Casualties in Scotland and, by him, passed on to the Exchequer at Westminster. A Register of names and estates of those attainted was to be drawn up and anyone unwilling to be examined on the subject could be sent to gaol without trial. Inventories of the forfeited persons' goods were to be made, auctions held of personal and moveable goods, and lists of debts were to be verified. Thereafter the Register was to be open for inspection at the Court of Exchequer, free of charge, between the hours of ten and twelve on any lawful day, as were the copies sent to the Commissioners of the Treasury and to the sheriffs of all the shires in which forfeited estates were to be found. If the king did not make due provision for the payment of lawful debts within twelve months, the Barons might sell parts of the estates to settle proven claims. Otherwise they were to sell under the instructions given in the act of George I's reign, which empowered the Barons of the Exchequer to sell estates forfeited after 1715 under the same rules as the Commissioners and Trustees.[17] These rules were laid down in the act of 4 George I, c.8., and provided that, after claims were determined, public notice was to be given of public roups or sales. Only Protestants could buy; the proceeds were to be paid into the Exchequer in England and conditions were also made about various legal technicalities which might affect property such as arrears, encumbrances, etc. The Barons in the meantime were responsible for day-to-day management, but only on a 'care and maintenance' basis, keeping the properties in good condition so that a good purchase price could be obtained, but not tying up money or land in long-term schemes of improvement which might discourage prospective buyers. For example, leases were allowed for only three years' duration.

A very important part of the whole process of forfeiture concerned the creditors of the attainted. Just as the Clan Act of 1715 had aimed at trying to ensure loyalty by offering inducements such as two years free of rent to loyal tenants of rebellious landlords,[18] so the government after 1745–46 wished to avoid penalising, and thereby possibly alienating, supporters who had had quite lawful dealings before the rebellion with persons who turned out to be active supporters of the Stewarts. Provision had to be made to pay all just debts. It was therefore enacted in the

Vesting Act that claims for money and goods must be made within three months from the entry of an estate in the Register and claims for real estate within six months. Written on parchment, all such claims were to be sent to the Court of Session, whose decision on their legality was to be final, though thirty days were allowed in which to appeal for a reversal or an amendment of their decree. This is one of those rare occasions on which one can point to a lesson learned from history. After 1715, creditors' appeals and counter-claims of the Commissioners when appeals against them were successful could be taken from the Commissioners who first handled all claims to a specially constituted Court of Delegates. The Court of Session could overturn the decisions of the Delegates and thereafter there could be recourse to the House of Lords. Apart from leading to interminable delays in settling claims and therefore in selling estates, the legal processes ate away much of the profit expected. This protraction of business was to some extent, though not wholly, avoided after 1746.

Rules for examining witnesses and for hearing cases were also simplified, the Court of Session being authorised to act 'in a summary way' and without the usual formality of a Court of Law. Justice had to be seen to be done, of course, and the King's Advocate or, in his absence the Solicitor-General, was to act on behalf of the Crown, while witnesses had to produce all relevant documents in court. Successful claimants were given certificates to present to the Barons of the Exchequer if money was involved. They were then given debentures in return for which the Receiver-General was to reimburse them from rents and profits in his hand. Where 'honours, castles, manors' or other real estates were concerned, the Court of Session could authorise the sheriffs of the respective counties to deliver the property to the claimants. The Court was also empowered to rank claimants, an essential step in cases where debts due far outstripped possible profits from rentals or purchase price.

Before the Vesting Act had been passed, the Scottish Barons of the Exchequer had been somewhat taken aback to receive instructions from the Treasury official John Scrope, in September 1746, that they should take steps to 'prevent waste or spoil' on estates of attainted rebels. Their response, two months later, had been the properly legalistic one that such an enquiry as Scrope advised could not be carried out until escheats and certificates of the persons attainted had been transmitted to them.[19] In the following summer, however, by which time the estates were vested in the Crown with responsibility delegated to the Exchequer Court, the Barons emphasised the need for speed and protested about the delay in their being informed by those officials who had the records. Their delay in answering Scrope's letter and, later, their complaints over Treasury dilatoriness were unfortunately omens of the standard of administration and of the relations between the two bodies which persisted throughout their association with the forfeitures.

Separate records of all forfeited estates business were kept in the Scottish Exchequer and the relevant minute books open on 3 August 1747.[20] Within a week, an office staff had been appointed specially to deal with forfeitures. They included a secretary, David Moncrieffe, a register, Wyvel Boteler, an auditor, John Philp, an accomptant, John McDougal, and George Clerk as a Clerk of

Discoverys (*sic*), i.e. discoveries of forfeited property. All had salaries of £100 per annum and clerks who earned £20.[21] The Barons also set out to find surveyors and factors with the stipulation that no man should serve in both capacities on the same estate. The surveyors were employed to produce the rentals of the estates forfeited or believed to be forfeited.

Immediately, of course, protests against forfeitures and claims from creditors poured into the Scottish courts. It was not to be expected that parents, heirs, widows and children of attainted persons would lightly accept the financial loss which would result from legal forfeiture and sale of the family properties. The last two categories of claimants particularly would in normal times on the death of husband or father have most needed and expected income from these lands. Another interested group included all the feudal superiors of estates affected who had remained loyal to the Hanoverians and had hoped to benefit by the Clan Act. John Farquharson of Invercauld, for example, claimed Monaltrie as subject superior, but he lost his case as he had been a rebel in 1715 and so could not say that he had 'continued' in 'dutiful and loyal allegiance'.[22] Few of these people left any legal stone unturned in their attempts to circumvent the government's intentions, while lawful creditors very properly sought their legal rights, and unlawful creditors did their best to save or make something from the forfeitures.

Mrs. Jean Mercer, the widow of Robert Mercer of Aldie who was killed at Culloden, claimed that that estate was her property and therefore could not be affected by his crime. After she died, her eldest son pursued the claim and had it sustained by the Court of Session in February, 1752.[23] The Clanranald estate was found not to be forfeited on the purely technical grounds that the attainder mistakenly named Donald MacDonald; both the clan chief and his heir 'Young Clanranald' who had fought with Charles Edward had the Christian name of Ranald. The mistake was venial, for the second son of the chief was also a captain in the rebel army and his name was Donald.[24] Alexander MacDonald of Keppoch was killed at Culloden, as was Lauchlan MacLauchlan of MacLauchlan, and their heirs claimed successfully that therefore the attainder and the succeeding forfeitures could not stand.[25] Keppoch was surveyed but rent was never collected by Crown officials and, when the Barons tried to remedy this in 1755, the Court of Session pronounced in favour of Alexander MacDonald's son, yet another Ranald.[26] The estate of John MacKinnon of MacKinnon, with a rental of £500.7.10⅓, the Barons admitted to having surveyed by mistake as he had remained loyal during the rebellion.[27]

None of the subject superiors succeeded in their claims, though the very fact of their having claimed prevented the payment of creditors. The Court of Session could determine debts only on estates definitely known to be forfeited. In the event, of the fifty-three estates surveyed by the Barons' officers, only twelve escaped forfeiture, despite cases being taken to the House of Lords.[28] Those finally included were widespread throughout Scotland from Roxburgh to Cromarty, though property in the Highlands and the north-east far outweighed that from the central and southern parts of the country.[29] They ranged in value, too, from the wide acres of the titular Duke of Perth to the pitiful possessions of Patrick Lindsay, a farmer at Wester Deanhouse in Peeblesshire. At the time the latter was executed, he owed £25.3.11 in arrears of rent and owned only £23.10.3 of household goods, mostly 'much wore and tore', broken or very old, including his deceased wife's old clothes.[30]

Settling the claims of creditors was a laborious task for, as the Barons pointed out in 1750, there were 'a Multiplicity of Claims of Debts' which 'must necessarily occasion a great deal of labour and Expence in discussing these Claims which is not less necessary, that many of the Claims may upon tryal be found good, which will diminish the profit of the Forfeitures to his Majesty'. This comment came at the end of a list of estates and attainted persons which could produce £16,285.17.7 in rent, £19,345.14.4⅙ of personal estate and claims for £277,127.4.8 in debt as well as claims for possession of whole or part estates on various grounds.[31] However, in 1753, it was claimed in a letter to the Treasury that the total value of the estates forfeited far exceeded the amount of debts claimed,[32] despite at least nine being found to be bankrupt.[33]

The final date for submitting claims was 22 July 1748, and in December, 1749, 1485 had been made, though many were eventually found to be fictitious.[34] They included every imaginable form of financial transaction. There were comparatively simple matters such as arrears of wages and accounts unpaid because the attainted person went off to join Prince Charles. A gardener at Murthly and James Drummond, a dyker at Bridgend of Earn, claimed that they had not received wages due them of £2.11.6 and £6.8.0 respectively.[35] William Drummond, an Edinburgh bookseller, wanted payment for £7.6.9 worth of goods supplied to Lord James Drummond before the rebellion.[36] There were, of course, many straightforward claims on bonds for large and small sums signed either by the forfeiting owner of estates or by his predecessors. Many Scottish landowners were accustomed to keep themselves in ready money by borrowing on the security of their estates; their heirs on succeeding then had to sign bonds corroborating the earlier bonds. Many lenders seem to have been quite happy to use this transaction as a type of bank, accepting interest with little hope of speedy return of all or indeed any of their capital, but content as long as land was in the background to back up the debtor's commitments. The defeat of the rebels and the resultant forfeiture of their estates removed this security as well as the income arising from interest paid. Many creditors must have suffered inconvenience, if not financial embarrassment and certainly alarm, at the unexpected threat to their wealth, and the disruption of a considerable number of normal Scottish financial arrangements must have caused as much inconvenience as the rebellion itself.

The position of debts on the Cromartie estate was complicated by the fact that the estate was entailed so that, in theory, payment of debts thereon was limited to those undertaken during the holder's life. Indeed, the Earl of Cromartie's creditors had had adjudication of the estate before the rebellion, thus exercising their rights under Scots law to get possession of a debtor's rents in order to gain payment of their just dues.[37] Annexation and the later special provision made by Parliament for the payment of all debts on annexed estates cut this Gordian knot.[38] Lady Balmerino not only claimed possession of lodgings and a yard in Leith as part of her jointure, but declared that she was due £102.2.11 $\frac{9}{12}$ besides, on the grounds that some goods sold with her husband's furniture had in fact been hers by a deed of gift.[39] At least one estate, Arnprior, was burdened with pensions to the widow not only of the immediate owner but of his predecessors.[40] Many of the wives, widows and children of attainted rebels were in dire need in the period immediately after Culloden, though many benefited from the king's generosity, being awarded sums under the Royal Sign Manual. By 1764 the Receiver-General had paid out £18,135.4.11 $\frac{3}{12}$ to needy relatives of the forfeited.[41] Helen Stewart, widow of Allan Cameron of Callart, received £168.15.0 in 1747, but repaid this generosity by retaining possession of her husband's estate and refusing to pay any rents. Her jointure, which she no doubt looked on as still legally hers, was a considerable part of the property. Her son made kelp, illegally in light of the forfeitures, and on at least one occasion, in 1754, the factor promptly seized it and sold it so that the profit came to the state. The factors, in this case Colin and then his nephew Mungo Campbell, were often on the horns of a dilemma, as were the Barons. Not without sympathy for people in such circumstances as Mrs. Cameron, the factors had to meet the Barons' demands for rents, just as the Barons had to account to the Treasury.[42]

Despite the work involved, and the complaint of the Barons that the Court of Session was not informing them of its decisions,[43] by November 1754, William Alston, the Barons' Solicitor for Claims before the Court of Session, was able to report to the Treasury that all the claims were determined except those on estates holding of subject superiors, over which the Court had no jurisdiction.[44] This was not in fact the case; Lovat claims were still being discussed in 1760[45] but at least considerable progress had been made. In 1780, the House of Commons was informed that £92,558.0.10 $\frac{3}{12}$ had been paid to creditors on the estates under the management of the Barons, which had been sold for £98,715.19.4 $\frac{6}{12}$. Debts to the small extent of £135.9.4 $\frac{10}{12}$ had not been claimed.[46] These sums did not include the claims made on annexed estates which were of similar magnitude, so the Court of Session had shouldered a heavy burden.

While the Lords of Council and Session struggled to settle the financial position of the Crown's new possessions vis-a-vis creditors, the Barons of the Exchequer did not delay their initial foray into management of these lands and other property. Undeterred even by the uncertainty of forfeiture in some cases, they arranged for their surveyors to set to work on over fifty estates, including personal and heritable property. Most of the surveyors appointed were writers, i.e. lawyers, from various parts of Scotland. All appointments had to be approved by the Treasury, to try to ensure that officials were both loyal and honest. Even such scrutiny did not wholly succeed in that troubled period. The sub-factor on Lovat, Mr. James Grant, was dismissed early in 1753 because of disorderly behaviour by himself, his servants and his family. Despite all the legislation, rules and regulations to the contrary, they had carried arms and worn Highland dress.[47]

On 9 August 1747, however, Francis Grant, brother of Lord Prestongrange, and David Bruce took the necessary oaths of loyalty as chief surveyors on all the estates, except those belonging to the Earl of Cromartie and Lord Lovat.[48] The

Treasury agreed to the Barons' suggestion that Hugh Monro of Teaninich should survey these two, as he spoke Gaelic and was a native of 'these estates'; presumably they hoped that he would find it all the easier to discharge his duties.[49] The instructions given to surveyors were comprehensive. They were directed to take full and true information of rentals, from rental books, tacks and leases, and on oath from those with no tacks or leases; to enquire into conditions of existing tenures, to find which tenants were sufficient, which not; to notice the conditions of the houses, barns, etc.; to take the yearly value of yards, orchards, parks, inclosures, meadows, any ground enclosed, dovehouses, coneygares (*anglice* – rabbit-warrens), or other properties, not under rental, as well as woods, fishings, lime quarries, coal and salt works and any other casual estates. They were also to enquire if any 'waste or spoil' had been committed on the premises. Further, houses and people were to be searched for goods belonging to the attainted, while all cattle, horses, sheep, etc. were to be sought and secured. Charters and other papers were to be seized and finally, at least once a fortnight, the surveyors were to remit to the Deputy Remembrancers an exact journal of their proceedings.[50]

The difficulties of such a survey in some parts of Scotland hardly need elaboration. At any time there would have been physical and climatic problems to increase the expense as well as the time required, and the surveyors' difficulties were not lessened by the political atmosphere. As Bruce pointed out, he and his attendant carried out their duties 'at considerable risque of personal injury and danger'. They had been obliged to 'ly for the most part in our cloaths, at best having no other bed than heath or straw spread upon the ground . . . and not certain when we lay down but our throats might be cut before morning'. They also had to carry food, as 'the prices were never so extravagant'.[51] The hardships they faced did not lose in the telling, partly because they had to tell their story so often in order to obtain their just dues. In the late 1750s and in 1760 the surveyors were still asking for their salaries, and must often have regretted that they had made no stipulation about payment before they began their work.[52] The 'inclemency of the weather and the bad accomodations' were trying enough; Bruce, in addition, had had to borrow £1208 to finance his expeditions. The Barons had not provided him with the wherewithal to meet demands such as that of the Sheriff of Argyll. This gentleman had insisted that his substitute with an attendant and a horse should accompany the surveyors on their trips to the islands, their subsistence being provided by the Barons' officials. Further they had to make him a payment of £40.

The Barons had their own difficulties where forfeited estates finance was concerned. When the Treasury ordered payment to Bruce, in 1755, for his surveys of estates found later not to be forfeited, the Barons asked pertinently what funds were to be used, as there was little lying in the Receiver-General's hand arising from the forfeitures.[53] The figure of £1,400 reported as expenditure on surveys in 1752 was kept so low partly by neglecting to pay the surveyors.[54] Without willing cooperation from all concerned, it would have been a difficult task to obtain a certainly accurate survey, even before 1745. Rentals and agreements about services were as likely to be carried in factors' and folk memories, as to be written; marches were not always clearly defined; the inhabitants tended to be argumentative. In the late 1740s, cooperation was the last thing to be expected. Tenants sometimes resisted appearing before the surveyors[55] and the evidence of those who did come was not always dependable. In 1754–55, James Small produced a rental for Cluny differing radically from earlier lists, because subtenants had finally admitted that they were used to paying far more than they had stated before.[56] Hugh Monro found the families of the forfeiting earls of Lovat and Cromartie so 'obliging' that his work was eased in one respect, but on the other hand, he could not obtain the Lovat estate books and rentals. The factor, Thomas Fraser of Gortuleg, had been excepted from the Act of Idemnity and not surprisingly refused to show face.[57] Some parts of forfeited property had simply disappeared. Lord Balmerino was reputed to have owned houses in Dundee, but they could not be found. It was assumed that in 'time out of mind' they had become ruinous and that the magistrates had disposed of them to anyone prepared to rebuild.[58]

Further complications in completing surveys were caused by the Scottish form of landholding called wadset. This was a type of extended mortgage by which the owner leased out land almost indefinitely on receipt of a lump sum. Some of the estates forfeited were affected by such arrangements and, in others, there was some doubt as to whether lands had been disponed irredeemably or in wadset. Lovat had disposed of several parts of his estate in 1744 and 1745. The buyers, all Frasers, protested against their lands being surveyed as forfeited, and the Barons' Clerk of Discoveries and their Secretary for Forfeitures had to settle the matter by comparing the names of the lands in the Books of Sasine with those in the survey. The Duke of Atholl claimed that part of Lochgarry had been set (*anglice* – let) in wadset by one of his predecessors and that he could therefore redeem it. As he had neglected entering his claim within the six months from the date of the estates being registered, as directed by the Vesting Act, he tried legal action before the Court of Session to cancel the survey so that he could contest the case.[59] Lochgarry was one of the estates annexed in 1752, however, and as he was found to be its feudal superior, the Crown bought the superiority, with those of other annexed estates similarly held, in 1770.

One of the surveyors' comparatively small problems was trying to put a value on some of the large houses and castles on the estates which were too large for tenants and not really suitable for private persons. Grant's solution was to leave them out of the valuation altogether, but this was not completely satisfactory.[60] Others were returned as personal estate, but this too led to difficulties, for the Barons then inquired about discrepancies between the valuation and the amounts recovered when such things were sold. The loss of just over £33 on the sale of Cromartie's furniture was of course nothing compared to the unobtainable £3120 valuation placed on the two houses included in the list of his personal estate (£1350 on Castle Leod and £1770 on New Tarbat).[61] The problem could only be overcome by sale but, as one percipient commentator pointed out, no-one was likely to purchase such houses until the estates on which they stood were sold.[62]

Despite these many obstacles in their paths, the chief surveyors reported in December 1748 that their task was completed.[63] They were over-optimistic of course. It could not have surprised Hugh Monro that the Lord Advocate advised the Barons in June 1749 that he had reason to believe that the estate of Lovat had not been accurately surveyed. We have already noted his difficulties with the factor, and Monro had already commented that the rental there was £1000 *per annum* less than he had expected and had always believed it to be.[64] 'Discoveries' of property legally forfeited but not found in the initial surveys continued for many years thereafter. In 1750, an oil mill in Angus was found to have belonged to Alexander Kinloch.[65] In 1756, Mungo Campbell, factor on Lochiel, was instructed to survey remote Barrisdale, as the earlier survey was considered illegal[66] and, as late as 1764, James MacPherson of Killihuntly gave information about money belonging to McPherson of Cluny. He may have regretted doing so, for some of the Cluny tenants took exception to his action and at one point he was chased across country by a throng of bloodthirsty women, who he claimed were men in women's clothes – a charge that finds itself often repeated in Highland history.[67] In this case, the factor, James Small, was ordered to protect him and prosecute anyone who further 'insulted' Killihuntly, but whatever the benefits of official protection, the social disadvantages following behaviour similar to his was such as must have daunted all but the most stouthearted Hanoverian. In an environment where good or bad relationships with neighbours did much to make or mar life, it was more comfortable to be in agreement with the majority, or at least with one's nearest neighbours. There can be little doubt that, in these years, the majority view in the Highlands was against the government, or at least against the changes being imposed by the government and its agents.

Concurrently and associated with the surveyors' problems went those of the factors appointed to manage the estates. In June 1748, John Campbell of Barcaldine, factor on Perth, Strathallan and Gask, wrote that those serving under him must carry arms for their safety.[68] The Barons were sufficiently impressed by his arguments to ask the Commander-in-Chief in Scotland, General Bland, for a licence for Barcaldine to keep eighteen stands of arms and, in 1749, the Barons' Secretary for Forfeitures, David Moncrieffe, wrote to Major-General Churchill, Commander-in-Chief of H.M. forces in North Britain, that it was impossible to levy rents on Dungallon and Lochiel without military assistance.[69] The type of reaction with which factors had to deal is vividly and indignantly described in a letter from Colin Campbell of Glenure, the first factor on Ardsheal, Callart and part of Lochiel, who alone among the officers of the Barons or the Commissioners for the Annexed Estates achieved posthumous fame by being murdered. He wrote to Baron Maule that he found that a decreet or any other legal step to levy the king's rents was treated as a matter for ridicule. The tenants on Kinlochmoidart had warned the bailies on that estate that they would blow their brains out if they dared take any part of the tenants' belongings for payment of rent. The crowning insult was a message from John Cameron of Fassifern, brother of the attainted 'Gentle' Donald of Lochiel, which was delivered to tenants in Campbell's presence, threatening them that if they paid him any rents – 'To me, the King's factor', he wrote in pious horror – it must be 'at their perral'.[70] Campbell must have thought this poor return for his risking reprimand from the Barons for disobeying one of their rules by letting a farm to Fassifern, a relative of an attainted person.[71]

The factors were burdened with relatively few rules and regulations, but one of the most important ones was 'You are on no condition whatever to sett a farm to any of the friends of the forfeiting persons', friends here having the Scottish meaning of relatives. Aimed at extirpating any remnants of Jacobite influence, this order could on occasion lead to results that were not economically desirable. The Barons wished to have Laurence Oliphant of Condie, a relative of the forfeiting Laurence Oliphant of Gask, removed from his tenancy on the estate of Gask, but they yielded to the factor's argument that he was the only substantial tenant on the estate and certainly the only one who paid his rent with any degree of regularity.[72] Nor was this attitude carried to its logical conclusion for, in 1753, Condie was allowed to buy the estate.[73] Sympathetic neighbours and friends had combined with him to put up the money to buy it on behalf of the rebel, having first spread rumours belittling its value. In this they enrolled the tenants' help. The purchasers had to sell two of the baronies comprising the estate to recover their capital and they then formed a trust to run the remaining barony of Gask. In 1763, Mrs. Oliphant of Gask was awarded a pension of £111 by George III, and her husband returned to his ancestral home, apparently with the tacit consent of the government. Though not master of his estate and not wholly satisfied with the management of the trustees, he lived there quietly until his death in 1767. The difficulties faced by the government in trying to wipe out Jacobites as opposed to Jacobitism is well illustrated in Gask's case. Not only sympathisers colluded in assisting Condie to buy his relative's lands; Lord Dupplin, a member of the government but also a neighbour of the Oliphants, refrained from bidding for the estate which would have been a convenient addition to his own property.[74]

A further attack on Jacobitism was the decision that no factor should be connected with the forfeiting persons or under the influence of neighbouring families.[75] The government would have liked to import Lowlanders and Englishmen to hold these posts, but wiser counsels prevailed. As Baron Maule pointed out, anyone but a Highlander would have needed an interpreter to carry out his duties properly, but the government remained suspicious. In 1751, Henry Pelham was still asking questions about factors who were Highlanders. Perhaps the murder of Colin Campbell of Glenure may have allayed some of his worries, but the discovery that John Rutherford, factor on Lord George Murray's estate, had been a rebel did nothing to convince him that any Scots could be trusted.[76]

The factors' duties naturally reflected the Barons' functions, which in turn were one manifestation of government policy, the rooting out of attachment to the Stewarts, the removal of their supporters where possible, and the maintenance of the estates in reasonable running order so that they could be sold as soon as possible, preferably to loyal subjects of George II. Hence we find the arbitrary orders for 1751: 'You are to make it your business to inquire which of the tenants have been in rebellion . . . If any of the tenants behave in a way not agreeable to you, you are to turn them out so soon as leases expire'.[77] A later list of 'Instructions given to the Different Factors on the Forfeited Estates', sent from the Exchequer Chambers in July, 1755, included also the order we have already seen concerning leases to relatives of forfeiting persons, and the following: 'You are never to give power of subsetting to any tenant to whom you grant a lease. You are to let all your farms for which judicial rentals cannot be got by public cant or roup, and one express article shall be in the roup that no person, though the highest offerer, shall be preferred unless he go voluntarily before a J.P. and take the oath of allegiance. You are to recover the rents as far back as the year 1745 and do ultimate diligence against them.'[78] None of these rules carried out to the letter would have endeared the factors to the inhabitants, and their frequent repetition may indicate that factors interpreted their orders with commonsense and sympathy or both, with regard to the realities of their situation, face to face with tenants.

Any person known or suspected to be connected with the rising, however remotely, was likely to be penalised. Such tenants were the first to be evicted or prosecuted for non-payment of rents. In 1755, John Campbell of Barcaldine was ordered to prosecute tenants on the Perth estate for arrears of 1752 and was specifically instructed to start on those who could not prove their loyalty.[79] And this was nine years after Culloden. Any official who had unauthorised dealings with relatives of the attainted was liable to instant dismissal, like the luckless ground-officer on the estate of Nairn, who sold trees on the estate and gave the money to Lady Catherine, wife of the attainted and long bankrupt John Nairn.[80] In the light of later certainty that no further Stewart attempt on the throne was likely to succeed, the fears evinced seem extravagant and the resultant repression vindictive, but this is a judgement made with hindsight. The Barons' attitude to any of the Crown's tenants whose loyalty was at all in doubt was only one facet of the many-sided attack on the possibility of further upheavals, and was imposed on them by the government. The officers on the ground – factors, baron bailies, ground-officers, foresters – did not have an enviable task. Factors' letters show how little sympathy they found in the Highlands, though the comparatively few lowland estates gave less trouble. The Lovat factor faced not only tenants' hostility but that of the local gentry. When fishermen from the north-east ports such as Banff tried to collect mussels from the Lovat scalp, first the local populace beat them off. The factor called in the military to protect the undoubted rights of the Crown and found himself ordered off by the local gentlemen who then sold the mussels themselves, stating that the proceeds were for the poor.[81]

Often the forfeiting owner as well as his wife managed to remain on his estate, a focus for old loyalties. They were also a handy recipient for rents, and tenants were much happier to pay them than the Crown's factors. The question of rests (*anglice* – arrears of rent) became a very vexed one. In 1749, the official estimate of rests due to the Crown was £14,445.10.4⅔; the total rental of forfeited estates was variously estimated but was probably about £12,000. In 1751, the Barons wrote to the Treasury that surveys had produced a rental of £16,285.17.6; £5000 had to be deducted for estates not forfeited or bankrupt before 1745, and they added that in fact very little rent had been paid at all.[82] A great number of the tenants declared they had previously paid the forfeiting owner, his wife or other agent, and they often had receipts to prove it. It soon became obvious that it was well-nigh impossible to exact rents for a second time from the poverty-stricken inhabitants, and adjustments had to be made. Mrs. Oliphant of Gask had uplifted the rents from that estate and all the Barons could suggest was that the tenants must pay up again and have recourse to her for recompense, but eventually receipts from wives and mothers were accepted.[83] For example, the factor on Kinlochmoidart was told that he could count such receipts for the years before the Barons took over, as long as the ladies or their factors were present to discharge their debts.[84] Similarly, in 1760, the Barons agreed to accept the receipts of John Gordon of Glenbucket for 1745–1750, when the tenants sent in a petition representing how little they were able to pay more.[85]

The Clan Act was another possible source of loss of income to the Crown until 1748. Then the parts referring to the rights of loyal tenants and superiors were repealed. For example, John Fraser of Bochrobine obtained a decreet from the Sheriff of Inverness on behalf of his ward, a Fraser of Inverlachine, authorising him to uplift the rents of the estate of Lovat for 1747. As a feudal subject remaining loyal to the Hanoverians, the Clan Act allowed him to obtain the use of his superior's land as a reward.[86] The Barons were further inhibited by the uncertainty about the ownership of estates which were being claimed by subject superiors and others – or so they said in 1751 when the Treasury complained about the lack of visible profit coming in. They were unwilling to risk the expense of legal action against dilatory tenants when they might discover that these arrears were really owed to some owner other than the Crown.[87] Collection of arrears certainly occupied a considerable amount of the factors' time, but it is arguable that this was normal,[88] as was the need to keep a close eye on tenants' crops and markets where victual rent was due.[89] John Campbell of Barcaldine was put out by being summoned to Edinburgh just when he was collecting rents, and told the Barons that the best time to see them was just after the harvest when he would be finished.[90] Even good tenants could face bankruptcy if all arrears were collected, and many believed like the Frasers that, by not participating in the rebellion, they were entitled to benefits under the Clan Act, such as two years free of rent. Barcaldine, however, thought that most would prefer paying to facing a lawsuit and he was given permission to try to collect arrears over three years.[91]

At the time neither general nor particular conditions favoured the Highland region where most of the estates forfeited lay. When owners joined the rebel army, ordinary estate business was perforce interrupted, though members of the family and factors did their best. The passage of fighting troops of both sides brought few benefits, and while what one can call an 'occupying force' in the post-45 period may well have been an essential factor in keeping order and preventing further outbreaks of support for the Stewarts, it could also be another source of trouble. General Beauclerk pointed out that deserters, for instance, became thieves because they 'can at no time live peaceably to get an honest livelihood in the Highlands'.[92] The delay in determining ownership after the passing of the Vesting Act did more damage, for it was unlikely that relatives or agents of possible losers would spend any profits they collected on repairs and maintenance. For their part, the Barons had often little or no cash available and were equally unwilling to risk what might have become illegal expenditure, if estates were declared not forfeited. Other losers in these troubled times were creditors on estates where there was doubt about the legality of the forfeiture and on those claimed by subject superiors. The Court of Session had no power to determine claims in either of these cases until ownership was settled, and this could be a question that took years to decide.

Even under happier circumstances, the temporary nature of the Barons' responsibilities was bound to be reflected in their approach to estate-management, and hence in the nature of the factors' duties. The Barons' main purpose was to sell off the forfeited estates as profitably as possible, pay creditors with the proceeds and hand over any surplus to the crown. As a result there was no concerted programme of improvement and certainly not one which would have involved any large, long-term expenditure. There was a veto on subsetting, which was considered to give the tenant too much power over those to whom he subset. Holdings were to be set at no lower a rent than before 1745 but no purposeful attempt was made to raise them. The prohibition on leases of more than three years was rigidly adhered to. Even a farmer like Patrick McIntyre, on Glenforstan in Kinlochmoidart, who could point to consistent improvement of his land and farm buildings, was rebuffed. The factors therefore had no need to oversee tenants' methods; their main concern was to collect rents and ensure that tenants were reliable subjects and regular payers. They also had to make sure that owners' rights were maintained for the future, as in specifying services of labour and carriage when setting new tacks.[93]

On the other hand, the Barons did countenance expenditure on essential maintenance, on improvements which affected neighbours who would bear their due share of the cost, such as straightening marches, on obligations which the forfeiting owners had shouldered voluntarily and on the usual public burdens of cess, stipends and schoolmasters' salaries. Woods were cared for, though Mrs. Cameron of Callart for one was critical of their management on her husband's estate and, on at least one occasion in 1752, took the law into her own hands and had trees felled. The factor, however, managed to stop John McKerlie's ship that was carrying the timber and repossessed it for the Crown. Woods were of course a profitable source of income when properly looked after. Robert Pringle of Clifton, a neighbour to the Graden estate previously owned by Henry Kerr, asked if a meadow on Graden marching with his land could be drained. As he made the very fair offer that he would pay half and in addition keep the drain in order during his tack, this was agreed.[94] When proof was given that Lachlan MacPherson of Cluny had mortified 8000 merks for a school at Ruthven, there was little hesitation in continuing the yearly allowance of 100 merks.[95] A rather large outlay on the estate of Pitsligo was queried. The factors' accounts for crops 1754, 1755 and 1756 included £379 for seven new boats, as those belonging to the estate had been 'dashed to pieces' in March, 1756, but an obligation to replace boats was laid on the owner, and appeared in the judicial survey. Also seven new houses had been built for the fishermen, the heritor and tenants sharing in the upkeep.[96] The library on the Perth estate was given an airing when it was reported that the books were 'perishing for want of air', and the factor was told to take one of the family with him when he went to arrange this.[97]

Of course, it was to the Crown's benefit to keep all these new possessions in good order to get a better price, and once all the necessary legal steps had been taken, then estates were advertised for sale in various newspapers, the *Caledonian Mercury*, the Edinburgh *Courant* and some of the London papers.[98] Unfortunately for the Crown's convenience, there was no York Buildings Company to step in on this occasion, as after the 1715 forfeitures, and in many cases buyers were hard to find. This was hardly surprising for, apart from the unsettled atmosphere in the north, the Company's example was not encouraging; it was still struggling with its unprofitable purchases. Some conditions imposed may also have lowered the attractions of the various properties for prospective purchasers. For instance, the clause in the Vesting Act reserving the patronage of kirks to the Crown was sensible in the context of increasing government influence in disaffected areas, but it removed a source of patronage which landowners enjoyed on other estates.

Even in more peaceable parts of the country, it was not always easy to dispose of the various types of property. The superiorities of Balmerino were offered for sale on several occasions in 1752, and eventually, at the creditors' request, the estate was offered in 'lots and parts', but it was some time before a buyer of repute appeared at the roup.[99] John Hay of Restalrig had £830 deposited in the Bank of Scotland and also seven shares in the bank. Hay had paid up only half the capital on these, £3,500 Scots (£291.13.4 sterling) instead of £7,000 Scots. They were worth $45\frac{1}{4}$% above par and by 1753 had accumulated £119.11.8 sterling interest. The secretary of the bank, James Spence, suggested they should be put up to roup for buyers to offer what they thought they were worth but the shares failed to elicit offers in 1753.[100] An odd situation arose in the case of the estate of Sir William Gordon of Park in Banffshire. His brother, Captain John Gordon, obtained the entailed part,[101] but bids were made and accepted for the unentailed lands of Brackenhills and Rothmackenzie in Fordyce parish and Thorax in Marnoch. Alexander Brebner, a Portsoy merchant, was the highest bidder in 1756, and he went into residence and remained in possession without making any payment at all.[102] In August, 1764, we find the Park creditors petitioning the Exchequer as Brebner had not yet paid for his purchase. He claimed that he had been misled about its value and wanted a reduction,[103] but the sale was declared null and void, the lands were once more advertised and they were bought by the Earl of Findlater and Seafield. Two years later, however, Brebner was still in possession and the authority of the Sheriff-Depute was required to turn him out. Tenants were ordered to pay their rents to this officer, who then handed on the proceeds to the Receiver-General, but it was March, 1769, before payment of the creditors was possible.[104]

So far, attention has been focused mainly on forfeited landed estate, and most of those attainted did own land and a wide variety of other types of property. But some were not landed proprietors and indeed, a few had neither land nor any other form of real estate. Nevertheless, their possessions were also vested in the Crown and had to be dealt with, though they did not involve management problems on the same scale. The largest purely monetary estate was that of David Wemyss, Lord

Elcho, eldest son of James, fourth Earl of Wemyss, who has obtained posthumous fame for his narrative of the campaigns of the Forty-five, *A Short Account of the Affairs of Scotland in the years 1744, 1745, 1746.* His father had settled £10,000 on him, which his brother, Francis Charteris, redeemed. Francis had taken the surname of his maternal grandfather on succeeding to the latter's estates.[105] The Barons proposed lending this capital to the British Linen Bank, but the Treasury refused to countenance allowing the money out of government hands.[106] Merchants like James Nicolson, vintner and coffee-house keeper in Leith, and George Abernethy in Banff had their wealth, such as it was, invested largely in shops and housing.[107] The same legal processes had to be followed, however, as were used in deciding ownership and value of the largest areas of land.

As one estate after another was sold, the work handled by the Exchequer officers was naturally less onerous. Similarly, as the number of cases determining claims decreased, if slowly, the Barons realised that there was no longer the same need for solicitors to act for them in the Court of Session. The validity or illegality of the greater part of creditors' claims had been determined, even though payment might not immediately follow. One solicitor was dismissed in 1752 and the other's salary was reduced by £50, though it was accepted that the secretary's work might thereby be increased until estates were sold.[108] Two years later, Wyvel Boteler's post of Register of Forfeitures was 'sunk' with Treasury permission[109] and, in 1760, there was a further reduction of various officers' salaries because of the decrease in the volume of work connected with the forfeitures.[110] There were still a few cases outstanding, such as that of the Park estate, and the creditors of Charles Gordon of Terpersie were not finally satisfied about the ranking of their claims until 1779,[111] but the bulk of business connected with estates definitely forfeited or found not to be forfeited was over by the time George III became king.

In June of 1754 the Treasury Lords encouraged speedy sale of unannexed estates to cut down the costs of management, but the Barons had had to remind them on another occasion that, on some estates, debts and claims had been adjudged twelve months before and, that if no provision was made by the Crown to retain the estates and satisfy creditors, they must sell.[112] Treasury dissatisfaction with and suspicion of the management of the forfeited estates in Scotland pervades correspondence with the Barons. We have seen that they were unhappy about the factors appointed; the financial situation was another source of worry. In 1749 there was a protest about £100 salary for the solicitor,[113] though it does not seem overgenerous when one thinks of the amount of business he had to deal with. Sitting in London, Pelham also thought the numbers of officials appointed excessive[114] and, in 1754, the Treasury expressed great surprise that the Barons could not provide a general view of the forfeitures because their solicitor had not yet supplied them with an exact full picture. The Barons were driven to the lame excuse that the solicitor had been dangerously ill, but that, in any case, they could not send any money to London until creditors' ranking had been settled, as they considered it would be unjust to expect claimants for small sums to go so far to collect their debts.[115] Treasury interest in the Barons' management of the estates was more intense at this date, as the Duke of Newcastle was trying to root out the corruption and inefficiency he believed, with some reason, to be widespread in official Scottish financial matters.[116] Administrative mistakes and delays were not all on one side, however, and the Barons, had they been so inclined, could have listed Treasury sins of omission and commission which had handicapped them.

In 1750, the Treasury urged the Barons to sell 'forthwith' lowland estates on which claims had been decided[117] and between 1751 and 1766, twenty-one in the Highlands and the Lowlands were disposed of. However, the sale of these estates affected by the Vesting Act of 1747 did not end the Barons' share in duties connected with the post-45 forfeitures. Doubts arose about the ownership of the whole of five and of parts of two which were annexed to the Crown in 1752, because of their being held of subject superiors. Implementation of the Annexing Act in these cases was delayed until the Crown bought the superiorities in 1770 and, in the meantime, their management was left in the hands of the Scottish Exchequer. Finally, in 1784, the Annexing Act was repealed and the Barons were once more involved in the financial aspects of forfeiture, an involvement which lasted into the nineteenth century.[118] But this is to anticipate, and we must now consider the passing and the working of the 1752 Annexing Act.

2

The Annexing Act

THE Vesting Act had been so worded that, if the government desired, the forfeited estates could be retained as Crown land. The idea of permanent annexation of at least some of them, particularly those situated in the Highlands, became increasingly popular among the Scottish ruling classes of every political persuasion, from Culloden onwards. There was no wish to see the former owners slipping back into possession, reinforcing the pernicious influences that most of those in authority aimed at eliminating.[1] Duncan Forbes of Culloden was active as ever in adopting and pressing ideas which he considered would benefit Scotland and the Highlands, and was one of the first to suggest annexation, in 1746, the year before his death. However, Argyll and the Earl of Findlater, speaking from opposite sides of the political spectrum, were best able to keep the idea of annexation, if not in the forefront, at least present in the mind of the ministry. Though Lord Milton initially thought the possible income from the estates so small that it would be advisable to sell them all, his own strong opinions on how the Highlands' problems should be solved induced him to work on a draft bill for annexing some of them, taking advice from both political allies and opponents. In addition, he and Argyll, whose spokesman and agent he normally was, thought it would be useful for the Crown to obtain by straightforward purchase a block of estates quite apart from the forfeitures, particularly where the proprietor's loyalty was questionable. Presumably an element of compulsion was considered, and the fact that a similar idea made its appearance among Cumberland's friends is an illustration of the agreement among the Scottish ruling classes on the subject of the Highlands.[2]

However united Scottish politicians may have been, it would have been quite impossible for them to enforce such a proposal as annexation without a considerable measure of government support. Such support became feasible only after Pelham's influence grew in domestic affairs, in comparison with that of his brother Newcastle's and Cumberland's, as their foreign policy ran into difficulties for some time from 1746 onwards. Pelham, who had what has been called 'a soothing influence on politics',[3] was, like Argyll, in favour neither of harsh punitive measures in Scotland nor of radical changes in the country's institutions. However, the warnings of one government spy, with the splendid pseudonym P.O., that the Jacobites believed the loss of their estates would not be permanent, were bound to give him pause. The Lord Chancellor Hardwicke, already predisposed towards radical reform, was also broadly sympathetic to any proposals which might assist his long-term aims so that the schemes propounded in Scotland met with his general approval. Pelham's conversion added to Hardwicke's convictions ensured that once a bill was formulated which met two conditions, then, at a convenient time, the government would assist its passage through Parliament. These two conditions were that, firstly, it must satisfy the large number of Scots who were just as tired as the English of the difficulties to which the social and economic structure of the Highlands gave rise and secondly, at the same time, it must avoid rousing too many English suspicions that treatment of the rebel Scots was softening. It was 1752 before a suitable occasion occurred.

In the meantime, in the years preceding the successful passing of the Annexing Act, the ultimate aims of annexation, the methods of achieving these aims, and arrangements for administering the estates were widely dicussed in Scotland. Lord Milton, with Lords Elchies and Tinwald and Lord Advocate Grant, who eventually introduced the bill into Parliament, produced one plan, co-operating at various times with the Earl of Findlater, and his son, Lord Deskford, as well as Lord Arniston, who were not often to be found in such agreement with the first group. General Bland, the Commander-in-Chief in Scotland, sent a paper entitled 'Proposals for Civilising the Highlands' to the *Caledonian Mercury* in June, 1747, but he seems to have been prompted by Milton;[4] a draft bill produced at Argyll's request was probably written by Milton, Elchies and Bland with Tinwald acting as the constructive critic, and it was the model for the eventual act. One of the Scottish Exchequer judges, Baron Reid, wanted a parliamentary grant of £20,000 for the purpose of building roads, schools, villages and harbours, something Parliament at the time was not likely to agree to. Most of these plans demonstrate a certain amount of altruism, but one may beg leave to suspect some self-interest, when Lord Glenorchy advocated that any such expenditure should be supervised by leading Highlanders such as himself.

Whatever the differences of opinion over methods, there was striking unanimity among all likely to be concerned with the administration of Scotland over the main evils that must be eliminated. Many conscientious men of affairs believed, like Duncan Forbes, that one of the first duties of a Scottish statesman should be the destruction of the distinctive, or what many Lowlanders and Englishmen would have preferred to describe as the deplorable, features of Highland society.[5] These were poverty, even more obvious than in the Lowlands, and the overweening power of the chiefs. The Society in Scotland for Propagating Christian Knowledge, usually abbreviated to SSPCK, would have added the prevailing religion and the climate, but had to accept that nothing could be done about the latter. It was thought that the chiefs' influence must be undermined first, because it was assumed that there was little hope of introducing either enlightened ideas on education, religion and politics, or practical assistance in forwarding modern industry and improving agricultural practices, so long as what the non-Highlander saw as the subservience of the commons persisted. Much of the repressive and punitive legislation was expected to erode the clan system and thus to start the process of freeing the ordinary Highlander from bonds which, oddly enough, did not seem to irk him. The process was bound to be a lengthy one and, in the early 1750s the Highlands, though no longer in a state of active rebellion, were hardly pacified. Garrisons were still necessary at Fort Augustus and Fort William; a new fort, Fort George, was considered essential, and information sent to the

Duke of Newcastle in 1750 declared that 'Highlanders seem more inclined to rebellion than ever'.[6]

In these circumstances and in light of English nervousness, it is remarkable that the Annexing Act reached the statute book, embodying as it did the second stage of the reformation of the Highlands, by the attempted alleviation of social and economic ills and modernisation with the help of the state. It was not new for government or Crown to attempt to control wild areas by granting land to known and trustworthy supporters, the Ulster Plantation and the Fife Adventurers of the early seventeenth century demonstrating the belief that it was possible to graft loyalty and obedience on rebellious shoots; but there was a novel conception in the philosophy of the majority of the proponents of annexation. This was that the proceeds of the estates should be devoted solely to benefiting the area wherein they lay, and not to filling the pockets of either the Privy purse or of those supporters of the monarch brave or foolish enough to risk their money and often their lives in the venture. The act shows unmistakable traces of philanthropy towards, and an embryonic sense of the value of, different regions of the United Kingdom, which has expressed itself in various guises from the foundation of the Board of Trustees for Manufactures and Fisheries in 1727 until it reached its apotheosis in 1965, as far as Scotland is concerned, in the Highlands and Islands Development Board. To ensure its passing, in the atmosphere of the late 1740s and the early 1750s, such bounty had to be somewhat disguised for the benefit of English M.P.'s and concealment was attempted by laying great emphasis on establishing law and order as well as 'civilisation', the usual contemporary description of the proposed transformation of the Highlands into a carbon copy of the Lowlands. Not only abstract ideas were to be introduced; Pelham seems to have suggested German 'colonists' and it was implied that immigrants from other parts of Britain, especially England, would be encouraged to create a situation similar to that in Ireland.[7]

There were abortive attempts to persuade the government to introduce an annexing bill before 1752. Political in-fighting which absorbed energies at Westminster was one cause of delay; the Scots were sometimes diverted and divided by other Scottish issues, and Hardwicke also claimed lack of Parliamentary time on one occasion. More immediately relevant to the question of annexation in the years between 1746 and 1752 were the problems of settling creditors' claims for repayment of their debts, a decision on feudal superiors' possession of some of the forfeited estates, and the funding of any financial outlay, should the proceeds from rents and purchase price be insufficient to pay debts or to buy superiorities. Also vital was the decision as to which estates should be annexed. The uncertainty which surrounded so many is well illustrated by the list proposed by Milton, Deskford and Lieutenant-Colonel David Watson, a friend of Cumberland's, who was Quartermaster-General for Scotland. They included one that was not to be forfeited, Glencoe, and several that were later sold, but none that could be described as Lowland.[8] The Barons, it will be remembered had been urged to sell off Lowland estates as soon as the rights of claimants were determined. The Court of Session's dilatory treatment of claims was one, though not the only, factor which protracted the Barons' handling of the forfeitures, and their slow progress threatened to delay annexation also. First Pelham and then Hardwicke displayed some anxiety, for it became obvious that the sums involved were very great when compared with the value of the land bearing the debts. The two English politicians had to be careful not to offend English parliamentary susceptibilities by appearing to make rebellion pay. Then, not least among the problems that had to be solved before annexation became politically practicable, was that of deciding the identity of those who would administer the estates.

Compromises and solutions were gradually worked out, largely by Scots, but once the government had accepted these, it was Pelham's control of the House of Commons which was of most importance in pushing the bill through. He was helped by the greater interest among M.P.'s at the time in subsidies to European allies but, even so, dislike of Scots in general and of the Duke of Argyll in particular pervaded the debate. The accusation that the whole affair was a Scottish 'job' must have been nourished by the clause allowing for payment of lawful creditors by aids granted by Parliament, especially when the amount due was disclosed. There was, of course, no other practicable way of dealing with the debts on the estates for, as the Barons of the Exchequer pointed out later, in 1756, if all the debts were to be paid out of rents, those on the Perth estate, for instance, being about £55,000 while the rents were about £3,000, then 'the Annexing Act will be rendered extremely pointless at least for some years'.[9]

Opposition in the House of Lords was more dangerous, and better organised by the Dukes of Cumberland and Bedford, who declared that if mild measures were applied to Scotland 'rebellion would become a national malady'.[10] But attitudes in the upper house really reflected English politics more than any true interest in Scotland. Cumberland, who had been prepared to stomach annexation as a police measure, had taken umbrage at the neglect of his opinions in formulating the terms of the act, and Bedford had fallen out with Newcastle in the summer of 1751; so both used the debate to demonstrate their antagonism to the government. Perhaps the most intelligent and pointed criticism came from the Earl of Bath who pointed out that, in the five years of forfeiture since 1747, no money whatsoever had reached the Exchequer, and that the Treasury's present calculations were vague in the extreme. Bedford's suggestion that estates should be sold to the highest bidder was summarily disposed of by Hardwicke. He argued that private persons would be unwilling to bid against friends of forfeiting families and, in any case, could rarely match the latter's offers; too many of the disaffected could afford to pay more, as they would not need to honour many of the genuine debts, such as settlements on wives and daughters, and they could assume too that false claims, which had slipped through the legal nets, would be dropped.

Government peers painted a glowing picture of the benefits which annexation would bring and their prognostications are worth noting for, elaborating on and in combination with the contents of the act, they foreshadowed practically every aspect of the policies followed by the Board of Commissioners appointed later to manage the estates annexed and carry out the intentions of the government. Hardwicke and Newcastle foretold that Lowland farmers would be enticed into the Highlands by long leases, which they believed would also induce indigenous tenants to resist the return of the chiefs. They envisaged inland towns built to provide billets for soldiers and tradesmen, and coastal villages to take advantage of the fishing and potential coastal shipping trade. Parishes would be divided to ease the propagation of protestantism; more schools would be erected; attention would be paid to the development of both land and water transport, by making highways passable in winter as well as summer and by improving many natural harbours. Hardwicke replied to such criticisms and summed up the official attitude and defence of the act in these words:

> When I consider the frequent and great dangers we have since the revolution been exposed to, from the Highlands of Scotland, when I consider what a vast tract of country lies there uncultivated, when I consider the rich mines of lead that may probably be discovered in these mountains, and when I consider the beneficial fisheries that may be established upon the western coasts and islands of Scotland and addition that may therefore be made to our naval power, I am astonished to hear it suggested that the utility to be expected is not worth the expense.[11]

The opposition went to the lengths of accusing Pelham of protecting Jacobites in public offices, in their attempts to defeat or at least delay the bill but, despite all they could do, the Act was passed 'annexing certain Forfeited Estates in Scotland to the Crown unalienably; and for making Satisfaction to the lawful Creditors thereupon; and applying the Rents and Profits thereof, for the better civilising and improving the Highlands of Scotland; and preventing Disorders there for the future'. It received the royal assent on 26 March, 1752.

Fourteen Highland estates were named in the act, but only thirteen were annexed, as that of Alexander MacDonald of Keppoch was found not to be forfeited. The thirteen were the lands belonging to Charles Stewart of Ardsheal, Francis Buchanan of Arnprior, Archibald MacDonnell of Barrisdale, Allan Cameron of Callart, Ewan MacPherson of Cluny, George, Earl of Cromartie, Donald MacDonald of Kinlochmoidart, Donald MacDonnell of Lochgarry, Donald Cameron of Lochiel, Simon Fraser, Lord Lovat, Francis Farquharson of Monaltrie, Lord John Drummond, brother of James the sixth earl and titular Duke of Perth who had died before the Act of Attainder took effect, and Alexander Robertson of Struan. The last named still lay under an earlier forfeiture of 1690. The Cromartie estate lay on the shores of the Cromarty firth on the east coast and round Lochbroom and Lochcarron on the west. Perth, Arnprior, Struan, Lochgarry, Cluny and Lovat formed a broken chain from six miles north of Stirling to Inverness and beyond. To the west of the chain were Ardsheal, Barrisdale, Kinlochmoidart and Lochiel, while in Aberdeenshire, quite disjoined and so small one wonders if the only reason for annexing it was to obtain a foothold in a strong Jacobite area, was Monaltrie.[12]

One of the most important compromises embodied in the act concerned the nature of the body that was to manage the estates. The Barons' administration of the forfeitures had impressed no-one, and there was no likelihood that they would be entrusted with this much more onerous and demanding task. There were reservations about the enthusiasm and commitment of an unpaid commission, but

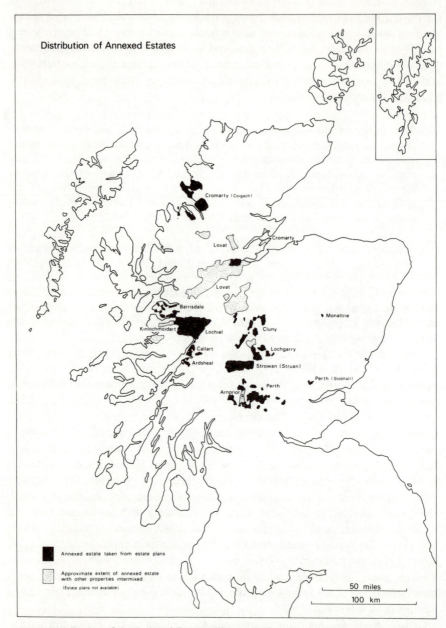

Fig. 1 Distribution of the Annexed Estates. The areas of the Lovat Estate and parts of certain other estates for which there are no plans in the Scottish Record Office are approximate.

these were counterbalanced by the fears that a salaried board might become merely another source of government patronage, without regard to the suitability of the appointees. Lord Milton did suggest that the Commissioners of Police who had no official duty should shoulder the administration of the annexed estates. There was, however, one very reasonable argument against this, reasonable at least in eighteenth-century terms: those who had accepted commissionership as a sinecure might feel aggrieved if they were suddenly expected to work for their money. An even stronger argument against this proposal was that the government needed the patronage available to them in the Police Commission. The final decision was that the commissioners, appointed under the Privy Seal, were to serve in an honorary capacity.[13] As it happened, several were Commissioners of Police, but that was irrelevant to their position on the board managing the annexed estates.

A note on nomenclature and identity may not come amiss at this point. The first Treasury commission was addressed to commissioners for the Forfeited Annexed Estates, though logicians would argue for Annexed Forfeited Estates.[14] It is unfortunate that the very existence of the Annexing Act seems to have escaped the attention of the editor of the Scottish History Society's selection of manuscripts dealing with both the 1715 and 1745 forfeitures, with the result that there has been a certain amount of confusion over the two separate bodies which dealt with the two very different operations.[15] The earlier commission was employed primarily to sell estates forfeited after 1715 and was dissolved in 1725, the members having been paid at the rate of £1,000 per annum. Throughout this volume, the honorary Board operating from 1755 to 1784, managing the estates annexed in 1752, will be given the unambiguous title of the Board for the Annexed Estates.

As it happened, not all the estates came immediately under the Board's control. Five whole and two parts of estates affected by the act remained under the Barons of the Scottish Exchequer until 1770, because they were held of subject superiors. These were Ardsheal, Callart, Cluny, Lochgarry, and Lochiel, the largest in the west, *in toto*, and Arnprior and Kinlochmoidart in part. The Lochgarry superior was the Duke of Atholl, and Arnprior's was John Erskine of Carnock. Kinlochmoidart, Ardsheal and part of Lochiel were held of the Duke of Argyll, while the rest of Lochiel and the other estates not in clear possession of the attainted, with the exception of Monaltrie, were held of the Duke of Gordon. Monaltrie's superior, John Farquharson of Invercauld, had been a rebel in 1715 so his rights were ignored, and the estate was included among those administered by the Board appointed in 1755.

Provision was made in the Annexing Act for the purchase of the other superiorities, to overcome any legal let or hindrance to the Crown's complete control over and ownership of these estates. In 1755, James West and Nicholas Hardinge, Joint Secretaries to the Treasury, were appointed to negotiate with the superiors,[16] but it was fifteen years later before these negotiations were completed and a parliamentary grant provided the purchase price.[17] The explanation for this time-lag lies in the spasmodic nature of the Treasury's interest in the annexed estates after 1752. When one of the two secretaries was replaced in 1757, the commission empowering his successor to make the legal arrangements was not renewed, presumably by neglect, not intent.[18]

It was 1770 before the Crown assumed ownership and the delay did nothing for the ultimate aims of the annexation. The estates involved were not situated in the most prosperous areas of Scotland and they were not ideally suited for the development of industry. Though Cameron of Lochiel is reputed to have made the most of his woods,[19] they were probably not the easiest areas in which to introduce improving agricultural methods. In the circumstances, however, continued management by the Barons of the Exchequer and uncertainty of eventual ownership gave them the worst of all worlds, the Barons' 'care and maintenance' remit providing little incentive for change, whether for better or worse. Certainly, after 1752, the Barons' records show more activity in that limited sphere than had been visible earlier and, after commissioners were appointed to manage the estates over whose legal status there was no doubt, the Barons and the Board for the Annexed Estates consulted each other over major projects, such as the Dalnacardoch inn, and over minor aspects of management. Yet these estates stood in an unsatisfactory position and, at the same time, the resources available for the purposes of annexation were substantially reduced, as the rents were about £1,200.

Before the bill reached Parliament, another compromise was forced on the Scots, who were mainly responsible for drafting it. Pelham refused to countenance the proposal that the Crown might purchase other estates. He seems to have doubted his ability to push such a clause through Parliament in combination with the undertaking to honour the debts on the estates already chosen for annexation.[20] The significance of the financial and legal technicalities which absorbed the attention of so many interested in the estates, and the need to attend to these interests, is illustrated by the fact that almost half the text of the Annexing Act is consumed in dealing with them. Eventually, however, the wider aims of annexation are defined rather more particularly than in the title, and the methods of achieving them are mapped out.

The somewhat uneven balance between general principles of annexation and attention to detail illustrates also the preoccupations of the influential. The goal to be achieved by the application of the rents of the annexed estates was 'the civilising the inhabitants upon the said estates, and other parts of the Highlands and Islands of Scotland, the promoting amongst them the Protestant religion, good Government, Industry and Manufactures, and the principles of Duty and Loyalty to His Majesty, His Heirs, and Successors, and to no other use and purpose whatsoever'. Freedom of action for the central government was preserved by the clause relating to rents which directed that profits from the estates should be applicable 'in the Manner herein after mentioned, or in such other Manner as His Majesty, His Heirs and Successors shall from time to time by Warrants under His or Their Sign Manual, be pleased to direct', but it seems reasonable to assume that the priorities of the would-be transformers of the north stand revealed by the order in which various duties, mandatory or permissive, are enacted.

Landholding and the power that ownership of land gave were already recognised as basic problems which had to be resolved before Highland society could be altered to achieve the consummation devoutly wished for by those outside it. The removal of the tenure of wardholding mentioned in the preamble to the Annexing Act was only one indication of this, and that the first power given to the commissioners was the ability to grant leases is a continuation of that recognition. Reforming agriculturalists considered, with some reason, that security of tenure was the first essential step towards improvement of agricultural methods, though as we shall see, that one step alone was insufficient. Probably more important in the context of annexation, the establishment of secure landholding, independent of chiefs, was seen as an essential move towards undermining the powers of chief and tacksman, to which were attributed the backward economic conditions, the lawlessness, the Roman Catholicism, or sometimes the paganism of the inhabitants of the north and west.[21]

Both these views can be illustrated in terms of the Annexing Act, which forbade subtenancy and gave specific encouragement in the shape of extremely long leases of forty-one years to tenants who would improve their holdings by spending five years' rent in seven years from the granting of the lease. Oaths of loyalty were insisted upon before leases were allowed, and a maximum rent of £20 was permitted for all holdings except for mines and fishing. The latter two conditions aimed at the avoidance of the emergence of a future type of tacksman, who could rent large areas of land, and as a result exert an influence that the government might not always consider beneficial. The regulations governing the appointment and behaviour of factors can also be seen as attempting to counteract possible subversive influence, for presents and services from the tenants were strictly forbidden.

In the general permission to make arrangements for appointing clerks and other officials, the order to have all the estates surveyed and proposed improvements reported on at least once a year to Parliament strikes an unusually detailed note, but a thorough knowledge of conditions on the estates and of their exact extent was profoundly necessary for efficient management. Some of the first steps taken by the Board were aimed at obtaining that knowledge.

The attachment of many of the Highland areas to the Roman Catholic faith, especially when combined with the Catholicism of the family pretending to the throne, had been a constant source of worry to the Protestant establishment. The inability of the Church of Scotland to attain complete conversion despite the activities of the SSPCK (the Society in Scotland for Propagating Christian Knowledge) gave rise to further clauses in the act. The commissioners were to be permitted to divide parishes that were too large for satisfactory pastorship by one man and to provide stipends for the new charges, where the whole parish was contained within one estate. No such parishes existed but provision was also made for similar divisions by application to the Court of Commissioners for the Plantation of Kirks and Valuation of Tythes in Scotland when others were interested – heritors, patrons or titulars of tiends, i.e. anyone with a legal title to the tithes in a parish. It is odd that this clause was in fact abortive. It was clear from its position in the act and as the first step mentioned in the commission under the Privy Seal, which both stipulated the maximum stipend, that this was initially considered a vital part of the programme of annexation. Yet in 1784, the Barons of the Exchequer had to enumerate, under the heading of 'Engagements remaining undischarged', the building of four churches.

There is a note of explanation by the Barons. They attribute the lack of activity to the fact that other proprietors were involved in the erection of the four parishes that were decided on, and they would have had to pay some part of the expense.[22] The king had authorised the expenditure of £420 maximum to build churches and manses in Strathgartney, and Lochbroom, and two in Ardnamurchan, in 1766. The Board had not been inactive, suggesting parishes that would be the better for being divided as early as 1756 and 1757.[23] Boleskine and Dores, Killin, and the united parish of Walls, Sandness, Papastour, and Foula in Shetland were among those mentioned either by the Board or by the local inhabitants or ministers concerned, but Lochbroom, thirty-two miles long and twenty broad with a population of 1,900 examinable souls, half of whom were on the annexed estate of Cromartie, was the first to be recommended positively.[24] The case for a new parish there was strengthened by the support of the Committee of the General Assembly appointed to visit the Highlands with a view to dividing parishes, as was that for Ardnamurchan by its largely Roman Catholic population.[25] In Lochbroom, lists were even made of tenants and 'catechisable persons' to assist the division, and a committee of the Board thought that the Moderator of Glenelg Presbytery should be told that the Board would erect a new parish in Knoydart but had no funds available at the time.[26]

The fact that the commissioners could report to the king, in 1766, that they felt there was no reason to fear the increase of Popery on the estates may have dampened any sense of urgency on the part of the central government. In any case, it was felt that only one parish could be erected each year, as the expense was so great. The General Assembly twice approached the Board,[27] but by 1781, when Principal Robertson was the emissary, they got cold comfort, for by that time it was becoming clear that the estates would be returned to the original familes, and the commissioners wrote that they could not undertake any action that would tie the hands of future proprietors. It cannot be claimed, however, that even before this date they had pursued this section of the Annexing Act's terms with vigour, and their early belief that Roman Catholicism was no longer a danger no doubt affected their approach.

The proper share of the various estates in bearing the usual burdens of church maintenance, paying stipends, and sometimes building new churches or manses was not neglected. In 1771 for example, arrangements were made with the other heritors in Callander to build a new church there costing £500. The factor's accounts at Martimas, 1772, show £153 for the steeple, £8.17.2 to Elias Scott, 'plummer' in Edinburgh, for iron 'spier' and cock for the steeple, as well as £6.6.0 for a gown for the minister. Probably the larger proportion came out of the Perth rental, quite properly, as the largest valuation in the parish was that of the Perth estate.[28] The commissioners also allowed £10 to pay an assistant at Comrie when the minister, Robert Menzies, became old and infirm.[29] Such subsidies were not extraordinary activities for the larger landowners in any area, but the Catholic

Drummond family of course might not have been very sympathetic.

Following religion, we next find the Annexing Act making provision for the Crown, in the persons of the commissioners, to improve the educational standards in the Highlands by building public schools, not only for the conventional purpose of teaching reading and writing English, but for what we may call technical education. Schools could be built to give instruction in agriculture and manufactures and, furthermore, the commissioners were to be enabled to set up residential establishments where they could maintain 'young Persons' (not merely young male persons it should be noted) while they learned suitable and desirable skills which might further the aims of the annexation. The school for agriculture was only talked about and never materialised; the only full-blown scheme for a school for manufactures was planned between 1755 and 1760, but it was first ignored by the Crown, despite the demand in the first set of instructions to the Board that plans should be drawn up for such purposes.[30] Then it was overtaken by the withdrawal from all Highland areas of financial support by the Board of Trustees for Manufactures. Nevertheless the encouragement of manufacturing arts and skills by paying teachers of spinning and knitting, by helping spinning schools and by subsidising apprentices and craftsmen, was a definite part, if not a very large part in financial terms, of the Board's activities, especially in the earlier years of the annexation.[31]

The teaching of English was a different matter and one to which the government of Scotland had periodically turned its attention since the Reformation. The resistance of the pagan or Roman Catholic, Gaelic-speaking Highlander to assimilation into the Protestant and Presbyterian, non-Gaelic culture of the southern parts of Scotland – resistance expressed sometimes passively by simply ignoring the central government, but often in active revolt, as in the Hebridean reaction to the Fife Adventurers – had been consistently deplored by the Lowland rulers whose aim had been peace and quiet and conformity throughout the whole realm. Equally consistently, this cultural resistance had been attributed in large measure to the retention of the Gaelic tongue. At the same time, the greater speed with which economic growth, law and order (as understood in the south) and the accepted Protestant established church had been welcomed south of the Highland line, had made it possible for those apparently benefiting by and making material progress on account of such phenomena to consider society developing on different lines as backward and uncivilised. The use of Gaelic, the people speaking the language, their preferred religion and the culture expressed in Gaelic had thus come to be condemned as barbaric and, from 1609, when the Statutes of Iona were signed, the elimination of Gaelic had been a cardinal part of the aims of many influential in government and church who wished to 'civilise' the Highlands. The church recognised earlier than the state, however, that a non-Gaelic speaking minister in a Gaelic-speaking area was not much use as a pastor.

The lawmakers were fairly explicit in the definition of their views and ambitions. The Statutes of Iona merely provided for the education of the sons of chiefs – or the eldest daughter if there were no sons – in the schools in the Lowlands where they could learn to 'speik, reid and wryte Inglische',[32] but the Privy Council by

1616 went further, expressing the king's wish that the 'Irishe language, whilk is one of the cheif and principall causis of the continewance of barbaritie and incivilitie amongis the inhabitantis of the Ilis and Heylandis, may be abolisheit and removit'.[33] The General Assembly in 1688 could include 'erecting of English schools and . . . rooting out the Irish language' among 'other pious uses',[34] yet only eighty years later a presentee of the Crown to Kirkhill was disqualified because he did not know Gaelic.[35] The SSPCK initially forbade the use of Gaelic even for instruction in English, a counterproductive ordinance one would have thought when companions and parents still spoke 'Irish'. This order was rescinded in 1767 but, like the Bourbons, the educational establishment were slow learners and, after 1872, until 1918, even five-year-olds were expected to learn their letters and numbers in what was to them a foreign language, previously rarely heard.[36]

To find that the annexation of 1752 maintained this tradition of the previous century and a half can hardly come as a surprise. The events of 1745–46 had seemed a particularly frightening example of Highland recalcitrance in face of southern forbearance after 1715 and 1719. Once again Gaelic is described as distinctly divisive and retrogressive, not indeed in the legislation, which merely mentioned instruction in reading and writing English, but in the general approach of the commissioners and their servants, especially the factors.

The clause following that on education provided that free charters could be granted to the proposed holders of land up to ten acres. It was realised only in so far as it enabled the commissioners the more easily to set up King's Cottagers.[37] The connection between the actual beneficiaries, the small pendiclers, and the envisaged builders of large houses, outhouses and gardens seems attenuated. The aim was no doubt to facilitate the settlement of a number of substantial loyal citizens at regular intervals throughout the Highlands, for anyone who could hold ten acres merely for domestic use and take a lease elsewhere was very surely not poverty-stricken. It came to nothing and indeed does not seem to have been seriously and practically considered at any time. The nearest approach to this idea, with a slight stretch of one's notions of just what it was meant to achieve, is perhaps the order to build new and enlarge existing towns and villages, included in the first set of instructions sent to the commissioners. Men of substance dotted over the area would be a further deterrent to disorder, for they could possibly be depended on to report on any signs of rebellion, just as concealment of such plans was considered less easy in urban settlements.

The 'prevention of disorders for the future', so clamant a need to those in power, was inextricably mixed in their minds with the existence of towns and of prisons. The lack of prisons was next mentioned in the Annexing Act as having been found a 'great Obstruction to the Course of Justice', though the heritable jursidictions were probably as great an obstruction, and power was given to the commissioners to build gaols and appoint gaolers. As for towns, the reasons for building them included the statement that thereby the 'inhabitants could help each other and secure their property against theft, rapine, that malefactors may be more easily detached and apprehended'. Similarly it had been suggested by the author of a manuscript of 1752 entitled 'Hints on Managing the Forfeited Estates' that the building of what today's planners would call 'nucleate settlements' would make it easier to protect newcomers and well-behaved tenants and to suppress evildoers, as ministers and officers would be constantly present.[38] A further benefit mentioned was the possibility of mutual defence of the inhabitants, and in 'any future rebellion of the clans' the troops would find good entertainment and refreshment in these towns, instead of the miserable fare obtained in the existing wretched 'cabbins'. This may be thought over-optimistic so far as Scottish inns were considered, but it does illuminate one of the ideas behind the annexation, the attainment and maintenance of peace and quiet in the Highlands.

The commissioners' adventures in planting new towns were hardly felicitous, as we shall see below in Chapter 8. They did build a few prisons, for example at Dunblane, for £77, and at Stonehaven,[39] and a court house as well as a gaol at Cromarty, the last costing £350. Repairs were carried out to others, £150 being spent on the Crieff tolbooth in 1765. It was logical also, in the quest for order, to grant the quasi-proprietors the right to appoint baron bailies, who administered what remained of local justice after the abolition of the heritable jurisdictions. The commissioners duly carried out their duties in this respect, throughout their administration.

The final clauses in the Annexing Act provided for the Receiver General for Scotland to reserve the rents for carrying out the Board's orders, in line with the powers granted in the act and according to the warrants and orders from the Crown. They also enabled the Treasury to use the rents in ordinary management of the estates and in any litigation that might arise over the claims of creditors.

These provisions seem comprehensive enough, but there were two important potential sources of economic development which were not specifically mentioned in the Act, but were discussed in the debates in Parliament. The first of these to which the commissioners turned their attention was the fishing industry, which will be considered in Chapter 8. The other was the possibility of finding and working minerals. Not the wildest eighteenth-century dreams could have imagined the twentieth-century North Sea oil and gas bonanza, but in the earlier period there was what Professor Smout calls gently 'a good deal of excitement', similar to what had prevailed two hundred years before in the sixteenth century.[40] Exploitation of wealth under their estates came as naturally to improving landlords as industrial and agricultural development above ground, and it was not uncommon for landowners to open mines at some expense, work them for a limited period and then leave them.[41] General searches were encouraged by at least one Duke of Argyll and a Marquis of Breadalbane, but unfortunately the particular prospector they favoured was of doubtful integrity. He was Rudolf Raspe, the Swiss geologist who created Baron Munchausen, and it was suspected that he first planted the specimens he then 'discovered'.[42]

Now the commissioners were the last men to be left out of any such contemporary excitement and, on request, they were authorised by the Treasury to spend £700 on coal-prospecting particularly. They did not apparently envisage operating mines themselves or even employing miners as their agents, but they saw their role as 'providing opportunities for adventurers', according to George Clerk

Maxwell.[43] Dr. Walker of Moffat carried out various surveys for them, as did John Williams, the mining engineer and surveyor, who was also at one time the tacksman of the Brora coalmine. Among the places he was sent to search for coal and minerals of any kind was the barony of Stobhall in Cargill parish in eastern Perthshire. He found only lime and marl. The hunt was still on in 1780 when Mr. Sandeman, the bleacher, was paid £20 as remuneration for Andrew Moir who had been surveying under his auspices in Luncarty.[44]

Eastern Perthshire was situated on the edge of the major coalfields of central Scotland,[45] but the funds of the estates were also directed to assisting a mine and adjoining salt pans that were already in operation, at Brora in Sutherland. Salt pans burned the dross that would otherwise have been waste, and the combination of the two activities when mines were near the sea was commonplace. In 1771, £220 was granted as an aid to the salt pans there, after a couple of years' delay when the sum had been diverted to what seemed to the commissioners more pressing needs. John Williams was paid £80 subsistence, particularly for his work in connection with the mine there.[46] The Brora mines were worked in the sixteenth century to provide fuel for the salt pans,[47] and were worked sporadically until 1974. The contribution from the annexed estates rents seems to have been of little immediate avail for, in 1781, Andrew Wight reported that 'At Brora, it grieved me to observe that the coal and salt pans are given up'. At that point in the mine's history, only the upper seam had been worked and it was too full of sulphur, taking fire when wet.[48]

Though lead-mining was a longstanding and widespread part of the Scottish economy, lead having been worked in almost every part of Scotland and referred to from the thirteenth century, it had never been of major importance.[49] The high prices in the late eighteenth and early nineteenth centuries, however, plus technical improvements in mining generally, opened up possibilities of further exploitation of any veins that were either known or newly discovered. The Board employed John McDonald to drive six fathoms north-east in an 'amino' vein in Dripan Glen, near Loch Venachar, at 10/- to £3 per fathom, the miner furnishing powder and candles and being responsible for clearing away rubble.[50] (The Board were ready to compensate farmers, however, for damage done to their land.)[51] There must have been a fair amount of activity, the factor James Small writing that 'they are everywhere underground', but the search was stopped by October, 1774 and the miner was not prepared to commit himself about the possibilities of the site without further trials. At the end of the year, John Williams was to have a look at the work done when he was in the area.[52] Nothing came of the venture, however, and it has to be admitted that, apart from the present growing market in semi-precious stones in making jewellery and the occasional silver and lead-working,[53] the Highlands have not yet divulged an eldorado.

Another type of search, this time on the surface, was also sponsored by the Board; this was a botanical one, which it was hoped would provide the key to types of vegetation and soils. James Robertson was the student of botany employed, and his journals are in the National Library of Scotland.[54] The significance of these searches lies not in the results, which can hardly be described as very valuable, but in the illumination they cast on those who planned the annexation and on the type of men to whom administration of the estates was entrusted. They were lively, curious and inquisitive about the world and about their country and were prepared to experiment. They were, in fact, very much men of the Enlightenment, an age which saw intellectual activity in Scotland to a degree never experienced before and probably never since, and much of their approach to the management of the annexed estates can be seen as an illustration of the contemporary frame of mind.

Their general philosophy makes all the more surprising a certain lack of perseverance in one field in which it might have been expected that both government and commissioners would have had a prime and abiding interest. Education was not neglected but, even at the beginning of the Board's life, it did not attract the amount of attention or the financial support that its place in the Annexing Act seemed to demand. When one considers how often the ignorance of the Highlander was deplored, it might have been expected that the provision of schools would have taken priority over many other worthwhile schemes. Yet, in 1755, in the questionnaire sent to the factors to obtain a fuller picture of social conditions than the scientific survey could provide, it is noticeable that the commissioners were far more concerned with law and order or, at least, with the means of maintaining it, than with providing education and religious instruction. The Annexing Act had admittedly been described as aimed at 'preventing Disorders for the future' in the Highlands but power to build prisons, for instance, had been far down the list of priorities. The Board, however, asked first about the presence of Justices of the Peace, the nearness of prisons, and the distance of estates from Sheriff-Substitutes, before mentioning churches, schools, whether preaching was in English, and what progress spoken English had made.

The factors' replies demonstrated the desire to replace one criticised form of paternalism, that of the wadsetters and lesser gentlemen, by another, that of the government agency and its officers. Captain Forbes, the factor on Lovat and Cromartie, accused the former group of wishing to keep the people in 'ignorance and slavery'. He obviously considered the introduction of schools, with the concomitant use and knowledge of English, as necessary to ensure what he saw as the 'freedom' of the tenants. He went so far as to suggest refusing tenancies to those who could not speak English, and proposed a clause in tacks (*anglice* – leases) insisting that children should attend school. However, he had sufficient sense of the realities of the situation to add that financial assistance should be given to indigent parents, to enable them to keep their families at school until they could speak English.[55] While Forbes had been employed by the Barons of the Exchequer as factor on Lovat and Cromartie, his interest in schools had been explicit. In 1754, after a visit to Coigach, he remarked that 'It is shocking to see such numbers of young ones going about in Rags, idle, and without one word of English or more care taken of them (scarce so much) as of their cattle'. And he added that he longed to see schools in the area.[56]

However, he was neither so enthusiastic nor so independent in this field as his counterpart in Struan, Cluny and Lochgarry, William Ramsay, who found only one school in Struan, with twenty to twenty-four pupils. Having described the area in 1751, soon after the Barons were able to take possession, as populated by 'inhabitants more uncivilised and addicted to rapine and theft than any other sett of people in the Highlands', he wanted to use the rents to set up both ordinary and spinning schools, and an application to be made to the SSPCK for yet another. The Barons did not respond speedily and positively enough for his liking and he set about realising his ideas without their consent, By 1754, he could report that the SSPCK had provided one and that he himself had arranged for six schools in Struan and Lochgarry, at his own expense. He claimed that 350 people, young and old, were now learning to read, write, spin and knit stockings. He had also set up a reading and spinning school on the Cluny estate, which he provided with dressed lint, bought at Inverness. This he sold at cost price to encourage the newly trained spinners, following the practice of the Board of Trustees for Manufactures and Fisheries which was later followed by the Board for the Annexed Estates. To Ramsay, too, must go the credit of employing Dugald Buchanan, at £20 per annum, which salary he had taken upon himself to guarantee for ten years, whether he remained factor or not. Buchanan was 'the most famous of Gaelic spiritual bards'.[57]

Unfortunately, such independent action was not likely to be received with acclamation in Edinburgh. Combined with unfavourable comment from the woodkeeper on Struan, James Small, the Barons' strictures resulted in Ramsay's resignation in 1754 and his replacement by Small, who was later retained in that position, with great success, by the Board for the Annexed Estates. Once appointed, Small had to admit that the setting up of all the schools was 'doubtless a right measure', which the people wanted to continue, but he added, somewhat unctuously, that Ramsay had been wrong to lay out money without orders and to attribute to himself 'a dale of merit', as if the money had indeed been his own.[58]

Small considered that the schools were particularly useful in 'learning the young ones English as the masters discharge scholars to speak the Irish'.[59] Not all the evidence corroborated his view, however. The information provided by the factors did not always demonstrate that schools were the only, or even the best, places for learning English. John Campbell of Barcaldine, factor on the Perth estate, admitted to surprise at the progress the language was making in Strathgartney, despite the lack of a school. The presence of a Society school in the barony of Strathpeffer, part of the Cromartie estate, seemed to be making little impact in this respect. Certainly the salary there was only £5 and the teacher elderly, but the idleness and poverty of the inhabitants, which the factor had deplored as leading to neglect of their offspring, would not encourage education, while the remoteness of the estate from areas in which English was normally spoken must have made the acquisition of the language seem an esoteric puruit to parents and children alike. Undoubtedly commercial exchanges, which involved contact with the Lowlands, demanded and resulted in some knowledge of the southern language. For example, all but two of the tenants on two farms on Strathyre, who had dealings with drovers, could speak English, while many of the wives and children had not yet acquired this skill. In the parish of Boleskine and

Abertarff there was only one charity school, at Fort Augustus. Perhaps it was not surprising that the only area in the parish showing any increase in knowledge of English was that round the garrison, since it was as likely to be effective in spreading the language as any amount of academic teaching.

The provision of schools on the estates that came under the management of the commissioners in 1755 was as good as could be expected at the time. While there was no parochial school in parishes such as Fodderty, Lochbroom, Kilmorack, Dores, Boleskine and Abertarff, each could boast one charity school and Dores had two. The whole of Knoydart had neither parochial nor charity school and this was typical of remote areas. The nearest school to the estate of Monaltrie, in Crathie parish, was the parochial school in Braemar. Perthshire was well endowed with schools, though in Dunblane the parochial school did the Perth tenants little good as it was too far away from them. On the other hand, many of the larger parishes were served by both parochial and charity schools. Ramsay's legacy of schools on Struan had been somewhat eroded, for the SSPCK had moved their establishment and the salary provided to Lochgarry, and the other four left had such poor salaries, ranging from £1.10.0 to £4, without a compensatory number of pupils, that masters were unwilling to stay. Nor were teaching conditions ideal. In Callander, the church was used as there was no schoolhouse, and this caused many complaints because of unspecified 'abuses' to the seats, for which the pupils were responsible. In Crieff, there was a schoolhouse, but it was in such poor condition that the master had to hire another for teaching purposes.[60]

Faced with such a clear picture of deficiencies, it might have been expected that a Board of such interests as the commissioners would have been pressing their officers to increase the numbers of schools and improve the physical conditions of the existing buildings. And it might also have been assumed that any expenditure on such objectives would have been easily and speedily approved. This was not to be. There was no problem about government authorisation for the first £200 per year proposed for educational expenses but, within a year, the Board realised that such a sum was hardly sufficient if the aims of the Annexing Act were to be adequately and efficiently carried out, and the decision was taken to request permission to allot a further £200 each year to providing schools.[61] There was no response from the Treasury at all, neither a direct negative nor even a suggestion that perhaps the sum should be reconsidered. It may be that the Board received an unrecorded hint from the central government that no further sums would be made available for education but, until some evidence appears, it can only be assumed that no-one on the Board was sufficiently interested to press the matter. The years went by, the Highlands showed no signs of further eruption, and the restriction of the income from the estates was increasingly felt. The provision of schools for the inhabitants may have seemed of less vital importance than it did to the legislators in 1752, and certainly of less importance to economic development than many of the other activities of the Board. Admittedly the SSPCK was operating on educational lines in the Highlands and Islands which were similar to those of the Board, but the Society, like the Board of Trustees, seized on the excuse of the Board for the Annexed Estates to husband its own scanty resources and 'resolved to discontinue their appointments to schoolmasters settled upon or in the neighbourhood' of the estates,[62] though this decision does not seem to have been strictly adhered to.[63]

However, the Board conscientiously carried out their duties as heritors, undertaking their full share of the public burden of building new schools, or paying masters in parishes where others were involved, as well as endeavouring to achieve the wider aims within the financial limits imposed. By 1765, the factor on the most remote estates could claim to have built schools at Inverie, Kinlochmoidart and Locharkaig. He had pointed out that the need in Barrisdale, Lochiel, Kinlochmoidart and Ardsheal was greater than anywhere else, as his factorship was in the 'most recluse and least civilised' part of the Highlands.[64]

Financial stringency was soon felt, however; in 1768, Glenartney tenants had to be told that the school fund was exhausted and they could not be given immediate help with the salary for the school built earlier by the Board. New Tarbat tenants could afford only £6 for their schoolmaster; despite the accesibility of the school, the children got little good of it as they found it impossible to keep a well-qualified master. They had had seven changes in as many years, and would have liked a grant of £20 to £25, which was quite beyond the resources of the Board. The most they could offer was £10, with three acres of ground if the factor approved.[65] The SSPCK expected proprietors to give a house, a cow's grass, a kailyard and a schoolhouse when they gave a salary. As landlords of extensive estates, the Board duly provided what the Society expected; it did not cost them much. They gave schoolmasters the use of a few acres to supplement their pay by enabling them to grow their own food, reserving their rights to such areas in leases and on occasion undertaking the enclosure of such crofts. They further attempted some insurance for the future by arranging in tacks that augmentations for both ministers' stipends and schoolmasters' salaries should be paid by the tenants even where sometimes no public burdens had been borne before.[66] They built and fitted out schools, with desks for example,[67] and the factors kept them aware of the need for repairs, an important feature of providing education at the time which was commended later by the SSPCK.[68] Towards the end of the annexation, however, the greater part of the expenditure on education was devoted to salaries. For the years 1777–78, £322.3.10 out of £479.18.10½ had been spent as follows: £97.10.0 on Struan, £75.19.10 on the Highland and £33.4.0 on the Lowland parts of the Perth estate, £8 on Lochgarry, £12.10.00 on Coigach, £30 in Fortrose, £21.13.4 on one school on Lochiel, £11.13.4 on Cluny and Barrisdale, and £10 in Ardsheal and Fort William. Clearly it was not a fat basic living that was provided, except perhaps on Lochiel, but this was not out of line with contemporary arrangements. Mr. Swinton had suggested that £10 with a few acres was sufficient salary, where there was no parochial school. And of course, the masters on the estates were able to eke out salaries by acting, as others did, as Session or Presbytery clerk.[69] The master at Muthill could count on £33.4.7.

The payment of teachers, however, was regarded as a basic duty, so much so that the Struan factor was instructed to pay salaries to teachers without submitting any application to the Board for permission.[70] Indeed, the factors' attitude to the dominies emerges as one of the admirable features of the annexation. In a memorial to the Barons of the Exchequer in 1791, the SSPCK noted that the teachers were well treated by the factors on the estates, and hence by everyone else. After the disannexation, houses had fallen into disrepair and the general position of schools and schoolmasters had deteriorated.[71] It was not to be wondered at that private proprietors were unwilling to spend the same proportion of their income as the commissioners on educating their own and their neighbours' tenants. About one tenth of the Struan rents, for example, was spent on schooling. What does astonish one is the complete lack of provision in the Disannexing Act for compensation to masters and for upkeep of schools that had been largely dependent on the funds from the annexed estates. This must have been an oversight, but it is strangely at odds with the emphasis placed on education in the Annexing Act.

With parochial resources stretched as far as the heritors would allow, the dismissed masters and mistresses could have recourse to only one haven, the SSPCK. The Society's spirit was willing but its funds were exceedingly weak. Eventually, in 1786, the government took steps to provide £2,000 out of the money paid by the returning heirs.[72] With this the SSPCK undertook to maintain sixteen masters, whose salaries amounted to £138.14.0, and eight spinning mistresses at £48. Six of the spinning schools were in the area of the Perth estates, one was at Kinloch Rannoch and one at Cluny. The ordinary schools were widespread, from Strelitz, the original soldiers' settlement in Cargill parish in the east, to South Uist in the west.[73] By 1790 none of this money had reached the Society – though they retained the teachers – because of delay in the proprietors' repayment, but it seems to have materialised eventually,[74] unlike the £20,000 promised from the estates forfeited in 1715.

What has been called an early attempt at practical or vocational education[75] will be considered in Chapter 7, where the Boards' attempts to introduce industry and improve craftsmanship will be looked at.[76] It may be noted here, however, that the conventional schools provided were not only for teaching English, for at Callander there were a few boys learning French and Latin. Girls were taught only English and the alphabet. Like so much of the work of the Board for the Annexed Estates, it can be said that the incursion into education achieved a certain amount, but not as much as was hoped in the days when 'The People Above' were laying their plans; and, as will be seen in all their other activities, financial stringency was a crucial factor in restricting their success.

3

Annexation and Administration

ALTHOUGH the Annexing Act was passed in March, 1752, it was not implemented until 1755. The delay can be attributed to a variety of factors which, like the opposition in Parliament during the passage of the legislation, reflect power politics in London and English suspicion of and hostility towards Scots. A further complication was Scottish dilatoriness, both in setting in motion the necessary administrative machinery for realising annexation and in settling the claims on the annexed estates. Pelham had first to ward off an attack on his power and his integrity regarding Jacobites in the Scottish revenue service; the resultant adverse reaction to all things Scottish prevented Lord Milton's travelling to London to make detailed arrangements for the administration of the estates, but his presence in Scotland did not speed up the production of plans in Edinburgh. These were eventually sent to London and usually sent back again to be altered. It was also difficult to reach agreement about the personnel of the Board. Preparations were nowhere near completion when Pelham's death and the subsequent reorganisation of the ministry protracted discussion still further. The Court of Session showed no sense of urgency in determining the claims on the estates until after Robert Dundas became Lord Advocate in 1754, and the Barons of the Exchequer were equally leisurely in providing the government with accounts of the annexed estates, which remained under their management, together with unsold forfeited properties, so long as the Annexing Act remained a dead letter. The Barons had some excuse, for there were doubts after 1752 as to whether they could use any of the rents, even for defraying ordinary costs of management.[1]

Once Newcastle became First Lord of the Treasury, despite being primarily absorbed in foreign affairs, he took steps to appoint a commission. There seems to be little doubt that he would have preferred a predominantly English and certainly a non-Highland board, and to that end his Scottish friends provided possible lists, which omitted such prominent Highlanders as the Dukes of Argyll and Atholl and the former's henchman, Lord Milton. In addition to being a Highlander, Argyll, as Pelham's ally, was doubly unwelcome as a member, but Newcastle's need for his support in Parliament produced a compromise over personnel resulting in a rather large commission of twenty-eight, which represented the interests of both.[2] Argyll, Milton and Baron Maule, also a close friend of Argyll's, were included, but Argyll attended no meetings of the Board, his voice presumably being ably heard through Milton's and Maule's.

If we ignore political affiliation, the first Board for the Annexed Estates was a promising collection, however tardily got together. It included several Scottish peers, some well known for agricultural improvements on their own estates as well as for their membership of the Board of Trustees for Manufactures and Fisheries, such as John, Marquis of Tweeddale and James, Earl of Findlater as well as Lord Deskford, Findlater's son and heir, who was an enthusiastic improver. Findlater may have expected to enjoy a vicarious sense of ownership by being on the Board, for in 1753 he had presented a petition to the king, detailing past faithful services and suggesting that he might be given the estate of Lord John Drummond as a reward; this was the highest rentalled of all the estates annexed in 1752.[3] However, he graced the meetings with his presence only once.[4] The Lord President of the Court of Session, the Lord Chief Baron, the Lord Justice Clerk and the Commander-in-Chief of H.M. Forces in Scotland were all *ex officio* members. In 1755, the last named was General Bland, who had been deeply concerned with the earlier plans for annexation. He was one of the most assiduous attenders at meetings of the Board until he turned ill and was succeeded by Lord George Beauclerk in November, 1756. Several Commissioners of Customs, two prominent Edinburgh citizens, William Alexander and George Drummond, Charles Hope Weir, M.P., the Earl of Hopetoun's brother, and one or two other Scottish M.P.'s, Lieutenant-Colonel David Watson, Quartermaster-General for Scotland, and a considerable number of lawyers made up the full complement of the Board, twenty of whom gathered together for the first time on 23 June, 1755. There was never again to be such a large attendance, and the Board provided a splendid example of what the Earl of Marchmont described as letting 'things fall by degrees into one or two hands covered under a set of respectable but unactive names . . .'.[5] Marchmont should have known, for between 1755 and 1760 he appeared only once.

Before any detailed plans could be formulated for achieving the wider aims of annexation, some administrative preparations were immediately necessary. Factors had to be appointed to the six complete and two part estates which came under the aegis of the Board at this time. An office had to be found, suitable both for meetings and for storing records; executive and clerical staff were required. At the first meeting, a letter from the Duke of Newcastle awaited the commissioners, suggesting a possible secretary, but the negotiations regarding this appointment and that of other servants of the Board have been shown to have been affected not so much by the suitability of the candidate for the post as by politicians' desire for influence on the commission.[6] An English lawyer, Stamp Brooksbank, son of a Director of the Bank of England, was Newcastle's nominee, and the salary proposed was £500 a year, which would have placed this civil servant in the same income group as the judges of the Court of Session. Argyll's party swallowed the man, but even Newcastle's friends choked over the excessive remuneration, and Brooksbank was appointed at a lower salary of £300 on 14 July, 1755.[7] Newcastle apparently managed to make up the extra £200 for his protégé out of the Scottish Civil List; he declared he 'never thought of the salary in any other light than as an inducement to a gentleman of Rank, Character and Ability to give up his whole time' to the position.[8] The secretary, however, gave up more and more of his time to the search for a more lucrative, less demanding post in England and in 1762, when he found one to his taste, he resigned and was succeeded by Mr. Henry Barclay of Collernie, who bore the brunt of most of the work of the Board. His son,

William Barclay, was clerk for fifteen years, becoming conjunct secretary with his father in December, 1771, when the former's age and health interrupted the 'necessary attendance to the Execution of the duties of his office'. William was sole secretary until his death in 1783, when John Clerk became the Board's last secretary.[9] Provision was also made for two clerks to join the establishment, a fortnight after the secretary's appointment, at salaries of £70 and £40. A further necessary expense was that of agents in Edinburgh and London. The first Edinburgh lawyer was William Alston, a friend of Lord Milton's, but his obvious merits had appeared when he was working for the Barons of the Exchequer, so that he was acceptable to the government. In 1771, Allen Macdougall succeeded him, the salary of £70 having been increased in 1762 to £100 because of increased business, as was the first clerk's. In London, Milward Rowe, another Treasury nominee, served as agent until 1782 for the fee of £20, when William Mitford replaced him.[10]

Before a permanent office was decided on, the Board met in the hall of the Trustees for the Funds of Widows and Children of the Church of Scotland, but in due course they found a solution to their accommodation problem. Various people with houses to let or sell had approached them or been approached, but all the negotiations fell through. Then it was realised that a house belonging to the Lovat estate and hence now under the Board's management was 'very conveniently situated' near the Tron Kirk in the High Street, Edinburgh. In November, 1755, Mr. John Adam, the architect, was instructed to inspect the house with a view to its being used as an office, and three months later the Adam brothers sent in a report and plan with their proposals for the alterations required. They were less than enthusiastic. The plan showed a six-roomed flat on one floor and their letter ended: 'The House is in very indifferent condition, so that to put it in proper order and to make the alterations necessary for converting it from its present shape into an office would require at least £300. At the same time we beg leave to observe that the accommodation would be very much confined and indeed less than such an office ought to have'.[11]

Nevertheless, the Board decided to go ahead and by 1757 the house had been fitted up by Charles Howison, Wright, for £340.2.3 $\frac{2}{12}$. This was reduced to £330.19.3 $\frac{2}{12}$ as six mahogany chairs, a chimney piece, 'pocker', tongs and fender were returned.[12] In 1774, when Major-General Simon Fraser, as he had become, had his patrimonial estates restored to him for services rendered to the Hanoverians, he invited the commissioners to continue using his house and consider it 'as much at their service as before H.M's grant'. (However, that did not stop his agent, James Fraser, making a sharp demand for overdue rent after the disannexation of all the estates). This 'house' or flat was one of the usual High Street tenements, and had a china shop below, presumably on the ground floor,[13] and other accommodation above, part of which was rented for a time by a 'doorkeeper', i.e. a caretaker, employed by the Board.

The office was fairly lavishly furnished. A quantity of Scotch carpet 'of the best kind' cost £4.12.6, curtains for the directors' room £1.10.0, and saxon green watered stuff for other curtains 17/4d. The rooms were all papered, some in pink diamond pattern, some blue-flowered, some with stucco-painted paper. Pewter inkstands were provided and the somewhat extraordinary number of seven and a half dozen purple Dutch pigs. Twelve elm and twelve beech leather-seated chairs cost £7.4.0 and £5.2.0 respectively, while decoration was not forgotten, with a bust of Shakespeare's head at 10/6d, £10 for a clock with a 4/6d pedestal and £2.5.6 for dove-coloured marble in the chimney.[14]

Once this office was in use, the commissioners had to employ a doorkeeper, and at first he had accommodation in the same tenement. When he had to move for reasons unspecified, he pointed out to the Board that he had to keep a servant to maintain his own house as a result, 'a great charge upon him in these times of scarcity'. So he was allowed an extra £2, making his wages £30 per annum. A few years later he complained that, because of the lack of room in the office for him and the distance of his own house from the office, he had had to hire a house in the same stair at a 'high yearly rent', so that he could keep adequate charge of the office, including lighting and extinguishing fires. This was apparently considered quite reasonable for he was awarded another £10 yearly. This man was not slow in seeing where he could add to his wages. When Princess Caroline died in 1758, he sent in asking for mourning clothes, and in 1760 for another £5 on the death of George II, 'as is given in all other public offices'. He also received regular payments for copying for the Board.[15]

As well as dealing with the necessary minutiae of administrative organisation, the Board almost immediately applied themselves to the wider issues involved in their commission, making all sorts of plans, according to their instructions, and as a first step arranging, as was statutorily necessary, that the estates should all be accurately surveyed. Lieutenant-Colonel David Watson was eminently suited to the task of overseeing this project, as it had been he who suggested to the Duke of Cumberland that there was great need for a proper survey of the Highlands, and William Roy had first worked on his staff.[16] Within a week he had produced detailed instructions for surveyors and had them approved by the commissioners. The first item recommended as necessary was that the surveyor 'reconnoiter the whole estate' and this alone, when one considers the extent of the annexed estates, would have accounted for the length of time and the expense that these surveys involved.[17] The boundaries of each farm had to be noted and attention had to be paid to the type of arable, meadow and wood lands; whether bogs could be easily drained, the nature of the woods, and whether ground was improvable or not. Fords, ferries, bridges, villages, farms and even cothouses within the estates were to be particularly surveyed; boundaries of the parishes, and the distance of the most remote parts of the parish from the church were to be noted. This last would have been essential if the commissioners had carried out the proposal to form new parishes where such distances were unreasonable.

Watson's instructions to the surveyors have been described as 'one of the most important documents in the history of Scottish surveying', for the landowners among the commissioners and their friends and acquaintances paid Watson the supreme compliment of copying them over the next few years, during which time Scottish estate management and agricultural methods became ever more sophisticated and skilful. Perhaps at the instigation of the Earl of Findlater, who described Peter May on one occasion as the best surveyor in Scotland, Watson proposed that this man should be appointed as the Board's surveyor on the estates of Lovat and Cromartie. May's influence on surveying, and hence on the changing appearance of the countryside, was widespread, both through his own work and through that of his apprentices.[18] It is probably not too far-fetched to attribute some of these changes indirectly to the annexation and to the composition of the Board.

The surveys produced very detailed pictures of the estates, as we can see from William Morison's description of part of Lochiel.[19] They were also very expensive. The type of country, and the weather, which was much bemoaned as 'inclement', were both blamed for the length of time needed to produce results; David Bruce told the Barons of the Exchequer it took him nine hours on one occasion to travel eleven miles.[20] Lack of cooperation from the inhabitants, and sometimes active opposition which required the support of troops, all combined to make this a heavy, if necessary, drain on the rents.[21] Without them, the commissioners' lack of knowledge of the terrain they were supposed to be transforming would have been an even greater disadvantage than it was. Surveyors were employed throughout the annexation whenever any divisions or amalgamations of holdings were under consideration, or during negotiations with neighbours over boundaries and *excambions,* the Scottish legal term for an exchange of land.

Apart from achieving adequate surveys of the estates and appointing their officials, however, the commissioners immediately ran into difficulties in putting any of their plans into operation. Their problem was the reaction of the central government, or more accurately the lack of reaction. There was nothing so positive as active obstruction that could have been attacked; there was simply massive indifference. One aspect of annexation merits attention almost equally with the actual policies planned and attempted, and that is the efficiency or otherwise of the administrative methods involved. Any results from government policy carried out by an organisation such as the Board for the Annexed Estates were bound to be affected not only by the policy itself but by the system of execution. In many ways, this Board was an embryonic form of the twentieth-century public corporation, for it consisted of members appointed by the central government, and it was expected to follow government policy as laid down in the Annexing Act and in the instructions given by the central government. These instructions, like the policy guidelines to the public corporation, reached Edinburgh in only very general terms initially, and the commissioners then had to formulate detailed schemes of economic, social and religious development within these broad outlines. The great difference between the responsibility of today's public corporations and that of the eighteenth-century Board was that the government then intended maintaining much stricter supervision over day-to-day management than does today's central bureaucracy. Had these intentions been realised or, alternatively, had more independence been granted to the managing board, better administration and possibly better results might have been achieved on the estates; but the long delay between the enactment of the annexing legislation and the appointment of the commissioners was only a foretaste of what was to follow.

The elements of centralisation and bureaucratic control that have tended to appear in any form of state management are strikingly present in the administrative records of the Board. The central government controlled the Edinburgh Board through the Treasury, which had to approve all expenditure and appointments, and through the Crown. Regular reports were required by the Annexing Act, describing past achievements and suggesting future policy. From its inception the Board sent statutory biannual reports faithfully to its agent in London, Milward Rowe, to forward to the Duke of Newcastle and succeeding First Lords of the Treasury, to be handed to the king. But the Treasury paid very little attention to these[22] and the Crown ignored them completely in the five years after 1755. There are no records of royal approval or disapproval in these years, and this is not because they have been lost in the various moves that have been the lot of this collection of papers in the last two centuries. There were no replies to lose. The report of 1758 repeats that the commissioners are anxiously awaiting reactions to the 1757 report, pointing out that their 'progress had been somewhat retarded'. The lack of formal approval meant that the Board and hence the annexed estates were in a state of suspended animation, for no major policy, economic, religious, social or educational, could be initiated without royal approval. Such large schemes as turning Tarbat House into a linen station, like the establishments set up by the Board of Trustees at Lochbroom and Lochcarron, never got past the blueprint stage.[23] That this was a blessing in disguise, as this plan would probably have used up the whole surplus of the estates and been as unsuccessful as these other incredibly situated factories, is beside the point. What is noteworthy here is that it was not even mentioned, when eventually a response came from London. It might have been a scheme which would have revolutionised the Highland economy but the Board awaited comments and approval or disapproval in vain.

Treasury interest in the annexation, or at least in the activities of the Board for the Annexed Estates, evaporated with incredible rapidity after the appointment of the secretary. Part of the explanation for this must lie in international events, for the problems of the diplomatic, military and naval manoeuvres in the years preceding the official outbreak of the Seven Years War in May, 1756 were sufficiently absorbing to distract attention from domestic affairs, even without Newcastle's natural predilection for foreign adventures. And George II was always more interested in Hanover than in the Highlands. It has been argued recently that the war had in fact little effect and that the main influence slowing down the impetus of the commission, in 1755 and 1756 at least, was that Cumberland had regained favour with his father and used his influence to petrify the Scottish Board.[24] This does not explain, however, why the Treasury continued to ignore the Board's reports in the last years of the decade, when Argyll's stature in the ministry waxed once more. Some evidence points to faults in Edinburgh, for the commissioners' own organisation was not blameless. Grounds for criticism are easily found, and it is difficult to understand an earlier description of their administration as brilliant.[25] It would be wrong to judge their filing system by the disorderly state the collection of papers was in before being recatalogued in the early 1960s by the

Scottish Record Office, for there had been moves from one repository to another, and a fire in the Exchequer where they were kept after the disannexation in 1784.[26] Against this apologia, we must face the fact that in 1768 one of the clerks, James Morison, was recommended by Lord Elliock for a bonus and commended for the extra work he had had in 'sorting the great confusion' in the office accounts. Even after Morison's work, confusion must still have reigned in some areas, for the following January the Barons of the Exchequer were threatening to take the Board for the Annexed Estates to court for omitting to send them due records of the money arising from the estates.[27] Several members of the latter Board were also Barons, so we can fairly assume that the Exchequer was not over-reacting to the first occasion when something of the kind had happened. In fact, much earlier, in the Minto papers, there is a very irritated, unsigned, undated – but mentioning the 1757 report – sheet of complaints stating that the Board had sent to the government no plans, no surveys, no reports or even abstracts of reports by factors or anyone else on the suggestions made in this report; nothing in fact on which any decisions could be taken.[28] This must surely have contributed to Treasury silence and demonstrates that carelessness and delay were not the prerogative of the central government.

On the other hand, the manner in which the central bureaucracy dealt with Scottish matters intensified any tendency to neglect on the part of ministers. Either the First Lord of the Treasury or one of the Secretaries of State handled the administrative details of Scottish business. In the Treasury, to which the Board was answerable, two secretaries supervised the work of about twelve clerks; but in 1761 Gilbert Elliot found that all of them were 'extremely ignorant about the common course of Scotch business' and they seem to have been equally inefficient and uninterested, as records and letters were not infrequently lost. To achieve any action, it was apparently necessary to bribe one of the clerks to nag the First Lord.[29] It is unlikely that such a situation arose overnight, so perhaps normal eighteenth-century bureaucratic methods compounded government sins of omission.

There was certainly no regular pattern or apparent logic in Treasury behaviour. Some suggestions were speedily approved, others ignored for long periods or even completely, like the request for an extra £200 per annum for educational purposes. Financial control was erratic, sudden unexpected rigidity and attention to detail occasionally taking the Board by surprise. They undoubtedly believed, particularly after 1760, that they would have more freedom of movement than in fact turned out to be the case. In 1762, Lord Milton had been sure that, if the sum allocated to Dr. Cullen for his research on cashube ashes was inadequate, the king would allow a further grant.[30] Possibly this was so, but when the Board did in fact lend money to several manufacturers without prior permission, to avoid delay, the Treasury's 'dead hand' fell flat and clammy and they were instructed to retrieve the £2,100 paid out. This particular episode illustrates not only the occasional emphasis placed by the central government on absolute control of the disposition of finance but is another example of the tardiness of reactions in London. Consider the dates. The Board reported the grant of money in March 1764; the minutes of

January 1765 record the reception of royal disapproval,[31] a time lag of almost a year. Without independent action by the Commissioners, some small undertakings, set up only because of guaranteed state support, might have collapsed, losing not only the advantages hoped for but money already spent. One sturdy entrepreneur, James Welch, a tanner in Inverness, threatened to give up, so disgusted was he at delay in receiving promised capital.[32]

This brush with the Treasury made the Board more cautious in future. Previously they had overcome red tape in smaller matters by making requests in their reports for permission to use a specific amount for very general purposes. In 1756, £200 per annum had been suggested for indenturing and supporting apprentices, though this did not, of course, become operative until after 1760. In 1767, £900 a year for three years was proposed for the encouragement of the linen industry, and this was approved.[33] This gave them a little more independence, though they did not even try to spend £900 in one year, as such a sum was not available in hard cash. But each year, in such cases, they added the annual allowance, said what had been spent, and gave the capital remaining. This ensured that if any large expense arose they had money ready, in theory at least. For example, in 1773, £77.4.10 had been spent on linen manufacturing from the fund of £1,804.4.7$\frac{6}{12}$, leaving £1,726.19.9$\frac{6}{12}$ from the original capital of £2,700, in itself the aforementioned sum of £900 a year for three years.

Two points are worth noting about these types of grants. First, the sums were largely theoretical as there was rarely the amount of money in hand that was mentioned. Secondly, detailed accounts were not usually demanded by the Treasury, and as a result the commissioners exercised a certain amount of discretion. Thus £50 allowed for 'encouraging artificers in Crieff and Callendar' in 1763 had been used for two years to support a mill in Crieff for making coarse paper.[34] It was easy to rationalise this expenditure but the original idea had undoubtedly been that individual craftsmen should be set up with a decent house and garden and some tools. Then when the apprenticeship scheme was abandoned, or at least cut down in some disgust, the Board did not apply to have the £200 yearly allowance made available for some other purpose. The entries in their Journal read 'To Henry Barclay [the secretary] for apprentices and incidents'. That could cover a multiplicity of expenditure.

In the earlier years, Treasury hesitation in activating the Board's policies may have arisen partly from the financial and legal questions surrounding the rights of creditors. Both the Vesting Act and the Annexing Act expressly protected these rights and the latter included the undertaking that genuine claims – 'sustained' claims – should be paid out of 'the next aids to be granted in Parliament'. There was some suggestion that the rents were the proper funds that should be used for this purpose, and it took some time for the lawyers to agree, or at least for the government to accept, that this use of rents was not possible, because of the wording in the Annexing Act that the proceeds of the estates were to be used for 'civilising . . . promoting . . . the Protestant religion . . . and to no other Use or Purpose whatsoever'.[35] The realisation must slowly have dawned too that the Barons of the Exchequer were correct in stating that, if rents were used to pay creditors, there would be little or no surplus left to carry out the purposes of the Act. In 1759, £69,910.15.9¼ was supplied by Parliament to pay the Perth debts and, in 1770, £72,000 to provide for the debts on various estates, an annuity for the widow of Coll MacDonell of Barrisdale, and the purchase money for the superiorities on the seven estates still managed by the Barons of the Exchequer.[36] The substantial amounts required lent some support to Clerk of Penicuik's view that the only thing certain about the rebels was that most of them were bankrupt.[37]

Eventually, in their first report of 1760, the Board pointed out that no plan or method of distribution of the rents could be put into execution until approved by a 'writing under Your Majesty's Sign Manual', and as H.M. pleasure had not been made known to them, they thought themselves in duty bound to stop further proceedings. They had not been completely idle, of course, in these five years, and on the accession of George III they sent in a long description of all they had in fact achieved and what they had so far proposed. The result was the appointment of a new Board, not noticeably different from the old one, with a few more eminent 'Improvers' – improvers in every field – but also lawyers again, such as Lord Kames and Lord Gardenstone and the Sheriff Deputes of Perth and Forfarshire. Throughout the life of the Board, as need arose, or as suitable people became available, new appointments were made, one very interesting one in 1771 being Archibald Menzies, Younger of Culdares, after his resignation from the post of the Board's General Inspector to become a Commissioner of Customs. The second-last appointment was that of Henry Dundas, in 1783. After 1760 there was usually some sort of reaction to correspondence and reports, but all through the period of annexation there were delays because of tardy answers from the Crown and Treasury.

In Edinburgh, too, there were signs of somewhat lackadaisical attitudes. Perhaps, of course, it was merely that the Adam brothers had been right and the accommodation was in fact quite unsuitable but, while it would probably be maligning the commissioners to say that they all resembled their London masters in showing indifference, the management of the annexed estates certainly did not have first call on their energies. One can hardly be surprised at this, for they were all busy, eminent men with professions or estates, or both, of their own to attend to, and their duties on the Board brought no material rewards. The lack of any sense of urgency can be seen in considering the attendance at Board meetings. The first meeting in 1755 attracted a large turnout, twenty of the twenty-eight appointed, but Board meetings were not infrequently postponed through lack of a quorum, which was only five, and on more than one occasion because no commissioners at all appeared. In the first five years there were monthly meetings only, which cannot have expedited business. The clerk wrote to one of the factors on one occasion in May, 1757: 'I find that the whole business of the Board on Monday was transacted in one line – Adjourned to Monday 20th June'. That meant two months between meetings. He went on: 'Yesterday, the standing committee consisted of Lord Milton and he adjourned himself to the first day of the session in June'. The standing committee had been appointed in 1757, it should be noted, to allow for a certain amount of specialisation and speedier transaction of business.[38] On December 18th, 1758, only Lord George Beauclerk and Lord Somerville attended, so the meeting was adjourned until January 8th, 1759, when no members at all appeared, as on January 15th, and eventually a quorum was achieved on January 22nd. In March, 1760 there was another adjournment until June, but at least the first clerk, John Robertson, was instructed 'in anything of an emergency' to apply for directions to 'any of the commissioners who might be about town'.[39]

The new Board commissioned by George III tried to overcome the difficulty of collecting a quorum by deciding to hold meetings at a fixed hour, on a fixed day each week. They were perhaps driven to this by their record in the first few months of their corporate existence, when they met twice in August and then again not until November. At least, with a definite unchanging day and hour, members could hardly plead previous engagements. Failure on this scale to attend meetings can surely be taken as indicating something less than intense interest in their commission. Small committees were appointed to look into individual matters such as leases, schools and bridges, minutes of their meetings being intermingled with those of the full Board.[40]

Treasury neglect must rank as an extenuating circumstance in explaining absenteeism among Board members. Any commissioner excited by the possibilities of the annexation must have found the enforced inactivity from 1755 to 1760 extremely frustrating, and meetings where no final policy decisions could be taken must often have seemed pointless and not worth attending. But politics affected attendance too. Newcastle needed Argyll too much to back up his own supporters in any disagreements, and his protégé in the secretaryship, Stamp Brooksbank, was eventually instructed to pay his respects to the Scottish duke.[41] Lord Deskford, initially an enthusiastic participant at Board meetings, if attendance and enthusiasm can indeed be equated, realised that his services were no longer of great importance to Newcastle and attended no meetings after the spring of 1756. He was persuaded to accept renomination by George III and explained his earlier retiral in a letter to another Commissioner, Baron Mure, on the grounds that 'some People possessed of more Power had very different Plans in view from mine'.[42] The most assiduous attenders were a Commissioner of Customs, Mansfeldt Cardonnel, closely followed by Lord President Craigie of Glendoich, and Joseph Tudor, another Commissioner of Customs. George Drummond, several times Provost of Edinburgh, Lord Somerville and the lawyers on the Board made the next most regular appearances, the short distance between the law courts and the Board's office no doubt having its effect on the last group.

Another somewhat surprising aspect of the Board's administration is that they definitely did not consider regular visits to the estates as a necessary, ineluctable part of their duties. There seem to be no records of official visitations by commissioners to the extensive areas under their control, though commissioners who were law lords sometimes wore two hats when on circuit duty. From the beginning, they conceived of the whole administration being carried out on their part by letters and verbal instruction to their staff, their views having been formed solely from consideration of surveys, maps, plans and reports from various officers. The end results can hardly be acclaimed, although, to give the commissioners their due, they were aware of the deficiencies of this approach. They could hardly be otherwise for, landowners as many of them were, it is difficult to believe that they managed their own estates by such remote control. This may be slightly harsh criticism to make in an eighteenth-century context, for even Grant of Monymusk did not apparently visit his estates every year, if we are to judge from the letter from his gardener, John Middleton, regretting his absence 'this season' as his presence had far more effect than 'twenty precepts'.[43] An obituary on James Ogilvie, Earl of Findlater and Seafield, considered it worth noting that he had 'for many years past resided almost constantly on his own estates'.[44] But to abdicate almost entirely from the necessity of personal supervision seems irresponsible.

To help overcome the disadvantages of absentee landlordism, the Board decided to appoint a Riding Officer or General Inspector as their substitute. Even here, central delays had their effect for, in 1758, they decided to delay his circuit because of having had no word of the king's pleasure with regard to the last report.[45] But their consciousness of the limitatations of their methods is clearly revealed in a paragraph in one draft of instructions to this officer which, even more significantly, was ordered to be struck out and not even minuted: 'You are also to keep in mind that you are appointed for this reason chiefly that the Trustees themselves consist of a number of Lords and Gentlemen who have other Employments, Business or Avocations and can but seldom have opportunity to see with their own eyes what is fit to be done or going forward in several parts in prosecution of the purposes of the said law' (i.e. the Annexing Act).[46] The General Inspector went out on a tour in the summer, first with a salary of £100 and 10/6 per day travelling expenses, then, when Menzies was appointed, £150 and one guinea a day. This officer had to make reports on the general conditions of the estates and on individual projects which were sometimes mentioned in his instructions.[47] This was not a continuous appointment, and even at an early date there was some discussion among the commissioners as to whether it was necessary. Francis Grant, the first appointed, died in 1762 and Archibald Menzies was appointed to replace him in 1764. When he resigned to become a Commissioner of Customs, he offered to continue his duties *gratis*, and no further official appointment was made until after his death in 1780. Then Adam Drummond of Gardrum was appointed on 20th November, 1780, but has left no records of any activity, only a demand for payment of his salary after disannexation. William Frend became an inspector and supervisor of the estate of Perth and left reports as well as a 1781 receipt for his term of inspection.[48] Menzies' reports ceased on his resignation, however, and this is unfortunate for they were revealing, and Menzies did not mince words in criticism of the management by the commissioners or anyone else.

Another means used by the commissioners to compensate for their absence from the estates was to demand the factors' attendance at the Edinburgh office, fairly frequently and expensively. The Struan accounts for example have regular entries of £25 for the factor's travelling expenses to Edinburgh. The other side of this coin was their apparent distrust of factors, who were on the defensive throughout their tenure of office. This partly arose from one of the aims of the annexation, that of 'infusing [the inhabitants] with a deep conviction of the Goodness of the present Royal Family', to quote one of the many who offered advice on managing the annexed estates.[49] Translated into administrative terms, this clashed vigorously with efficiency and undermined the position of the Board's representatives, especially the factors, vis-a-vis the tenants. In the mysterious way that such information gets about, the tenants of the annexed estates got wind of it and boasted that, now they were the king's tenants, they would be much better off than anyone else. There was even a rumour that rents were all to be reduced by one-fifth, or even a quarter.[50]

Rumour was not too far from the truth. There was general attention to tenants' welfare, such as buying meal in times of scarcity, and in 1757 the Struan factor was instructed to buy meal and, in addition: 'As for the poor in general, you are to join with the neighbouring heritors and be as forward as any of them for their relief'. In 1765, when the Perth estate was divided for administrative reasons into Highland and Lowland Divisions, William Lawson, clerk to the dismissed factor, John Campbell of Barcaldine, was directed to take up the very large arrears of rent 'without hurting the tenant'. How this was to be reconciled with earlier strict instructions from the king that, for the future, 'factors be upon no consideration or pretence whatsoever excused from settling' is uncertain.[51] The 'pretence' referred to was the '*alledged* (my italics) scarcity of money in the Highlands arising from the bad sale of cattle', an attitude that seems to denote a certain ignorance of the Highland economy with its fluctuations and uncertainties. One of the most significant and influential elements in the Board's attitude to their commission was their conception of their duty to the king's tenants. Among the earliest instructions to the factors was the reminder that their responsibility was to promote not just the civilising but the happiness of the inhabitants. It was unimaginable that the Board of Commissioners for the Annexed Estates would tell their factors, as did the Barons of the Exchequer, that any tenants who 'behaved in a way not agreeable' to the factor should be turned out when their leases expired.[52] This type of Board/tenant/factor relationship may have had its unfortunate results administratively, but socially, if the aim was to assist in the reconciliation of the northern inhabitants of Britain with the Hanoverians, it should have had only good effects.

Needless to say, the vision of the good landlord as seen by an eighteenth-century board predominantly composed of Edinburgh lawyers and landowners was essentially paternalistic but, in its contemporary context, it was not contemptible. For example, adhering to the belief that the 'deil finds wark for idle hands', happiness and leisure were not equated. The factors, while remembering that the happiness of the inhabitants was a worthwhile aim, were also to 'use all due means and incitement to keep people from being idle especially in the winter nights from close of evening to bedtime'. General health in the estates was attended to, in that tenents were inoculated against smallpox;[53] suffers from the cevennes – veneral disease – were sought out and given treatment. Prospective patients were sometimes reticent about the latter complaint, but treatment was dealt out in various districts. No-one in Barrisdale would initially admit to having the cevennes, but eventually the factor showed £5.3.8 $\frac{2}{12}$ spent on treatment; and £30 was paid to Alexander McDonald, the Fort William surgeon, for curing the cevennes in Lochaber.[54]

The Board also did their duty as heritors, in respect of other relief; they paid their proportion of the poor rate to the collector in Callander, Robert Buchanan. There are also examples of particular charity. Patrick Drummond in Dalchrune was allowed £2 travelling expenses to Edinburgh Royal Infirmary to have his leg amputated in 1772, and two years later was given 10/- towards buying a cow, 'he being a very poor man and had his leg cut off in Edinburgh Royal Infirmary.[55] No doubt, one quite considerable allowance of £10 to £12 a year to a widow to maintain her children until they were old enough to benefit by the Board's apprenticeship scheme was largely inspired by the desire to save her and the children from popish principles; her sole known source of support was a brother, a Jesuit priest who had already sent one of the boys to Douai. This son returned home, though the several members of the Dingwall Presbytery who wrote to the Board about him used the more emotive word 'escaped', and the factor thought he had prevailed upon him to attend the established church and take up an apprenticeship to a ship's carpenter.[56]

The factors were perhaps less likely to have felt so charitable as they struggled in close proximity, day by day, with apathetic, reluctant improvers, recalcitrant soldiers and uncomprehending peasantry. John Forbes and James Small had both been in the army and Small particularly, who was a competent, hard-working, conscientious man, was in favour of keeping the Highlands 'in proper subjection'. He felt that the Highlanders had too recently been under 'very despotic government' for it to be safe to let them have similar freedom to the rest of the country: 'If they are not brought by proper degrees to absolute freedom, that freedom may turn into a licentiousness that may give more trouble than people unacquainted with their dispositions may think of'. Quite a disciplinarian, even near the end of his life Small was prepared to recruit thieves and evildoers forcibly for General Fraser's regiment, but not surprisingly the Board would not give approval to this suggestion.[57] On the other hand, there is no doubt of the factors' compassion in face of the famines, in 1783 particularly. Henry Butter's letters in 1772 and 1783 show horror at the situation, and he tried to impress on the Board the need for speedy action. He was not alone in this.[58]

The commissioners persisted in their attitude throughout that loyal, Protestant tenants must always be well-treated and be seen to be so, whatever the inconveniences thereby inflicted on their servants. It is difficult to criticise them for the underlying philosophy, but simple to show that their benevolence sometimes outweighed commonsense and efficiency and thus minimised the benefits of some of the steps they wished to take. One particular aspect of this tenderness towards the tenants may have been intensified by there being so many lawyers on the Board. A complaint from a tenant about any of the officers' actions immediately set off a series of enquiries, charges and countercharges, expensive correspondence and visits to Edinburgh. The complainants were often inspired by what the factors considered sheer contrariness. Archibald Menzies had a fairly good idea of the difficulties the factors faced and he gives a very sympathetic description of what they had to contend with in his reports for 1767–68. He says: 'The factors upon these estates have been at great pains to divide the farms . . . and have tried to carry out a number of other articles for improving the police of the estates but they have been very much discouraged from pushing those articles by the licentious dispositions of the tenants'. Apparently, whenever any decision was taken not entirely to the liking of the tenants, they got an agent to draw up a long paper of complaints and grievances to lay before the Board. Thereupon the factor was ordered to report, 'things are suspended until factors are further examined and after all, tho the tenant is found in the wrong no further notice is taken. Things are come to such a pass upon these estates that no order of the Board if in the least disagreeable to the tenants can be executed without going through all the different courts'. Note that the factors were 'further examined', not the tenants. Factors are never heroes in the Highlands, but the weighting was very much against them on the annexed estates.

Menzies directed the Board's attention to their accounts to consider the great expense they had been put to to have their 'orders executed and ended by the ruin of the litigating tenants' and he tried to convince the commissioners of the necessity of supporting their authority in the persons of their factors. No tenant, he thought, on being ordered to remove, ever looked out for another possession nor, if an exchange was ordered, was a removal thought of until the tenant had tried all the courts. Tenants knew that if their case were proved unjustified they would still get the first farm ordered. Menzies was on a similar tack when he wrote to the secretary from New Tarbat asking him to get the Board to defer action on complaints until he returned from his tour, 'so preventing the disagreeable situation we have been in for some time past of doing one day and undoing another'.[59] He added that his only motive was to save the tenants from a 'parcel of Agents who squeeze the very life out of them'.

The factors' duties were heavy and responsible, as we can see from the Struan factor's list in 1759 of only some of the things he had to do: 'Attend meetings of the Quarter Session and of neighbouring Gentlemen and J.P's to concert measures for the Police of the Country, the personal attendance to every new Work, carring on in the estate by order of the Board' and – here perhaps a touch of bitterness – 'even to reparation of a tenant's house, expense of sending money to the Receiver General and other things of that nature'. All rents from the estates had to be sent to the Receiver General. Small added that the estate of Struan was so situated that it required 'constant attendance and application to keep the inhabitants in a due respect and obedience to the laws'; and this made frequent visits to the different corners of the estate necessary to become personally acquainted with them, to hear their complaints and grievances and to procure 'assistance and redress', all of which incurred expense apart from 'personal trouble'. Other duties included assisting in recruiting men in 1756 and 1757 for the forces.[60] Factors had to be resident on the estate they factored for the greater part of the year, a reasonable condition, and they had also to refuse gifts of any sort from tenants, to preclude bribery. When John Campbell of Barcaldine eventually lost his factory of the Perth estate in 1765, one of the accusations was that he had accepted 'presents', but he had also been very lax in sending in accounts, 1761 not being cleared until 1764. When an inquiry was made, considerable discrepancy was found between his lists and that of the Inspector General, who was eventually sent off with one of the clerks from the Edinburgh office to investigate.[61]

Despite the somewhat doubtful reliability of Barcaldine, it is worth quoting his letter to Lord Milton, regarding a breach in the banks of the River Earn. It does illuminate the difficulties the factors worked under: 'If I was acting for a single person I would go on with the work and expect his thanks, but I do not know that I might be found fault with if I exceed my order'. The factors had little confidence that their masters would support them. Even after Menzies' comments, Thomas Keir on the Lowland division of Perth was not prepared to press a warning against a tenant in Auchinglen who had cut down a 'good thriving ash tree', had not brought rent due when he said he would and had been very insolent. He needed definite orders. On another occasion, Barcaldine sent in asking for instructions and advice, very legitimately, and he got very little positive assistance. He wondered if he was at liberty to accept the 5/- and 10/- notes from the banks of Perth, Dundee, Auchtermuchty and Kirkliston, etc., as this was the only money he was able to collect. The commissioners' first reaction, astoundingly, was that they refused to give directions as to what notes the factor should take. Then one of those present, Mr. Drummond, produced the information that the Bank of Edinburgh (*sic*) had agreed to give their notes for those of the Bank of Ayr and the three banks of Glasgow, the Old, the New and the Thistle. So the Board relented but only so far as to direct the secretary to write to the factor accordingly.[62]

The factors had not only to defend themselves against tenants and Board. In 1765, the Lovat factor was faced with a court case, as a complaint had been laid against him for acting as a Commissioner of Supply in the County of Cromarty. He was liable to be fined £20 for every time he had attended if it was proved that his attendance – as the Board's representative – was not legal. He had been advised to 'offer a reclaiming petition' and hoped the Board would 'join their appearance in this case'. All that is noted in the minutes is 'Read', cold comfort for someone whose annual salary would have paid only five of these fines.[63]

The pay too was uncertain, for it was calculated as 5% of the rents, and these varied annually according to the increase and decrease of the price of meal and barley of which the greater part of the rents consisted, at least at the beginning of the annexation. In 1770, three of the longest-serving factors were given a considerable bonus – £100 per annum extra to Captain Forbes of New 'for his great Zeal and activity in civilising the Highlands', the same to James Small and £80 to Henry Butter. This mark of appreciation must have been the more welcome by comparison with the attitude revealed in 1766, when it was thought that the factories were too extensive and that the factors with the smaller salaries were more diligent. Further, there was even a suggestion that allowances for houses, clerks, postage, and visits to Edinburgh were not warranted by law.[64] Of course this was reaction to the realisation of Barcaldine's sins of both omission and commission, and the same paper recommended the division of the larger estates. This administrative change was made; James Small was made factor on Struan and the Highland Division of the estate of Perth, and Thomas Keir on the Lowland Division of Perth, the highest rentalled estate, at the end of 1766.

Certainly also, the factors were not all blameless. We have noted Barcaldine's dismissal; Ninian Jeffrey's cautioners withdrew their surety as they had heard rumours, correct as it turned out, that he had fallen into considerable arrears with the Coigach rent. Also, he and Henry Butter were reprimanded for holding tenancies of more than the Board thought proper.[65] But the overall impression is of hard-working, honest and conscientious men who did their best under difficult conditions. When Small died in 1777, a list of the orders he had not carried out included two questions of disputed marches, one in 1774 and one in 1776, neglecting to purchase a drill and hoe for a labourer in 1776, and failure to prosecute three tenants for keeping goats. The list is somewhat longer in 1777 when presumably his last illness hindered his working.[66] It is not a bad record and merits the remark of Leslie, the surveyor, on 'Mr. Small's well-known complaisance'. Indeed when one considers the behaviour of the Edinburgh Board, it may be thought surprising that Small had done so well, for dilatoriness at the centre can have an infectious reaction at all levels.

Keir, in an effort to overcome delay on one occasion, was driven to deviousness. He wrote to the secretary that a process commenced against tenants had been sent to the Board about two years previously and no answer or order had been received. He suggested that the secretary should examine the minutes and, if there were no orders and nothing had been done, they should simply renew the process '. . . without giving the Board any further trouble about it or waiting for this copy to be laid before them'. A few years later he wrote that he was 'much surprised' that the Board had not come to a resolution about the rent of Muthill,[67] but one cannot avoid the suspicion that the expression of surprise was mere courtesy. By 1773, when this letter was written, the picture that emerges is one of flabbiness in the administration, too much centralisation combined with insufficient attention both in Edinburgh and in London, delay and procrastination. These organisational and administrative mishaps and misjudgments, however, were to emerge in the course of the years of annexation and were certainly not anticipated in 1755. At that date the commissioners, once appointed, began their work energetically in an atmosphere of enthusiasm and optimism.

AGRICULTURE

4

Landholding

AMONG the varied activities of the Board for the Annexed Estates, management
of the estates as agricultural units was perhaps the most time-consuming, and
rightly deserved to be so. Society in the area covered by the estates was
agriculturally based in 1752 and, over two hundred years later, agriculture is still
an important part of the Highland economy in one form or another, despite the
Dounreay complex, hydro-electricity, tourism and the current developments in the
exploitation of oil. If the direct effect on individuals is considered, agricultural
change was the most important and far-reaching of all that the commissioners
attempted. Some few industrial entrepreneurs were to benefit directly from the
Board's largesse; roads, bridges, schools, all contributed to the quality of life in the
area; but land was still the vital element and, on it, all were dependent in the last
resort, for the only income available to the commissioners came from the land, in
money rent, services and casualties. Their management was clearly of vital
importance.

Sensible of this fact, and also aware of their basic ignorance of conditions on the
estates, the commissioners' first task was to discover, to the best of their ability, the
true state of affairs, technically and socially. Peter May and John Leslie were the
two men who carried out most of the scientific surveys; others employed included
Francis Grant, who also worked for the Barons of the Exchequer, William
Morison, and David Aitkin.[1] For additional social information, however, the
factors were required to answer a long list of questions put to them by the commissioners; this list included enquiries about every aspect of life on the estates, and
they were also asked what they would recommend in the way of improvements.[2]
Although the social aspect will assume a less important place here, it must always
be borne in mind that it is almost impossible to separate agricultural and social
organisation in the Highlands at that time. This is amply demonstrated in the
factors' reports, which refer to the estates that were under the commissioners'
management from 1755, and not to those held of subject superiors. The factors
employed at the time who returned reports were John Campbell of Barcaldine for
the Perth estate – by far the largest – William Monteath on the parts of Arnprior
not held of a subject superior, James Small for Struan, Captain John Forbes of
New for both Lovat and Cromartie, Mungo Campbell for Barrisdale and
Kinlochmoidart and James Mackdonald (*sic*) of Rineton for Monaltrie, the
smallest estate, only about 'two miles in circumference'.

The questions put to the factors regarding agricultural practices give some
indication of the type of policy the commissioners were likely to follow. The first
query concerned the types of leases on the estates, and any subletting connected

with the lessees, the next the number of wadsetters, and the effect on the people of having 'these lesser gentlemen' living among them. Thereafter, each barony had to be described by size, situation and fertility; the grain it cultivated was to be noted, and the pasture. The factors were asked to find out if lime was burnt for manure, or if indeed any limestone had been found; had flax and potato raising made any progress; was grass sown or hay made; if there were any enclosures, how large they were and how they were made. On animal stocking, information about the type and value of the cattle kept was requested and, following this, what use was made of milk and dairy produce. Mills and woods had also to be looked at from the point of view of convenience and value, and the penultimate query was what carriages of bark and other services should be reserved in leases.

Allowing for local differences in soil and climate, as well as in the character of the inhabitants, the factors' reports showed remarkable similarity in some aspects of husbandry.[3] Potatoes, for example, were universally grown, even in Barrisdale, the most inaccessible of the estates annexed, and there the dung was put on the potato ground. Small claimed that it was only through his initiative, in the previous two years, that Struan tenants had been persuaded to plant both potatoes and lint, lintseed having been obtained through the Barons of the Exchequer at prime cost, while very few potatoes were grown in Monaltrie. Near Dunblane, on the other hand, enough potatoes were grown to produce a surplus for sale. Another common factor was that no grass seeds were sown and little hay was made, even where the greatest dependence of the tenants was on their supplies of black cattle and the milk yield, as in Coigach, where the tenants made butter and cheese for sale in Tain, Dingwall and Contin, and in the Barony of Stratherrick, lying largely on the south side of Loch Ness. Black cattle of average quality, even if small, seemed to fetch much the same price all over the estates, namely thirty to forty shillings, except in places like Auchterarder where they were not fit for marketing, hardly producing enough milk for the owner's family, or in Glenartney, where the quality was high and the price might reach forty-five shillings.

Bere and oats were produced in varying quantities and quality, almost everywhere from Callander to Coigach, the results depending on the soil, the climate and the tenants' energy. In Lix, in Killin parish, no matter that they bought in good seed, there were poor returns. The barony lay on high ground, north-facing over Loch Dochart, and only a hot, dry season saw the crops ripen there. If less than three bolls of oats gave one boll of meal, that was reckoned a good return. And these tenants limed their grounds, using the plentiful peat to burn the equally easily obtained limestone. The use of lime, of course, was conditioned by the availability of fuel and, in Strathyre, an eighteen-mile carry for coal effectively restricted the tenants' use of that particular form of improvement. In the far west estate of Barrisdale, the little arable land that there was provided the inhabitants with grey oats to keep them in bread all winter and spring, through spade culture and the use of sea-ware for manure. In the summer, they made enough money from butter and cheese, sold to Sleat, to buy oatmeal. But the factor, Mungo Campbell, considered that the arable land would not respond to any treatment, and the only improvement he recommended was dividing the farms.

E

What one might term the outline of landholding did not differ much from south to north, in that the size of the holdings seems similar overall and the intermingling of one proprietor's lands with another's was widespread. Barcaldine says little about runrig or the size of holdings but, in Strathyre, the farms which were leased for nineteen years and not subset had so many tenanats in each that there was not much milk. On the estate of Lovat, too, Captain Forbes had to write that the holdings were far too small and in runrig, so that only division and enlargement would make the farms economic.

In general, it can be said that, the farther north the estate, the more backward by 'improving' standards were the agricultural methods used, and the less interested the inhabitants in change or improvement, though there were of course exceptions. Throughout the annexation, the tenants of Muthill, for example, in the heartland of the estate of Perth near Castle Drummond, got few good words from anyone. In 1755, the only agricultural enterprise they showed was in watering their ground; they used none of the stone marl that was in good supply for manure, they burned no lime, and their cattle were poor, though some cheese and butter was sold in the Highland part of the barony. They made a little hay, but even the stone dikes round some enclosures in the vicinity of Drummond Castle were poor. Neighbouring baronies could show very different attitudes, for while Dunblane and Muthill had similar soils and could be expected to respond to similar methods of improvement, the tenants were very different, those in Dunblane being 'frugal and industrious'. In the barony of Stratherrick, on the Lovat estate, good soil and good pasture made some of the tenants self-sufficient in grain despite the poor climate, and ensured good supplies of butter and cheese, but Forbes' view of the tenants was so low that, to counteract the effect of the over-small holdings which led to the wives and children having to beg, he could only suggest introducing strangers from other parts of the country, as death or removal left vacant possessions. This advice was apparently taken and seems to have been effective, as the General Inspector was able to report in 1766 that the new tenants were in fact improvers. He attributed this mainly to their being separate from their own clan and needing the Board's support, which only their industry would gain.[4]

James Drummond, the former owner of the estate of Perth, had been an interested improving landlord before he became involved in the 1745 and, as a result, leases and enclosures were not unknown on the estate. The greater part of the barony of Callander was under tack, the leases having six to eight years still to run, though Balquhidder, slightly farther north, had none. Most of Stratherrick (part of Lovat) was set to tacksmen and wadsetters, but Lowland eyes did not see them as improvers. And enclosures were more conspicuous by their absence or, as in Monaltrie, by their being allowed to go to ruin, in the last few years.

The most striking visual difference between the areas most likely to have felt Lowland influences and those in the north and west must have been in the appearance of the houses. All over the Perth estate, Barcaldine mentions good or tolerably good stone houses, and when Menzies is travelling over the estate, he talks of all the Highlanders in Perthshire being good builders of dry-stone dikes, as they were used to building and repairing their own houses. The other reports hardly mentioned houses but, in Barrisdale, 'the whole houses of the country are made up of twigs and manufactured by way of creels called watling and covered with turff'. In 1767, Menzies stated that, in all the Highland estates, there were only creel houses, and one of his greatest objections to these was that the frame was made of only pliant plants, mostly young trees.

One other local element which conditioned the use of lime was the availability or otherwise of fuel. It was not surprising to discover only one man burning limestone in the Barony of Stobhall, when peat had to be carried five or six miles, and coal from still farther away, from Perth, even though it was obtainable at any time of the year. Farm implements and presumably tools for all trades were also affected. In Lix, the lack of wood was explicitly given as one of the reasons for the poor tools; the tenants could provide themselves with these, but from a distance – where exactly was unspecified. And clearly the time and effort involved would inhibit their being over-particular.

The factors' reports served as a basis on which to plan how best the aims of the annexation could be achieved on the estates themselves. 'Ever so very contemporary',[5] the commissioners shared what Malcolm Gray calls 'the singularly unanimous abhorrence which the articulate thinkers of the eighteenth century held for anything but individual and permanent tenure of land'.[6] Unable fully to understand the Highlander's concept of landholding, and disliking and mistrusting what they did see and comprehend, this panel of mainly Lowland improvers and lawyers had little doubt about their first agricultural priority and, of course, neither had their masters in Parliament. If the Highlands were to be 'improved', 'civilised' and brought into the mainstream of British life, it was essential that the inhabitants should become more independent of their chiefs and of the tacksmen. The one certain way of ensuring this state of affairs, in Lowland eyes at least there was no doubt, was to provide them with security of tenure of the land they cultivated. In the Lowlands as well, the system of landholding was considered one of the worst evils of the unimproved agricultural system by all the active improvers of the eighteenth century. Leaseless, undivided land held in runrig, in tenements of any size, large or small, whether farm, croft or pendicle, provided no incentive to tenants to increase the yield by good husbandry of any kind, by weeding, manuring, or sowing better seed, when there was no certainty that the improver would reap the benefit of his expenditure in time or money. As a result, it was thought that one of the first objects of those managing the annexed estates should be to grant leases to tenants, directly from the Crown, and especially to cut out subtenancies, with their dependence on the favour of a middleman.

The Annexing Act showed the importance attached to this, for the first positive step towards change that was mentioned was the desirability of granting leases and the qualifications that lessees must have. The term of the lease was to be a maximum of twenty-one years, or forty-one if the lessee was prepared to lay out not less than five years' rent on the holding, either on buildings or other improvements, within seven years of the date of the leases. To prevent over-large farms, only mines or fishing could be let at more than £20 per annum. Then the leases could be made void, if the tenants sublet even part of their holding; if they were non-resident; or if they were found to have 'paid anything other than the rent' expressed in the lease, in consideration of having obtained it. This delicate method of saying 'No bribery' was emphasisied when the factors were given instructions by the commissioners that they must under no circumstances accept 'presents', and John Campbell of Barcaldine's breach of this rule was an important consideration in his losing his post on the Perth estate.[7] In addition, leases were to be 'absolutely void', unless the lessee had taken the oaths required for qualifying persons to execute offices of public trust in Scotland. These had to be sworn before the Quarter Sessions or before the Sheriff Depute or his Substitute. This step may seem like the proverbial sledgehammer and the nut, but the Barons of the Exchequer, who could statutorily give only three-year leases or longer leases with a three-year breach, had also instructed factors that farms being rouped for letting because of uncertainty over the rental were to be set only to those prepared to go voluntarily to the Justices of the Peace to take the oath of allegiance.[8] The government was determined to be sure of the inhabitants' loyalty, before they could have security of tenure. The restriction of the size of lands held by one man, by specifying a maximum rent, was likewise an attempt to prevent the establishment of possible dissident influences.

Later a change in the value of holdings allowed had to be made. In 1774, the upper limit of £20 was increased on account of the rise in the value of horned cattle and in recognition of the rise in the general value of land, through 'inclosure improvements'.[9] It was unfortunate that the price of grain dropped quite considerably soon after, in 1777 and 1778, so that the total produce of the estates fell instead of rising as anticipated.

Ensuring that the estates were accurately surveyed was a statutory duty placed on the commissioners, one that was necessary in the narrower context if landholding was to be made more precise, and desirable in the wider, with the mapping of the Highlands still imperfect. With surveys fairly complete as they thought and factors' reports before them, by 1757, the Board informed the King and Treasury that they had begun to grant leases. In accordance with the aims and terms of the Annexing Act, tenants had to be chosen with care and, as the Protestant religion had to be forwarded by all possible means, there are examples of Roman Catholics being turned off on account of their faith. Duncan Stewart and William Riddoch are only two of these. Early in 1758, one lease at least was held up until the would-be lessee's religion was ascertained, as this seemed dubious from the factor's comments. As loyalty to the reigning monarch was also a *sine qua non* for security of tenure, tenants such as David Ross and his brother were evicted in 1756 on suspicion of having sheltered rebels.[10] The notion, too, first expressed by Captain Forbes in his report on Lovat and Cromartie, of mixing 'some strangers with the old inhabitants' persisted, the hope being that the former would set an example in hard work and perseverance, the lack of industry on the part of the tenants being regularly deplored by the commissioners and factors. During his tenure of office, Inspector Menzies commented that there was little hope of improvement in the estates with the present 'ignorant, aukward, lazy inhabitants'.

As the factors' reports showed, leases were not unknown on the estates, though the number varied from one district to another. Struan could boast only two, and one of these was for fir woods, but in Ardsheal, in the part claimed by the subject superior, there were leases of eighteen, nineteen and twenty-nine years' duration, granted from 1735 onwards.[11] But by 1761, despite delays and reservations over the legal steps necessary,[12] the Board felt able to report to His Majesty that they had been 'particularly attentive' to their instructions regarding leases, granted for a limited time in place of the 'dependant precarious possessions which formerly prevailed'. They duly attached schedules showing the conditions of the leases and the rules and articles for managing corn farms.

In 1760, Charles Dundas, who was considered a skilled agriculturalist, had been appointed as Director for agricultural improvements, and he was sent to examine farms on the Perth estate. He had also been employed to examine tenants who might be 'proper persons' to hold leases from the commissioners and to decide what methods of cultivation should be used. Their reaction to his suggestions was sensible and humane for, recognising the poverty and ignorance of the larger part of the Highland population, they aimed at leases that would not load tenants with too many restraints and obligations, and yet would gradually teach them the value, on corn farms initially, of fallowing, enclosing and sowing grass. They also proposed the use of estate funds to carry out improvements, which would be interest-free for the first three years. However, perhaps too much was expected from tenants, even with this principle in mind, for in 1770 James Small, factor on Struan, where improvements had been considerable, felt it necessary to point out that the tenants were 'like overgrown lads, first sent to school', who could not carry out some of the tasks their contemporaries were skilled at. He suggested that very gradual steps should be taken to push them into the improving methods, perhaps just enclosing for seven years, with prizes for industry, another step in the next seven years, and then in the next seven one could reasonably expect more general competence.[13]

Certainly these leases, though the Board claimed their aims were gradual, embodied all the steps necessary in the eyes of the improver. No subletting was allowed, thirlage was to be equitably commuted, marches were to be straightened, through excambion if essential, and gates and fences were to be kept up by the tenants. On corn farms, sheep were to be kept only if they were in enclosures with sufficient stone walls; all beasts were to be herded in winter as well as summer, and housed at night. Rules were made about regular fallowing, at least five acres annually per plough. Red clover was insisted on and two-fifths of the arable land was to be in grass seed, this proportion to be ready for incoming tenants, and to have been in pasture for at least three preceding years. Dung had to be left, but the outgoing tenants could use the steading for threshing their last crop and for keeping their horses at the time. Assistance would be given for building houses, only if the roofs were of thatch, fern or heather. This was to discourage the wasteful habit of ruining the best grass lands by using turf or divots to roof houses.[14] Carriage of bark, peat and coal, 'from the usual distance and the accustomed places', was still reserved in the leases, but this was only realistic before good roads and transport were common, and had been decided on in 1755. All the factors had advised this too in their reports. The vagueness, in a legal document, of the expression 'the accustomed place' must have led to more than one argument of the type that arose when tenants on Perth declared that they had been used to carry only forty stone of the eighty proposed in their lease and forty more only if the family needed it in the spring. These early leases were for seven, eight or nine years, but had a covenant to extend them to twenty-one years if the tenants proved satisfactory.[15] Later, some small tenants asked for leases of crofts, and if the factor gave a favourable report, they were admitted as King's Cottagers, a category of holding that had two parallel aims. It could give security of tenure to even the least important of the king's tenants, or provide subsistence for craftsmen, who could not be expected to look after a large farm and practise their trade as well.[16]

In 1763, the government's response to the Board's report emphasised the desire of the central government to facilitate the granting of leases. If the initial duration was less than twenty-one years, the tenants should be 'absolutely intitled' to a prolongation, as long as they had kept the terms of the original. The aim of lessening the dependence on chiefs and tacksmen was re-emphasised, 'It being as we have already signified to you a principal object of our attention to render these possessions as little precarious as possible and to accustom the tenants to consider themselves as depending upon nothing but the exertion of their own industry and the performance of their engagements for the secure continuance of their tenure…'. The commissioners took this duty seriously and, within a year of obtaining the control of the estates held of a subject superior, they began to grant leases. In Arnprior, for example, leases carried the usual provision that five years' rent should be spent on improvements in seven years.[17] Usually, leases were of twenty-one years' duration but, as late as 1784, the year when the estates were returned to heirs or to pardoned proprietors, some were being granted for forty-one years. Earlier, various factors other than doubts about tenants' abilities and qualifications had delayed the granting of leases. Government silence before 1760 was one; George II's death was another; then in August 1761 the commissioners decided not to extend any leases already in operation to the Perth estate until all the debts for that estate were paid.[18] There was further delay in 1765 when it was reported to the king that farms already leased had not been fairly rented; until the factors and the General Inspector had compared and reported on this, there was to be a moratorium. In 1769, one of the commissioners' several attempts to kill two birds with one stone was incorporated in the provision that anyone beginning or just carrying on any useful branch of manufactures on the annexed estates was to be given preference in obtaining a lease.[19] The Misses Campbell of Tomperran had been granted a lease for Garrichrew dependent on their industry and perseverance in carrying on the manufacture of linen thread. An attempt was also made to control improvements by stipulating that enclosing and improving should be carried out as the commissioners or their factors directed, but later investigators found that this condition was not always adhered to.[20]

The granting of long leases is generally held by later commentators to have been one of the many contributory causes of the agricultural improvements that swept through Scotland in the late eighteenth and early nineteenth centuries, but the immediate benefits were not so obvious to the commissioners' servants. In 1769, Small noted that once tenants on Struan were granted leases they promptly gave up thoughts of any further improvements, and he considered that it was vain to imagine that binding them to carry on, in their tacks, would have any effect. Later, William Frend, Inspector on the Perth estate from 1780 to 1784, remarked that tenants had built the dikes insisted on by the terms of their leases, but 'in a superficial manner', and were not all careful about maintaining them. They adhered to the letter, not the spirit, of the leases and were thus enabled to retain the additional rents. He suggested that the Board should not pay for such improvements until after inspection and approval, and this somewhat obvious step Lord Stonefield and Mr. Oliphant, who were making comments on his report, could only recommend. Other tenants were mentioned who, it was claimed, did not care what became of the ground, as long as they got the advanced rents.[21]

This lack of cooperation cannot simply be ascribed to dislike of state management. Other proprietors had met with a similar response, the Earl of Perth among them when he had tried to introduce more modern methods on his estates before 1745. Campbell of Shawfield had let on long leases on the island of Islay in 1720 but, by 1764, the only improvement was the introduction of flax, and that had been due to a compulsory clause. Another landowner, Sir James Macdonald, eighth baronet of Sleat, proposed introducing shorter leases on his lands in 1763, on the grounds that the length of those formerly granted served only to 'lay the tenants asleep'.[22] Nor did all tenants rush to obtain leases. One reason given for lack of enthusiasm was that, once leases were granted, tenants sometimes found themselves bound to action they disliked. In 1778, an attempt to divide farms and tidy up the marches was foiled by eleven families on Meuvie farm. A 'contentious, disobedient set', they had no leases, and refused to agree to any suggestion of exchange while their neighbours, who had tacks, were constrained to accept the alterations, however contentious they may have felt.[23]

Long leases, then, were probably not the cure-all they are sometimes believed to be, unless the tenants were either prepared to obey instructions or were inclined towards making improvements themselves. But the Board aimed at encouraging industrious farmers. In 1764, they indicated the type of improvements they wanted, pointing out that anyone effecting some or any of these would recommend himself for a long lease. Listed were divisions of runrig, uneven marches to be straightened, draining and winter herding, and on arable farms the Board demanded summer fallow, grass to be sown on outfield as well as infield, and turnips, potatoes and green crops to be sown. On Highland farms with only a little arable land, small areas in the glens were to be dug over with the spade to raise corn, hay and green crops to increase the winter fodder.[24] Would-be lessees on the other hand promised such improvements as sowing Lucerne grass to help persuade the commissioners to favour their case.[25]

Desite all the activity and the undoubtedly large number of leases that were discussed, a report on the annexed estates balances after the disannexation stated that the great proportion of the farms on the minutes of the Board had no formal leases drawn up, and it would be very difficult to ascertain the terms. Whose was the greater responsibility for this is difficult to decide, weighing the leisurely business methods of the Board against the dubious temper of the tenants. In 1774, the commissioners reported that many leases had been sent to tenants and not returned, but on the other hand, in 1782, some Perth estate tenants sent in a petition claiming that they had been waiting some years to have their leases written out as the Board had ordered.

Intermingled with the question of granting leases was that of the innumerable subtenants, who comprised a large proportion of the inhabitants, but who do not appear on rent-rolls. To would-be improvers, social and economic, there were two main criticisms that could be made of the system of subletting; first they disliked the power given to the main tenants over the subtenants and, secondly, the inefficiency. In 1756, several complaints had already been received by the commissioners that heritors had been accustomed to let large pieces of land to one tenant, who subset to others at a much higher rent than he himself paid, and then 'grievously oppresses' these subtenants.[26] Such oppression required redress when it came to light, but as long as both sides making the arrangements were prepared to be reasonable, there was a fair amount of satisfaction, and the system would not have lasted as long as it did without satisfaction, even allowing for the Highlander's reverence for old customs.

The possibility of such satisfaction was not recognised, however, in any improver's manual. To the power implicit in the tenant's and tacksmen's hold over the subtenant, because of the latter's lack of any legal standing, the Lowland improvers attributed the late Rising and the whole social fabric of the Highlands – which of course they deplored. This power was equally assumed to lead to inefficiency, not just in the Highlands, as a subtenant would have to work for the tenant at a time not necessarily convenient to himself. If all crops were ripe, the tenant would have prior claim on the subtenant's labour for the harvest, and to the lack of security of tenure could be attributed the delay in accepting modernisation and progress. The methods used by the commissioners in tackling the problem illustrate the lack of understanding by Highlanders and Lowlanders of each other's social organisation.

It is fair to say that they cannot have been over-enlightened by reports like that of John Campbell of Barcaldine, the Perth factor, which declared that he, a Highlander, was 'at a loss' in making such a report.[27] To start with, the term 'subtenant', so he said, was understood differently in different countries, and in the Highlands the only person looked on as a subtenant proper was he who had a proportion of a farm set to him, which he managed in grass or corn with his own stock, independent of the principal tacksman. The only difference between him and the tenant was that he paid the tacksman instead of the proprietor or his factor. The subtenant could stock and manage a farm on his own, unlike the steelbollmen, for example, whom Barcaldine describes as merely servants of a more substantial kind; they were provided by the tacksman with stock and crops and had to leave these as they found them. Without such capital assistance, they would in fact have been servants. Barcaldine also mentions pendiclers, crofters and cottars, some of whom had some grazing and some of whom had only what was called a dryhouse, that is only a house and kailyard, another of the type to whom the Annexed Estates Commissioners gave security as King's Cottagers. Most of the classes of smallholding mentioned in the report could be held of either the tacksman or the proprietor and many pendiclers were main tenants but, usually, the smaller holdings were occupied by subtenants. Wadsetters had the legal right to subset, so their subtenants were in a different category.

The siting of subtenants' holdings was sometimes a disadvantage and a nuisance when they were mixed up with the tenants'. Peter May had been ordered in his survey of Coigach to measure these separately, but found this almost impossible, as they were so interwoven with one another and in runrig with the tenants' land on so many farms that little could be done exactly.[28] Not everyone was so provident as General Skene, the Inspector of Roads, who had his cottars on Dalchonzie – 'a very pretty improved place' – fixed on the outskirts of his ground so that they had no communication with his enclosure. More often the cottar was likely to have to cross the tenant's or proprietor's land to gain access to arable land for his cattle. A smallholding in the middle of a farm could completely upset a good plan of improvement.[29] One estate that did not have to cope with the problems of subtenants was Barrisdale. According to Henry Butter, when he was factor, few had to pay a rent of more than £4 so there was no subsetting. Cottars and workmen assisted the tenant in tillage and had a small portion of arable ground and the grazing of a few cattle in recompense for labour.[30] This sounds remarkably like some of Barcaldine's categories of subtenants, bearing out his contention that the term had different connotations in different parts of the country.

Some indication of the lack of viability in the size of the farms is given in 1763 by Small, the Struan factor, for he knew of no subtenants who had been removed whose holdings could be set as separate farms. He maintained that their holdings were too small and described them as 'starving on oversmall farms', but in the social conditions prevailing in Rannoch he did not recommend turning them out of their farms, as their poverty and 'habits of idleness' might lead them into outlawry. Instead he proposed employing small tenants at £2.10/- per annum and two pecks of oatmeal a week on any public works the Board might undertake.[31]

Unfortunately for many of the subtenants, it soon became known that the commissioners meant to eradicate this type of holding and, as a result, from 1756 the chief tenants began to try to rid themselves of subtenants. The delay caused by the central government's lack of response to the Board's communications had repercussions that speedier action could have prevented. It was 1762 before the factors were asked to give a formal report on subtenancy in general and, by then, while some of the subtenants may have been kept on as hired servants if their status had been lowly enough, others had been thrust out into beggary, emigration, or near starvation. In 1762, the Lovat factor was ordered to try to provide for deserving cases among evicted subtenants, but it was already too late for many.[32] Earlier in 1762, Barcaldine had written complaining that, had the Board's orders to the factors to employ legal methods for keeping subtenants in possession been received by the previous term, it might have benefited many who were dipossessed then. He also pointed out what had been happening during the past years, as the tenants rid themselves of subtenants in self-protection.[33] The order he refers to can be found in the minutes of 11th February, 1762, and states expressly that, to prevent tenants who got tacks from dispersing the artificers and day-labourers residing on their farms at the time, the houses and yards of these should be specifically exempted from tacks. These men were not to pay rent but should be obliged to uphold their houses and, to give them some independence, the Board wanted to reserve in leases one-eighth of each farm for houses and byres for artificers and day-labourers. Some subtenants had been lucky. On one farm, Garrichrew, the main tenants had been dispossessed as they were Roman Catholics, and the subtenants took over.[34]

Initially, the commissioners saw only the disadvantages, the uneconomic aspects, and the oppression possible in the system of subletting, but its advantages soon became obvious when the subtenants were removed. Misfortune overtook many of them, while the ambiguity of their situation remained unresolved until the Treasury communicated with the Board and then the Board with the factors. In addition, there were complaints by 1762 that the tenants could not manage their farms, for they had lost the mainstay of their labour force in the subtenants. Smaller tenants, too, had been in the habit of coming into the larger farms to help out but, in 1765, Archibald Menzies, the General Inspector, wrote that, in an area where labour was scarce and becoming scarcer on account of emigration abroad and to the Lowlands, the tenants were deprived by the loss of subtenants of much-needed labour. The crofters on the other hand might have become independent, but they could not now plough their land; one of the returns they received for services rendered was that the richer tenant or master ploughed for them. Now the former masters would not do this, and the crofters who had neither the implements nor the money to buy them were thus reduced to poverty.

Hence the tenant lost his labour force and the smaller man the use of utensils which only his more highly capitilised neighbour could provide. Admittedly, the labour had been only moderately efficient, the crofter sometimes dragged away from his own land at an inconvenient time, and the ploughing possibly done only when it suited the tenant, but at least the labour had been there and the ploughing done. The other side of the coin of oppression also appeared on occasion; the power of the tacksman had included some necessary discipline. In Coigach, for example, where the subtenants were made independent of the principal tacksmen, the result was, temporarily at least, some disintegration of any improvements that had begun. The new smaller tenants generally disregarded the rules of herding, and stopped maintaining any enclosures they had made.[35] Another benefit to the tenant and subtenant was that, when specie was scarce and goods to buy hardly plentiful, payment of rent and payment for labour in services or in kind were often much more convenient than the straight money bargain. When tenants had to pay money wages, it was discovered that they could not really afford them. To the economist this may illustrate the economic inefficiency of the system, but rapid change was not practical in eighteenth-century conditions in a society to which economic growth meant nothing. The Board did in fact quickly accept that the labour question was a serious one and tried to solve it by the institution of the new class of tenant mentioned earlier – that of King's Cottager. Each of these small tenants was to have a small, commodious house with a byre and a few acres for garden stuff. This proposal was approved by the King and Treasury, £500 being allowed initially towards building houses and enclosing ground, and another £500 for the same purpose in 1766. By enclosing the holdings, the expense of leases was avoided.

The commissioners, then, had begun the destruction of subtenure from their earliest days in 1755, and other landlords generally made this a 'central theme of their policy' from the 1770s. However, Dr. Walker may be expressing a not uncommon, if extreme, view of the matter, in that he thought the proprietor cut himself off from all other methods of improving by clearing an estate of subtenants and cottagers. He thought that in place of a labour force the landowner might well find himself burdened with an 'adventurer' insufficiently well-stocked.[36] He eventually decided that the best solution would be the occupation of a large part of the land by smaller farmers holding leases, while larger farms were managed with the help of regular hired servants.[37] The difficulty, of course, in the Highlands during the transition from the old to the new social and economic system was to find the servants. It would seem therefore that in the Highland economy, whatever the situation in the Lowlands, subtenancy had some merits, both for the tacksman in providing a stable labour force and for the subtenant, who found himself slightly higher on the social scale and materially better off than he would have been as a hired labourer.

As the whole economy moved gradually from subsistence and barter to the modern concept of cash exchange for goods, rents and services, the subtenant in his older form was bound to become an anachronism, but wholesale abolition of the position was too drastic a step in the middle of the eighteenth century, with results such as have been described. This the commissioners soon had to recognise. Their compromise was the provision of the holdings for the so-called King's Cottagers at the same time as they maintained their policy of ridding the estates of unofficial subtenants, by forbidding subletting in leases and at least warning refractory tacksmen, such as James Clephan of Tomaknock, who continued the practice, to desist. In 1780, he was believed to be subsetting, as men from an adjoining farm were seen entering the farm buildings of Tomaknock.

There were other aspects of landholding which produced problems for the Board; among them were rents and the size of holding. The Board and their officers were greatly concerned over the correct size that farms should be, for they had to balance the need to produce viable economic units with the social aims of the annexation. In *The Highlands in 1750*, it was suggested that no-one should have a farm larger than he could cultivate with his domestic servants, thus lessening the tenants' and chiefs' influence over the people,[38] and the clause in the Annexing Act forbidding rents over £20 as well as multiple holdings also had that end in view. On the economic side, however, there was an argument for larger holdings, and one of the most noted improvers of the eighteenth century, Grant of Monymusk, was adamant that 'A large farm is the only way of making an estate by husbandry', pointing out that on a small one the charges and the family's subsistence ate all the produce.[39] This was the landowner's point of view, but James Small's picture of the Struan economy gives that of the small tenant with much the same implications. Farms there were so small that the dairy produce was for home consumption only; and it was not as good as it would have been if farms had been larger with resulting increase in milk supplies and more frequent churning. In summer, too, there was a meal shortage, but this was less important, as the poor people then lived on milk and needed less food since they were idle. Despite this, Small did not put forward a case for very large holdings; he suggested only that the farms when properly enlarged would be enough to keep the tenants 'as happy as it is necessary they should be' and, on the contrary, pointed out that farms that were too lucrative would not be good examples, because they would be uncharacteristic. This would 'take away their being exemplary'.

By the mid-1760s, as Jacobitism faded and Charles Edward was not recognised as King even by the Vatican on his father's death, so did the paranoiac fear of the power of the Highland landowner and large landholder. Government and the Board began to give more weighting to purely economic arguments. One good reason for increasing the size of farms was that the expense of the animals needed for a plough was too great for any holding that had under five bolls' sowing, and the Inspector General had written in his report for 1767–68 of the bad effects of keeping a plough on too small a farm. The tenants had to borrow and ended with the costs of a large farm and not even the profits of a small one. It was suggested that as tenants died their possessions should be amalgamated to bring about a gradual increase in size and, in 1771, Lord Kames went so far as to say that he thought men of substance should get large farms. However, he proposed that, in future, special regard should be paid to the nature and extent of a farm, avoiding division if one plough was sufficient to work the ground. If a farm would support the use of two ploughs, then it it should be divided so that industrious tenants would increase in numbers.[40]

The statutory veto in the Annexing Act on rents of over £20 and on multiple holdings had the effect that, while smaller holdings were amalgamated over the period of annexation, others had to be separated initially. For example, on the Perth estate, in 1755, Alexander Buchanan of Duilater held two farms, Nether and Upper Bochastle at £49.10.8 rent, and Offrans, Coshambie, Duncraggan and Portneallan were in the hands of one man, Mr. Stewart of Annat. Their rentals were £16.15.3 $\frac{4}{12}$, £5.7.5 $\frac{8}{12}$, £5.14.6 $\frac{8}{12}$ and £8.15.5. Offrans at least had a sub-tenant. By 1767, Upper Bochastle had four tenants and one King's Cottager, whilst Nether Bochastle had a single tenant, with the mill attached. In 1773, Upper Bochastle was divided into two larger and two smaller holdings but, by 1775, there was one main holding with cottagers, for by that time legislation had been passed enabling the commissioners to charge larger rents.[41] From 1775, all the rent rolls have columns for the additional rents imposed thereafter. It was to be hoped this was an improvement for, in 1774, Wight had described Bochastle (Bohastle he spelled it) as the worst managed he had ever seen.[42] Mr. Stewart too, had to give up his multiple holding and, in 1767, Coshambie was held jointly by two brothers, or at least by two men with the same patronymic, and Portneallan was also a joint holding. By 1770, Portneallan was clearly two holdings, one with two names. In 1767, Duncraggan had two tenants and two King's Cottagers, with another cottager added by 1770, when the schoolmaster was provided with a croft on the main farm; 1770 saw a change, however, for then there was only one tenant, besides the three crofts, including one for the schoolmaster and one for a smith. Runrig was attacked too, and by 1764 the Board could report that Kinbuck and Auchterarder were divided.

Over the whole of the Perth estate during the annexation, there is a slow kaleidoscopic movement of tenants and boundaries, not consistently in the direc-tion of larger-sized holdings.[43] In the part of Muthill parish included in the Highland Division after the estate was allotted to two factors, many farms had a completely different organisation of tenants in 1784, compared to what had existed in 1767. Some were very similar, of course, like Glenlichorn which had five tenants in 1767, but which in 1784 was divided into Easter, Wester and Middle: three farms but still five tenants. However, there are examples of amalgamation in plenty. Blenror or Blainroar had five tenants in 1784, compared to nine in 1767, while Culloch with three tenants in 1767, one holding half the farm, the other two a quarter each, had only one main tenant in 1784 but five cottagers. Straid had four equal parts to it in 1767, but only one tenant in 1784, but the farm of Cornoch which had one tenant in 1767 had five in 1784, including one widow and one smith. The greatest single consistent change in this area is in the disappearance of the many pendicles and small possessions that existed in 1755, in Auchterarder and Muthill. On the other hand, the commissioners were not averse to dividing up what they thought suitable areas, like the Parks of Drum-mond, to provide smallholdings. Clearly the Board, surveyors and factors used their discretion, within their legal limits in the estate of Perth, at least, to form holdings of a sensible size suited in many cases to the individual tenant, while not leaving too much power in one man's hands. Their flexibility can perhaps be further illustrated by the treatment of two farms in the same area, Lendrick and Drippan. In 1755, each of these had two tenants, but by 1767 Lendrick was in one man's name, while Drippan had three tenants, two with quarter holdings, one with half the farm.

As Wight pointed out, however, in the Perth estate it was possible to dispossess small tenants in the knowledge that they would find employment in industry and as day labourers; in the north dispossession would have led to depopulation.[44] He did not add, as was probably the case, that depopulation would have been preceded by beggary, and to reduce the people in the estate to further misery was as emphatically not the policy of annexation, as emigration either to the Lowlands or abroad was not then considered an answer to the 'Highland Problem'. On the Lovat estate, the tenants in 1766 seemed to be little affected by the Board for, in that year, Menzies had little to say about the farming on the estate, except that no original tenants had carried out improvements, and that the low-lying farms were still small and were being made smaller by the possessors dividing them to provide for their children. A few years later, in 1774, the estate returned to the Fraser family and so passed from the aegis of the Board; there had hardly been time for extensive changes.

On the Cromartie estate, the changes in the numbers of tenants holding any particular farm were minimal between 1755 and 1764. By 1773, however, the introduction of the soldiers' settlements established after the Seven Years War had in fact increased the number of tenants, and may have decreased some holdings by the granting of crofts to soldiers. Ardwall had eight tenants in 1755 but by 1773, with the same number of tenants, had also four soldiers' lots extracted. Auchterneed, with eight tenants in 1755, had nine in 1773 and in addition three soldiers' crofts. In the barony of New Tarbat, several farms were affected in this way, for Tullich had sixteen soldiers and two tenants in 1773 but three tenants in 1755; Polnicel had still only one tenant at the later date, but had added the doubtful blessing of eight soldiers, and Kilmuir had seven. On the Mains of New Tarbat, which in 1755 had been held with Castlehill and included a pendicle for the doctor who also rented part of the New Tarbat House, there were three tenants and thirteen soldiers, and the doctor was still there at the later date. It has to be remembered of course that some of the soldiers' settlements were aimed at bringing uncultivated land into use, so that it is possible that their existence did not make much difference to the tenants' holdings, while the proprietors' rents were increased. The fact, too, that the grass was most valuable in that estate would perhaps indicate that additional tenants on a holding, who were supposed to be increasing arable land, would make little difference to the original tenants, but there are few signs on the estate of Cromartie of enlargement of individual holdings.[45]

The method of paying rents was another part of the management of the annexed estates that the commissioners would have liked to bring into line with contemporary improving practices. Ideally, they hoped eventually to have all rents paid in cash but such a transformation was not likely to be attained speedily, where specie was short and old customs died hard. The realism that allowed services of carriage of bark and fuel to be continued was able to accept gradual adjustment here too, and in 1774 payment in kind was still being stipulated.[46] Some steps towards the achievement of a cash economy had been taken before 1745 on the Perth estate, where James Drummond, Earl of Perth, had tried to convert all rents to money payment at the same time as he had started the process of raising rents on his lands.[47] On the Cromartie estate, on the other hand, a high proportion of tenants paid no money rents at all. In 1755, the parts of the estate in Kilmuir Easter parish paid £4.16.5 $\frac{8}{12}$ in cash, but over 290 bolls of bere, 267 bolls of meal and 30 of malt brought the total to a value estimated at £249.18.3 $\frac{7}{12}$ with services in addition. In the Barony of New Tarbat in Logie Easter, the money rent was 7/6 and the total £29.10.10.

The practice made for practical difficulties for the factor. In 1759 and 1760, he had faced the problem of storing rents, for he found that the tenants made a habit of paying only if farm victual was taken off their hands when they offered it. He suggested repairing a few rooms in New Tarbat House for the purpose, though this can hardly have been the ideal solution and, in August 1760, he sent an estimate, which was approved, for a granary at Beauly. Eventually in 1765 a granary was built at Portleish, estimated at £180, but costing over £300.[48]

Even without the added complication of storing rents, their collection was a continuous problem for the factors. It seems unlikely, for example, that they could effectively have insisted on delivery of meal immediately after it was ground, as apparently was the custom on some estates. The proprietor benefited thereby from the weight gain in the six months after grinding.[49] In 1758, Barcaldine wrote that in good years accounting was easy, and all the money was paid between January and March, with not a penny the rest of the time. In bad years, however, every little market had to be watched. Barcaldine's book-keeping was hardly impeccable, but this was probably a fair assessment of the situation. In 1766, Forbes declared that the bulk of the rents paid in victual were usually bought by the tenants themselves, which seems odd when he had made such a fuss about the storage problem. In 1769, he wrote to the Board that there were no rents for Cromartie for 1768 and very few from Lovat, so that he would have difficulty in paying the public burdens, schoolmasters' salaries, etc.; and in 1771 he complained to the ground officers that the most positive orders he had had from the Board to clear his account for the 1770 crop by July, 1771 would be impossible to obey, if the tenants did not deliver their victual payment in kind and pay their rents at Whitsunday. The most substantial tenants, particularly those with leases, had not paid anything.[50]

Later, John Campbell of Lochend, factor on the Highland Division of the Perth estate, declared with some justification that collection of rents was the least important part of the factor's duties on the estate he was concerned with. Factors certainly had a multitude of duties, but the problem of obtaining prompt payment of rents was one that was always with them, and one that the Board, responsible after all for public money, checked fairly carefully. Accounts were examined each year and explanations were sought for discrepancies. In 1773, for example, Lord Stonefield examined the accounts of Thomas Keir for the Lowland part of the Perth estate, and found £787 in arrears.[51] By this time, the Board were beginning to realise that all such situations were not necessarily to be attributed to the factors' misdemeanours, and it was recommended that tenants without leases should be warned about their arrears, but those with tacks should have the most effectual legal steps taken against them. But factors must have been wryly amused by the instructions from the central government in 1764, that 'tenants were not to be allowed to run into arrears for the future'. After the disannexation, the Barons of the Exchequer were still dealing with factors' accounts and the question of arrears into the early years of the nineteenth century.[52] The tenants' belief too that, if they paid within a year and a day after the rents were due, they were in no danger of being removed cannot have helped the factors. Any attempt to convert rents to a purely cash transaction had also to take into consideration the tenants' resistance to such a charge. Menzies provides an interesting sidelight on this viewpoint, for he suggested that the rent on Lovat should be converted to labour. He declared that the people were not fond of work but yet preferred giving £5 in work to paying £2 in money.

By the 1770s, wherever possible, farm rents were calculated with the addition of an allowance for the amount of meal due; on the Perth estate, for example, the market price was 8/10 per boll in 1776, 13/4 in 1777 and down to 10/- in 1779. On the Lovat and Cromartie estates, this process was combined with the process of raising rents to a more economic height, according to the surveyors' valuation and, in 1768, the General Inspector wrote that he and the factor on those estates had begun to prepare the tenants for the proposed increases. Half the victual rent was to be converted at eight marks to the boll, which Menzies described as 'a bait that took'. The rents were still going to be higher, as additional rent was to be charged to make the estate conform to Peter May's evaluation, but the chance of an apparent bargain was tempting to the tenants. Another piece of encouragement was that tenants who had begun to enclose had their rents reduced.

Whatever tenants felt about it, however, the practice of paying rents in cash instead of in kind had been growing throughout the eighteenth century, largely for the proprietor's convenience,[53] and as a modern innovation had become accepted as 'improvement'. It was gradually to spread throughout the whole of Scotland, and had already affected the annexed estate of Perth. The commissioners were almost inevitably bound to start the process on the estates under their management, and the two differences between them and other proprietors lay, firstly, in the very large area over which they could introduce this change and, secondly, in the proceeds being spent on the Highland area and primarily on the estates annexed, instead of on proprietorial living expenses, riotous or otherwise, in other parts of the kingdom.

The commissioners met some opposition in their desire to make all the rents payable in cash, partly, as has been noted, because of the short supply of cash and partly because payment by labour, food, and services, such as carriage of fuel, was in many ways a far more convenient method of exchange between landlord and tenants at the time. This, as we have seen, the Board speedily discovered in their attempts to eradicate subtenancy. Services and victual added to the apparent value of an estate, for the Barrisdale rent in money in 1755 was detailed at £79.3.4 sterling, but by the time the bishop's teinds, the kitchen cow, the May present – quite large at £3.15.10 – 21 stones of butter, 42 of cheese, 43½ sheep, plus 372 hours of service at 6d. per day had been added, the total gross rent amounted to £133.11.3. This was deceptive, however, for according to Francis Grant's report to the Barons of the Exchequer in 1749, when services were not performed the tenants were not expected to pay a conversion, while those who did have to cut and carry peats – a great time waster in the commissioners' opinion – were given an allowance of meal and money for doing this. This picture is far removed from that of the tyrannous landlord demanding his due, regardless of the needs of the tenants, which was the one the improvers carried in their minds. When the factor in Barrisdale tried to exact cash payment for services not rendered at 6d. per day, not surprisingly the tenants refused to pay, and the Board accepted that compulsion was impossible, though they resolved at the same time that leases granted in the future on the estate should reserve services as on all the other annexed estates.[54]

Clearly, for the convenience of the factors, the commissioners would have had to try to make some other type of arrangement for collecting rent. The troubles of the Lovat and Cromartie factor in storing grain we have already seen. Jean, Dowager of Perth, on her life-rented estate received money rent of £1,502.6.8 Scots but the total rent was £3,991.19.0 Scots, and she can have had little need to provide much food for herself and her household when her tenants had to supply 38 capons, 5 weddars, 5 lambs, 256½ poultry, 70 chickens and 384 eggs as well as over 400 bolls of meal, bere and oats. This was wealth to her but would have have been something of an inconvenience to factors to collect and dispose of.[55]

The factors found out the inconveniences of being without the carriage service, for to avoid extortion on their part they had to have the Board's orders to tenants to carry for them. Coal was quite a difficulty, and Small pointed out that without being granted this carriage he had no other method of being supplied. Ten years later, he had to send in a memorial to the effect that he had had no coal carried for three years, and he did not think it would be a hardship to the tenants, nor that they would object, as the carriage had been reserved in the leases, and the rents as a result made less. This was read in December 1775 and then again in July 1776, so it is to be hoped he did not suffer overmuch from cold in the meantime. But, as he pointed out, the carriages had been reserved. Recognising necessity, the early leases required the tenants to lead loads of bark, peat and coal, or to pay for each undelivered load, at the rate of 1d. each stone of coal and 2d. sterling for each undelivered load of peats.[56]

One service, however, was almost universally resented and condemned and that was thirlage, the servitude that bound tenants on certain lands to have their corn ground at one particular mill and to help with the repairs of that mill. The grasping miller of fairy-tale and folklore is so common and cosmopolitan a character that one feels there must be some grounds for the belief that all were untrustworthy and most were rogues. When weights were not uniform or subjected to independent scrutiny, so that both farmer and miller had only their eyes to depend on, it is easy to understand, especially in a subsistence economy, that the bag of flour or meal produced from the hopper usually seemed less than it should have been, and that the portion claimed by the miller, who took no risk in producing the corn, seemed more than he deserved. Further, the miller considered himself the master, not the servant, of his customers, and let 'his humour rather than a sense of his duty' regulate his conduct. He knew that 'the yolk is wreathed so hard about their necks that they dare not pass his door'.[57] The commissioners saw thirlage as the most burdensome of services and they were determined from the start of their period of duties to 'relieve' the tenants. In 1762, they reported to the king in Schedule No. 2 that they were anxious to free the tenants on the annexed estates from thirlage and, in the minutes, they had recorded their intention to abolish it whenever a proper scheme was agreed on. As a result, they decided to let mills for only one year at a time.

There were plenty of complaints about millers and thirlage, like that of the tenant thirled to a Cromartie mill where John, Earl of Cromartie, had in 1714 extended the thirlage to include not only the corn grown within the sucken, the district thirled to a mill, but also to all corn imported, bought or stored within it. The petitioner also complained that his lands were a long way from the mill, but that he only wished to show how oppressive thirlage could be made. He lived in a bad area from the tenants' point of view, however, as Symon tells us that the thirlage in Ross-shire was sometimes one-eighth.[58] Millers were tenants too, of course, and had to have their interests defended. The inclusion of the repair of the mill and the lead to it in thirlage made abolition far from simple. Surprisingly too, not all tenants were as enthusiastic about the removal of this 'burden' as one might have expected them to be. The tenants of Monaltrie, when faced with the choice of paying more rent for conversion of thirlage or of remaining under thirlage, preferred remaining astricted to the mill and this concession they were allowed. Similarly, the tenants on the Perth estate in 1765 were said to be 'of very various and variable minds' on the subject, and in 1782, when the Crieff inhabitants wanted to be freed of thirlage, the factor thought it would be better to leave things as they were as he reckoned it would be impossible to satisfy them all. One estate, Barrisdale, did not have to make any adjustments on this service, for the inhabitants used querns and there had never been a cornmill on the estate.[59]

However, so important did the commissioners consider the question of abolition that it was one of the first items dealt with, in the rules and articles registered with the Court of Session in connection with leases for the improvement of Highland farms. Tenants were to remain thirled and to pay the same multures and perform the same services as before, by use and wont but, whenever new leases were granted to mills without astricted multures, tenants had to pay a proportion of rent to make up the diminution of the mill's profits and they had still to perform the repair services. This was another recognition of reality, the lack of workmen. This having been agreed, tenants would then grind at the same mill or pay at another if it was more convenient, as they and the miller arranged. Thirlage, however, was still in operation at the end of the annexation, and it was 1799 before legislation allowed for commutation.[60]

Changing patterns of farming were in evidence as early as 1757 and affected millers perhaps more than any other tenants. For example, where grass was grown in place of corn, the miller's earnings were greatly reduced. Changes in the communications system could also affect a mill's intake, as at the mill of Tonbea, which gradually became redundant once the new bridge built at Callander made the Gartchonzie mill more convenient. But by 1780 the miller at Gartchonzie had his own complaint. Tenants formerly thirled to his mill were now at liberty to carry their corn to any they cared, but other proprietors, not quite so disinterested as the annexed estates commissioners, would not allow their tenants to bring their custom to him.[61] It must have been a novel experience for the miller to find himself in such a situation, and the more annoying as his fellows on other estates were carrying on as before. The response of both tenants and other proprietors to the proposal to abolish thirlage is another illustration of the strength of custom in rural communities and illuminates the magnitude of the task facing the improver. That the commissioners once again could only initiate and introduce the idea is not surprising.

The hands of the commissioners were always tied in their search for improved agricultural practice and efficiency by their need to aim at the happiness of the tenants. Commutation of victual and service led to an apparent rise in rent, and was not likely to be popular for, as we have seen, services and cash were not always equated by the Highland tenants. In their defence, it has to be remembered that making arrangements to sell their meal to obtain cash was likely to weigh on the smaller tenants perhaps even more heavily than finding cash to pay wages did on the larger. To the general rise in rents, partly real, partly due to commutation of services and rents and hence not a true increase, was generally attributed much of the 'fever of emigration' affecting the Highlands in the second half of the eighteenth century. We have Dr. Johnson's word for this, when he spoke to one of his hosts, in Anach, in Glenmoriston.[62] The same attitude is expressed by one of the surveyors employed by the Board. William Morison described Barrisdale in 1772 as 'very disjoined' with shealings at a great, inconvenient distance from the farms and, though he was supposed to be looking at the estate with the aim of preparing an increased rental, he spoke against too high an addition, as he thought this would make the inhabitants desperate or, like their neighbours, emigrate to America. As he rightly assumed, this was the opposite of the Board's intentions. He gave an estimate of £160.7.8, a rise from £138.19.4, which the Board reduced by £9.8.6, but then they added £29.4.2,presumably for improvements.[63]

At the beginning of their term of office, the Board faced a complicated picture of rents, for initially it was not clear whether the Barons of the Exchequer could collect rents from 1752 until the appointment of the commissioners. In fact, they had continued doing so and had also used the money to contest claims of creditors in the Court of Session. It was eventually decided that they had been within their legal rights to do so,[64] but the uncertainty encouraged tenants to try for abatements, for one reason or another. The question was an even more vexed one on the Perth estate, because of the unfortunate coincidence of the rents having been raised just before the turmoil of the Rebellion. As a result of the confusion then, some of the tenants had never in fact paid the augmented rents. Some kept the money until 1748, when the factors appointed by the Barons under the Vesting Act took control; others felt optimistically they would never have to pay the extra amount and spent their money. The factor making his report in 1755, John Campbell of Barcaldine, was very critical of Drummond's scheme, saying there had been no regular plan of improvement and no encouragement to the tenants. Rents in Callander had been so far raised that the tenants were not in very good circumstances, and many petitions appeared in the Board's office asking for relief, especially in 1757 when there was a scarcity of meal. Even a miller on one holding needed help then, and the holders of Dalclathick who had their rent raised from £9.13.4 to £20 said they had only kept on the farm because the factor persuaded them to. They succeeded in having their case considered.

The tenants no doubt seized on the general atmosphere at the time of the annexation to try to have their rents reduced. The Board must have been convinced that there were some grounds for complaint for, in 1763, the Perth factor was told to make up a list of farms that he considered too highly rented, with the reductions he thought possible, but he also had to say which he thought could be raised, so that the rental could be kept up. The last sentence points the dilemma which the commissioners had to try to resolve over rentals in their management of the estates. On the income from rents depended all their activities aimed at achieving the 'civilisation' of the Highlands, good government, the Protestant religion, and the multitude of other benefits set out in the Annexing Act. They could not afford to be over-generous in cutting rents, however much that might contribute to the happiness and to ensuring the loyalty of individual tenants, also an aim of the annexation. Rents did rise throughout the period of the annexation, as a result of rising values generally, and as a result of the interest charged by the Board on money lent for improvements. For instance, in 1753, the gross rent of the estate of Struan was £504.8.3. From 1759–1765 it remained at £522.0.1 and was then raised to £552.18.7, to £585.17.7 in 1767, reaching £662.19.5 in 1775. The drop in prices shows in the reduction to £543.5.3 in 1777, but recovery began in 1778 when £587.9.10 is recorded, followed by £630.16.3 in 1779 and an eventual maximum of £682.5.9 in 1782–83.[65] However, the opinion of many neighbouring proprietors and tenants was that 'kindness' to tenants had outweighed the desire for efficiency and increased revenue.

The effect of lower than average rents lasted, of course, for tenants with leases could hold their farms at the original rental even after the return of the estates to the heirs of the attainted, and writers in the *Old Statistical Account* reported on the fact that the farms on the Perth estate, for example, were 'allowed by all to be low rented' and certainly so when compared with the rest of the county. The minister of Cargill was extremely critical, for his view was that, when the barony of Stobhall was under the direction of the commissioners, the lands were so low in rent that they were 'no spur to industry or excitement to exertion'. According to him, if the farmer could pay his rent and 'live like his neighbours' without changing his methods, it was only seldom he would do any more. Rents had been raised considerably in the few years since the disannexation, one farm from £33 to £200 and another from £23 to £90, thus calling for activity and skill on the part of the farmer. He implied that it was only since the disannexation that 'a spirit of industry was diffusing itself over the whole parish'.[66] As we shall see, it was not only in Cargill that farmers on the annexed estates seemed to lack enterprise and ability, even as late as 1784.

5
Divisions, Enclosures and Stocking

THE factors' reports in 1755 helped to highlight the aspects of farm management and the practices of husbandry on the estates that required amelioration. While the establishment of security of tenure by means of granting leases was seen as part of the process of eradicating social malpractices,[1] it was in fact indivisible from all the other strands of the Board's attempts to make the agricultural system on the annexed estates more productive, both quantitatively and qualitatively. Leases without insistence on improving habits might have made some impact on the social organisation of the estates but it is likely that they would have been singularly ineffective, agriculturally speaking. Indeed, even with mandatory clauses attempting to control the worst features of the older style of farming, they must be seen as only part of a general movement towards modernisation, which demanded close attention to such matters as dividing and enclosing lands and straightening marches, improving the management of animal stock, obtaining better and bigger yields from crops of all kinds, and improving farm buildings and farm implements. Of these four categories, the first was probably the most important in the Highland area, for doubts about boundaries could have a deleterious effect on relations between tenants and neighbouring proprietors, in a society where cooperation was more beneficial than controversy. Equally, division and enclosure of land gave the individual the benefits of his industry, while also protecting crops from roving stock and stock from harassment by herds or dogs.

Enclosing farms and fields can be described as the most continuous of all the Board's activities. Every year, large amounts of money were spent on fencing, diking and ditching. This was the first of the commissioners' many activities that was of fundamental importance, and their interest in it was maintained throughout the annexation. Their reports to King and Treasury list the amounts spent. In 1768, £624.18.10 was laid out on the Perth estate, £9.10.0 on Cromartie and £39.15.10½ on Struan. In 1771, the expenditure on Perth had gone up to £845.15.10 $\frac{9}{12}$, Coigach had absorbed £28.13.7, and £35.12.4 had been spent on Struan and Cromartie, all of this earning in theory 5% interest on the capital spent as extra rent, though the rent roll of the last-named ignores this.[2] Thereafter the sums tended to decrease, varying from sums like £584.15.5 spent on '5% improvements' on the Lowland Division of the Perth estate in 1767–8 to nothing at all between February 1780 and June 1782 and again in the last year of annexation. Most of the estate must have been affected by this part of the Board's policy, and the larger amount included enclosing and planting muirs, which was entered separately from the next year, but a large proportion was spent on diking. Dikes were not always within farms or between proprietors; in 1771, £58.18.0 was laid out on a dike on the King's road. In 1769–71 accounts, £80 was paid to a man who had built dikes on each side of the King's road from Lagg to Bridgend of Crieff, and £18.9.3 was used to build a dike built round the acres taken off Fintalich farm for some of the inhabitants of Muthill. 6/- per rood was the price, in 1775–76 at least. Damage done when quarrying was also indented under 5% improvements.

Among the practical difficulties that had to be overcome in diking, there was the problem of carriage of stones. When Barcaldine was having a dike built at Drummond, he wrote suggesting that it would be cheapest to buy two horses and a cart, as the country people would not bargain to do the job. Their horses were so weak, they could pull only small loads in single-horse carts, and he thought hiring by the day would turn out to be very expensive. However, for his pains, he was told that the Board did not approve of this suggestion and he was to build dikes as best as he could, a singularly unhelpful comment.[3]

Considering the area over which the Board was supposed to exercise control and the amount of money paid out on this very necessary aspect of improvement, it was almost inevitable that dikes and ditches did indeed 'gradually change the face of the land'.[4] That the dikes were neither efficiently built nor particularly well placed for efficient farm management, either within the annexed estates or between them and the neighbouring proprietors, seems clear from the comments of later observers. Andrew Wight and William Frend on their travels round the estates were none too complimentary about the work done. The commissioners had no doubt that the additional rents obtained from enclosing would greatly enhance the value of the estates, and probably this would have been the effect in time, but perhaps not under a Crown Commission whose actions were restricted and whose supervision of improvements was not all it might have been.

The response of tenants was varied, of course, in different parts of the country. Some tenants were keen to improve, even in the northern parts of the estates for, while still under the management of the Barons of the Exchequer, some Cluny tenants had complained of the lack of head-dikes and the resultant danger to their crops from wandering stock. They were prepared to build head-dikes at their own expense if they were given the security of seven years' possession.[5] In 1780, Wight remarked that on the annexed estate of Cluny 'improvements make a figure', with neat commodious houses on each farm, sufficient stone walls, good pasture for good stock of well-looking cattle. In addition, he felt that the people were aware that the Board had no intention of rack-renting them, so they were prepared to make the most of their possessions.[6] Wight seems inclined to give the Board the benefit for such a welcome sight, but the tenants' earlier actions indicate that the credit should perhaps go to them, for Cluny had been held of a subject superior, the Duke of Gordon, and had been managed by the Board only since 1770. William Tennoch surveyed the estate for the commissioners in 1771 and leases were granted from 1774 onwards; nine years of the Board's management were not likely to have transformed the estates in any great degree, and the records do not show any great amount of activity. The tenants should for once be given some credit for industry and enthusiasm.

Further south, in Auchtermuthil, on the Perth estate, we find tenants of a very different kidney. According to Frend, they built dikes just well enough to entitle them to the additional rent and then took no trouble in keeping them up. Very little enclosing had been done in the area, for most of the land is described as entirely open; Drumdowie, 100 acres, had no enclosures. The need for supervision was clear and it is a little disconcerting to find Frend, in 1780, suggesting as a new idea what Archibald Menzies had told the commissioners was necessary on his first visit to the estate in August 1765. Frend thought that the money paid out for work on dikes should be withheld until they had been inspected, and after his report the two commissioners commenting on his proposals could only agree.[7] But Menzies had already – without effect, it would appear – realised this and had thought the byrlawmen could have carried out the necessary inspection. Frend, in addition, did not altogether approve of dikes. He thought that ditches were a cheaper method of dividing land and that, with one process, drainage was also provided, without which, he said, the farmer would get little profit from dung or manure.[8]

However, not all tenants were totally resistant to change. Mungo Campbell, farming at Auchleskine, had spent £50 on building a farmhouse and necessary outbuildings, and as he wanted to continue his improvements, he asked for a division of the infield which was in runrig between him and his neighbours.[9] What the neighbours wanted, however, is not on record in the minutes. It was easiest to make changes when the mood of tenants was propitious. Two years earlier, Barcaldine had suggested that the opportunity should be taken to make a proper division of the land held in runrig at Auchterarder with the Duke of Montrose, as all at that time were so well disposed to change.[10] The favourable inclination of tenants was a vital element in successful improvements and it was not always present. The lack of uniformity, both in tenants' responses and in the results attainable, can be seen in the difference between Cluny and the parts of the Perth estate mentioned. Later, not all that far from Auchtermuthil, the village of Comrie is described in the *Old Statistical Account* as being partly enclosed, especially that part belonging to Mr. Drummond of Perth, who entered into possession of the estate after the disannexation.[11] The commissioners' continued maintenance of expenditure on enclosures all through the annexation, however well or badly this was done, would not be without some effect.

Runrig and open land were not the only problems of the organisation of the use of farm land that had to be dealt with. For example, many farms were not properly proportioned for efficient management, some having too much hill pasture, some too little, and surveyors and other officers had to take thought about this type of division too. Sometimes small holdings were allotted to inefficient tenants who had not been successful in their original land, and their rents were adjusted accordingly.[12]

Another difficulty to be overcome was the intermingling of the land of various proprietors, something that was not uncommon all over the Highlands. It is clearly simpler to build a dike round one large piece of ground rather than round several small bits, dikes being rather less flexible than the modern wire-netting, and a burn was a splendid boundary when it divided two properties instead of meandering from one to the other. Many attempts were made to rationalise marches, both between farms on the estates and also between the annexed estates and those of neighbouring proprietors; excambions were made whereby boundaries became straighter, and new channels were cut for streams to ensure that all the land of one proprietor lay on one side of the water.[13] In this matter, as in other aspects of the management of the estates, the length of time between the forfeiture, the annexation and the appointment of commissioners had unfortunate effects. March lines were at any time only vaguely known, especially on the higher ground; for example, in Barrisdale, the boundaries were stated to be known only by custom and tradition.[14] The delays of the initial years were an invitation to even greater uncertainty and to encroachments by neighbours, either innocently or by design. Fraser of Struy tried to absorb some of Lovat's land. The Duke of Atholl and the Struan factor had 'a trifling difference' about marches.[15] This latter dispute seems to have been resolved amicably enough for, in 1765, the General Inspector was instructed to visit the Duke to thank him for concurring so readily in adjusting the marches.

Political expediency also had unfortunate repercussions here. The veto on any participation in the management of the estates by members of the families who had previously owned them almost certainly deepened the ignorance of officers as to what had traditionally been considered the correct march lines. In the neighbourhood of the estate of Lovat there were many small proprietors ready to make their own boundaries, and a court case was needed to settle the extent of the mosses of the barony of Beauly.[16] In 1766, Menzies discovered another complication arising from this lack of certainty, when he found what can only be called squatters settled on the boundaries of the estates. These people informed the neighbouring proprietors that they were the king's tenants, and the factors on the annexed estates were told that they were tenants on the neighbouring estates; hence they paid rents to neither. Of course, until there were enclosures and sheep farms, the exact lines of estates' boundaries had been less important, and it was only as the hill grazings became more valuable that much detailed attention was paid to them. The Board's experience illustrates just how vague boundaries had been.

Some disputes were hangovers from longstanding battles with the original owners, like Sir Robert Menzies' claim to exclusive rights to the fishing of Loch Rannoch, and the privilege of drying his nets on the Struan side of the loch. This affected the Board, as he threatened to prevent the boats and timber from being carried to the sawmill at Carie, on the grounds that they hurt his fishing. Like the internal enclosing, the question of settling marches went on throughout the annexation and, even in the previous few years, there had been quarrels with neighbours involving surveys and plans and, eventually in some cases, the due course of the law.[17] Despite the realisation of the need both of recognition and of the rationalisation of boundaries, the Board's intentions were more admirable than their execution of these, or their officers' performances, and Archibald Menzies criticised the fact that the marches had not been cleared with neighbours before some enclosing was carried out. Apparently his words of wisdom were not heeded or no corrections were made, for Frend in the 1780s had equal strictures to make, pointing out that a more determined effort should have been made to achieve more sensible boundaries. He thought much of the money would be found to have been wasted because of the irregular lines between properties.

Various excambions were proposed, both by the Board and by neighbours, and some were effected.[18] One quite extensive one was the exchange of the barony of Fernan, part of Struan, valued at £3979.13.9, and Lix, part of the Perth estate, valued at £1054.17.3$\frac{4}{12}$, for the lands of Pitkellony, part of the estate of the Earl of Breadalbane. The Crown had to pay the difference of £5354.0.3 and, thereafter, the rents were included in the Perth rental, but on disannexation Pitkellony was granted to the proprietor of the Perth estate, on payment of £3979.13.9 to Colonel Robertson, the owner of the Struan estate after 1784.[19]

Later comments on the divisions made are an implicit criticism of the surveyors, who had been employed extensively by the Board, not only to find and measure boundaries but to suggest improvements. Several men were employed regularly. Initially, William Cockburn and Francis Grant, before the latter was made the first Riding Master and General Inspector, did many of the surveys, but later John Leslie declared that he found so many omissions in the survey of the estate of Perth that he was rather cautious in using it. Peter May and William Morison were also kept busy. They did not always have an easy time; apart from the difficulties arising from the weather and tenants, they had sometimes a long time to wait for their due emoluments. Leslie had three years to put in before he received his expenses for 1767 and was paid fully only in 1774 for about three years' work.[20] As the sum involved in the latter case was over £400, the man was considerably out of pocket.

Reports and recommendations were not always equably received, even by the factors. In 1770, John Forbes complained that Peter May had rented many farms at too high a rent and had augmented rents where tenants had carried out their own improvements, when the Board had decreed that such tenants were to be free of any increases.[21] Leslie had to deal with the tenants round Callander, known for their fractiousness despite their reputed attachment to the factor James Small. Other tenants ploughed over the lines he made one year, a straightforward method of non-cooperation, claiming that they thought he had finished and that there would be nothing further done. Others again, he thought, prevented any real improvements for fear of the additional rent they might have to pay.[22] Leslie, like the factors on occasion, was reduced to the plaint that he wished he had been working for any of the Board as private proprietors, when he might have had more encouragement. At least he was able to say he had divided all the Struan farms on the south side of Loch Rannoch by 1774; but there had been a good start there for, by 1766, Menzies had reported on a considerable amount of division and enclosure on the Struan estate. The factor was somewhat handicapped, however, as Leslie had left him no plans, and the tenants had removed most of the surveyor's marker cairns.[23]

The expense of surveying was necessary wherever new divisions of farms or decisions on boundaries had to be made, but it was a fairly costly essential, as Leslie's accounts show. Some surveying costs were not purely for agricultural

purposes. In the accounts of all improvements in the Lowland Division of the
Perth estate in 1771–72, the £60 for surveying costs includes £20 to George
Young for surveying a canal between Coupar and Perth, while the land surveyor
was paid £40. The 1772–74 surveying costs were £167.3.0, and those of 1774–5
included ten guineas to the library at Innerpeffray for books on husbandry, out of
a total of £29.10.0, an odd entry in the context.

More rational and clearer division of holdings was also necessary if animal
husbandry on the estates was to be improved. Despite its fundamental importance
to the whole Highland economy, this was marked by little skill on the annexed
estates. The factors' description of the management of stock is similar to that prevalent all over the north of Scotland. Stocking, until the mid-eighteenth century,
meant largely black cattle. Pigs were uncommon, though it would seem that some
were kept; the Perth rental for 1747–8 has a space for them and a conversion rate
of £6 Scots. The factors list one on Monaltrie and nine on Lovat, but this was
negligible compared to the forty-four goats on Monaltrie and the 4,332 sheep on
Lovat. The Highlander at the time had a loathing for pig-meat, quite inexplicable
by him or anyone else, so that little use was made of this invaluable food-supplier;
a change gradually took place so that, by the time James Robertson was writing in
1799, he could claim that the dislike had greatly worn off.[24]

Goats were numerous and did particularly well in Rannoch, where the ground
was too wet for sheep,[25] but they were not popular with improving landlords
because of their depredations on woods and plantations. In 1762, tenants of
Dalclathick on the Perth estate, in the neighbourhood of Glenartney Forest, had
always been in the habit of keeping a large number of goats pastured on the ground
'comprehended under the name of the forest'. Not surprisingly, when the forest
was let, the lessee, Colonel Graeme, had the goats driven away or poinded, much to
the annoyance of the tenants, and to their distress. They claimed that a considerable part of the support of their families and payment of rents depended on the
profit from the goats. The factor was set to finding whether this use of the forest
ground was by right or merely by toleration of the former possessors of the forest.[26]
But, when faced with a choice over goats, there was no ambiguity in the commissioners' reactions. In leases for Highland farms, laid out in 1774, no goats and
no sheep were to be allowed upon parts enclosed with hedges or where enclosures
were ready for young woods, and, indeed, where there were woods of any kind,
goats were expressly forbidden.[27] Tenants who persisted in keeping goats were to
be evicted, though they were given an opportunity to vindicate themselves. It was
unfortunate that the inhabitants of the estates were such poor controllers of their
bestial. Where goats were kept there seemed to be a much better supply of milk and
cheese than could be obtained from the poor cattle. But, by 1794, in southern
Perthshire at least, that is from the Forth to the Braes of Lednock, south to north,
and from Fife to Dunbartonshire, east to west, the goat had almost entirely
disappeared.[28] The Board for the Annexed Estates would not be alone responsible
for their elimination there, for there were plenty of other improvers active in the
area.

Women's thrift apart, cows were the money-spinner. When sold they paid the rent and in some areas, not only in the annexed estates, they were the only source of hard cash.[29] And yet they were ill-managed. There was no attempt at selective breeding and little at effective herding. The best and worst fed together and ate their respective owners' scanty crops together, as well as their neighbours' whenever a breach was found in the head dike and there was no herd to chase them off. The basic problem was that of overstocking, and this the Board recognised, trying to regulate the numbers of cattle and, of course, of all other livestock kept by their tenants. Theoretically, pasture lands were soumed and roumed; that is, they were assessed for the number of farm animals they could bear. Thus the optimum, or at least the maximum, stocking that each piece of ground could sustain was decided by estate officers. Tenants were supposed to abide by the agreed stocking; allowed to understock, they were not supposed to overstock. Owing to the profusion of fodder in summertime, it was a common and universal fault all over the Highlands to keep a larger herd than the winter scarcity of grass merited. 'The Honourable Board might know that the value of all highland farms depends on the accommodation of grass belonging to them in summer and winter and more depends on the winter grass than on the summer,' wrote General Fraser's factor when he was negotiating for a lease for the best winter farm on the estate of Lovat, Meikle Portclair.[30] This lesson was apparently never learned by many of the smaller tenants, despite their almost annual experience of dearth and death. It may have been a perverted form of optimism that made them stock each year as many and more cattle than the winter grazings would feed, knowing full well that during the winter they and their animals would go hungry. In 1755, one of the main points regarding agricultural improvements made by the factor on Lovat was that, when leases were granted, no overstocking should be allowed. This, too, was in an area that he considered much better suited to cattle than to arable farming.[31]

Captain Forbes' suggestion, made in 1755, was undoubtedly correct, and fifteen years later, in 1770–71, a new souming of all the larger annexed estates was carried out. Even had conditions of animal husbandry been much more admirable than on the estates, this would probably have been necessary, as a result of the various changes in boundaries and land allotment that the Board had carried out. There was a drastic reduction in the official number of animals as a result of this, and the new souming of Slisgarrow in Struan, on the south side of Loch Rannoch, was 1,267, as opposed to the previous 1,613. The qualitative distinctions remained the same, however, one cow counting as one soum, and a horse two, while six sheep equalled one.[32] Also, each number was calculated as including the 'followers' of the original soum – animals that were of their own rearing, and only one calf between every two cows; but male animals were not to be included in the souming. By 1779, this calculation had to be reconsidered; if the tenants kept to it, it had turned out to be too low. *If* the tenants kept to it. Judging by the factor's lists in 1778, this was rare.

The gradual infiltration of better methods and management did begin to have some effect on tenants' attitudes, however. In 1783, William Frend was able to report that the tenants of Strathgartney thought their souming was too high and they had found it beneficial to reduce their souming of cattle by one-fifth. Such a sign of initiative was encouraging, even if late in the annexation. Quality and quantity of cattle varied, of course, depending not only on the methods of care used by the tenants, but on the type of farmland. In 1755, James Small reported that in Struan the chief dependence of the country was on cattle and grass, and the tenants desired no more corn than would keep their cattle from starving in the winter. They had good pasture among the woods near Loch Rannoch and on the hills where there were woods, but most of the grass was long spiral grass growing from the moss, good for the cattle in the spring when it was tender. Then the cattle pulled it out and ate the roots. He decided later that far more and better cattle still could be kept if this young grass was used more. In 1755, however, despite reason-able conditions, he had to say that the cattle were generally small as they remained out on the hills most of the winter and were poorly fed then. The price they fetched was £2 with a calf in springtime or if sold after harvest.[33] On the Perth estate, the black cattle were small in Lix and indifferent in Auchterarder, but few and very good in the barony of Kinbuck, near Dunblane. Muthill, twelve miles further north, had generally bad cattle, but Muthill people generally seemed to be bad farmers. William Frend had little good to say about them, their lack of energy, and their improvements conspicuous only by absence, towards the end of the annexa-tion.

Apart from the numbers involved, other elements in the management and care of animals were treatment of pasture land and protection of the arable from wandering flocks. In his report of 1767–8, the Inspector General Menzies had made it clear that he thought little of the tenants' management of their grass lands, and he also criticised their lack of provision of proper herds. Conditions in leases were inserted in an attempt to remedy such defects. In the model lease for Highland farms, set out in 1774, clause 12 directed that all grazings should be divided and separated as much as possible between tenants and, where division was for any reason impossible, then the land should be soumed and roumed. Clause 13 demanded herding in winter as well as summer and clause 15 that all tenants paid a proportion of public herds.[34] In Rannoch, each farm-town was to have its 'hill and straith poindler' to round up stray beasts and see that tenants did not exceed their souming. Herding had not been unknown in the estates before, and it had been differently, it might be said indifferently, organised in various parts. In one area in Lovat it had been the practice for the cows to go in with the laird's or larger tenants' young cattle, and each of the cottars' wives herded or kept them day about. 'But, though they saved a herd, they paid dearly for it, because the whole grass was overrun at times, and after all they are but ill-served and ill-pleased.' In other areas tenants merely chased the beasts off their own crops. The unsettling effect on the animals of being harried by tenants and dogs was another evil of the prevailing practices that the majority of the population in the north could not be brought to appreciate.

The Board tried to improve the stock that was there by encouraging better winter feeding, through having grass sown and turnips cultivated, and by offering prizes for the best animals.[35] Ninian Jeffrey claimed in Coigach that, by feeding his black cattle better in winter, he had increased their size considerably since he had come north.[36] Whether he had thereby convinced neighbouring tenants of the benefits of his methods, he did not say. The improvement of a breed of cattle is a slow business even in skilled willing hands. On the annexed estates there were none skilled and few willing, so that it is not surprising to find that in Frend's reports on the Perth estate, 1781–84, there are few encomiums on the quality of beasts. Some of the hill farms such as Easter and Wester Glentarken received praise as good for grazing; they cost little in terms of running expenses and thus were of greater value than low farms. But for most of the animals that he saw the usual description was 'middling'. Unfortunately he was employed only on the estate of Perth, so we do not have any comments from him on Struan, where, before 1770, better bulls were being imported from Skye.[37] Andrew Wight of course was employed to consider only corn farms in detail. The rise in the rents to take into account the increased prices from horned cattle was parallel to a general increase over the country, and not particularly the result of the Board's policies.

That the possibilities of sheep farming were at least considered we can see from their Particular Instructions to Archibald Menzies, the Inspector General, in March, 1765, to report on the suitability of any Highland farms for sheep. His report, read in July 1767, told of the Perth tenants' deplorable habit of tathing, that is bringing in the flock at the beginning of harvest time from the outlying parts of farms. They thus wasted good grass available at the shealings, and ate the grass round the house, which should properly have been left for winter feeding. But on the general potential of the area for sheep farming he voiced the opinion of south country shepherds that, in Perthshire, no farm was too high for sheep and only mismanagement prevented their thriving. They gave little wool, they were housed all winter, and were allowed out to grass for only a few hours daily, so that in the spring they died of hunger. William Boutcher, who was sent with Charles Dundas, the director of improvements on the Perth estate, to measure out a proposed garden at the Park of Drummond, reported among other things that the tenants of two farms particularly, Corsecaple and Cambuschinnie, kept sheep but they got little good from them as so many died in winter.

Charles Dundas had in fact suggested that sheep should not be allowed in the 'Low Countries', or 'there will be no such thing as rearing of hedges', and the barony of Kinbuck became forbidden territory for sheep.[38] The commissioners tried to improve the existing management of sheep by laying down regulations about keeping them in enclosures, housing them at night and herding all the year round. It must be admitted, however, that the herding and night housing were aimed as much at preserving hedges and woods as at improving sheep farming, although, until 'vermin' (eagles and foxes) were exterminated, night housing was essential protection.

One obstacle any attempt to improve sheep farming encountered was the contempt with which the average Highlander viewed the animal. Any queries met with a typical response that the tenant did not know anything about them – 'My wife has sheep with leave'. And yet, even at that early date, sheep did well in Lovat and Cromartie despite bad management.[39] There were, too, quite a number of sheep on the estates: 648 sheep to 127 cattle on Monaltrie, 161 sheep to 142 cattle on Kinlochmoidart, 4332 sheep to 3852 black cattle on Lovat, and 4997 sheep to 2000 cattle on Struan, despite the contention that it was too wet on Struan for sheep. In Struan, too, there were 1515 goats and 62 swine.[40]

Ninian Jeffrey, having come from the Borders, was very much aware of the possibilities of sheep farming. He thought that nobody in the Highlands understood sheep farming, and consequently could never make as much out of it as a proper sheep farmer could. He suggested that it would be a service to the barony, and to the Highlands in general, if a sheep farmer could be encouraged to settle in Coigach by being given the forest of Coigach rent-free for some years. He proposed himself too as a tenant of Tanera, one of the Summer Isles, as a sheep farmer, for two reasons. The first was that such a policy would mean the importation of a hardy breed of sheep from the south, but he offered as his second reason the additional inducement that more sheep would mean fewer black cattle, which would then be better maintained during the winter, would be brought to a better size, and would mature earlier, being able to take the bull at two or three years old instead of at five or six. When we look at the gay abandon with which tenants ignored the official souming, this can only have been a pious hope.

The commissioners failed to give Jeffrey any practical encouragement, however, and in 1771 he was still writing asking for a suitable farm for sheep. His suggestion that the forest of Coigach should be let to a sheep farmer was approved, but on easy terms, not rent-free.[41] Over-encouragement of sheep farming, with consequent evictions and displacement of large numbers of tenants, would in fact have been inconsistent with the main aims of the annexation which included ensuring a happy tenantry and did not demand a much increased rent-roll as a mark of efficient management. Improvement of the existing stock and hence of the material prosperity and happiness of the tenants was enough. Individual tenants were reported as having reasonably large sheep flocks, but the Board neither could nor should have had any intention of throwing the estates into sheep runs and dispossessing large numbers of inhabitants. This would have contravened the aims of the Annexing Act. They did disjoin shealings from the farms below and made separate tenements from them, as the factor on the Breadalbane estates informed his master when he was trying to persuade him to do likewise, adding that even the commissioners did this who 'upon all occasions showed more lenity to the tenants under their charge than any others' (other proprietors).[42]

By the 1770s the pros and cons of sheep farming were being widely discussed. The *Scots Magazine* had several articles on the subject in 1774, one in October, by 'Agricola', advocating it as one method of improving the Highlands.[43] This writer thought that no industry was likely to succeed in what he called a thinly populated district, unless it worked up the native product of the country, a practical approach the Board eventually began to appreciate, and he also advised sheep as more suitable than cattle, decrying many mistaken beliefs about sheep-rearing, such as that only rich pastures gave good wool. He also carried on to give advice on how to deal properly with sheep – feeding them all the year round, providing dry fodder in snow, etc. By the time sheep rearing and sheep runs were becoming more usual policy in the Highlands, however, the Board was no more. Rent-rolls do not show signs of formation of huge sheep farms, with resultant disappearance of small tenants, in those later years when the introduction of sheep on a large scale might have been expected, even in Coigach. One tenant who did try sheep farming in Coigach found it turned to no account, despite his long lease and low rent as a tenant of the Annexed Estates Board.[44] During the annexation, general improvement in the type of animal and its care were all that would be looked for. Other proprietors were introducing sheep farmers in Perthshire, but drastic alteration in the Board's policy and statutory duties would have been necessary before 'Clearances' on any large scale could have taken place.

Horses and oxen were also kept on many farms, mostly uneconomically, but this habit, where pride and interest in the particular animals are involved, was one which was still prevalent in 1924. Miss Grant described a twenty-acre holder maintaining a pair of horses for ploughing when one and a half pairs could cope with 60 acres.[45] The Inspector General had pointed out that tenants who kept ploughs on insufficient resources of land and income had all the expense of a large farm but only the profits of a small one. They had to borrow, as they had insufficient fodder for their working animals, so that 'unless he thiggs from his neighbours he must starve'. Probably as a result of this the Board ordered that no-one with less than five bolls' sowing should keep an ox, as Menzies had said that an eight-oxen plough could manage 40 bolls' sowing.

Changes in the management of livestock could not be carried out without impinging on all other aspects of husbandry. Pastoral farming was by far the largest and most important part of Highland agriculture, but we must now consider the Board's policies in the fields of arable farming, and the provision of farm buildings and farm implements. All of these were bound to be affected by the numbers, size, management and feeding of animals, as well as by any developments that were occurring independently and intrinsically within these areas of farm management.

6

Arable Farming

THE pendulum of historical orthodoxy has recently swung away from wholehearted acceptance of the opinions of eighteenth-century improvers. They held that Scottish agriculture, before their activities transformed it, was calculated to obtain the least possible returns.[1] Today we find judicious adjustments to such a picture, which explain the rationality behind under- rather than over-production, when there was little or no possibility of marketing a surplus from remote areas, and proving that, in the Lowlands particularly, seventeenth-century Scotland had been laying at least some foundations for eighteenth-century modernisation.[2] The descriptions of agricultural practices on the annexed estates, however, give more support to the older than to the modern theories. Despite the dependence of man and beast on the harvest of grain and grass, and the famines that occurred periodically, indicating the need for better yields, it cannot be claimed that the best use was made of the cultivated ground. The division of farm land into infield and outfield with the resultant overcropping of the former and the neglect of the latter, runrig, insufficient feeding of the soil, fallowing that was merely leaving nature to take over, usually with weeds as no grass was sown, lack of root and green crops, a primitive rotation of oats, oats, barley, combined with the retention of the poorest grain as seed for the next year's crop because of the overpowering immediate demand for food; all those bad habits could be found in the annexed estates and they were compounded in the Highland area by adverse weather conditions and the conservatism of the people. Sowing, for example, was late, the date often fixed by custom as much as by climate, so that often the harvest was later than it need have been.

Garden vegetables, despite their potential as a food supply, aroused little interest. Lochiel was reported to have had a garden in 1734 as well as, somewhat surprisingly, a watermill,[3] but in 1755 the factor in his report on Barrisdale found that the tenants had never seen green kail, cabbage or anything peculiar to garden growth. Peter May, when surveying Coigach in 1756, thought the tenants should have small yards near their houses for cabbage and turnips, something previously unheard of.[4]

While the grain crop for the whole Highland area might not have been of much financial importance to the tenants in general who depended on their animals for cash, it was of no little importance to the commissioners. Apart from any missionary zeal for improving yields, it was very much in the interests of the final intentions of the annexation that crops should be improved; rents were paid in kind and any famine would have to be relieved at the expense of the proceeds of the estates. This happened on a large scale in 1783, when £1,750 was spent on grain for the relief of the starving tenants. In 1773, the Board was explaining to the Treasury the variations in the gross rents for the Lovat estate between 1764 and 1770. The difference was entirely due to the change in prices when rents were paid in bere and oatmeal, and fluctuated from a minimum of £2087.15.1 in 1768, when a Scots boll made only ten shillings, to £2449.12.1 in 1770. Teind duty too was paid in grain.[5]

To increase the yield and improve the quality of crops, the commissioners tried several methods of encouraging tenants to help themselves. In 1762, for example, they arranged the purchase of 1,000 lbs of red clover and 1,500 lbs of white clover seed, to be distributed at half-price to the tenants on the Perth estate.[6] Three years later, in the Board's report, they pointed out that there was great ignorance of sown grasses and considerable difficulty for ordinary tenants to obtain them, because of the great distance from markets. They therefore suggested buying and providing grass seed at cost price, a low price or free, depending on the state of the area they were dealing with. Three years later again, in 1768, they were allowed to give £26 in rewards to tenants for sowing clover and other grass seeds, as well as for signs of improvements in breeds of cattle and also for turning moor ground into viable arable land. In 1774, £386.6.7 was approved for meal and seed corn for the tenants on Lovat and Cromartie, to be sold to them at prime cost. In leases, as we have seen, the sowing of clover was insisted on, as was a rotation including flax, barley, oats, clover and grass. They were prepared to countenance experiments, such as a new method of growing potatoes by cutting out the eyes, using the rest for food, then laying the eyes on dunghills in February. Once these had sprouted two or three inches, they were to be planted on previously prepared ground. The benefit of this was that it was supposed to bring on potatoes a month earlier than usual.[7]

The value of natural grass was recognised by almost all the inhabitants of the Highlands. Barrisdale tenants were described as 'botanists', so careful and knowledgeable were they in their treatment of grass[8] and, in Rannoch and Glen Lyon, though no grass seed was sown, the inhabitants were described as paying more attention to their grass than anything else.[9] This was of course because of the vital importance to their animals of a good stock of grass, though their haymaking was cursory and perfunctory, and the use of turf for roofs an apparent contradiction.

The inclusion of flax in schemes of rotation was not purely an agricultural matter. The growth of flax was encouraged to save national expenditure in importing it, again by selling the seed cheaply. The manufacturers involved in the spinning industry handled a great deal of the seed, giving it out to tenants and buying the crops.[10] Even though the leases signed in 1774 included flax in the rotation, by the time Wight was carrying out his survey there were doubts about the effect of this crop on the soil and, in 1794, James Robertson was quite firm in remarking that it 'impoverishes the soil to a great degree'.[11] So flax-growing may have been of little benefit to the already maltreated soil of the Highland area, even though the practice of raising it and spinning the yarn was reputed to pay all the rents in Perthshire at least.[12]

In insisting on proper rotation of crops, the commissioners showed that they knew what was needed, as did the factors. Writing these into leases was one way of trying to make tenants conform, but this was not wholly successful. In 1794, Robertson complained that, though for fifteen years leases had had conditions insisting on better regulation of arable land, these had not been enforced for various reasons. One of these was inefficient legal competence in the writing of the leases, but even more important, he thought, was the landlord's absence. Rotation of crops was not everywhere equally efficient. Most good farmers had similar rotations but others could be said to have no fixed rotation at all. Worse, if we are merely trying to obtain a favourable assessment of the work of the Board of the Annexed Estates, he reported that round Drummond Castle, the heartland of the Perth estate, on which most time and thought were lavished by the Board and where, if anywhere, their work should have shown very positive results, the rotation still included two years of oats which, as Robertson said, no good farmer should follow and no tenants should have been allowed to.[13]

There was also room for improvement in preparing the ground for crops. Apart from any thoughts on the type of implements to use, the tenants' methods were also faulty and, in 1780–81, Frend wrote in his journal that he had never seen such bad ploughing as in Mr. Keir's part of the estate of Perth. The seeds were not even covered after they were sown. It was also necessary to treat the land more kindly, to give it some care to help it return to its natural wealth, so dressing and manuring were to be encouraged. The use of manure was not unknown in the Highlands, but its use was neither thorough, nor systematic, nor sufficient. Tathing was the chief method, and house and farm dung were used, as well as discarded turf roofs, but the difficulty of transporting any type of manure in large quantities to a farm, that might lie many miles from a military or a reasonable country road and in addition be inaccessible by boat, was an almost insurmountable one. In fact, it was not unheard of for the factor to deny a tenant's claim regarding the quantity of lime he had used, on account of the distance it had to be carried. All manure used in Barrisdale, for example, had to be carried there on men's backs, and this would put obvious limits on the amount that could profitably be used.

The commissioners used one of their usual methods to increase the use of approved manures – they awarded prizes for the largest quantity of dung or lime laid, the greatest quantity of shell manure used, the most marl.[14] In addition to these three, there was some use of water-flooding, but it was least important. It had disadvantages and, though Menzies declared in 1767 that it had increased in Perthshire, it had fallen into abeyance by the 1780s. The possibility of obtaining marl aroused some ambitious projects for draining lochs. Mr. Adam Drummond of Megginch proposed taking a lease of the loch of Balloch, to drain it, as the other tenants could not sustain the expense.[15] Small was somewhat cynical about this, as he thought it was not feasible to drain the loch, and the only marl he knew of was on the bottom, which he could not see. £10, £6 and £3 were the amounts offered for the greatest quantities of shell manure used.[16]

The greatest efforts were made with regard to lime. Here the difficulties in ensuring adequate use were twofold. In the existing state of communications, the transport problem was almost insuperable in dealing with large quantities of lime and, where a limestone quarry might be at hand, even when the quality of the lime was suitable, there was often insufficient fuel nearby to burn it for use. When both lime and fuel were available there was no problem. The reports to the king and the Board's minutes mention the various proposals made to encourage and increase the use of lime – by building kilns, opening quarries and giving financial aid to tenants who might offer to open quarries on their own responsibility. Mr. Stewart, the minister at Callander, was allowed the limestone quarry at Tarndownan rent-free for nine years, to compensate for his trouble in opening it up. At the beginning of that year, the Perth factor had been ordered to carry out experiments in burning and caking lime in such parts of the estates as seemed suitable. When a new vein of lime was found, as was reported in 1767, prizes were instituted for the tenants who laid down the greatest amount; £6 for the largest and £4 for the second largest amount was substantial encouragement, when the whole rent could not exceed £20.[17] Measuring efficiency in laying manure by the quantity was not invariably completely successful, and over-enthusiasm was criticised. Keir, for example, the factor on the Lowland Division of the Perth estate, had his rank corn attributed by Frend to over-marling. This was an unusual state of affairs, and, throughout the annexation, the Board found more occasion for encouraging a greater use of fertilisers than for cutting down the quantities recommended. The presentation of prizes to obtain this goal remained a favourite method with the commissioners; in 1774, £10 was paid to Lt. Kenneth Sutherland on the Mains of New Tarbat for laying the greatest quantity of sea-shell manure with dung on 'lee' (i.e. untilled) ground, at the rate of over 300 bolls to the acre.

Another method of encouragement, which used private enterprise, was to give a subsidy to any entrepreneur who would sell lime cheaply. Charles Freebairn was offered 6d. on every boll up to 2,000 per year for three years, if he would sell lime on the Perth estate 30% cheaper than he normally would have done. The Inspector was supposed to enquire into how this scheme was working, by finding out what price the tenants paid compared to the situation where no premiums were allowed. However, Menzies, who was a very efficient and conscientious official, for once seems to have committed the sin of omission, and the report he produced after his tour in 1765 makes no mention of Freebairn, though he did comment favourably on the working of a quarry in the Barony of Kinbuck. Then, as the Board recognised the practical difficulties of obtaining access to many quarries, financial help in building roads was granted to remove that hindrance from use. Monaltrie improvements in 1777 include £10 towards a road to a limestone quarry; an undated report mentions the benefit to Callander from a quarry since a road was made and, in 1783, £10 was a continuing payment on Struan.[18]

One unusual experiment was made in an attempt to overcome the difficulty caused by the lack of fuel. It was proposed that £50 should be expended in making a machine to pound limestone down to the required minuteness, using water power instead of the usual method of burning it. This suggestion was eventually approved and the device became a perpetual, if fairly small, drain on the Board's resources, until it was carried off in a flood about 1778. Erected in Rannoch, it cost almost three times the estimate to build, £141.1.10, and in the Struan accounts every year had an entry for its upkeep and repairs, from £3.0.6 to £92.5.0.[19] Neither James Robertson nor William Marshall was particularly enthusiastic about the machine. Robertson said it had not been there long enough for its effects to be known – ten years – and in any case, the water power was insufficient, despite the ultimate fate of the device. Marshall found that the inhabitants of the area were most disparaging about it but added revealingly, 'but it was a new thing'.[20] In the circumstances, it can only be described as an interesting anticipation of twentieth-century use and practice in liming and a further example of the Board's readiness to experiment. It seems likely that they were not overly impressed, however, for after the machine's disappearance in the flood, no attempt was made to erect another.

Other manures used included potash,[21] and near the coast the use of sea-ware was always advocated, before kelp-burning became so profitable. The tenants on Coigach, for example, were well aware of its value, and strenuously resisted any attempt to wrest this privilege from them. Ninian Jeffrey would have liked a lease of the kelp himself.[22] Another petitioner for a lease of the shore was told that the tenants had the right of the sea-ware and that he must bargain with them. But the factor was to encourage them to use shells as an alternative.[23] Apparently the Earl of Cromartie had left the tenants their share of the ware as manure, even when he had kelp made, and the minister of Lochbroom reckoned that without this they would certainly have starved. Gradually, however, the financial rewards to be gained from other uses of kelp persuaded the Board to reserve kelp as well as woods, in Ardsheal, for instance.[24] By 1779, the shores were being let in Coigach for kelp-burning, though the tack required that tenants be left a proper quantity for manure. The shores of Corpach were also let on similar conditions. While the estate of Kinlochmoidart was still under the Barons of the Exchequer, the factor there, Henry Butter, had been making representations to them about what he considered a waste of the estate's resources. The tenants did not pay anything for their yearly cutting of wrack, and he thought that the farms were so cheap that it would be no hardship for them to be asked to give some token for it. He added somewhat ominously that, if they would not, others could be found.[25] In their resistance to kelp burning the tenants were wiser than the improvers, for kelp left only the tangle for manure, neither so suitable nor so effective as the fresh weed. It has also been claimed that the burning process and the general disturbance on the shores drove away the fish.[26]

By the end of the period of annexation, there is no doubt that there was a measure of improvement in some of the tenants' approaches to arable farming. Some were industrious in trying new crops and applying manure; others were not. In 1781, Frend found that rape was sown and the tenants of Stobhall were becoming 'fond of clover', but Robertson's description of the rotations of crops in general use in Perthshire shows that improved arable farming was only in its initial stages, even in the areas that received most attention from the Board and the Inspector. Of course, as Walker remarked in 1808, any alterations for the better had occurred only in the preceding fifty years.[27] The degree of improvement attained on the annexed estates can only be judged by comparison with that on similar neighbouring estates. Conditions varied, but no-one said about the farms on the estates, as Wight did about Forfarshire, that it would be too tedious to describe all the farms that were improving.[28]

One further step was needed to improve cultivation, and this was the provision of better farm implements. The factors had not been asked in 1755 to specify in detail what types of tools were used and, though it could be argued that such a specification should have automatically been included by them when they were describing methods of husbandry, none in fact did so. The only mention of tools in Barcaldine's report was that the lack of woods in the barony of Lix involved the tenants in long journeys to obtain their labouring implements and any tools for husbandry. Barrisdale was noted for having only one plough, but there was no comment on its quality. It was unlikely, however, that the farmers on the Board were unaware of the problem, and they took several steps to try to improve implements. One method used was to indent apprentices, another to employ properly trained men to make proper ploughs and harrows on the estates. Charles Dundas, employed to oversee improvements on the estate of Perth, like Barcaldine in his report in 1755, suggested that tradesmen should be settled at Crieff. James Duncanson was employed to teach ploughwrights and smiths, being allowed one guinea a week by the Board. The Inspector was told to look at this man's work, in 1765, and also to see if the tenants who were given free ploughs were making proper use of them. When he was reporting on this, Menzies seemed to suggest that, in one part of the estate at least, none of the tenants had got any ploughs from the Board, though this scheme had been in operation from 1762, and some, who had used them, found they were adequate only where the ground was not stony. Another ploughwright, Magnus Morris, who made similar ploughs, had distributed fifteen, which were also described as not answering in stony ground. Menzies did not think much of the workmanship, yet they had cost the Board about a guinea each.[29]

Tenants in Kinbuck, on being granted leases, had been presented with ploughs of an approved design, and also with harrows with iron teeth.[30] They had to undertake to use these or similar implements throughout their tenancy, and to leave them in good condition at the end of their tack. Any tenant who could prove that he was using approved modern farming techniques, such as turnip-growing, flax cultivation, or a newer model plough, i.e. one with more iron in its construction and pulled by one or two horses instead of several oxen, or who would promise to herd his animals, was well in the running for being given a lease.[31] Menzies suggested too that, instead of giving money in particular districts, it might have a salutary effect to give out improved farm implements as rewards for industry. Perhaps it was as well that this advice was not taken in the prevailing economic climate, when tenants were so slow in recognising the benefits that might arise from improved methods but knew hard cash when they saw it.

Indiscriminate use of the plough was not advised, however, for the Board took heed of the known and accepted fact that, in many parts of the Highlands, there were mountainous and boggy areas where spade and hoe cultivation produced much more plentiful corn than the plough.[32] In Barrisdale, the factor had shown that the ruggedness of the ground as well as the bogs prevented the use of horses over most of the estate.[33] Cottars who were given holdings on outfield could be ordered not to use ploughs, as was the former subtenant, who was to hold a piece of the farm of Straid rent-free for seven years, provided he used spade cultivation.[34] Walker, publishing his comments half a century later, was to make the point that it was sometimes not so uneconomic or so inefficient to make do with primitive instruments. The situation of the country, the lack of materials both for making and for forging tools, and the lack of communications so that these could be easily imported, outweighed the benefits from the expense and effort needed to improve them. He thought the caschrome produced better crops than the plough, certainly better than those from any plough seen in the Highlands when he was writing.[35] The commissioners seem to have been prepared to accept this thesis too.

The various steps taken – the employment of the smith in the Perth estate to train apprentices, the ploughwright in Auchterarder, the free gifts of decent ploughs – must all have helped, marginally, to improve the situation. In 1774, however, Wight was still complaining of bad ploughs and harrows, though it must be said that his worst strictures were for the conditions on Stobhall, where the greater part of the barony had been life-rented until a couple of years before. There the instruments were 'as bad as could be devised'.[36] There were no enormous strides forward in the use of better implements, and Sir John Sinclair could describe the implements of the tenants in general as 'miserable imitations of approved utensils', in the northern counties, which did include the annexed estate of Cromartie. Drastic, speedy change at this period in the history of agrarian change was not to be expected; the commissioners probably did all they could within the limits of their resources to give their tenants a gentle nudge in the right direction. It was not an easy task and even in Struan, where Menzies reported great improvement, the quality of implements was still 'extremely bad'.[37]

One other physical improvement that the commissioners wished to see on the estates was better housing, both for human and animal inhabitants. With the animals and their dung under the same roof, the houses were hardly satisfactory by human standards of hygiene, and tenants could not be brought to understand that by keeping their stock in such conditions they perhaps got more manure but lost pounds of stock. It was a habit that lasted in the Hebrides until the early years of the present century, when there was sometimes not even a wall between the byre and the living quarters.[38] Peter May wrote from Coigach in 1756 that the houses were so full of vermin in the summer that there was no sleeping in them.[39] These houses were also an offence to the eyes and minds of the would-be improvers, on account of the methods used in construction. The Board tried to eradicate the practice of using good turf for roofing by ordering that those who persisted in this should be turned out, but how far the order was carried out is uncertain.[40] Achievement of such total change would have been a marathon task, and turf roofs can be seen on outbuildings in Shetland today. The creel houses did not last for many years, and only the most pliant plants were used for the frame, usually young trees. This meant spoliation of plantations and was bound to be unpopular.[41] In leases, the Board included building improvements among others that would entail the tenants spending five years' rent in seven years, and they gave loans, quite large loans in some cases, towards new houses or towards rebuilding. John Porteous, the tenant on Mains of Strageath, proposed building a house 42′ × 19′, 14′ high with a slate roof, the cost being estimated at £50 exclusive of timber, and he was awarded £50, with 5% interest added to his rent. But a John MacLeish was advanced only £15 to rebuild his house in 1777.[42] On Lochiel, Butter had tried to encourage the tenants to build stone houses, but his success must have been limited, for William Morison's survey in 1772 comments on the fact that most of the houses were creel huts, despite the easy availability of a good supply of stones.[43]

Menzies also complained of 'slovenly biggings' which consumed a great deal of wood, because of their short life and the need for repairs. The Board encouraged tenants to build better barns and byres, giving them a proportion of the money spent, but scaling such grants to the size of the holdings. £20 was lent to one tenant on Arnprior for his barn and byre.[44] Not only did the commissioners want better houses; they wanted to see them more conveniently placed on farms in the interests of efficiency and time-saving.[45] Some steadings were not even on their respective farms and, in 1780, George Nicolson, the gardener and surveyor, mentioned the expense of moving them to more convenient places on the farm. Removal of even the more primitive type of steading was likely to be expensive and, on at least one occasion, the official surveyor's suggestion was dismissed by George Clerk Maxwell on the grounds that the factor's plan obviated the removal of the steading.[46]

The effectiveness of the Board's housing policy cannot be judged only by the money advanced out of rents, for this gives no idea of the lasting quality of the buildings. We must also consider the comments made towards the end of the annexation and afterwards. In some areas the verdict must be favourable when these later reports are studied. In 1783, William Frend could move round the estate of Perth, remarking that in the main the houses were in good order. The crops and the cattle might range from the middling to the tolerably good, but the comfort of better housing seemed to have had its own impetus. It should be remembered, of course, that the tenants on this estate had a head start, being largely housed in stone buildings in 1755.[47] It was the only one of the annexed estates about which this could be said. The reports made to the Board of Agriculture from 1794 onwards show that, the further north and west, the worse the houses, though Sir John Sinclair thought there had been some slight improvement where timber was easily got, as landlords had 'recently' begun to make allowances for improvements.[48] His survey included Ross and Cromarty. In Inverness-shire, even in 1808, the gentlemen and wealthier tenants had well-built houses, but those of the poorer were 'mean beyond description'.[49]

Apart from Wight's few words of praise of Cluny estate, where he does not specify what houses are made of but is hardly likely to have voiced an enthusiastic few words about creel houses,[50] the most northerly estates managed by the Board do not seem to have been conspicuous for good housing. It must have been much simpler to encourage better building where there was already a tradition of stonemasonry, as in Perthshire; more attention to the more remote estates in the north and west might have been immediately less rewarding and certainly more difficult but more truly an attempt to carry out the aims of annexation. The change that took place in this respect on Struan showed what was possible. By 1765, Menzies was very enthusiastic about all the improvements going on there, and declared that all the tenants were now in neat stone houses, while five years before, on his last visit to the area, there had been mostly creel houses. Unfortunately, the energy and enthusiasm of the factor and overseer, which had a great deal to do with the speed of improvement, were not equally effective on all the estates.

However, as Robert Heron remarks, the commissioners were not idle[51] and they explored every avenue of improvement imaginable in agriculture and, in accordance with the terms of the Annexing Act, not only on the annexed estates. In 1764, the king's approval was asked for £1,000 in 'premiums' for those showing a 'spirit of improvement in agriculture' in the counties of Argyll, Bute, Caithness, Sutherland, Ross, Orkney and Shetland, as well as in Inverness-shire, where so many of the estates lay. Nothing came of this, as the king's approval was never expressed, but it illustrated the Board's comprehensive conception of their duties – a Highlands and Islands Development Board in embryo. Prizes to encourage many forms of industrial activity were common, of course, in the eighteenth century; the Board of Trustees and the various improving societies all made a habit of offering premiums, and it was not surprising that the Board for the Annexed Estates, who were no strangers to the other troupes of improvers, followed that custom too.

One other important form of 'improvement', not purely agricultural, seemed essential. The idleness of the Highlanders, which was such a source of worry to factors, inspectors and commissioners, needed to be remedied if possible, and several methods were applied to this. One suggestion was that, in place of repaying loans in additional rent, the tenants should be obliged to perform additional work.[52] That proposal must have made the factors shudder. Then it was thought that, if 'strangers' were given farms among the native inhabitants, the newcomers would set an example of industry. The newcomers obliged but, unfortunately, the example was not followed by the older-established tenants.[53] One such import was a protégé of Lord Findlater, who brought him up from Norfolk to introduce the Norfolk plough and turnip cultivation into Banff. Once he had done this to Findlater's satisfaction, the Earl was prepared to pay his fare back south, but the man, Philip Girling, wanted to stay in Scotland. Unfortunately, he had 'lived like an Englishman, though sober', so he had saved little money. With such a recommendation, Girling was to be given a holding on the estate of Perth.[54] On the other hand, inefficient tenants and unruly members of the community were liable to be removed. Evictions were threatened for various reasons, including being bad neighbours, refusing to divide runrig, becoming bankrupt, getting into arrears of rent – though this was a perpetual state of affairs – or stealing wood. All such types of behaviour were likely to advert against good husbandry and improvements, and hence met with disapproval.

In their general scheme for raising the standard of workmanship in the areas under their management, the commissioners also included apprenticing men to farmers. It was suggested that it would be desirable and praiseworthy to train some of the young men, especially the sons of chief tenants and better-off farmers, in the rudiments of farming as practised in the Lowlands. In the report to the king in 1761, apprenticeship in farming was among the schemes put forward. Once the scheme was approved, surprisingly quickly, the Board also moved at high speed for once and, by November 1761, they were able to report that the necessary steps had been taken to bind apprentices to farmers in the Lowlands. Tenants who wanted their sons to be trained were asked to write in, and those who were accepted were sent off at a fairly high cost of £25 per annum.[55] This apprenticeship was not confined to the sons of tenants, for one of the sergeants, who had been employed in enclosing in Kinbuck, asked for assistance. As he was prepared to go to England, he spent two years in the south on an allowance of £20 a year. He had to send in quarterly reports and, when he did ask for a farm, he was allowed yet another year's training and was promised the tenancy of the first proper farm vacant on the estate of Perth.[56] Ninian Jeffrey, once again on the track of improving sheep-rearing, suggested in 1765 that some of the Coigach tenants might well benefit by being sent to other sheep-rearing areas, so that they could learn how to use the extensive, dry hill-grazings in the barony. He thought they should also be given a general training in agriculture, but this idea was not taken up.

The idea of training farmers in improving methods was good enough, but does not seem to have borne much fruit. A few of the trainees, like James Robertson, are mentioned as being employed later on Struan, but £25 was a large proportion of the annual sum of £200 allocated to the apprenticeship scheme to be spent on one individual and, when the commissioners formally abandoned the idea in 1775, there was no mention of farmers having returned to the estates in a greater proportion than other apprentices. Those who did return must surely have been affected by their Lowland training but, in the inspector's later reports, there is no recognition of better farmers having been apprentices – nor of the worst for that matter. Despite the cost, however, it seems a pity that it was not pursued with greater vigour, as the money for apprentices was rarely exhausted.[57] The apprenticing of farmers was aimed at counteracting the ignorance of good farming practice in the estates, and a further onslaught on ignorance was made by purchasing instructive texts on agriculture. Some were sent to the factors for lending to the tenants; some were given direct to tenants, and Young's writings, Dickson's *Treatise of Husbandry* and Wight's *Husbandry* were among such volumes.[58]

One very dramatic improvement was envisaged, similar to Lord Kames' draining of Flanders Moss. This was the draining of what was called the Moor of Rannoch but, after a few years, the factor was inclined to be cautious about laying out too much money on this.[59] It had been suggested that the moss between Rannoch and Glenorchy was not one large plain but about 10,000 little mosses, each one of which would need two or three drains. Little seemed to have come of the experiment, however; what are known as 'soldiers' trenches' are possibly the remains.[60]

As behoved aspiring model landowners, the commissioners were very interested in the encouragement and full exploitation of existing woodland, accompanied by planting for the future. They did not initiate afforestation; that example had been set already in Scotland by proprietors like Lauderdale in the seventeenth century and Grant of Monymusk earlier in the eighteenth.[61] They needed no prodding into activity, however, for while planting and caring for woodland were expensive pursuits, they were also a worthwhile investment. Not only were plantations expected to increase the income from estates through the sale of timber and bark, but their aesthetic value was also considered and, while the Board did not neglect this latter aspect, neither did their senior servants. One contract for cutting the woods near Castle Drummond reserved sixty old oaks growing together there, and Archibald Menzies on his own initiative directed the tacksman of the woods to leave others of about the same age and size that were scattered around singly. He said he was 'perswaded the Board never meant [them] to be cut, as they are a great ornament to the country'.[62] Some years later, a surveyor proposed a mixture of oak, ash and elm on one part of Strathpeffer, adding that even firs alone would be an ornament as they would cover an ugly ridge of black hills to the south. The factor's detailed descriptions of the woods on the estates, particularly on Perth and Struan in 1755, show that Dr. Johnson's strictures on the treelessness of Scotland contained much exaggeration.[63] The woods on the estate of Perth were described as valuable – with reason, for those near Drummond and Balloch had been sold at their last cutting for £2,000 and would be ready for the next sale in about seven years. Where transport was a problem, however, which meant over most of the Highlands, the bark was more valuable than the timber in commercial terms, as it could be carried more easily; bark carriage was one of the services that the factors advised should be retained, as its potential value was so great.

Much of the woodland area had suffered maltreatment after the Forty-Five, according to the factors, on Lovat and Cromartie especially, though Stobhall in Cargill parish was also mentioned in this respect, but the woods demanded continuous attention to preserve them from the depredations of tenants and their stock. Tenants were so convinced of their rights to various perquisites from the woods, such as brushwood for firing and timber for their houses, that Barcaldine was moved to the suggestion that only sealing off the Stobhall woods would save them. The proprietors were not blameless, for one at least of the previous proprietors of the annexed estates, Robertson of Struan, was said to have taken 'a very fatherless care' of his valuable fir wood, the Black Wood of Rannoch, supposed to be over 2,000 acres.[64] He not only cut more than he needed himself but allowed his tenants to cut indiscriminately. But then John Williams, the mineral surveyor, declared in 1771 that woods were neglected all over the Highlands. Indeed, successful forestry calls for as much specialised skill and care – in planting, weeding, thinning and appropriate felling – as any other use of land, and this the commissioners set out to supply, like any other improvers of the time.

The first essential was to discipline the tenants in their use – or perhaps one should say their abuse – of woods, and another priority was to ensure that tacksmen adhered to their contracts. Thomas Campbell was appointed baron bailie on the Perth estate in November 1755, at £5 per annum, but concurrently his work as overseer of wood grieves and woods was much more highly rated at £15. For this he was expected to see that the underkeepers were diligent, which would involve watching the tenants' behaviour, and ensuring that purchasers of the woods adhered to their contracts.[65] The supervision of contract work was no empty gesture, for several lessees lost their contracts when they had not cut at the prescribed time, and complaints were made about too high or too much cutting.[66] The commissioners were also prepared to look for methods of distracting the tenants from their depredations on the woods, and several ideas appeared, such as planting the tenants' yards with timber for their building and Lord Kames' notion that firs might be planted near Callander purely for fuel. Goats were the great menace to young plantations, and there was apparently no compunction on the part of the Board in having any that did appear killed.

The commissioners also began a positive programme of building new nursery gardens and repairing established ones at Drummond, Beauly, Callander and Balloch to provide young trees for their own use and for sale to neighbouring proprietors such as Stirling of Keir.[67] These were under the care of specially appointed gardeners and they hoped to economise by finding men who could measure land, so that they could help tenants lay out their ground, something that surveyors usually had to do. They also spent a great deal of money on enclosing and planting moors, £1,900.7.10½ on the Lowland Division of the Perth estate alone, between 1768 and 1784, and by 1773, on Small's Division of the estate, about £1,000 had been spent on planting.

It would be too much to expect that the programme of afforestation should have proceeded without any interruption, and it is not surprising to learn of several mishaps. The first gardener at Drummond, John Bruce, had to be dismissed for indolence; the gardener at the colony of Strelitz was reported to have planted trees so badly that half failed, though this was refuted.[68] The sawmill at Carie, rebuilt in 1759 to replace the 'Gothic' construction there, was perpetually in arrears, probably because the tacksman was also a drover.[69] Tenants with leases had to accept the reservation by the commissioners to enclose woods without receiving any abatement of rent for what they lost thereby, such as the grazing;[70] but long-established traditions were hard a-dying and Frend expressed concern in 1780 about the tenants' prevailing habit of peeling the bark from trees, which was as bad for young trees as goats were. Few of the plantations, however, seemed to do too badly, though 93 acres of firs failed one year because of a bad over-dry season, and the Board's work here compares well with that of other proprietors in an age that thought of planting trees in millions, not hundreds. Wight claimed that every eminence near Castle Downie, on General Fraser's estate, had been planted by the Board, and furthermore all were prospering.[71] And Frend's comments on the woods between 1780 and 1784 must have sounded like a paean of praise in the Board's ears after his somewhat dampening views on the progress of general agricultural improvements. Most of the woods, unlike the houses, the cattle and the crops, were 'tolerably well kept', 'promising well' or 'in good order'.

How can we measure the success or failure of the commissioners' agricultural policy? Certainly not by merely counting up the money that was spent on diking and on improvements generally, or by counting the length of dikes that were built. We must look at comments made by inspectors during the annexation and by reporters such as Andrew Wight, and also we must consider accounts of the areas involved in the annexation after 1784. Factors' reports of what was going on must be treated with a certain amount of reserve, for they had their reputations and their positions to consider. The General Inspector, Archibald Menzies of Culdares, toured the estates each summer from 1765 to 1768, visiting parts of Perth in the first three years, Struan in 1765 and 1767, Lovat and Cromartie in 1766 and 1768 and Barrisdale in 1768, having hired a ship, the *Woodhall*, for this last expedition. Better paid than the factors, at £150 p.a. with one guinea allowed daily for expenses, independent and self-confident, his reports serve as an interim commentary on the progress made on the estates at about the halfway mark. Despite his apologia in the introduction to his first report that 'As this employment is entirely new to me, I hope the Honourable Board will pardon the many mistakes I shall make', he was quite prepared to make pungent comments on the Board's policies, as well as on the tenants' and factors' reactions.

His first point was that conditions varied greatly in different parts of the estates but, at the same time, he seemed to consider all the tenantry as basically 'ignorant, aukward and lazy'; they would make it difficult to follow the best general plan of improvement. In his first year's tour, Menzies certainly paints a very mixed picture. One condition was general and that was that the tenants lived poorly, and he thought that giving them an unspecified area for garden stuff would help them. The Board and its officers he criticised, firstly, for indiscriminately establishing subtenants as king's tenants, as he considered many of them were only suited to being servants; and secondly, for not having cleared marches with neighbours before beginning enclosure. Some good dikes were being built but many were indifferent, and dividing farms did not automatically lead to improved farming, for in Auchterarder barony, divided, the tenants were no improvers, while Callander, undivided, was full of improving if quarrelsome tenants, some of whom had even stopped making a distinction between infield and outfield, which was very advanced farming in the 1760s. Muthill, as usual, was farther back in farming than any other area.

There were farms where the tenants 'took care to overstock', but in Lovat and Cromartie, where the tenants were mostly idle and the few tradesmen described as 'the dregs of the country', several tenants had wholly enclosed their farms. In the barony of New Tarbat, however, he had to admit that only one tenant showed any interest in improvement. Charles Dundas had written in July, 1762, that all the tenants on the estate of Perth were bad farmers, and though Menzies does not give quite the same impression, he did comment that one man, John Dun, showed a spirit and intelligence rarely to be met with in that country. The few years between Dundas's writing and Menzies' inspection may have seen some improvement in the tenants' attitudes, but it is noticeable that Andrew Wight from 1774, and William Frend in his reports from 1780–84, consistently convey the impression that most of the good farmers they met with were either tenants on or proprietors of other estates. Thirteen years of formal annexation had made little difference to Monaltrie, too, where the tenants were 'the most beggarly wretches' who scourged a poor light soil with one crop of barley and two of oats.

The one truly encouraging report on the progress of improvements was on Struan, where Menzies was able to say that it gave him great pleasure to see the remarkable change in the country since his last visit about five years previously, presumably before he was employed as Inspector. He had a cheerful tale to tell of farms divided, cattle and sheep soumed, head fences of timber, stone dikes, and stone houses replacing the universal creel huts previously seen. Admittedly, farming equipment was still poor, but a plough-and-cartwright had settled at Kinloch, so it would be possible to train an apprentice. In a period of five years, short in breeding terms, it was unlikely that the cattle would show much signs of increase in size or milk yield, but the arrangements being made to bring in bulls from Skye, where a standard higher than the usual Highland one was maintained, were expected to improve the breed.[72]

Andrew Wight was the next semi-independent observer to set out on a tour of the estates to report on their conditions. It is somewhat surprising, considering the amount that had already been spent on surveys and on Menzies' inspections, to find Lord Kames proposing, in 1773, that still another survey and inspection should be undertaken.[73] Admittedly, on this occasion, special attention was to be paid to the corn farms on the estates, but most of the information the Board asked him to report on could have been discovered from the factors: methods of culture, instruments of husbandry, types of grain sown and the return, the manure used, the climate and seasons, the price of labour and provisions, and how far farms lay from markets. However, as his reports were eventually published as *The Present State of Husbandry in Scotland*, historians should perhaps not quibble, though the immediate returns for his labours may not have been commensurate with the expense.

Wight set out on August 12th, 1773, and his preface in the published work was very optimistic. Fifty years previously, he pontificated, such a survey would have been of no avail, because the practice was the same everywhere. Fifty years thereafter, he thought, nothing would remain to be learned.[74] Certainly, a great deal remained to be learned still on the annexed estates. He started off in Stobhall, most of which had been life-rented to the Dowager of Perth, who was not an improving farmer; some years after her death it was said that she would not bestow a farthing on repairs of any kind, for if her beads were in order all was well.[75] She had sold marl to her own tenants, but had been uninterested in any other type of improvement and, as the barony had been under the Board's management for only a year, it was hardly likely to be a model. All the usual features of unimproved farming practices could be illustrated in the barony of Stobhall, and even Alexander Robertson of Brunty, whom Menzies had singled out for praise for his energetic building and planting, had corn no better than his neighbours, and as full of weeds.[76]

The next part of the Perth estate Wight visited was the barony of Auchterarder. The Board had been in charge here since 1755 and, though the tenants seemed to be industrious and ready to change their methods, there was not a vast difference between Auchterarder and Stobhall. The ditches that had been dug to enclose farms had been poorly planned and were now half-filled with earth that had been allowed to fall in. Even hard-working farmers either used the same methods of cultivation as their neighbours and so got little more produce though they had enclosed, or they overcropped. In Kinbuck, Wight reckoned that the enclosure had been carried out 'without any judgement' and that the tenants were reaping no benefits from the interest they were paying. He suggested that if the Board were serious in having ground properly enclosed, what was already done would have to be abandoned. However, in 1755, there had been no enclosures in the barony, so division and enclosures, even if unsatisfactory by the high standards of Wight of Ormiston, must be considered an improvement.

When he reached Callander in the summer of 1774, it was seen that the slightly more efficient and energetic tenants there had maintained their superiority, described in earlier reports. Wight assumed that the greater enterprise thereabouts was the result of the presence of Mr. Small, who had a small tenement near Callander. Small was a popular factor, who among other gifts was an amateur physician, and according to Wight the tenants tried to please him by keeping their farms in order.[77] In this assumption, however, he underestimated the inhabitants, for they had shown signs of interest in better husbandry when Menzies visited there some years before, and their very quarrelsome reputation makes one suspect the likelihood of such agreeable behaviour; almost ten years later, when Frend supervised the estates of Perth, he mentioned good crops, well-kept houses, and the use of lime there, but he was critical of their dikes and ditches, lack of repairs, and only 'middling-well' grazed cattle. But there were few better farmers on the estates. Indeed, Wight eventually remarked in some despair that, since he had had occasion to mention so much imperfect husbandry, he would close with some instances of good – but these were not on the annexed estates.[78]

The Board found Wight's survey sufficiently interesting and useful to employ him on a similar study of the whole of the country, and it was 1780 before his travels took him to any more of the annexed estates. He set off then for the far north of Scotland, and from his reports it would be difficult to believe that, in the county of Cromarty, there was an estate under the control of his employers that touched both east and west coasts. The extensive lands of the family of the erstwhile Earl of Cromartie were never mentioned, and the only reference to the annexed estates is in connection with the subsidy made through George Ross, the Cromarty improver and entrepreneur, towards building Cromarty harbour.[79] The Board may not have totally forgotten the existence of their most northerly responsibilities but, in the last ten or twelve years of the annexation, there is a marked diminution of interest, as illustrated by the decrease in the volume of records relating to this period.[80]

Wight's comment, too, that the inhabitants on the estate of Lovat had been reclaimed by the commissioners from ignorance and indolence must be weighed against the information Menzies gives about the comparable behaviour of the old and new tenants there. None of the original tenants by 1766 had done anything about improving their farms, and Wight himself states a few pages later that Beauly, on the Lovat estates, furnished 'not a single good example of husbandry'. A few years before, Alexander Shaw, the manufacturer at Glenmoriston, had categorised the people of Beauly as an 'idle, drunken set', whom he would have removed to make way for industrious tenants. The afforestation on Lovat, round Castle Downie, was successful, however, and General Fraser, who had had his ancestral lands returned to him in 1774, was beginning to give nineteen-year leases.[81] So far, we must agree from such evidence that, as Professor Youngson says, improvement had only begun.[82]

In the same year that Wight made his way north, the Board decided to revive the post of General Inspector. The Perth bridge was no longer absorbing its annual subsidy, so the salary for the post was once again available.[83] Adam Drummond of Gardrum was duly appointed and took a salary, but what he did for it is difficult to discover. From 1780 onwards, there are detailed descriptions of the estate of Perth from William Frend, appointed to advise on improvements there.[84] He traversed several parts of Perthshire more than once in the few years to 1784. There were undoubted signs of improvements, though Frend's comments on the astonishing change for the better that took place between his first appearance in 1780 and in his last reports may be treated with some reserve as special pleading. There were some well-kept houses and mills, for example Drummond; the tenants of Stobhall were 'becoming fond of clover' and were sowing rape, while Robert McNeil in Balloch got two bolls more yield to the acre than before he marled. Even the Muthill tenants were beginning to enclose: beginning, it may be noticed, in 1780. However, the Muthill houses were not recommended and they had dreadful cattle. Auchtermuthil tenants were condemned as indolent and cultivated their ground 'after the worst manner I ever saw'. In 1783, he was able to say there had been some improvements, including the sowing of clover and rye-grass, for which he implicitly claimed credit,[85] but these annual reports make it clear what uphill work it was to introduce new methods. One aspect of the Board's policy met with his approval: the hill farms of Easter and Wester Glentarken were apparently successful, and he thought them of much greater value than Lowland farms on account of the low management costs. It seems likely that Thomas Keir, the factor on the Lowland Division of Perth, was not the best of farmers, whatever his other merits, and without good examples, tenants were not usually inclined to improve. Keir, as we have seen, had overdone the quantities of marl on his grounds, so that his corn was rank. In 1780 and 1781, Strathgartney, under Campbell, was in better condition, no doubt helped by the better soil in parts of Balquhidder for, in 1783, Frend could report mostly only dike-making; one farm had good turnips. Back in Stobhall, the dikes, badly built in the first place, were going to ruin and only Lady Rachel Drummond continued improvements; the others had shot their bolt and were doing no more.

There were undoubtedly improvements in farming practice and changes in organisation on the annexed estates under the Board's management. How much was achieved, particularly by comparison with the work of other improving landlords, is difficult to assess. Negative evidence is not without value, and it is perhaps significant that only one writer reporting for the Board of Agriculture from 1794 paid the Board of Commissioners for the Annexed Estates any compliment on their management of the estates. This was Robert Heron, who did not officially inspect any of the counties wherein the estates lay.[86] Those writing about central and southern Perthshire, Inverness-shire, Ross and Cromarty were suspiciously silent.[87] Of course, agricultural change, by its nature, and in the eighteenth century by the nature of the human material involved as well as the animal and vegetable, was bound to be a slow process. That James Robertson found a great deal of the land between Stirling and Crieff for the most part unimproved in 1771, much of this annexed, only sixteen years after the appointment of the commissioners, is not too reprehensible.[88] Whether the Board should have been quite so slow in some of its reactions is something that is more open to criticism. In 1774, Lord Kames produced a paper of comments on Andrew Wight's report of that year; it included his somewhat belated reaction to Menzies' reports of the late 1760s. Highly critical of Scottish agriculture generally, he expressed the hope that, if the commissioners persevered in their plans, they would be a blessing to their country. But the Board for the Annexed Estates was to have only another ten years of life and, at this point, two-thirds of the way through its existence, he had to talk even in Perthshire of spirits depressed by poverty, though rents were low; of tenants who showed no activity in, and had no knowledge of, cultivating their lands well. 'They languidly go on in the old beaten track and it never enters their thoughts that there is a better method.' Nineteen years of state control, exhortation, and encouragement had little to show so far for all the effort in that area where most might have been expected.[89]

The Perth estate was the one approaching nearest to good farming practice, where the previous proprietor had made some token steps at least in the direction of improvement; one would have thought it the place most likely to display change and yet, ten years later still, Frend's descriptions of conditions do not convince one that thirty years of expenditure had achieved significant results. Admittedly the Board started off with unfriendly tenantry, poorly husbanded land, and a tradition of lethargy, but other proprietors in the same area faced almost identical problems, and Wight's comments on the estates of neighbours, like the Duke of Atholl and the Marquis of Breadalbane, do not show the annexed estates shining by comparison. Hugh Seton of Touch had been in possession of his lands only sixteen years when Wight visited him in 1777, and while he was certainly working with potentially rich carse land, it had been worn out when he went into it; his tenants were as ignorant and indolent as those on the annexed estates; and yet he had worked wonders.[90] Of work done on the annexed estates, a similar comment was made only by Menzies and referring only to Struan.

It would be unjust to assess the Board's work by what happened on those estates that remained under the Barons of the Exchequer until 1770, but those were the most remote, the least advanced in agriculture, and presumably most in need of all the processes the annexation was meant to set in motion. Yet, following the surveys made immediately after the legal rights of the subjects superior were bought over, no inspector visited them; there were few reports thereafter. Certainly leases were granted very quickly on Lochiel, Cluny, Kinlochmoidart, Lochgarry (from 1778). Callart, and Ardsheal[91] but, as we have seen, leases were no guarantee of improvement, especially on estates so far away from immediate supervision. The return of the Lovat estate to the Fraser family may well have led to a certain lack of interest in any very active policy, especially on the estates newly acquired in 1770, and possibly even an unspoken assumption that, if all the estates were to be returned, then members of the respective families could well be left to make the best of them. Certainly in 1774, the whole of Ardsheal except Ardsheal farm itself and Lettermore was leased to the family.[92] Four years later, Francis Farquharson of Monaltrie was offered the factorship of his own estate. He refused it, suggesting his nephew William Farquharson of Bruxie instead[93] and, while Monaltrie was not in the same category as these other estates, having been under the Board since its appointment in 1755, this step may be another pointer to the direction the Board's collective mind was taking.

More reprehensible, and something that must be a serious charge against the efficiency of the Board's management, was their comparative neglect of the estate of Cromartie, especially in the later years. This estate may have demanded much of their attention – even though such attention was somewhat lopsided – in the first few years of the annexation, but it did not last.[94] In 1779, the abstracted rental shows only £7.11.9 being paid in interest on money advanced for improvements, when the total rental was £772.18.10 $\frac{8}{12}$. And this is the first rental of those available that shows any expenditure of the sort on the estate, though earlier reports to the government implied that Cromartie had shared in 5% improvements. Rents had certainly been raised, but seemingly only on the basis of the increased valuation that took place all over the estates in the 1770s. There had been consistently discouraging reports on Coigach, except for Jeffrey's belief that sheep would flourish there and, in 1772–73, the surveyor, David Aitkin, thought that the Forest of Coigach justified no expenditure whatsoever. Lord Macleod, the eldest son of George, third Earl of Cromartie, who received his father's estates on the disannexation, is said to have had to begin their restoration, as Tarbat had been 'much dilapidated' during the forfeiture.[95]

Comparisons with other improving proprietors, implicit in Wight's survey, for example, are not wholly encouraging. Nor did the estates pass highly in what has been called 'the true test of the progress and importance of improvement', the response of the small man.[96] The annexed estates were not, of course, unique in that; neither did all their neighbours'. A history of Monzievaird and Strowan, written in 1784, talks of the failure of the inhabitants to follow the gentlemen in fallowing and sowing turnips and grass.[97] What can probably be said is that the annexed estates made as much progress as the average by 1784. Not all improvers were successful, in either the Highlands or the Lowlands, and the commissioners were not alone in making mistakes and misjudgements. Mackenzie of Delvine, for example, employed Captain Lawrence Day as his factor, and Day was allowed £200 by the Board for his own improvements as well as being involved in training apprentices. Mackenzie, however, became increasingly worried about Day's competence, complaining that, whatever his genius, he was idle; his farm was going to waste and destruction. He reckoned that Day, who was a plausible Irishman, had gained no advantage from his activities and he, Mackenzie, had lost much. A further source of his disapproval of his erstwhile employee was the belief that he had left his wife in financial straits.[98] There may have been other such instances, possibly influencing Lord Kames to write of Campbell of Shawfield's agricultural plans that the idea of attracting skilled farmers to remote areas had a 'plausible appearance' but seldom succeeded. Kames thought that it was not skilful farmers who would be attracted, but adventurers who were unsuccessful at home. Instead, he recommended the employment of an overseer, preferably one experienced in looking after gentlemen's grounds.[99]

The Board took this advice themselves in some measure. They attempted to compensate for the lack of personal supervision by appointing overseers of various kinds and standards. Charles Dundas was director of improvements on the estate of Perth for some time, and William Roy had a similar position on Struan, with a salary of 1/6 per day. On that estate, he and the factor, James Small, can be said to have come nearest to realising the aims of the Annexing Act.[100] At the top of the pyramid of inspection came the General Inspectors, Francis Grant, Archibald Menzies and, finally, Adam Drummond, who apparently was not expected to work for his money. It was regrettable that the commissioners did not accept the logic of their earlier appointments. As Frend pointed out, it was a mistake to have left the position of General Inspector vacant, after Menzies resigned in 1770, for frequent inspections such as he carried out, with the resultant fear of an unfavourable report to the Board, could have acted as a 'spur and an auband' (awe-band) to the tenants.[101] Menzies offered to continue his duties unpaid, but there are no further annual visits to estates, with their illuminating descriptions of the effects of the Board's works, after his elevation to the post of Commissioner of Customs, even though he did become a member of the Board.

Among the commissioners there were many articulate and able improvers, Lord Kames perhaps outstanding, but in the last analysis they were absentee landlords and, further, absentees who did not hand over to their factors the absolute control that many proprietors did, like the Sutherland family.[102] This could lead to abuse, but lack of support for the factors did not help efficiency.[103] Barcaldine wrote on one occasion, when he was seeking authorisation to repair a breech in the banks of the River Earn, that if he had been working for a private proprietor, he would have gone ahead at once and expected his thanks. An omen of what state control might lead to was also explicit in a communication to the Barons of the Exchequer in 1754; Forbes wrote that he had had the mills on Strathpeffer repaired 'as frugally as tho' it had been done on a private gentleman's estate'.[104] An energetic factor, like Small on Struan, assisted by an overseer specially appointed for agricultural duties, could to some extent overcome the handicap of there being no resident proprietor, but it is arguable that private landowners, with a personal interest in the estates, would have been just as effective improvers as the Edinburgh Board, however capable, enlightened and successful individual members might be on their own lands. If any single cause were to be picked on for the lack of overwhelming success in achieving agricultural change and improvement, it should probably be this: the absence of resident proprietors.

In thirty years of control, the state might have expected more from such an eminent group as comprised the Board for the Annexed Estates, but it must be remembered in all fairness that simple agricultural efficiency was not the sole, or even the first, aim of annexation. The commissioners were never free agents. They were restricted initially by the terms of the Annexing Act, which posed the dilemma of weighing efficiency against achieving the 'happiness of the tenants' and their loyalty to the Hanoverians. After 1774, when the Lovat estate was returned to the son of the Red Fox, there was always present the realisation that the annexation might be overturned, so that long-term policies would never in any case come to fruition; the Treasury even suggested in that year that no more long leases should be granted. It was not the best recipe for agricultural improvement.

INDUSTRIAL DEVELOPMENT AND FISHING

Aid to Industrial Development

THE need for good, profitable estate management was implicit in the whole concept of annexation. Explicit in the Annexing Act, and in government orders to the commissioners, was the exhortation to accelerate the social and economic transformation of the Highlands by introducing industries, as well as the habits of industry, to the area. The Board for the Annexed Estates was not of course the first or the last organisation, public or private, to face this task; in the previous century, the Scottish Estates passed laws which aimed at the promotion of manufacturing industries and the improvement of craftsmanship in the Lowlands as well as the Highlands. Royal encouragement was granted to the fishing industry, and Miss Dean points out that 'One of the most surprising and indeed one of the most pathetic features of Scottish political life in the seventeenth century is the persistence with which, even in the midst of dangers of all kinds, those who were anxious to foster Scottish industries kept urging their plans'.[1] But in 1755 it was still possible to agree with Wodrow, who had remarked earlier, 'I have seen frequent attempts of this nature come to very little'.[2] However, long before the half-century mark, individual landowners had begun to take an active interest in improving not only their agricultural methods but the whole economy of their estates and the surrounding country. Cockburn of Ormiston, Joseph Cumine, and most significantly in the context of the annexation, James Drummond, the titular Duke of Perth, were among those who tried, perhaps only instinctively, to produce a balanced economy on their estates. Drummond established a large linen factory at Perth, which was destroyed by the military guarding the town in 1746, and he had also built a 'large house for carrying on a linen manufacture' in Crieff.[3] New industries needed new implements and new craftsmen readily available to make and mend more elaborate tools than the natives were accustomed to handling. A new type of society was also an essential.

So these heritors built small towns, feuing out land to craftsmen, who would be provided with a house and a piece of ground. Wheelwrights, spinners, weavers, blacksmiths, would grow on their crofts the primary products necessary to feed their families but, as their main occupation, they would be expected to practise their crafts, repair the tools of the less skilled and in addition train apprentices. On the annexed estates, Callander was a Drummond creation and Crieff's redevelopment after 1716 was largely due to that family. Other proprietors worked on a smaller scale. Sir Alexander Mackenzie of Coul, for example, on whose grounds the Board of Trustees had established a spinning school at Lochcarron, was reported by John Neilson, the Trustee's inspector, as having given out wheels and reels to his tenants and he had also asked the SSPCK for assistance in establishing tradesmen.[4] It was taken for granted that the process of weaning the Highlanders from what Lowlanders and Englishmen considered their 'long habit of sloth and inactivity' and reconciling them to the love of labour, industry and good order should be an integral part of all such plans, whenever Highland proprietors were concerned.

In this atmosphere the factors, in 1755, answered the commissioners' questions on the progress of manufactures in the estates. The references are minimal and discouraging.[5] From east to west, the same tale is told, but the further away from 'civilisation', as it was understood south of the Tay, the less likelihood there was that the factor could describe any profitable commerce or industry. In Monaltrie, the 'generality of the people are idly inclined', and commerce and industry are 'come to no great length' – not surprising, considering the size of the estate. On Struan the factor, James Small, declared that commerce and manufactures could scarcely be said to have reached Rannoch but he could say that there had been some improvement, in that 'the women who were wont to do nothing but look after the cattle when the men were idle or perhaps worse employed' had betaken themselves to spinning and industry, especially in the winter, and the men looked after the cattle. In addition, he thought that the men were 'labouring their grounds and of late do many things about the family which were formerly lookt upon by them as women's work but which they chuse to do themselves rather than take the women from the spinning'. A little optimistic perhaps. Small thought a village at Kinloch Rannoch was a necessity but, discreetly, found himself 'unequal to the task of saying what should or should not be done in Rannoch'. One reasonable, if not wholly practicable, recommendation he did make was that several types of manufactures should be introduced to give the youth of the neighbourhood their choice of occupation.

In Cromartie, in the barony of New Tarbat, there was some spinning; in Strathpeffer, the women 'spin but little' and were quite idle in winter. In the estate of Lovat, manufactures were introduced partly in Kirkhill, but little progress had been made in Kiltarlity, though there were plenty of stills. In the smaller estates, farther west, Kinlochmoidart and Barrisdale, spinning was hardly mentioned. In Barrisdale, the only commerce was the sale of black cattle and the exchange of butter and cheese for oatmeal from Skye. No linen was made and the multiplicity of whisky stills was one reason, it was suggested, for the poverty of the inhabitants.

It is only when we come south to the Drummonds' extensive lands in Perthshire, that commerce, industry and manufactures, in the accepted sense of the word and then in only the most rudimentary way, became a part of ordinary life. And in this estate spreading over forty-six miles, in the western, most Highland parts, in the barony of Lix, in the parish of Killin, and in Balquhidder, there was 'no commerce or public manufactures', though the inhabitants did buy lint for the women to spin. The yarn was sold and this was their only way in a subsistence economy of making money. One of the few references to wool-spinning relates to Balquhidder, but in this rather damp part of Scotland, the plentiful water was unfortunately inconveniently situated for bleaching, so that the linen manufacture was handicapped.

The Duke of Perth's foundation, Callander, was in a better position, since the opening of some communications between the Highlands and Lowlands of Scotland, and the factors felt it was reasonable to hope for some development there. A few craftsmen had settled on the feus granted by Lord James Drummond, and linen yarn was the principal commodity at the yearly fairs. Strathgartney had two meal mills, and 'a good deal' of linen yarn was spun. The same pattern emerged in Comrie and Strowan parishes. In Muthill the honesty of the inhabitants was admitted – the very fact of this being mentioned may be a testimony to the rarity of such a quality – but alas, they showed industry only in spinning linen yarn and in watering their grounds. This latter activity would seem to be a singularly unnecessary pastime in Perthshire.

Stobhall, most of it life-rented to the Dowager Duchess of Perth, had no sort of commerce, other than three meal mills and linen yarn, spun and, unusually, woven into cloth. In Auchterarder, there were signs of commercial initiative, a number of shops selling small merchandise, and there were middlemen, for some of the inhabitants were described as 'buying linen yarn up and down the country which they send to Glasgow'.

The town of Crieff, however, was obviously considered the most promising spot in the whole of the annexed estates, if not in the whole Highland area, Inverness excepted. There was a large amount of Perth property there, in the barony of Milnab, and it was apparently at the time the most thriving, certainly the largest, population centre in the estates. It was the hub of the road system; there were already established merchants in linen, wool and skins, and dealers in victuals; there was a fair, a convenient gathering place for merchants, farmers and pedlars; the drovers gathered near Crieff; there were tradesmen of all sorts – bakers, butchers, wheelwrights. A fairly sophisticated town for eighteenth-century Scotland! The factor quite clearly thought this a splendid place. There was even a surplus labour supply and he recommended a spinning and stocking-knitting school, as there were 'crowds of little girls here that stroll about the streets playing at hand ball' and other such employments and diversions who would be much better guided into industry. Already, quantities of yarn were brought to Crieff to be sold and sent to Paisley and Glasgow. Why not manufacture it on the spot? A tannery could be built and should do well, as there was plenty of bark as well as a good supply of skins. His excitement and enthusiasm must have been infectious.

Among the statistics the factors were asked to provide in the early years were the numbers of persons in each estate able to spin. Not a surprising request, considering the obsession with the linen trade, but one's sympathies must be with the factor struggling round the remoter parts of Kinlochmoidart, for example, trying to find how many of the antagonistic natives could use a spinning wheel or even a rock and spindle. However, they all managed to produce some figures: 2,376 on Perth out of a total population on the estate of 6,191, 112 of 293 on Arnprior, 73 of 249 on Barrisdale, 488 of 2,199 in Strathpeffer, 389 of 1,253 on Struan, but in Kinlochmoidart none claimed such skill.[6] As with all the more complicated or 'civilised' pursuits, the nearer to central Scotland, the more prevalent the skill, and nothing is said in this purely statistical reckoning of the quality of the spun yarn. That it was generally indifferent stuff we can fairly assume from later reports and from occasional remarks by the inspectors and manufacturers who corresponded with the commissioners in later years, by which time it may be hoped some improvement had been made. When James Glass asked to be made an Inspector under the Trustees, in 1768, his memorial stated that 'Most of the yarn spun in his neighbourhood is so ill-spun it is unfit for any branch of the linen manufacture'.[7]

With the factors' information in front of them, the Board set to work. Various influences combined to keep their industrial plans within the fairly narrow paths marked out by the Board of Trustees and other improvers, notably the fact that many of the commissioners were also members of other groups, particularly the Board of Trustees. Central government control of financial outlay, with resultant delays in releasing funds for industrial development, was a considerable disadvantage and a restraining influence. The limited financial resources available from the incomes of the estates came as a surprise; this was a very severe handicap and one that was not immediately appreciated by everyone involved. The end result was a decided lack of originality in the Annexed Estates Board's approach to all industrial development. It would probably have been unreasonable to expect anything else. Considering that many of the active members of the Board were also Trustees, any great divergence in the policies of the two bodies must have indicated either severe opposition from the other commissioners or a high degree of inconsistency in those members who served on both bodies. In any case, whether through lack of confidence in their own knowledge, lack of interest or, quite simply, merely a sensible division of labour, questions regarding industry and manufactures were almost invariably referred to a special committee, not always formally constituted, of members who were also Trustees for Manufactures and Fisheries.[8] This was an amicable arrangement which ensured that the industrial activities of the Board for the Annexed Estates were in fact merely an extension of the work of the Trustees. But of course, while industry and, to a lesser degree, fishing were the sole interests of the latter group, these aspects of Highland life were only two of the many the commissioners had to deal with, in addition to the day-to-day management of large estates.

The most elaborate of the abortive plans made before 1760 is perhaps worth examining, as it illuminates various facets of the outlook of the commissioners, especially their close adherence to the practices of the Trustees and the scale on which the Board envisaged itself working before government indifference and financial stringency curtailed such ambition. This was 'A plan for establishing and carrying on a manufacturing station at the house of New Tarbat, upon the Annexed Estate of Cromarty', which was expounded in the report to an unresponsive central government in 1757.[9] This was a comprehensive scheme, encompassing every branch of the linen industry, from the raising of flax to the final bleaching and weaving of the coarse kinds of linen thought to be necessary. An outlay of £4,209 over nine years was planned and, during these years, it was thought that 900 girls would be taught to spin, while 192 apprentices would learn the various trades of heckling, scutching, bleaching and weaving, under a skilled entrepreneur, who was not expected to make any profit for several years, despite the assistance that was proposed. It was realised that the apprentices would begin to earn anything towards their keep only in the second year of their training, so it was proposed that maintenance should be awarded on a sliding scale; bedding, clothes, food, utensils, yarn were all to be provided. Not only the resident apprentices but also the tenants in New Tarbat were to be taught how to prepare the ground for flax and how to crop it. In addition, remembering their mission to 'civilise' the inhabitants, the Board 'supposed' that a schoolmaster should be appointed to teach the children to read and speak the English language, and to instruct them in 'the principles of religion and loyalty to H.M. person and government'. The Trustees left religion and education to the SSPCK, but the moral approach was explicitly ordered for the Board in the Annexing Act.

Lacking approval from the Crown, however, this plan came to naught and, in any case, it is certain the funds would not have borne such an outlay, without the other activities of the Board being disproportionately curtailed. The failure of this scheme to materialise had one unfortunate effect. The house of New Tarbat was left to become ruinous despite the local doctor's tenancy and, according to the *Old Statistical Account* writer for Kilmuir Easter, this was a great loss to the area, as it had been 'the most elegant and best finished house in the three counties'.[10]

It was inevitable that, initially at least, the Board would lay most emphasis on encouraging the 'staple' of Scotland, the linen trade. Scottish interest in that textile had grown during the seventeenth century, and the Scottish Estates passed several acts to aid the trade.[11] Despite such assistance, the industry was declining at the beginning of the eighteenth century. There were a variety of reasons for this, one of the most potent, perhaps, being the poor quality of linen exported, combined with an exaggerated description of its goodness. Foreign merchants had a not surprising prejudice against the Scotch product as a result of the misleading advertising.

From 1727, when the Board of Trustees for Manufactures and Fisheries was set up, the Board's revenues and later, in 1742, the Bounty contributed to the expansion of the industry. The Trustees were justifiably proud of the increase in the quantity of linen produced, but it was perhaps more to their credit that the quality improved largely because of their practice of appointing stampmasters for the various districts where linen was spun in any appreciable amount.[12] An act of 1727 for 'The Better Regulation of the Linen and Hemp Manufactures in Scotland'[13] had provided for the appointment of stampmasters, but it was the Trustees' activities which made this an effective step.

Their most difficult task was that of controlling and expanding the growth of flax, and then its preparation for spinning. Miss Dean declared that very few farmers and crofters did not have their field of flax,[14] but the Trustees allocated £1,500 of their first year's income towards premiums for growing the crop.[15] In addition, once seed was in the ground, those cultivating it were not as careful as such a difficult crop deserved and, as Patrick Lindsay put it, 'Every Fault, every Failure in the Flax is an error of the first Connection not to be cured afterwards by Skill and Labour'.[16] When we consider the agricultural methods of the day, it is not surprising that flax was badly cultivated. A crop that needs care, skill and attention was unlikely to thrive when the humble oat was abused. Not only did much depend on temperature and rainfall, but careful weeding was essential, and this was not a very popular occupation among the ordinary farmers in Scotland in the eighteenth century.

Harvesting, too, caused difficulty. There was no general agreement as to the best time for picking. In Scotland, it was believed that the flax should be pulled first when the blossom fell, and the General Inspector on the annexed estates was greatly tried by the tenants' leaving the crop in the ground until the seeds had developed, as lintseed was such an expense for them. This he was sure 'hurts greatly the quality and lessens the quantity of flax'. Warden quotes Postlethwayte, however, as castigating the more general belief, saying that too quick gathering made for poor flax, as the lint heckled to nothing, having 'a fine appearance but no substance'.

The next processes of drying, scutching and heckling were also carried out roughly and imperfectly. The General Inspector also described in horror scutching done by merely beating the flax over the back of a chair with a wooden stick. The Trustees, too, had had to tackle this aspect of production before they could hope for an increase in the manufacture of good-quality, fine linen. They gave premiums to those who would grow the crop in the first place, employed flax-dressers to teach heckling and scutching, encouraged by prizes any improvement to instruments used for these processes, established spinning schools, and arranged for foreign weavers to come to Edinburgh to teach the art of weaving the fine linen produced abroad.[17] The fine ladies of Edinburgh flocked to Broughton Loan, now Picardy Place, to learn the art – and having accomplished this gave up practising. This was hardly the aim of the Trustees, but it did show the keen interest there was – or perhaps in this instance it was a whim of fashion.

In their programme for the improvement of the textile industry, we even find industrial espionage. Mrs. Fletcher of Saltoun had gone to Holland especially to discover the secret of fine weaving, and to find the proper method of bleaching. Royal approval was also obtained to spend some of their funds in sending a 'very ingenious and deserving young man of this country bred in Holland' to procure the secret of this final process. The implication was that he was to use fair means or foul for this purpose. Unfortunately, the Dutch masters 'with the greatest secrecy locked up the mistery of whitening from him'.[18] Despite the concentration of resources and specific geographic concentration needed for the bleaching trade, as this report suggests, the 'misteries of whitening' were unknown to the Scottish bleachers and remained mysterious until the end of the century when, in 1790, the use of chlorine was discovered.

Other people were also spreading the gospel of industrialisation. In 1738, the SSPCK, on the grounds presumably that an idle Christian is a 'prodigious contradiction', was granted a second patent that enabled the society, primarily an educational and missionary one, to encourage the manufacturing arts as it thought proper.[19] The Society therefore combined both its functions by establishing spinning schools. Other groups not government-sponsored, such as the Glasgow Highland Society and the Honorary Society of Improvers, which dated from 1723, were working along the same lines. Small local societies did their best to improve the skills needed in spinning and weaving, and the British Linen Company, incorporated in 1746, later the British Linen Bank, was notable both for its effectiveness and its longevity. It became a bank as it found this the most practical way of doing business but, initially, the company handed out linen and material to its members and debtors.

Despite all this assistance and encouragement, the industry did not show as much improvement as might have been expected. The allocation of £3,000 a year for nine years out of the unallocated funds of Scotland in 1753 was aimed at giving added impetus to the industry in the Highlands.[20] The Trustees planned to use £2,520 of this money to set up four linen manufacturing stations in certain parts of the Highlands, in the shires of Inverness and Ross, 'where it has not hitherto been introduced', at an estimated cost of £630 for each station. In the second year, when three had been established at Glenmoriston, Lochbroom and Lochcarron, £420 was allotted to their upkeep. Each one combined technical school and factory and illustrated the policy of the Trustees and, later, of the Board of Commissioners for the Annexed Estates in encouraging industry. Experienced craftsmen were to be employed to teach the various steps in the process of converting flax into linen yarn and cloth, prizes were to be given for quantity and quality of work produced, and wheels and reels were to be distributed by the managers to those who could not attend the schools.[21] The fourth station proposed for Glenelg never materialised. Robert Campbell, who had been appointed to take charge there, joined the army and, at the end of the Seven Years War, appeared in Callander as a beneficiary of the Board for the Annexed Estates. He was awarded £182.10.0 towards promoting the linen industry there, and was also to have houses built at an estimated £261.6.0 However, he was never a satisfactory operator, being unable to obtain workmen. The linen produced round Callander was very bad and Campbell was eventually threatened with legal action ('diligence') for non-payment of rent.[22]

At each of the Trustees' stations, a 'principal undertaker', a mixture of manager and entrepreneur, was appointed. Ninian Jeffrey from Kelso was in charge at Lochcarron, John Ross at Lochbroom and Alexander Shaw at Glenmoriston, when the Board for the Annexed Estates became actively concerned with their financial organisation. This involvement arose after the 1753 grant ended. The Trustees had to announce then that the limitations of their funds obliged them to discontinue the appointments which had been made in former years at Glenmoriston, Lochcarron and Lochbroom. The manufacturers at these stations pressed their need for continuing aid and asked the Trustees to recommend that the Board for the Annexed Estates should supply the deficiency. The latter body had asked and been granted approval to spend £1,200 on encouraging manufactures in the Highlands and, at a meeting on 29th June, 1763, Lord Milton reported that £977 of this sum would have to be paid over to the Secretary of the Trustees, Mr. Flint, to support the three stations already established and to introduce manufactures into Badenoch, Strathspey and Braemurray.[23] This, it should be noted, tied the hands of the Board for the Annexed Estates, as only £223 was left free for other industrial development, until they received a further note of approval from the Treasury for any of their proposals.

Their report to the king for 1764 gave an account of how this money had been allocated and it includes the following:–

Lintseed distributed at Lochbroom, Glenmoriston, Lochcarron, Badenoch, Strathspey and Braemurray	£73.6.8
Itinerant flax-raisers and dressers at the said stations	£50
Spinning mistresses, ditto	£25
Rent of two spinning schools	£6
Maintenance of scholars at said stations	£108
Premiums for scholars	£22.10.1
Wheels and reels distributed at said stations	£127
For wheelwright	£30
For promoting weaving in Badenoch, Strathspey and Braemurray	£15
For boatmen at Glenmoriston	£10
For employers of spinners for Glenmoriston, Strathspey	£22
For premiums and salary to undertakers	£321.10.0

Of the £223 left, £6 had been spent on the manufacture of linen thread at Tomperran, £50 on the same at Inverness, £13 for distributing wheels and reels at New Tarbat, and £100 on promoting the spinning of coarse linen there. That left £106.17.11 reserved for any unknown expense at the Trustees' stations, out of the £1,200 allowed.

Some years later, in 1766, the Trustees remitted to the Board an account for £306. This expense they had incurred in assistance to linen trade in the Highlands, and they represented to the Board that they expected to be entirely relieved of any financial burden in the Highland area, as their funds were rather too small for their commitments in the 'Low Countries'.[24] The commissioners accepted this and resolved that when the king authorised the use of a further £1,000 they had asked for manufacturing purposes, they would honour this debt.

From this time, the Trustees had little or no financial interest in industrial development in the Highland parts of Scotland. The Board for the Annexed Estates was the sole official body for promoting manufactures in the Highlands until the disannexation, in 1784, and most would-be entrepreneurs, inventors and tradesmen were directed to this Board for financial assistance. The Trustees had still some statutory obligations. They were responsible for giving commissions to stampmasters but, when James Glass was appointed in that capacity, in Crieff, in 1768, it was funds from the annexed estates that paid his salary of £5 p.a. There were other occasions when the two bodies cooperated, as for example in 1770, when the Board gave ground and a house to a hosier in Callander, while the Trustees gave machinery. Similarly, the Trustees had also suggested to the Board that they reward one of the Trustees' clerks, Robert MacPherson, who had invented a machine for dressing flax. The commissioners employed Angus Macdonald to study this, and he reported that this machine would obviate many of the dangers in lint mills, where fires were frequent, as were the numbers of occasions when men lost an arm. As both committees approved, MacPherson was awarded £100, provided he did not take out a patent in Scotland for the sole privilege of making and vending the machine.[25]

Even before the official transfer of financial responsibility from the Trustees to the commissioners, there had been some contact between one of the stations, Lochcarron, and the Board for the Annexed Estates. In 1756, a petition was received in Edinburgh on behalf of thirty-eight people who had gone north from Kelso with Ninian Jeffrey, the 'undertaker'. The petitioners asked for meal from the estate of Cromartie as they had suffered a series of mishaps. First, instead of travelling all the way by sea, they had been forced to disembark at Stonehive (Stonehaven), on account of bad weather, and travel overland had used up both their cash and subsistence quicker than they expected. On arrival at Lochcarron, it was found that the architect had misjudged the quantity of lime required for building, so they had had to live in earthen houses during the winter. Next their crops were 'defeated by the weather'. They were obviously feeling very sorry for themselves, though the minister gave attestations of their good behaviour and they claimed to have had a good reception from the local inhabitants.[26]

The problem they encountered of obtaining food supplies where agriculture was carried on at subsistence level was one that faced all would-be industrialists in the Highlands. In 1757 Alexander Shaw, the 'undertaker' at Glenmoriston, also wrote of the need for meal, and he returned to the subject in 1770.[27] In a letter recommending Thomas Munro of Beauly, another manufacturer, for the tenancy of a farm, he proposed that the commissioners should maintain a storehouse for meal on the Lovat and Cromartie estates, as he found that the people engaged in manufactures were 'straitened for meall' and a 'good time' was spent travelling round looking for it. He suggested that, if his proposal was acted on, manufacturers should have preference in buying this grain. Munro, pleading on his own behalf, declared that there was 'no market for ffewel or any kind of vivers' and his servants had to go looking through the country for food that sometimes could not be found or had to be bought 'very dear'. He had not even a kailyard – this seems to show a certain lack of enterprise on his part – and he meant to remove unless the Board rented him a farm and granted him aid in prosecuting his business. Another logistic problem Munro mentions must have troubled all the manufacturers. This was the need for horses and carriages. The country people were not in the habit of hiring and were often 'averse to go'. If they did 'go', their hires were not very good beasts; but there was no scope for bargaining, and what they asked had to be paid.[28]

The commissioners soon realised that the money spent on the three manufacturing stations had been wasted. The managers kept on producing encouraging figures but they accompanied these by requests for more support. Ross claimed that at Lochcarron 2,500 spindles of yarn had been spun in 1765 and that the quality was improving yearly;[29] Jeffrey showed in his records from October 1763 to December 1764 the spinning of 2,802 spindles of yarn, $5,188\frac{1}{2}$ lb of lint and 4,568 lb of tow and 135 lb of briards. He had not produced enough to qualify for the subsidy of 3d per spindle but he was hoping nevertheless to receive it on the grounds that neither wheels nor reels nor lint had been seen before his arrival in 'this remote corner', that flax had been 'extravagantly dear' in Holland, and that he had high carriage costs.[30] The factory of Coigach was probably not the only reason for Jeffrey's later financial difficulties.

The last question, the difficulty of transport to both the west coast situations chosen by the Trustees, had been emphasised by their surveyor, John Neilson, who made it quite clear to them that the road system was very poor and that the expense of remedying its deficiencies was too great for statute labour to bear. As well as the cross-country roads to Lochbroom and Lochcarron being bad, the main road to Dingwall, Inverness and the south was 'so remarkably bad that a horse with a load on his back would find it difficult to travel it'.[31] The Trustees chose to ignore his warnings, however, and the painful and expensive business of cutting their losses was left to the Board for the Annexed Estates. Once the latter were responsible, the continuous pleas for more help served only to convince them that further subsidies would merely be a method of throwing good money after bad. The original plan after all had envisaged self-sufficiency of the stations in a comparatively short time.

The final blow was probably dealt by the Inspector's report in 1767–68. He wrote that 'Considerable sums have been expended on that country, I am afraid to little purpose farther than it will be easy to teach a person already instructed in spinning yarn, to spin wool'. He had visited both Lochbroom and Glenmoriston and learned that Lochcarron was in the same state. 'Immense sums of money expended in building magnificent structures to carry on manufactures where there were hardly any inhabitants and to push a branch by high premiums which had fallen to the ground as soon as left to itself as the country has no access to raw materials.' He was not so scathing about the outstations of Glenmoriston – 'In a most unfit situation itself' – Urquhart, Fort Augustus, and The Aird. When Pennant made his first tour in 1769, he found Glenmoriston reasonably flourishing, reputedly operating six looms and teaching forty girls to spin every three months.[32] This is not wholly inconsistent with Menzies' description, as the success of the outstations would help the viability of the centre, but it closed in 1791.[33] Shaw, the manager there, certainly remained active in the industry long after official support for the station was discontinued and, even in 1767, his business was sufficiently healthy for him to be employing more spinning teachers than the number for whom he was allowed salaries.

The importunities of the undertakers did jar on the Board members and Lord Kames was constrained to write to Jeffrey at one point, saying that 'Mr. Jeffrey himself cannot but know the impracticability of establishing the linen manufacture at those stations that can never support itself without foreign aid'. Jeffrey may well have felt hard done by, for he claimed to have had support for only five years of the eight promised and to have had to pay out of his own pocket for a wheelwright and an 'intaker' – an employee who travelled round collecting spun yarn from the country people. But he got cold comfort, for the final response was, 'With regard in general to the two stations at Lochbroom and Lochcarron, we have learned by woeful experience that they are unfit places for carrying on any

Branch of the linen manufacture. The climate, the barrenness of the soil, the dearness of all sort of provisions, even oatmeal, the distance from commerce are all of them obstacles which in conjunction are insurmountable. It is for that opinion that I [Lord Kames] am of opinion to abandon these stations altogether and lose no more money upon them.'[34]

In retrospect it is incredible that the obstacles mentioned by Kames were not considered more before the stations were built at all, and the blindness of the Trustees can only be explained, if not excused, by the general Scottish obsession of the time with linen, and the particular Lowland obsession with the need for the injection of industry into the Highlands. It can only be regretted that the annexed estates funds were used at all in what has been described as the Board of Trustees' 'tragic error', the three Highland stations.[35] The sum of £1,200 spent seriously depleted the limited amount available for industrial development, without compensatory gains. The positive results that presumably ensued would be the skill gained in spinning by individuals and the small financial gain to the spinners, but these were not commensurate with the expenditure.

While the largest outlay on linen manufacture had of necessity been directed towards the three stations inherited from the Trustees and hence wasted, there had been other outlets for the funds. Several manufacturers who operated on a fairly large scale took full advantage of any assistance they could get from the Board. Among these were William Sandeman, who had factories and bleachfields near Perth, John Montgomery, his associate at New Tarbat and Fortrose, and Duncan Grant. Sandeman and Montgomery had experimented with producing fine yarn, but bad wheels among other things seem to have defeated them. They tried coarse weaving at Fortrose[36] but this did not last long, and in 1766 Sandeman was trying to sell to the Board the utensils left there. They included a shaking post and 'hake' (a hook) for drying yarn, a yarn cooler, yarn 'boams' (wooden frames) for shaking and drying, a large 'vatt' with iron hoops, an ash lapping table, a heckling lanthorn and scales, a pot metal boiler for yarn with a broken timber cover, and heckles. He was paid for these in 1768 and they were to be given to Montgomery, but it was August 1771 before anything was done about them. As they had been lying outside all this time, it is not surprising to find they were worth little, only 'where they ly', and some not much even there.[37]

Sandeman wrote uniformly depressing letters to the commissioners. On All Fools' Day, 1763, a letter from him said, 'I am afraid from my experience herein, it will turn out a losing trade on account of great outlay of money and charge attending correspondence and distance in transporting flax and yarn'. He thought he was always about £1,000 out in advance, which gives some idea of the scale of his business that he could even think of affording this. In January, 1765, he wrote that he had shipped £500-worth of cloth of 'sundry fabricks' to London but prices had fallen and he had not even covered his costs. He added that he was extremely sorry to have occasion to write in this tone, but he felt the Board should know the true state of affairs.[38]

Duncan Grant, who was allowed £300 in March, 1764, to introduce flax-spinning in Badenoch, Strathspey and Braemurray, managed to gain the trust of the Board, the local Justices of the Peace and the Trustees. Grant had a merchant's business in Forres, and was always 'thought in a peculiar manner a proper person for doing business in the Highlands because he is a Countryman and of good Relations there, being a Gentleman, his turning his hand to Manufactures will be of useful example to the country'. But Grant was regarded less favourably by the Board's employees and by others in the district. He was accused of embezzling and, incidentally, one of his defences was that the carriage was 'unsupportable by me' as horses were difficult to obtain. He quoted expenses as $3\frac{1}{2}$d per stone for ten to fifteen Scotch miles and on one occasion produced a testimonial from the local J.P.'s and a signed assurance from the Secretary to the Trustees, Mr. Flint, dated 7 March, 1767 that he had done more than the other entrepreneurs. He also stated as a reason for his being pilloried that his activities in training spinners raised the servants' wages, and some even sent the constables to remove girls from the spinning schools. He claimed that there had been no flax raised before he started his business in Forres and Braemurray in 1763, and that not a peck of lintseed was sown before the Trustees gave him an allowance.

The factor had a different tale to tell. He said sourly that there was more lintseed in Badenoch before Grant appeared, and that in fact the situation was worse now as he was depended on for seed and never had enough, 'not one third of what was demanded'. In addition, Small had heard of no premiums being awarded, girls were reported to spin for him for nothing, and flax-dressers had remained in Badenoch for only a short time. It was not surprising that the Board became a little suspicious. Grant did not always cover himself; he put in his plan in 1764 an allowance for 'Premiums of cloathes, etc.' and then wrote in 1765 that he did not give cloth but only lint, so that the spinners could improve their skill. As a further explanation of some of the extraordinary expense he had incurred, beyond his allowance, he claimed that in 1764 the Supervisor of Excise met his agents carrying lintseed to Castle Grant and Cromdale at a 'little alehouse', promptly suspected smuggling and pierced the casks, thus damaging the seed. It transpired, however, that Grant had been acting on instructions from the Board of Trustees, whose letter of authority gave privileges different from those the Annexed Estates Board customarily granted. As a result, he continued to act for the commissioners.

Like most of these entrepreneurs, Grant was mainly interested in spinning, as some of his reports make quite clear. Of 9,668 spindles of yarn spun, only 122 were woven into cloth. Of the rest, 1,910 were sent to thread makers, 3,156 to cloth makers, and 4,255 to the Glasgow and London markets.[39] As a result, any success either Board achieved had little effect on the male labour market[40] and, even where spinning was concerned, Archibald Menzies had by 1766 become very dubious not only about the possible benefits of the programme of promoting linen manufactures but about the integrity of the manufacturers themselves. He re-read the earliest reports from the factors, those sent in 1755, and discovered that in the eastern parts of the estates of Lovat and Cromartie, where most of the entrepreneurs operated, spinning had been quite well established at the earlier date. Ten years later, his view was that it was much further advanced than 'would be imagined from the continued aids still granted and craved from' the Board of

Trustees and the Board for the Annexed Estates. Continuation of grants seemed to benefit only the manufacturers so assisted; other dealers had to give up in light of unequal competition so that the former obtained a monopoly. This allowed them to deal with their outspinners just as suited them best and Menzies did not think the spinners were being fairly treated. Flax-dressers too had been settled out of public funds and yet flax-dressing cost more than anywhere else in Scotland. The only advantage he could find from the whole programme was that the distribution of lintseed, free or at half-price, had helped tenants. And then they ruined their fine crops by harvesting at the wrong time and by inefficient dressing.[41]

As we have seen, the Inspector's report in the following year was instrumental in stopping the waste of funds on the linen stations. Shortly after receiving his scathing indictment of their policies in the general encouragement of the linen manufacture, the Board decided that, considering the state of spinning in the low parts of Lovat and Cromartie, they would cease paying salaries to spinners.[42] Lord Kames also produced a more positive suggestion that, as spinning had made such progress, the bulk of the money allocated to developing the linen industry should be devoted to the encouragement of flax-culture, as foreign flax from both Holland and the Baltic was becoming increasingly expensive and difficult to obtain.[43] In August, 1767, the Treasury granted the Board permission to allocate some of the fund for the general encouragement of wool and linen manufactures to the improvement of flax husbandry. There was never enough money in hand to develop a large-scale programme, however, and the expenditure did not reach any great heights. The factors' accounts show continuous outlay of small sums on lintseed and on spinning and weaving. For example, in Kilmorack in 1768, £13.19.9 was spent on $279\frac{3}{4}$ pecks of flax at 1/- per peck while, in Stratherrick, the gentlemen and tenants spun only $33\frac{1}{2}$ pecks for which they were rewarded with £1.15.4. Private manufacturers and other interested individuals continued to act as agents for the Board in distributing lintseed and in competing for prizes and subsidies. In 1768, Shaw at Glenmoriston and Montgomery at New Tarbat were paid £29 and £8 respectively for distributing lintseed at cost, at £1 per hogshead, and two months later Shaw was awarded £25.17.9 as a premium at 3d per spindle of yarn spun from Scotch-raised lint. Mr. Campbell the younger of Aird was allowed £20 to furnish the people of Morven with hemp, flax-seed and utensils for their manufacture in 1769. Despite the 1767 allocation of such large funds for the purpose of raising flax, the last single entry in the commissioners' Journal regarding this was £9 in 1770 to Duncan Grant for lintseed he had given out in Badenoch and Strathspey; and 1772 saw the last individual entry regarding textiles, when £12 was recorded as being paid to Grant's agent for looms and weaving utensils that he had provided for Lachlan M'Pherson at the behest of the Board of Trustees, the Board for the Annexed Estates underwriting the cost.

The disappearance of such details from the Journal is an indication of the commissioners' declining interest in what was to have been their major industrial contribution to the Highland economy, a decline undoubtedly hastened by lack of success. Kames put a brave face on the matter by proposing increased help for flax cultivation as a logical complement to the expansion of spinning skills, but the Inspector made it clear that little credit could be claimed by the Board even for that technical advance. The true beneficiaries, perhaps the only beneficiaries, of a considerable outlay of public money had been the subsidised manufacturers. The notion of a widespread flourishing linen industry with all its accompanying ramifications in the north of Scotland had to be forgotten. The climate, resulting in lack of raw materials, and the lack of nearby markets, with a deficient system of communication, were an unconquerable combination and, having tacitly accepted failure, the commissioners turned their attention to less ambitious industrial ventures, mostly initiated by individual entrepreneurs. It must be a severe criticism of the Board of Trustees that the question of whether the methods of improvement and the industry proposed were ideally suited to the localities was one they did not probe, despite Neilson's discouraging survey. Equally, the Board for the Annexed Estates uncritically accepted the burden of the linen stations and discarded them only after a long series of disappointments.

As long as the commissioners were concerned with improving the textile industry, they were bound to pay some attention to the finishing processes, and one of these, bleaching, gave less than satisfactory results. One method of whitening linen was to boil it in ashes, and a great deal of thought was given to finding the type of ashes that would obtain the best bleach. Sweden and Russia provided most of the supplies and it became a matter of national interest, both financial and chauvinistic, to try to produce a home-made substitute. In 1757, the proposal was made that £200 should be spent in bringing over a foreigner skilled in the craft of making 'cashube' ashes as they were called, in building a suitable oven and trying to use the brushwood left after tree-felling. After this sum was authorised in 1761, a committee was set up to execute the scheme. Various contacts were made with Mr. Alex Hogg, a merchant in Danzig, for information about both methods and tradesmen, and he suggested sending a tradesman and bringing back a Polish workman, an easy matter as wages there were so small.[44] Dr. Adam Drummond of Gardrum sent in his instructions for using fern in December, 1761, and in June, 1762, Lord Milton impressed on the Board the urgency of the need for a local product as foreign ashes were both dear and in short supply. At the following meeting, however, Lord Kames suggested approaching Dr. William Cullen, Professor of Chemistry at the University of Edinburgh, as he had already carried out some experiments on procuring ashes, in Rannoch.[45]

Hardly encouraging at the first meeting at which he said he had met with unforeseen difficulties, Dr. Cullen sent in a detailed report the following spring. He and his assistant, Dr. David Millar, who had worked in Rannoch for four months, had tried burning every type of vegetable matter they could lay their hands on, from potato stalks to birch, and found none completely satisfactory in their alkaline content. His comments on the results of burning kelp, which he can hardly have found in Rannoch, are interesting in the light of later events in Scotland. He describes it as 'so very foul in its ordinary state' that it could be employed in bleaching only in the first steps of the process or for the coarsest manufacture. 'Nothing but want of wood will lead us to practise on kelp.' The ashes which resulted from the experiments were taken to Edinburgh where the

Board arranged for trials by bleachers. At Salton one of these, Archibald Horn, reported that Dr. Cullen's ashes produced a parcel of cloth 'in a small degree whiter' than that bleached with cashube lye. As Dr. Cullen's cost 7/6 per cwt and the others 14/- per cwt, he felt they would be 'of use to the country'.[46]

Small, the factor on Struan, thought that an allowance of $\frac{1}{2}$d per pound for several years would attract several people to the work, and he was ordered to make estimates for the expense of houses and necessary equipment, but there the matter seemed to rest.[47] Commissioners and factors just about then became absorbed in making arrangements for the soldiers' settlements and, as Small had had to give board and lodgings to all those concerned with the experiment, he may not have been very enthusiastic in pursuing the matter. In addition, Lord Milton had been the main instigator of the scheme, and his decline into senility cannot have helped it. In 1780, however, Sandeman the Perth bleacher forwarded a letter to the Board from James MacIlvride in Crieff who wanted to make bleachers' ashes from small brushwood, so the idea had not completely died.[48] Had the experiment been a complete success, of course, the soapmakers too would have been interested as the ashes would have been of use in making hard soap, the main commendation for which being that it would be entirely the produce of Great Britain, whereas soft soap was chiefly made of more expensive foreign materials.[49] The experiment was certainly undertaken with a view both to improving the bleaching process and to helping the country's financial situation.

Textiles are of course coloured as well as bleached, and in January, 1764, two brothers, George and Cuthbert Gordon, approached the Board with proposals concerning dye-making. Describing themselves as patentees of a 'cudbear manufactury' at Leith, they claimed to have made discoveries that would enable them to improve such estates in the Highlands as 'abound with rock, water and heath, so as to double the present rate and also defray the expence of improvement in two years' time'.[50] 'Cudbear', they explained, was a name derived from his Christian name by Dr. Cuthbert Gordon, who had obtained a patent for a purple or violet powder used for dyeing various materials. The dye was prepared from several types of lichens, and the collection and preparation of the powder would not inconvenience tenants in possession, who could go on farming both grass and arable land as usual. The brothers therefore asked only for a title such as 'Inspector-General of the Improvements of the Highlands and Islands' and an annual salary commensurate with the importance of their discovery. They also disarmed suspicion by stating that they did not want 'a shilling paid' until they had demonstrated the success of their discovery – though they did hope the payment would be backdated. A contract was drawn up and signed, not offering the grandiose title but arranging tenure of farms up to the value of £500 per annum. Presumably this meant only the right to gather the necessary materials on these farms. No money was to be forthcoming from the Board after twenty-two years and, if the Gordons did not work for any six months continuously, 'total abandonment' of the scheme would be understood.[51] Despite a penalty clause of £100 in case of default, the brothers do not seem to have been very active on the estates but they may not have given up completely, for David Loch in his own house watched

Cuthbert Gordon demonstrating the use of his dye on cotton velvet, making it a fine crimson colour in a few minutes, and showing he could dye or stain wood, linen, leather, cotton or even vegetable substances. Loch was very pleased that the cudbear could be made from Scottish plants which, he said, showed that the 'prejudice that we cannot equal the English in colours is without reason, existing only in the imagination'. Unfortunately, Loch does not date such encounters so, though his essays were published in 1778, this incident may have taken place up to thirty years before. George MacIntosh is given the credit for having established the manufacture of cudbear in 1777.[52]

Thread-making was another branch of the linen industry that both the Trustees and the Board were prepared to subsidise. It was mostly women who seemed to be interested in this, and women of some social standing at that. The Trustees passed on an account for £60 to be paid to Mrs. Campbell at Tomperran towards promoting the manufacture of thread, and their secretary, Flint, recommended Helen and Lydia Thomson, threadmakers in Inverness, on the grounds first that a great deal of yarn was made there but scarcely any was woven or 'otherwise manufactured'. Further, he considered this an ideal trade for 'gentlewomen of small portions' who had difficulty in finding a 'business they can prosecute'. The Thomsons were quite successful, operating a bleaching ground in connection with their threadmaking and selling a high proportion of their produce in London, £110.3.1½ out of a total of £114.7.4½ in one year. In the *Old Statistical Account* of Inverness a thread manufactory is dated as having been established about ten years before the account was written. If the minister was right in this, he was not describing the Thomsons' firm, as they were in business from the 1760s, but the organisation he mentioned was certainly a busy concern, employing 10,000 in heckling, spinning, twisting, bleaching and dyeing.[53]

Yet another textile factory operated in Inverness. A hemp factory had been granted £100 after a favourable description by the Inspector, who related that the 'manufactory of sacking, bagging and ropery at Inverness is carrying on with spirit'. The manufacturers had spent a considerable sum on sheds and warehouses and had a number of girls already employed in spinning 'after the Montrose manner'. A ship in the harbour was reported to have 150 tons of hemp aboard despite the various difficulties the makers had had to cope with. These included having to rebuild their long shed after it was damaged when the river bank burst, difficulty in obtaining tools, and finding that those they had employed as instructors were worthless, so 'abandoned' in fact that they had had to be sent away. The £100 sent them must have been very welcome, and it is likely that it was the same firm that was described in the *Old Statistical Account*. Apparently they managed to increase their capital from £1,200 to £15,000. The manufacture of hemp was new to Scotland in the 1760s and it is encouraging to find one success. Lord Kames had been in favour of sparing support as it was not yet properly established, but he felt it might be a useful trade for poor people who had no means of acquiring knowledge in the finer branches of textile-making.[54]

As far as wool was concerned, the Board for the Annexed Estates made only a few tentative suggestions towards encouraging the industry. There were suggestions for promoting wool-spinning in Lochaber and for wool manufacture at Callander. £20 was proposed for wheels for spinning wool in Barrisdale, and Lord Kames was asked to 'bring in a plan' for developing the industry in Rannoch. Nothing seems to have come of this, Kames was unenthusiastic,[55] linen was of predominant importance in most people's opinion and funds were scarce. English woollens in the eighteenth century were so much superior to the Scottish product that it is understandable that it seemed a more attractive proposition to encourage a different type of textile north of the Border, rather than face unequal competition. David Loch's was one of the few voices crying in the wilderness that wool had much more potential than linen in Scotland.[56] Archibald Menzies, the Inspector, was another wool enthusiast, remarking at one point that he thought money had been thrown away in teaching people to spin flax, except that it made it easier for them to learn to spin wool. He thought sheep would thrive in the west where much of the ground was 'too craggie' for cattle. Some prizes and subsidies for wool-spinning would soon overcome, he thought, the Highland farmer's belief that sheep were below his dignity and his pretence of lofty ignorance of the animal accompanied by the offhand statement, 'My wife has sheep with leave'.

There was some suggestion in 1772 of establishing a wool-based industry at Callander. The factor had compared wool to flax very favourably in that area. The linen was very poor but two hundred women 'made their bread' by spinning wool (as well as some lint) for tartans, coarse grays and plaids. Some fine worsteds were also sold in Stirling, for which the wool was combed locally and well done at that. Fifty stones of English wool were spun near Callander, as well as the three hundred or so produced within ten miles. In 1774 further favourable comment on the possibilities of wool-manufacturing there pointed out the near vicinity of the Stirling carpet-makers and the walk-mill at Kilmahog. But Kames was lukewarm, and prepared to countenance wool only because the inhabitants seemed 'more addicted to it' – with reasons one would think – and already had sheep.[57] He and the factor were to discuss the matter but no more was heard of it, and the suggestion that £400 or £500 would be needed must have helped put the idea out of court at a time when the Board's funds were already overstretched.

In retrospect, it is easy to see how unfortunate it was that the commissioners and, before them, the Trustees for Fisheries and Manufactures did not in fact give some more positive encouragement to the woollen industry. The Board usually listened to Menzies but in this case his words of wisdom fell on deaf ears. The large sums spent on the linen station by the Trustees and the smaller, but still substantial, amounts from the annexed estates funds might have had more positive results had they been devoted to an industry that had indigenous raw materials and a climate that encouraged these, instead of one where there was insufficient suitable ground to raise flax. In any case, the 'immense rains' destroyed the crops.[58]

Despite the obsession with linen, other industries did receive intellectual and financial attention from the Board, though the first did not necessarily include the second. The second half of the eighteenth century was a period of general expansion in the financing of industries, old and new. A. W. Kerr records that, between 1746 and 1751, several manufacturing companies were formed in Scotland for the prosecution of trades 'hardly attempted previously'.[59] He included in this list rope and sailcloth, iron, gold and silver, sugar refineries, herring and whale fisheries. A glance at the index to the inventory of the Forfeited Estates Papers, 1745 shows that, of Kerr's group, only sugar refining did not at some time attract the commissioners' interest but, having decided to cut their losses over the fiasco of the linen stations, the Board's philosophy towards the developing of new industries changed. Slightly soured, one feels, and also more conscious of the comparative slightness of their resources, they 'shut the door against unreasonable demands' and decided, as did the Trustees, that 'the most effectual method of laying out public money' was to engage gentlemen 'of patriotic spirit' to assist them by overseeing the application of sums allowed, especially if they were willing to contribute.[60] Even where such characters existed, great caution was exercised. Daniel Campbell of Shawfield was informed in reply to his request for financial aid for Islay that, while he could have a grant towards fisheries and harbours which were for the general public good, the introduction of manufactures into such a small area must be entirely his responsibility. His emphasis on what his grandfather had done for the linen industry may not have helped his case.[61]

The Board practised their new approach, however, with several industries including leather, the working of which has always been important in Scotland generally, though not in the Highland area, where the same lack of incentive to traders existed as in other consumer-oriented manufactures. For instance, where shoes were worn there, they were usually made from untanned dried skin, simply turned inside out so that the hairy side provided warmth and comfort. By the time of the *Old Statistical Account*, shoemakers were regularly mentioned, but they must surely have imported their hides, for even in the 1780s there were few tanneries north-west of Perth. Loch mentions two at Inverness, three at Dunkeld, and a small one 'on the increase' at Elgin, but a more typical reference is the Kilmallie minister's list of the disadvantages of the parish, which includes the want of a tannery.[62]

In 1755, the factor of the Perth estate thought that a tannery would have a very good chance of success in Crieff, for two reasons. The presence of woods was one. The town would be 'commodious for bark', vital for the tanning industry. The second reason given was that hides were easily obtained. And, of course, the demand for bark would increase the profits obtained from the commissioners' woods. This was discussed at a meeting of the Board in January, 1762, and the factor declared that, before the roads were made to Stirling, the Highland carriers and pedlars brought skins of all kinds to Crieff – goats, sheep, kids, lambskins, deer, roe, fox, otters and martins. Some of these had formerly been dressed and manufactured there, and the rest sold at other markets, but now they apparently all by-passed the town in favour of the larger markets to be found further south.[63] It was just at this time that Crieff's pre-eminence as the centre for the black cattle market at Michaelmas was waning. The commissioners were sufficiently aware of this to ask for the king's approval for their ordering the abolition of customs for five years, as one of the reasons for the loss of trade was considered to be the comparatively heavy dues. The royal approval of this suggestion to abolish tolls was received, but three years later, in January, 1765. The removal of tolls might well have been an encouragement to dealers, and a tannery would have ensured a market for slaughtered animals, but the only immediate positive result evoked by the Crieff petition was a visit from Mr. Welsh, a Dalkeith skinner, who was initially employed by the Board to go to Inverness.

This latter town seems to have had its fair share of energetic inhabitants. Not only had the magistrates requested help for their spinning school, over which they had already taken action, but now we find them supporting one of the firms in the town that was endeavouring to obtain government help towards establishing a tannery. A memorial arrived on the Board's table, from William Cummins, Convener of the Incorporated Trades of Inverness, and James Dunbar, a tanner and leather merchant in the town, setting forth the 'expediency' of having a tannery there, and the benefits it would confer on that part of the country. £400 would be required, but they undertook to put £200 towards it and to find proper security for the money.[64]

This was precisely the type of approach the Board admired and, on this occasion, Lord Kames suggested that Welsh should be sent to Inverness to investigate the position, looking at Crieff on the way. For this responsible task he was to be granted £5 travelling expenses, though in fact in November, 1762, the minutes record that he was paid £6.18.0 for his journey.[65]

Welsh's report was not particularly favourable to either town. He wrote that he was dubious about the number of skins that could be obtained near Crieff, and Inverness afforded only the 'probability of success'. The town was still in decay after the rebellion, there were no workmen of capacity and, as most good skins were now exported, the manufacturers would have to attract the trade back to Inverness. Despite this lukewarm testimonial, he had resolved to 'make a trial of the matter', 'so much was I pleased with the manners of the town'. He had been sufficiently attracted by the personalities of Cummins and Dunbar, or by their business acumen, or by both, to enter a ten-year contract with them.[66]

These entrepreneurs had initiative enough for the annual report to the king to be able to say in 1765, 'The tannery at Inverness is carrying on with probability of success', and it was proposed to lend £200 free of interest for a term of not more than five years. But the following year the commissioners had to report that they had advanced £200 of private money to Welsh, because of the delay in receiving the king's approbation. However, they thought that, if he could keep the money for a longer period than five years, he and his partners could extend their trade 'which with other articles must tend to spread industry among a people that have hitherto been better acquainted with the arts of war than peace'. They added hastily that they never gave assurance that 'the money was to be his for ever' but, if His Majesty approved, they would consider the money to be well spent, for Welsh had threatened to give up the whole idea as it took him so long to obtain the required capital. Whatever caused the change of heart, by the following year the £200 lent is described as 'bestowed' upon the tannery and the industry seemed to be in a flourishing state. The *Old Statistical Account* as well as Loch mentions two tanneries operating in Inverness, though it had to be admitted that the industry did not employ many hands. Later, Joseph Mitchell talks of an Inverness tannery run at the beginning of the nineteenth century by a Mr. Welsh, 'a very jolly member of most parties', who had come 'from the south'. It is pleasant to think that this must be the same man, prosperous and still delighted with the society he found in the town.[67]

With one success on their hands, the commissioners tried to establish more tanneries, asking at once for £300 towards the same purpose in Crieff and Callander. Crieff was, of course, the more favoured spot, but there were no results until the 1780s when eventually £300 was granted for the use of a tannery there, a sum which had not been fully paid when the estates were disannexed. In the records of engagements which the Board had not fulfilled by the passing of the Disannexation Act, in the second list stands: 'Balance of £300 for the tannery at Crieff – £100', although, according to the report sent to the king in 1784, £243.11.6 had already been paid out.

This delay had been hard on the tanner David Blair, for he had to keep asking for his money and it was only in December, 1782, that inspection of his factory was ordered. Blair's venture had not been all plain sailing. He had not got on well with the factor, who reported that his prices were the highest in the country. Blair, on the other hand, claimed that someone, nameless, who had failed to obtain the contract for the tannery, had spread false rumours about the amount that was to be allowed him by the Board, with the result that the masons had 'heightened their estimates'.[68]

The tanners may have suffered from unnecessary delay in receiving their subsidies, but another Inverness industry, soap-boiling, became embroiled in a bureaucratic and somewhat peevish demand from the Treasury for repayment of money lent by the commissioners without previous approval by the central government. In 1764, a petition of a rather unusual kind was received at the Edinburgh office. William Henderson wrote that, earlier in his career, he had been a bleacher, but as that involved only half a year's work he had gone to Glasgow to learn soap-making, which he reckoned would combine well with bleaching. However, he had been captured by a French privateer on his way back from Leith to Inverness and, as a result, lost all his savings. While he had now started his business, he was short of money, and asked for a loan, interest-free, of £50 or £100 for ten years, and two boilers of thirty-gallon capacity.[69] Two months later, we find a letter acknowledging the loan of £100 for three years, naming as his cautioners a jeweller and a goldsmith – an interesting indication of Inverness society – but saying he was 'uneasy' at not receiving the money as the kelp-burning season was approaching. A year later he was not merely uneasy – he was 'confounded' at having been asked to repay the loan, and declared that it would be easier for His Majesty to 'recall all his disbanded troops' than for him to collect enough cash to repay the loan at the time. However, this was eventually straightened out favourably to the borrower and, in 1776, Alexander Shaw vouched for Henderson's work, saying he had done well and the money had been well bestowed.[70]

Paper-making was yet another industry subsidised by annexed estates funds. This was a fairly novel venture in Scotland. The first paper-mill was built in 1590, at Dalry, but the industry did not develop quickly and Bremner reported that in 1763 there were only three mills near Edinburgh. Before Peter (or Patrick) Arnot, a Crieff merchant, built his mill in that town, with the help of £50 in each of the two years 1765 and 1766, there had been no paper-mills north of the Forth. To make up the deficiency in the home supply, foreign paper had to be bought and the Board suggested that the country could save £1,000 by using a home-made product. Arnot seems to have been enterprising, competent and successful. He could produce letters from satisfied customers enthusing about the superior quality of his goods as well as their cheapness compared with London and Newcastle. Though he started off making coarse brown paper, he very quickly turned to finer stuff, laying out £200 of his own money on frames and reserving his finest rags for the purpose. He employed a labour force of eight, who turned out six or seven reams a day, which the factor declared he could sell as fast as he could get it made.[71]

Nearly twenty years later, another would-be paper-maker in Crieff was apparently not so successful. The Inspector of the time, William Frend, had to report in 1783 that John Cock was finding that the paper-work in the country did not quite answer to his expectations, and he was hoping he would get 'some encouragement' from the Board to convert his paper-mill into one for boulting (sifting) flour. Frend was in favour of this change as the growing of wheat was beginning to take hold in the neighbourhood and, if there was a convenient mill, this tendency was more likely to develop. There were four bakers in Crieff, one in Muthill, and one in Comrie, all of whom had to take their wheat to Perth for milling, with the result that the size of bread in Crieff was smaller than in Perth. But 1783 was too near the end of the Board's existence for any action to be taken on this.

Wherever the Board turned to look at the economic life of the Highlands there were crying needs. In the primitive state of the eighteenth century economy, more was needed than the introduction of new industry, and the Board did give some attention to other necessities that would help develop a flourishing and energetic economic life. Until communications became more efficient and sophisticated, small mills serving their immediate locality were part and parcel of the fabric of Scottish economic life – meal-mills and sawmills, as well as the various types connected with the textile industry such as lint-mills and walk-mills for fulling. These mills provided a market without which the full commercial value could not be obtained from the produce of any area. In 1781, for example, some of the tenants on the estate of Perth near Crieff were finding it very difficult to sell their lintseed, as there was no oil-mill near. In 1780, the Board had paid £124.9.8 (plus £2.7.0 for an inspection of the work) as half the price of a mill at Gartchonzie,[72] but this was of no use to tenants near Crieff who were having to accept very low prices.

The proprietor of a lint-mill at Callander claimed that his mill had decreased the price of dressing lint below 2/- a stone which, of course, was of benefit to the neighbouring community. His letter also declared that his mill was the first built at the mill-proprietor's expense.[73] Mills also provided a comparatively high proportion of the landowners' wealth. There were twenty-one of various kinds on the estate of Perth with a rental of £343.18.4$\frac{10}{12}$, nine or ten on Lovat paying rent of £237.6.6, and seven on Cromartie with valued rent of £213.14.7$\frac{8}{12}$[74]. Of course, arrears of rent for mills as well as for any parts of their estates were a feature of life that landlords had to accept. A new sawmill had been built at Carie on the estate of Struan in 1758 to prevent wastage of the profitable Rannoch woods. The tacksman there, however, was never as successful as might have been expected and his rents were always considerably in arrears, despite or perhaps because of his other occupation, droving, which may have led to neglect of the timber trade.[75] It must certainly have ensured regular absences from the mill.

The Board did a certain amount, then, in respect of maintaining, building, or helping others to build, mills and they also tried to encourage markets to encourage trade generally. As we have seen, the Crieff market dues were reduced at their instigation, though they were too late to save the Crieff cattle trade. They certainly envisaged regular markets at any towns they planned, as did most eighteenth-century landlords, although these did not always materialise. As in most of their activities, they were following a fashionable contemporary trend, and they formed no general pattern or plan by which they might for example have gradually extended the number of mills evenly over the estates, or helped inject industry logically over the area. After the failure of the linen venture, piecemeal is the only description that can be applied to their industrial policies and, furthermore, initiative had to come from outside in the shape of requests for assistance from private individuals. The Board showed little or none themselves. This is not what was envisaged in the original concept of annexation.

Parallel to the commissioners' encouragement of what one might describe as 'factory' development ran their schemes to improve the quality of workmanship in the individual. Artisan skills were undoubtedly present in larger settlements in the Highlands and Islands, but many men living in smaller ferm-touns – perhaps the majority of men – did their own building and carpentering. They also repaired their own tools, which may have been crude but were sufficient for the work asked of them. As long as there was no radical alteration in the agricultural basis of the economy, there was little occasion for change in the equipment. In addition, in sparsely populated areas, the few specialists who did venture to set up shop and ply their trade found there was little enough money and less desire to use any available to pay them for their work, as more than one discovered on the annexed estates. However, as more sophisticated methods were introduced, both in agriculture and manufactures, the necessity for better husbandry, better tools and better workmanship were very soon obvious. Equally, it was soon realised that until money was more plentiful, any tradesman who was expected to earn his living by practising his trade, as opposed to subsisting from the produce of his garden or croft and earning a little on the side, must receive more concrete help than encouraging generalities. The Highland 'Jack-of-all-trades' would not overnight become the customer of the trained craftsman.

The Board for the Annexed Estates spent a fair proportion of their time and the resources at their disposal in trying to improve the general standards of craftsmanship, and in endeavouring to establish trained workmen in the Highlands, especially on their estates. They had four main lines of approach. The first was to apprentice boys and girls from the Highlands to tradesmen and farmers in the Lowlands; the second was to encourage and help 'artificers' to come north to practise their trades; the third was to set up or to assist existing schools, elementary examples of the type we would now call technical colleges; and the fourth was to build new towns or villages, where tradesmen could work and sell their skills to a conveniently placed set of customers. This last idea was somewhat distorted by the attempt to combine it with provision for demobilised forces after 1763 and will be discussed in the following chapter.

In none of this was the Board a trail-blazer. In 1755, the Board of Trustees for Manufactures and Fisheries had provided salaries at Lochcarron for various tradesmen, including a ploughman. The ploughman was to 'instruct gratis' all who might offer themselves for instruction, and the others were to train and maintain a certain number of apprentices at the expense of the S.S.P.C.K. But they taught only two apprentices, and they were dismissed for this and other reasons at Whitsunday, 1760. At Glenmoriston, a gardener and a smith had also been employed but the encouragement there too had been withdrawn by 1762. Other societies and individuals also dabbled in training schemes, including the Glasgow Highland Society which put out twelve boys to trades at their annual general meeting on January 10th, 1760. The Countess of Sutherland on at least one occasion gave assistance to a deserving case.[76] Once again we find that the Board's ideas reflect contemporary practice and, in 1756, they requested permission from the government to 'expend £200 per annum for binding apprentices to farmers in the Low Country such of the principal and most substantial tenants' sons in the Annexed Estates as discover the greatest genius for agricultural improvements'. It was expected that these boys would return to their native areas and set up 'in the country where the useful arts have hitherto been unknown and by a suitable encouragement given them by Your Majesty's Commissioners' improve their own lands to their own profit and advantage. Also, as it was believed that 'example is a stronger instructor than precept', they might be expected to spread the spirit of industry and improvement, the skill necessary to acquire riches and, further, 'the love of liberty and of depending only upon the protection of the law'. Part of this sum was to be used for apprenticing poorer children to smiths, ploughwrights, wheelwrights and other artificers. By these means, quick progress in agriculture was to be hoped for, and youths were to be weaned from their former idle ways and 'by degrees take pleasure in industry' by being put into the paths of acquiring property through virtuous toil. At this point, while the Treasury was paying no attention to the Board, nothing could be done but, when the central government did at last condescend to respond, the suggestion was immediately adopted. In August, 1761, the minutes record the king's approval of this plan.[77] On completing their apprenticeship, these young people were to be allowed premiums to enable them to set up and carry on their business. This last condition was likely to be the most tempting, if the General Inspector was correct in his surmise that nothing would be more likely to persuade tenants to put their families to a trade than the possibility of their becoming 'proprietors'.

The scheme was to be advertised at the church doors but it did not attract a flood of applicants. Indeed, one apprentice wrote in 1762, 'Your Lordships know that there was none but me ventured from the inrest of Pearth'. Even when the scheme had been underway for a year or two, in 1764, there were only three apprentices out of the large estate of Perth, which might have been expected to be most enthusiastic, being nearer the Lowlands. A stocking-weaver in Edinburgh who wanted two apprentices could get none. It was also impossible at that time to persuade boys to become ploughwrights. This reluctance on the part of boys and girls or their parents to enter into formal apprenticeships slowly broke down, and a later list shows nine cart and ploughwright apprenticeships from the Lowland Division of Perth and five from the Highland with three others, origins unspecified, as well as coopers, millwrights, a blacksmith and a ploughwright.[78]

Initially, a certain amount of care was taken both in choosing suitable boys and girls and in fitting them to a trade. Ludovick Grant's two sons were to be examined as to what would suit them when he requested apprenticeships for them, and they were promised 'a compleat set of clothes' if they behaved themselves. The selection processes cannot have been too successful, however, for the two Grant boys failed to take up the position arranged for them with Mr. Sandeman of Perth[79] and, in August, 1762, one master wrote indignantly that 'I propose having no more to do with any of them'. He was prepared to keep this particular apprentice only because Lord Kames had recommended him, but 'I think I have paid well enough . . . in maintaining one idle man those nine weeks'. He added bitterly that he wished the commissioners would be able to find 'apprentices thats as willing to be bound as their to bind or else they'l never do well'.[80] His last sentence was unfortunately prophetic.

The Board seems to have looked after the apprentices fairly well, paying fees, and providing clothes, medicine and tools. Tools were expensive. The list necessary for a smith included £5.5.0 for bellows, £4.10.10 and £2.10.0 for a small and large anvil, the total cost being £18.6.7. A weaver needed £14.13.11 to set him up. £200 per annum would not cover many boys at that rate, though the masters furnished food and bedding. So did a cooper at Leith, the Board having paid £16 indenture fees and provided clothes. Of course, not all were so expensive as the engineer who lost all his tools and clothes, when the boat in which he was travelling to the pier at Cromarty was dashed to pieces off Portsoy. He needed an extra £20.[81]

Ninian Jeffrey, the factor on Coigach, was very interested in improving farming, and especially in trying to introduce sheep-farming. He never missed an opportunity to push his point of view and the apprenticeship scheme for farmers was a splendid platform for him. When Kenneth M'Kenzie, the wadsetter of South Langwell, asked Jeffrey to recommend his son to the Board, 'who he is inclined should be bread to husbandry and as he has a large family is not in ability to educate him to purpose in that way', Mr. Jeffrey was delighted to add, 'As I humbly apprehend that little improvement in husbandry will ever be carried on in the Highlands without some such plan of educating their young and settling stranger farmers amongst them'. On at least one other occasion, he pointed out that Coigach had very extensive hill grazings, and 'these generally very drye', so boys should be sent to the best farmers in 'the highlands of Teviotdale, Selkirk or Dumfriesshire' to learn the management of 'that useful creature' the sheep,[82] and his advice was taken.

Apprentice-farmers involved the most expense per head. In 1765, the Board reported to the Treasury, that of the annual allowance of £200 they had spent £123.4.1, £40 of that going to Robert Menzies, in Northumberland, learning husbandry; an apprentice-ploughwright had needed only £6. Others were bound to flax-raisers and dressers, weavers and shoemakers. In 1767, Helen Campbell was apprenticed to be a midwife for only £10.13.6.

As well as sending boys and girls away from home, the Board tried to induce skilled craftsmen to venture into the northern parts of the country, both to practise their trade and to train others. The Perth factor sent for one, 'James Duncanson, a remarkable man for making all sorts of labouring utensils, particularly plough-shares and plough-irons', who promised to come to teach the smiths and wrights in Crieff to make ploughs.[83] He was to be subsidised at the rate of one guinea per week, given ostensibly for cutting timber for making the ploughs, and he had agreed to take two apprentices to be bound for four years, at £5 and £6 fees. Improvement in such basic skills could hardly be expected to be attained quickly, and in 1767 the General Inspector was still reporting unfavourably on the 'utensils of husbandry' used by the tenants in the Highland estates so that it was considered the more necessary to bind apprentices in making such tools.

The idea that young people should be given a training of some sort – suited to their station of course – can hardly be criticised even if, according to a memorandum from Small, the main motives were to induce 'the second sons of Highland gentlemen and the sons of their better sorts of tenants to abandon their dogs, guns and idleness'. The ideal was never fully realised, however, either for the poorer or the richer. The fund of money allocated was never fully spent, though it would not have been difficult to spend £200 on tools alone. There was always a credit balance in the apprenticeship fund, possibly only a theoretical one, but a credit just the same. In 1771, £168.7.1 was spent from the fund of £522.13.0; in 1772, £534.5.11 was available and £403.19.0 was issued. In the usual accounting fashion of the Board, £200 was added in the books each year, from the time that permission was granted to use money in this way, in 1761. Gradually disillusion-ment, combined with indifference, set in. It became necessary to put the king's mark on all the tools given out, as some of the apprentices disappeared with them. Other unexpected charges arose when apprentices were taken ill and masters claimed for the care they gave them. Eventually the Board refused allowances for medical care.[84] Some masters also found themselves involved in releasing apprentices from the press-gang. In 1773, the committee on apprentices decided that if a man left the annexed estates his tools should be kept. Two years later, in January 1775, the committee decided that the Board would not be liable for any expense for apprentices after the expiry of their indentures and, two months thereafter, practically wrote the whole scheme off. At a meeting on March 6th, 1775, the committee proposed, and on the same day the Board ratified, the deci-sion that 'As very few of the apprentices bred by the Board have ever settled on the

Annexed Estates, that as they are a continual burthen on the Board after their indentures are expired and their being present a great number under indentures, no more ought to be received until the present sett are settled'.[85]

The type of 'burthen' the Board meant can be illustrated by a very few examples. A blacksmith, William Paterson, trained at the Board's expense, was preparing to return to the Cromartie estate; he wanted money to cover the carriage of iron and, further, he asked the Board to 'order his house and shop to be ready as soon as possible'. The factor was in a dilemma: 'I am at a loss what to say . . . for these artificers are so avaritious and have such an inclination to impose that it is impossible to satisfy them'. On this occasion, however, a ploughwright, John Davidson, had already been established. As one without the other was practically useless, the metalworker's skills being essential for the ploughwright, he had to recommend, obviously against the grain, that it was 'absolutely necessary to do something'. Davidson had been equally demanding and, even worse, had been one of the ringleaders in a small local riot, when the mill lead at New Tarbat had been destroyed. The factor's sentiments are understandable, and he would have liked to see Davidson evicted.[86] From a rather different part of the British Isles came another plea for additional help. An apprentice farmer in Yorkshire wrote that the usual £3 for clothes was not nearly sufficient to cover the cost of clothes there, and he was awarded double that for both himself and his brother. Then he wandered off to Norfolk, claiming, perhaps honestly, that he had been increasing his skills, and he wanted money to get back.[87]

The decision to halt the apprenticeship scheme was tempered with sense and mercy and it was never brought to a complete stop, despite the Board's disillusionment. After all, some of their protégés realised their aims, and deserving cases could always depend on some support. James Small's assurance that a cart and ploughwright was much needed in Callander resulted in £10 being allowed to Alexander M'Robie for tools and, when Small himself died, his servant of long-standing who had no trade was given a training, the rules about age on entry being rather less rigid than today. In that context, it is interesting to find an older man being allowed a shorter period of training as a ship's carpenter, at the higher fees of £30 for a three years' apprenticeship, where a five years' stint would have cost £20 a year. Then, as late as 1780, a widow in the Benniebeg settlement with 'more than six' children had one provided for as an apprentice cart-and-ploughwright. On the other hand, the Duke of Argyll's overseer, who could hardly have been in want, was referred to the Board's decision of 6 March, 1775, when he asked for help in sending his son to England to learn farming.[88]

Unfortunately, the benefits envisaged in 1755 and 1761 did not materialise. It would be interesting to know why so few apprentices did in fact return to the estates, or like the son of Lovat's piper left a master very quickly, in this case in ten days.[89] We can only guess, for the commissioners and their officers did not understand why the scheme was not a resounding success, when even the lure of being set up in business on their own with reasonable encouragement, like the deplorable cartwright, Davidson, did not tempt many back. Some presumably seized on the opportunity of subsidised migration to the Lowlands or England;

others seized on their free tools. Fees were supposed to be repaid if apprentices did not return, but the fact that the S.S.P.C.K. put a clause in their indentures insisting that apprentices they supported must return to their home area shows that the Board's problems were not unique; such a condition must have been difficult to enforce. The Board continued spending small sums on the support of those already indentured and on the few who were added to their lists but, in 1783, only three were provided for. In the last year of annexation, 1784, £144.8.0 was spent and this largish sum included £20 for a millwright, £15 for a stocking weaver and £20 to the son of a former servant of the Board, who would be considered as meriting privileged treatment.[90] The would-be craftsmen do not shine in this story, but the masters must surely share some of the blame for the failure. Some certainly asked for apprentices when they had not enough business to provide teaching opportunities, and there must have been faults of character on their side as well, although their presumably greater articulacy has given us a picture weighted in their favour.[91] It must also be added that had every penny of the apprenticeship fund been spent, had every apprentice been a model of virtue and industry and returned to the estates, the paltry sum at the Board's disposal could not have made much impression on the Highland area.

It can be argued that the second string in the commissioners' plans for making the Highlands a hive of skilful industrious craftsmen was marginally more successful and effective than that for training and enticing young people back to their home stamping grounds. To their credit, they realised very early that, while larger holdings might increase efficiency among farmers, a resultant disadvantage might be the disappearance of the 'day-labourers', who did a little casual work for payment, but depended on their holdings for food. Further, when the long-term plan of converting all services to money rents eventually took shape, there would be even more need for labourers, independent of the tenants, to carry out the work previously proffered as part of the rent. At the same time, craftsmen evicted from their small holdings might well leave the area where they were uncertain of making a living in purely financial terms. It was no part of the Board's aims to denude the Highlands of people, trained or untrained; Malthus had not yet spoken, and skilled men were considered a great part of a country's wealth. In 1766, a cooper and merchant in Montrose were tried for 'enticing artificers' to go to Sweden.[92]

To counteract these possible evils, to 'help multiply the inhabitants and prevent the dispersion of artificers and day labourers now residing upon the estates whose small possessions as cottars are altogether dependent upon the tenant', the Board suggested that £500 should be used to except some lands from leases, to build 'small commodious house with cowbyre and a few acres of garden stuff for their families, forage for a cow', and in addition to enclose the ground. Any willing to settle were to be considered, not merely the present inhabitants, and all were to be classified as 'King's Cottagers'. They set the factors to work and various pendicles were preserved for craftsmen. Tenants had to be prepared to give up some of their land for this purpose and, while it might seem an inconvenience at first glance, it would be to the tenant's advantage if a sufficient labour force could be maintained thereby. There was not universal approval for this suggestion, however, and the correct extent of such a holding was difficult to decide. The acreage had to be enough for the craftsman's family's needs but not so great that it would distract him from what the commissioners or any other subsidising or improving body considered his proper trade. William Sandeman, the manufacturer, argued that even three acres of ground was too much for a trained man, for 'by having it he neglects the business he was bred to and disappoints his employers'; he reckoned that only a kailyard should be provided. This problem caused the British Fisheries Society some heartburning and is perhaps not fully resolved today. However, the commissioners had to be realistic and they knew that the tradesmen could not yet depend on a money income to buy grain and meal; it was essential that those they settled could be sure of enough food, and manufacturers, with far more capital than these small men could ever aspire to, had had their difficuties in that respect.[93]

One of the financial problems facing artisans in the Highlands arose from the unsophisticated nature of Highland society, where every man was of necessity a jack-of-all-trades. There was a certain lack of respect for these skills, a reluctance to use them and an even greater reluctance to pay for them when they were used. Men who had to purchase the raw materials for plying their trade found themselves in straits too often for comfort. The blacksmith at Kinloch Rannoch, David Gow, was one of the Board's apprentices who did return to the estates, but he complained that the tenants would not pay as much as 'will make me live'. The Board allowed him £2 per annum as the tenants refused to pay him the same rates as they did his predecessor. A wheelwright on the estate of Lochiel declared he came to repair spinning-wheels at the request of the inhabitants, but could not make a living without being granted a house, garden and 'some other small sum or benefit'. Henry Butter, the factor, agreed with this wright, Duncan Lothian, that his work was necessary, and further suggested that a cartwheel-mender should also be given a yearly aid of £5 or £6. Other tradesmen too could argue that a cash subsidy was necessary.[94]

A man who could repair spinning-wheels was considered an essential member of the community by the commissioners, obsessed as they were with the need to encourage the linen industry and, while the inhabitants of the Highlands seem to have been able to do most running repairs to their elementary tools, wheels were apparently beyond them. In 1764, in Rannoch, it was declared that 'Everybody in this country by their being ignorant how to use or even spin with their wheel, put them wrong almost every day'. In Coigach, it was the bad houses that were blamed for the damage to wheels.[95] But whatever the cause of the breakdowns, only qualified wheelwrights could mend them.

Robert Anderson, a Maryburgh weaver, had different problems. Because of the expense of provisions, he could not in 1765 on his existing income support apprentices, and he hoped for looms and 'individual encouragement' from the Board. By 1767, he had been provided with a 'good and sufficient house' and eight looms, but he still lacked assistants, and claimed that there was not a tradesman in the whole country who could work linen cloth. The neighbourhood being

K

so 'excessively poor and extravagant', he could not persuade anyone to come and had to depend on such tradesmen as were serving with the army in the area at the time. This was, needless to say, a precarious means of finding workmen and on occasion all his looms were idle, so once again he asked for help towards supporting apprentices. However, Mr. Anderson had additional troubles. The tenants of Lochiel and Ardsheal complained in 1772 that his behaviour had made him obnoxious, goods were 'embeazled' or 'abstracted from his house', and employers and customers got no satisfaction. They felt they were worse off than when they had no weaver. The factor bore out their complaints and, despite or perhaps because of Anderson's plea that his wife was an alcoholic who carried off everything she could lay her hands on and 'drinks it', recommended that he should lose the Board's support. The man's personal misfortune, dishonesty, or inefficiency does not alter the picture of the lack of skilled men in the area and the lack of money to pay any who did appear.[96]

Blacksmiths faced heavy carriage dues and were much sought after as the army needed their services. In February, 1773, a petition was read from John M'Lean, the smith and harrier at Coshieville, applying for smithy coal *gratis*, as he was so far from fuel and had to go to Perth or Stirling for steel, iron and coals. The factor thought he had 'always been paid for his pains', probably because he had dealt with the military, but added fairly that he knew Coshieville was far from coals and peat. Another smith, Alexander M'Naughton, however, would have found living impossible without the Board's assistance, the factor thought, and he was 'no richer than we found him' despite a good house and smithy.[97]

As well as the subsidies given to more isolated workmen, the Board proposed, with the king's approval which was granted in March 1762, to spend £100 each year in settling tradesmen and artificers of good character in Callander and Crieff. These two relatively large centres of population were considered suitable development points for trade and manufactures and, by settling industrious individuals there, the commissioners hoped to increase both population and productivity. Like the day-labourers in the countryside, these men in the towns were to be granted ground and a house. It was also hoped to spend £50 each year in premiums for them. The types of workmen wanted there were for example a stocking-weaver, who was given £100 to enable him to start a business at Crieff, a heckler who went to Callander with £25 of the Board's money, and a manufacturer of linen cloth there who got £30.[98]

The third strand of the Board's policy, that of setting up schools specially to teach spinning and in addition employing men and women to teach various crafts, was one that had been conceived earlier in the century and practised by the S.S.P.C.K. since 1738, when the society received its second charter. The Board had, in fact, avowed their intention of following the methods used by the Trustees for Manufactures and Fisheries,[99] and the funds of the estates were simply another boost to the various eighteenth-century onslaughts on poor craftsmanship. Spinning, stocking-knitting, and sewing white seams were all taught with the assistance of the Board, both in schools and by peripatetic teachers.

The largest single outlay of £133.5.0 each year for three years was made to the

Inverness magistrates, who had shown some initiative in providing premises for a school there; 184 girls were taught to spin there in 1765, and 120 in 1767. An allowance for maintenance for fifty girls from outlying districts was included in the grant, but none for those whose homes were in the town, though wheels and reels were to be bought for poor girls. Schools of this type were often attached to factories and in this case the entrepreneur, a Mr. Falconer, got no financial encouragement except the house provided by the magistrates and his salary as a manager. This school was judged reasonably successful, and it is mentioned in 1775 as having had good effects on the spinning skills in the area.[100]

The commissioners were asked for £30 per annum to help the spinning school on Lewis, on the grounds that tradesmen refused to come to such places without a subsidy,[101] and £57.10.0 was given to the Leishmore island school in 1765, but later expenditure tended to be concentrated on the south and east. Regular salaries were paid to schoolmistresses to teach sewing and spinning and knitting stockings on the Perth estate, and there was at least one man, Malcolm Fisher, teaching 'nitting' stockings at Callander. There were also what could be granted the name of 'technical schools' in twentieth-century terminology at Auchterarder, Borland, Muthill, Dunblane and Crieff.[102]

The Board's tendency to neglect the more remote estates can be illustrated in the location of these schools. There was one at Beauly in Lovat, and the manufacturers taught spinners in those northern areas, but the greater number of schools were in Perthshire; admittedly the larger, most lucrative estates were also in Perthshire, but manufactures were already in at least an embryonic stage there, and there were opportunities for learning. In 1775, Henry Butter wrote bitterly that there was far greater need for a school for white-seam and stocking-knitting in Fort William and it would be difficult to refute this. It is even easier to sympathise with his frustration when it is remembered that he had pointed out just such a need eleven years before without any result.[103]

The attendance and proficiency of the scholars varied but fortunately few were so handless as poor Agnes Graham, who could not learn to spin after a full three months' stay.[104] The numbers reputed to have learned spinning must be treated with caution, for the Inspector found that experienced spinners attended the school attracted by the 1/6 per week allowed for maintenance. It is interesting to note that the same problem arose in the spinning schools established by the Irish Linen Board in the same period. Menzies also commented, as we have seen, that spinning was much further advanced in both Lovat and Cromartie than the stream of demands for subsidies from the funds seems to indicate. Just as the teachers were unwilling to send away girls who they knew could spin, so the entrepreneurs were prepared to grasp any financial aid they could.[105] The benefits to the Highland economy in general or Highland skills in particular were marginal.

The *Old Statistical Account* is the first obvious source for immediate results of the commissioners' assistance to industry and manufactures in the Highlands, and it must be admitted that therein there is a deafening silence, except perhaps in the Inverness account. In Perthshire, there are some signs of life in the manufacturing industries. In Callander, woollen and linen yarn 'are much spun by the poor'. In Comrie, the writer claimed that the linen yarn was the staple manufacture and tartan plaid and hose were made partly for sale, partly for home use. In Callander, however, the Stirling carpet makers bought the wool, and linen was sent to Glasgow. In Fortingall, it was recognised by the end of the century that no manufactures were possible because of the scarcity of fuel, but even in Crieff, which it may be remembered was considered during the annexation the most promising site for industrial development, the *Old Statistical Account* described manufactures as having had 'hitherto little effect on the population', but – ever optimistic – 'in comparison with what they will probably soon have'. This 'little effect' was in spite of the presence of three corn-mills, three fulling-mills, and malt, barley and lint-mills, not to mention a tannery, for which £300 had been awarded out of annexed estates funds, and a similarly subsidised paper-mill. But this last employed only eight hands, after all. Further north and west, the ministers were still convinced that the introduction of manufacturing industry of one kind or another would improve the life of the people. In Kilmallie, the disadvantages of the parish are listed as the want of a quay, of a good regular market, good water, and not least, a tannery, a sawmill and a 'manufactory' of any sort.[106]

The impetus for introducing manufacturing industries which animated the Board in the early stages of its life soon died away. The commissioners' Journal of their daily expenses and the accounts of individual estates show this very clearly, and the fund of £2,700 allowed for encouraging the textile industries had a theoretical credit of £1,000 in 1784. During the last decade of the annexation, it was rarely that as much as £100 was drawn out of this in a year. This is misleading, for it should be noted that the Board's accounting practices were somewhat peculiar; grants were made to individual entrepreneurs, some undoubtedly working in textiles, and these were debited separately. One also finds that there was on occasion a very broad interpretation of what particular sums could be applied to. In 1783, the sum recorded as spent on manufactures included the cost of killing vermin.[107] But there was no doubt about the general diminution of interest with a corresponding decrease in expenditure in the 1770s.

During the whole of the annexation, the only large-scale industrial plans formulated were connected with linen, notably the abortive school and factory at New Tarbat, and once the Trustees' stations were seen to be foundering, the Board tended to ca' very canny indeed. In the circumstances, it is difficult to see what else they could have done. Shortage of money, Treasury dilatoriness, the handicaps the north of Scotland still suffers from – lack of raw materials (oil excepted), lack of markets, poor transport – all proved obstacles to industrial development. In the mid-eighteenth century, a further stumbling block was the lack of interest among the inhabitants in what the rest of the country considered the material essentials of the good life, and hence the lack of energy in trying to obtain these. It is possible to understand the conundrum of how the Board could believe, as did the Trustees for Manufactures and Fisheries, that they could establish much viable industry against such odds, only by considering the vitality of Lowland Scotland at the time, and the absolute determination of those in power to transfer some of that vitality, or at least its apparent results, to those whom they considered less fortunate and certainly misguided.

It can be argued that the Board's expenditure was not wholly wasted. Crieff and Callander no doubt felt the benefit of having £176.6.0 laid out in one year in setting up two stocking weavers, a heckler and a manufacturer of linen cloth. If a few women retained their spinning skills, if only to transfer them to wool; if a few men made a better living by heckling and weaving; if the tanneries and mills that the Board financed remained in operation into the next century and made for an easier, more convenient life for some of the inhabitants, then there is some justification for their work. John Knox, however, had some grounds for his general strictures on the Trustees' and the Board's efforts and exertions, by which, as he said, 'no effectual permanent settlement or even the appearance of it has been established and many thousands of pounds have thereby been lost to the public'.[108]

Unfortunately, it is well-nigh impossible to assess exactly the effects of the Annexed Estates Board's work, partly because it was only one among many groups and individual heritors working for change in the Highlands, whether for altruistic or for selfish ends; and further, the results of the commissioners' work were inevitably dispersed over the Highlands and Islands, because of the terms of the Annexing Act. Archibald Menzies pointed out that their methods may well have been attended with 'proper consequences', but such dispersion rendered these consequences practically invisible. The blacksmith who could not without their subsidies have made a living in a remoter sparsely populated area, the odd lintmill or other small factory, dotted here and there over the Highland area and employing half a dozen hands, can have made only a very slight, localised impact. Menzies also pointed out the greatest handicap laid on the commissioners, which happened to be the only measureable element in their story; this was their income, which was far too small for them to be able 'to render such improvements visible and exemplary'. Menzies was also about the only person who asked explicitly the vital question which no-one on the Board seems to have pondered although, to be fair, their commission from the government did not allow for much in the way of theoretical musings. He wondered if any money at all should have been spent on introducing manufactures into the area.

Menzies argued that 'It is more probable, had as much money been expended for introducing a proper knowledge of agriculture into the Highlands, establishing of villages and making of cross roads [i.e. as on manufactures], that manufactures, which must always be considered in a secondary light, would have followed of course with very little assistance'.[109] He had no crystal ball to foretell the future of industrial organisation and that of economic and technical developments, which give posterity leave to doubt his conclusion that more attention to the infrastructure of the Highland economy would have provided the complete solution for all the ills the Board was trying to cure. And from 1755, the Board had indeed spent consistently and, in light of their financial situation, lavishly, on all aspects of the Highland communication system, but their prime concern and that of the government, which gave unquestioning assent to all proposed expenditure on roads, bridges, ferries and inns, had been to secure the peace by making the

Highlands more accessible. In this context, advancement of the economy was incidental, though the century had seen growing support for the theory that better communications would soon eradicate the difference between Highlands and Lowlands.[110] Town building was also part of the programme set out by the government, but the commissoners' contribution to the stock of eighteenth-century planned towns must be counted as among the least successful examples of their activities. As the last strand in their attempts to encourage manufacturing industry and craftsmanship in the Highlands, it must now be considered.

8

New Towns by Land and Sea; Fishing

WHILE the foundation of new towns was by no means a novel pastime for landowners, it was one of the passions of the improvers of the eighteenth century, and one from which the commissioners could hardly be expected to be immune, even without express directions in the Annexing Act and in the first instructions sent to the newly appointed Board in 1755. Individual landowners who embarked in town-building occasionally indulged in some self-glorification, as we can see from the names of some of the new towns, such as Colinsburgh, Archiestown and Grantown, but behind even these eponymous titles there were often sound economic reasons for choosing particular sites. There was a fairly confident assumption that manufacturing industry would prosper better in a town than in open country, for the town would provide both a labour supply and a market both for agricultural produce in the vicinity and for the goods manufactured in the town. Estate rentals were also expected to rise as the population increased and the greater potential of land was realised, particularly if the landowner had made use of the extra hands to reclaim waste land on his property. Such expectations were not always fully or even partially realised, for many of the builders, like Alexander Dirom, the founder of Bridekirk, can be criticised, as J. D. Wood comments, because they never asked themselves, or indeed thought of asking themselves, even in contemporary terms as opposed to twentieth-century planners' jargon, 'What were the threshold requirements of the functions essential to the prosperity of a sizeable place in a predominantly agricultural setting?'[1] Statistics and the 'dismal science' had not at that time become the controlling genii of planners.

The public aims, however, were envisaged as more than economic. Just how radical a change it was hoped the annexation would make can be gathered from the reference to town building in the parliamentary debates on the annexation, and from some of the suggestions in the manuscript already mentioned giving 'Hints' on managing the estates.[2] In the third section of this document, it is suggested that the Trustees should 'fix proper passes', build bridges there, then churches, workhouses, i.e. factories, schoolhouses and prisons, and stone houses, with glass windows. Into these new settlements, *all* (my italics) the present inhabitants were to be gradually received and allotted new houses in which they could see to work during the winter – on account of the glass windows – whereupon their 'present dark smoky cabins indisposed for industry and work' were *all* (again my italics) to be destroyed. When one remembers that the last inhabited black houses have only recently been evacuated, the grandeur of this vision becomes awe-inspiring. A truly authoritarian society was described by this author, in which the 'junction of the people together' would provide stewards, factors and masters of crafts with convenient opportunities to propagate the mechanical arts and, even more important, a spirit of industry amongst them, especially as they would be 'easily overlooked and deprived of their usual recesses for sauntering and slothfulness'. The document had, however, the considerable merit of being realistic about finance, for the writer suggested that £10,000 should be advanced for this purpose, from the Treasury, interest to be paid out of the profits of the estates.

As the government gave the Board explicit instructions to erect new settlements, the commissioners made an early appointment of a sub-committee of four to take particular charge of the 'enlargement or new erection' of towns and villages and, in 1757, four places were suggested as suitable – New Tarbat, Callander of Menteith, Kinloch Rannoch and Beauly. Prisons and schools were to be erected at each place. Only two of these, strictly speaking, would have been new foundations; Callander had been the creation of James Drummond, former owner of the Perth estate, about 1730, and 'Beaulie' is stated in *Origines Parochiales* as having been in existence in 1562, though the present settlement is not necessarily on the precise site of the first. Kinloch Rannoch had only eight tenants and the proposed site for New Tarbat was part of the policies of the house of the former Earl of Cromartie. Some time later Ullapool was proposed as preferable to New Tarbat but, in 1761, when the first signs of royal approval for these particular plans were shown, New Tarbat was the favoured spot – probably because someone in London had been looking up old reports, not at minute-books.[3] Only general approval was elicited for the 'ends and purposes' these settlements were calculated to promote. To enable the government to make 'distinct and precise' judgements about the probable benefits of these and any future proposals, in relation to their situation, expense, type of manufactures proposed, and populousness, the commissioners were asked to send more information, such as plans of the estates, taken upon actual surveys, copies of properly authenticated rentals, and abstracts of the factors' reports; in 1755, the factors had been asked to comment on suitable sites for villages among all the other information the Board wanted.

The planned villages of the eighteenth century have been classified as falling into four categories, comprising those associated with agriculture and estate interests, manufacturing villages, fishing and other settlements connected with the coastal trade, and finally, inland spas, tourist and residential centres.[4] Many foundations fell into several categories, as most landlords hoped to increase the wealth of their estates by encouraging manufacturing industry as well as by improving agricultural practice, a perfectly feasible ambition before the days of mass-production. The commissioners had to take into account the possible social consequences of any urban development they assisted, in addition to considering economic aspects. Even so, four of the first five sites they proposed were fairly conventional by the standards of the time and, if Kinloch Rannoch is not yet either a thriving market town, an industrial centre, or even an important spa, a largish village in the Rannoch area was not in the 1760s a wholly unreasonable suggestion as a possibly potent agent of social change. As it happened, before any positive steps had been taken to start any building, the change in Britain's international position when the Seven Years War ended resulted in another element affecting the Board's town-planning, an element that was to be almost wholly destructive. The provision of holdings and employment for disbanded members of the army and navy became inextricably intermingled with what were often referred to as 'colonies' on the annexed estates. What solution could have seemed neater than placing these returning heroes in new towns in the Scottish Highlands, particularly if they were natives who could be expected to have benefited from the experience of 'civilisation' in other parts of the world?

Some evidence points to a degree of concern, at least among the governing classes, at the prospect of demobilisation. An act was passed enabling officers, mariners and soldiers to exercise their trades anywhere in Great Britain, an unusual privilege which may well have been aimed at dispersing at least parts of regiments.[5] Some Scottish landlords besides the commissioners encouraged servicemen to settle in specific towns and villages on their estates, such as Portsoy and Macduff, by offering bounties.[6] This was not pure altruism, of course. It was assumed that these men would bring craftsmanship and discipline into the settlements. Also, the question of providing for disabled soldiers had been brought up by Campbell of Barcaldine, the factor on the Perth estate, some time before the end of the Seven Years War. Early in 1760, he wrote to the commissioners that several Perthshire men who had served in America in the Highland regiments had lately returned home wounded and unfit for further service. They had applied to him for small holdings for themselves and their families, and he thought them quite able to manage a small farm. One advantage he saw for himself in giving tenancies to such people was that their pensions would enable them to pay their rents punctually. The Board approved and he was ordered to divide the farm of Morell to take several soldiers. Barcaldine had declared himself 'pretty positive' that the soldiers would set an example of industry to their neighbours, but his idea was never proved. In January, 1763, he had to report failure. He had tried to make an equable division of a farm, Drumlaken, as, for a variety of reasons, Morell had turned out to be impractical, but when the Chelsea Pensioners, as he termed them, foregathered for this purpose and found one of their proposed co-tenants without an arm, another without a leg, and no doubt others with similar handicaps, they 'took such an aversion to being brought together', that he had to give up the scheme.[7]

The commissioners did not read the omens correctly, however, and the factor's idea took a firm hold of the Board. Their onslaught on the problem began in 1763, when, in their report to the king, they proposed spending £3,000 to provide houses, each costing £5, 'Necessaries' estimated at £3 for three hundred married soldiers and a cash bounty of £3 for two hundred unmarried. Each of the soldiers was to be allotted three acres of ground for spade cultivation, and the ground adjoining the houses was to be enclosed and laid down in grass for pasture for cows, allowing two acres for a cow. Houses were to be rent-free for life. Farm ground, also rent-free for the first three years, was thereafter to be let at 5/- per acre. The unmarried men's bounty of £3 was to be paid out in three annual instalments. It was also proposed that £5 should be lent to deserving and indigent soldiers to maintain them for the first year, and to help them stock their holdings. It may be noted that the policy of giving land to craftsmen (and to fishermen) soon aroused criticism on the grounds we have already seen expressed that only a kailyard and potato croft were necessary, and that any more land would drive men from their proper business, making for inefficiency in both agriculture and trade.[8]

By this scheme, it was expected that the population would be increased, and that there would be introduced upon the annexed estates a number of good workmen for the various types of improvements envisaged, who would, 'by raising the spirit of emulation among the present inhabitants', promote industry, 'hitherto at its lowest ebb'. The commissioners were in for a rude awakening. One early dissentient voice was that of James Small in Struan who, significantly, had been an ensign in the army before becoming factor. He reported in 1763 that he had no land for them in the current year and he was obviously well pleased that he could say this. He forecast that five-sixths of the soldiers would be the greatest blackguards, in no way amenable to civil discipline, 'only the rod having kept them under control'. Further, he anticipated that they would sell their whole possessions and squander their money on drink. His prophecy was largely borne out in the next few years and, when the new towns were still embryonic, he was able to tell the commissioners that already, on the strength of the 'great things to be done for them', returning warriors were borrowing money in every public house on the road to Struan – from twelve to fifteen miles. Captain Forbes also disapproved. He wrote in November 1763, 'I do not much admire the grand plan of sailors and sogers being persuaded it will not easily execute'.[9]

However, in 1763, there was little likelihood that these Cassandra-like voices would be listened to and the 'colonies' as they were called were begun. It was unfortunate that, with the benefit of hindsight, the Board could not have read the words of wisdom of James Wilson that 'It is probably much more difficult to plant people than potatoes',[10] but even allowing for initial over-optimism, a great many of their actions in connection with this plan were unnecessarily precipitate. The first step taken was to insert advertisements in the Edinburgh newspapers and in the *London Gazette*, in March 1763, intimating that such provision was to be made for demobilised soldiers. Any interested were asked to apply to the secretary in the Edinburgh office, or to any of the factors and, within a few days, by March 30, several had appeared at the office. But no definite plans had been made for their reception, no inquiries had been sent to commanding officers of regiments about to be 'broke' as to the likely response from those being disbanded, and all that could be done was to ask the agent, Mr. Alston, to make plans for their immediate settlement on the estates. Previous to this, all that had been done was to give removal notices to tenants whose farms were wanted for the proposed settlements.

This had roused protests not merely from the tenants. In May the factor on Lovat pointed out that it was impossible to find holdings for soldiers without distressing the present inhabitants. He also suggested that the improvable muirs should be used, as the present farms were so small that taking off a few acres would make them 'no farm at all'. On the tiny estate of Monaltrie most of the tenants refused to give up any part of their ground. In November, four months later, the factor therefore had to report that he still could not get land for the soldiers, as the tenants were holding on to their possessions, and he had only six houses built, although there were far more than that number of soldiers on the estate.[11]

At the beginning of 1764, the Monaltrie factor had to defend himself against complaints from the soldiers that they had had no wages, and that their houses had no doors or windows. He was able to clear himself on both counts; the wright responsible for the houses had fallen sick and no wages had been paid because the men were absent from work. Also some had taken payment in meal. After it had been shown that the whole estate of Monaltrie was only sixteen oxgates and that some poor people held only one quarter of an oxgate, which with any land taken off to accommodate soldiers would be quite insufficient, the Board began somewhat belatedly to realise that 'there seems to be a difficulty in providing for all the soldiers' settled upon Monaltrie and told the factor to give them the opportunity to remove to other estates. In character with their general behaviour, none of them would then move. By May, 1765, however, some had disappeared, but they had disposed of their furniture and locked up their houses behind them, so that no-one else could inhabit them. The factor was instructed to apply for a sheriff's warrant to break down the doors of the locked houses.[12] The following year saw another voluntary clearance from Monaltrie when the Board ordered that no more money was to be given to the soldiers as loans; they were to be paid just as other workmen were when employed in public works. This drove a number of them south to solicit the Board in person. On the larger estates, a similar picture emerges.

In the meantime, in Edinburgh, Henry Barclay, the secretary, was bearing the brunt of the onslaught of the demobilised. In the special minute book, kept from April, 1763 to March, 1765, solely for business referring to the settlement of soldiers and sailors, there is a copy of his long report on his activities during the Board's adjournment in 1763.[13] He had dispatched 242 married and 78 unmarried soldiers, to the various estates, and the applications were increasing daily. What he dscribes delicately as the 'general importunity for being received' showed there would be no difficulty in finding sufficient candidates. One qualification was that the best recommended soldiers should be accepted, but Barclay and such commissioners who looked in at the office – 'casually attended' was Barclay's phrase – soon realised that they could not operate on a first come first served basis, as this might exclude some regiments that had distinguished themselves in the war but had not yet been disbanded. They inserted a further advertisement therefore that only old-established corps would be received in the meantime.

The next difficulty arose from the factors' correspondence, which plainly showed that they were facing very considerable problems in getting suitable accommodation for such numbers of settlers, as they had not been allowed time to build houses. In 1764, John Forbes complained that soldiers and sailors with their wives and children came every day 'in shoals' to his house, sometimes late at night, starving, when he had to lodge them and feed them, at least for one night. It was obvious that to relieve the factors there must be some delay in accepting any more prospective settlers. Despite yet another advertisement in the newspapers and a letter sent to the commanding officer when Keith's battalion was dismissed, numbers came crowding to the office and, no doubt because of their 'importunity', the beleaguered secretary judged it expedient to satisfy them by giving them seventy-six billets, most of this regiment expressing a preference for Cromartie. Again the newspapers were to be used to let them know when they could apply to the factor, as places became available. Many of them were unfit for work; others had travelled a considerable distance and had exhausted their allowance for travelling home. As it was the hope of the bounty that had attracted them, it was thought only reasonable to give some a few shillings to help 'carry them home to their friends' and to recommend others to the infirmary.

Another mistake in the original concept was discovered when the cheapest estimate for houses on the Perth estate appeared to be £16 each, and on Lovat and Cromartie £12–£15, while the commissioners had calculated on £5 each house. Other landlords avoided such an outlay by leaving it to the settlers to build their own houses.[14] The secretary had to report further that on the Struan estate some soldiers had already proved disorderly, and two were dishonest, while further unexpected expense had arisen when the Crieff surgeon's services had had to be called on for the sick on the Perth estate. He also advised the Board to give pecuniary encouragement until houses could be provided; like the doctor's fees, such expenditure had not been provided for in the original estimates. The one bright spot in this lugubrious tale was that at Whiteley, a farm on the barony of Stobhall, the eastmost part of the Perth estates, in the parish of Cargill George Young of Coupar Angus, who had been employed to oversee the settlement proposed there, had arranged for houses to start being built. He had got contracts and, as there was a stone quarry near, costs could be kept down.

Ever-optimistic at this point in the history of the annexation, the Board reported in 1764 that the scheme for settling the soldiers had succeeded. 276 houses had been built and 249 men, married and unmarried, had been provided for. The commissioners' main worry was that they had spent over £2,000 more than had been originally authorised. The original estimate stood at £3,000 but the actual costs had risen to £5,214.0.9 $\frac{5}{12}$, which included £1,042.4.1$\frac{11}{12}$ on travelling and subsistence, £2,619.16.7 $\frac{6}{12}$ on houses, and £1,552.0.0 on bounties. The next year's report was less sanguine. The success in settling the soldiers did not now seem so assured, and this about-face from 1764 had to be explained. Many quite defensible excuses could be produced. Bounties had been planned for stocking small holdings but instead had been used by the settlers to buy necessary furniture and for subsistence. There was no work available, so there was no money to buy seeds and, in any case, many were unable to work as they were 'valetudinary'. As a result, the Board had had to employ the able-bodied in enclosing heath or moorish ground for plantations on the annexed estates, in making fences for their settlements and in other 'New Deal' activities. Forbes, on Lovat, was at his wits' ends to know what to do with soldiers in the winter. Invalids were given enough to keep them alive but not 'sufficient to indulge them in idleness'. Many colonists had needed additional money to buy cows or the tools of their trades. The sole benefits the Board could enumerate in 1765 were that they expected the rents of the houses to correspond in a few years to the interest on the sums laid out – they must have forgotten that they proposed initially that the soldiers would live rent-free – and that the population was increased. The soldiers had been encouraged to marry and there were 368 children 'who in all probability would have been lost to the kingdom' without these colonies. However, to prevent further expense, they had decided to bring in no more soldiers, but they asked for permission to spend £500 more to complete what was already begun.[15]

Though the commissioners may have been satisfied with the progress made in settling soldiers in 1764, it is doubtful if the factors were ever happy about the conditions of the colonies or colonists, or if the majority of the beneficiaries were ever particularly appreciative. Nor was this unreasonable. It must be clear from the preceding pages, and especially from the quotations from the secretary's reports, that the central handling of the scheme was not well thought out, if indeed it was thought out at all to its logical conclusion. It was inefficient from its initiation; soldiers and factors and, as we shall see below, sailors too, had all legitimate grounds for complaint.

One of the worst features of the arrangements made was the type of ground allocated to the new settlers. It was realised that all would need some ground for subsistence, but even experienced agriculturalists would have had difficulty in dealing successfully with what faced them at Benniebeg, for example. In 1756, Barcaldine had described this farm as a 'small piece of bad meadow ground'. Though the rent had been brought down over the years from £20 to £13, the possessors still found themselves losers and had given up their tenancy. The soil was hard and gravelly and was eventually valued at £10. Other sites were not more promising. The area available at Kinloch Rannoch the Struan factor thought too small, and he suggested two hundred acres of 'muir ground very improveable', belonging to another proprietor on the south side of the loch. Borelandbog Park on the Perth estate was proposed as suitable because it would dispossess no-one but, though it had good soil, it was so interspersed with large stones that the factor thought they would have to be taken into account when the holdings were being measured. The Lovat factor had been given explicit instructions that he should settle soldiers without distressing the present inhabitants and he too suggested 'improveable muirs where the soil is good and may be turned to good account by ditching and trenching'. Later, in the history of the settlements, Menzies, the General Inspector, reported that those on the outskirts of Callander, who were local tenants' sons, had had trouble. He thought they were sober and industrious but because they 'had not been importunate and troubled the board with petitions' – unlike all the other colonists, it should be noted – they had been overlooked and their land was 'very difficult to improve'.[16]

The siting of the New Tarbat settlement was perhaps not so bad, though the farmer who was given notice to make room for soldiers and sailors had used it only for pasture. But the soldiers on Strathpeffer sent in a heart-rending petition to Lord Kames, describing their bad lots, stony and watery ground, and telling him they had been obliged to 'strip our backs to feed our bellies or els die for want, your lordships not fulfilling promises . . .' In 1768, some of those settled in the estates of Cromartie let the Board know that they had had to give up their ground on the Moss of Conon because it was 'entirely covered with water'. And these were men who had managed to improve other parts of their holdings. Skilled men, carefully supervised, might have been successful in these conditions but, by 1765, it was admitted in the minutes that on 'stony moorish, some swampy ground', the soldiers were not of themselves capable of improving without the help of the Board.[17] It is significant that the settlement which was most immediately success-ful was Strelitz. Named in honour of Charlotte of Mecklenburg-Strelitz, the wife of George III, it was built on reasonable ground, on the farm of Whiteley in Cargill parish and, from the beginning, George Young of Coupar Angus was engaged as supervisor. He kept a close watch on all the settlers' activities and by 1766 there were almost 300 inhabitants.

Neither were the houses as sound as the commissioners had hoped, for the haste with which factors had had to work to provide so many, with material and workmen not always at hand, had militated against that. Timber for building at Beauly and Conon had to be carried twenty-four miles over bad roads. On Coigach, the factor complained bitterly of the inefficient mason work and carpentry (wright work) on the soldiers' houses. Villages were not always laid out well, sometimes because the factors were not skilled town-planners – something they could hardly be blamed for. It took one of their servants to suggest to the com-missioners that a surveyor should be employed for these purposes. Admittedly this suggestion was immediately agreed to but previously the Board had merely ins-tructed the factor to set about designing and building a village. The results are not surprising. Borelandbog houses were in the 'upper part very ill-disposed running crooked and close . . . access to the houses very inconvenient not having space to make a sufficient broad road. Soldiers cannot let a chicken out of their houses but on their own or neighbours corn'. Some of the houses on the Perth estates had their slates set without sarking, the wood between the rafters and the slates, so that they would be uninhabitable in winter.[18]

The last essential element in the settlements was the human one, and it was no more satisfactory than the others. The only group of settlers who received any official or other commendation were those in Callander, and they may merely have shone by comparison with the original inhabitants, whose reputation was that, though they were usually at variance with one another, yet they joined in distress-ing any stranger settled amongst them. Previous knowledge of this trait of the Callander people may have been the reason for sending only locally born there in the first place, and of the first fourteen, none remained, as there were no houses built when they arrived. For the rest, there is almost universal condemnation, borne out it should be said by detailed descriptions of their conduct. In Strelitz, in 1765, George Young wrote that some had left and carried away their tools, officially government property, but they were 'troublesome, idle people'. He did add in some mitigation of their conduct, that they also had the worst lots; but, though he had promised them lime, they had lost patience and gone off to Dundee. The following year he reported that he had sold looms that he had recovered from some runaways[19] but, at least, these had remained for a couple of years. On Cromartie, by July, 1763, two had deserted and in 1764, in the sixty-nine houses built, only six sailors remained, while twenty left after receiving the bounty. The Monaltrie factor described them as a 'thankless pack', while Barcaldine explained his delay in sending his intromissions for the forfeited estate of Gask to the Barons of the Exchequer in 1763 by saying that 'ever since these plaguy soldiers came upon me, I could not get half an hour at a time free of some one or other of them'. He wrote even more feelingly in 1768, that he would not go through the same experience again for triple the sum, and he was surprised the Board would grudge an allowance for his trouble about those soldiers' settlements. He thought he was poorly paid for the effort it had cost him.[20] It is a welcome relief to hear of £20 being given to George Sinclair, 'an industrious soldier', a dyer at Ullapool, for a waulkmill, even though he was cheated by those he employed; and of another who on his own initiative opened a small store in Benniebeg. In 1766, the last year the soldiers were to be free of land-rent, those in Coigach had exhausted the money given them, had run into debt with the country people and would be unable to sow their acres if the Board did not assist them, but the factor added that 'such idle fellows are not worth countenancing'.[21]

By the spring of 1766, one can appreciate the commissioners' thorough disgust with the whole project. It had cost more than they had calculated – the wildest optimist could hardly have prophesied success by this time – and the Board was faced with asking once again for allowances to be made for their having spent more than had been authorised – £500 extra on this occasion. They decided to combine the plans for settling soldiers with that for establishing craftsmen and labourers and to call all soldiers in future merely King's Cottagers, using the fund appropriated for the latter type of tenant.

They were not so easily free of trouble from soldiers, however, and complaints and petitions carry on throughout the annexation and beyond. Even in the nineteenth century, the remaining inhabitants of Strelitz expressed dissatisfaction with the accommodation provided specially for them in the loft of Cargill church.[22] There was never enough produce from their lots to keep them. James Small had given warning of the dangers of over-small holdings, saying it was better that tenants should be employed on the roads rather than starve on their farms, but this had made no impression on the commissioners. They undoubtedly felt some moral obligation towards the colonists, however, and as they were ultimately responsible for the deficiencies of their holdings, they felt that work and wages must somehow be found. This involved the factors in laying out quite large sums, for wages mounted up at 4d per day; £204 was needed on Lovat and Cromartie alone between May and December, 1763.[23] One soldier at least went off to work in the Ayrshire mines, leaving his wife in possession, but he was killed. Millers complained that they could not obtain their thirlage from the settlements; in 1776, the inhabitants of Benniebeg were still applying for assistance in buying seed, while the villagers of Black Park were to be warned to remove in 1781, as they would neither pay additional rent nor work for it, and observed none of the regulations of the barony, and most went 'abegging through the country'.[24] Also they refused to do their statute labour.

This 'Utopian' scheme of the commissioners, as Pennant sneeringly described it, achieved very little in either the short or the long term. There were four planned villages on the Perth estate, Strelitz, Borelandbog Park, Benniebeg and Callander. When William Frend the Inspector visited the estate, he had to report that the soldiers' houses and land at Borelandbog were in general in very bad order. At Strelitz, a great number of the houses were ill-kept, the ditches were neglected, and the park land was flooded. There was much the same sort of comment on the soldiers' houses and ground at Callander with the additional disapproval of the dung being still kept before the doors of the houses. At Benniebeg, a rather odd situation had arisen, for James Glass, a linen manufacturer from Crieff, had by 1773 obtained the let of seven lots. Quite early on in the history of the village, one couple who had left had returned to find their house broken open, by order of course, their goods rouped, and Glass's looms installed instead. When Frend reported, he found that seven houses under the factor were reasonably kept, but Glass had begun to let or rather to sublet the houses he had, and they were very poor, with no thatch. The reason for this was discovered in 1783. Glass was charging a very heavy rent and would not allow the tenants to use the pasture.[25] Such a situation was hardly envisaged in the original plans.

Benniebeg, once all the inhabitants were dead or removed, was flooded by a Lady Perth, who presumably could no longer bear the sight of what must have been an unattractive lot of hovels on the avenue to Drummond Castle. When Pennant travelled that way in 1772, many of the houses were already empty.[26] Now the Pool of Drummond covers the site. Callander may be counted a reasonably profitable town in Highland terms, but the site was not chosen by the commissioners but by the titular Duke of Perth, about 1730. The Board added to it, the factor reporting in 1764 that he had marked out 45 acres, 2 roods and 3 falls on Murdieston and Ballanton to the north-west of the existing village. In 1800, Callander was described as having a 'neat, cheerful appearance', the writer pointing out the sudden change to the Gaelic tongue and Highland garb and, even worse, the bad and extravagant inn. The village of Boreland was occupied almost entirely by weavers by the time of the first Statistical Account.[27] As the original settlers left all the settlements, the factors were ordered to let their houses to the country people.

By the time Wight visited Strelitz, some of the inhabitants were unable to work, which was not surprising considering they had been there since 1763, and had been in the army before that. Others, he thought, were unwilling, but as a result they all had to hire labour, which kept their work behind as they had to wait until the labourers' own work was done. On the other hand, he gave a reasonably favourable description of the state of the village, especially of the nursery garden, which both Frend and he thought well-kept.[28] After the restoration of the estates to the heirs in 1784, Burrelton, a nearby village, grew and the name of Whiteley was apparently resumed locally,[29] though in the 1863 Ordnance Survey it is marked as Strelitz, and a farm of that name still exists.

According to Thomas Hunter, the soldiers here were notorious smugglers; and he also tells that they instituted an annual march to remind them of old campaigns, 'marching through the parish to the strains of martial music, the demonstrations generally ending in not a few bloody Fontenoys on a small scale'. This promenade gradually changed into a ploughman's festival and then merged into Burrelton Market and finally Burrelton Games. Unfortunately one's faith in this highly coloured story is somewhat lessened by his making the statement that the country people would not take the holdings the soldiers left, for Young seems to have had no difficulty in letting the houses, and Wight explicitly says that there were country people there in 1778. In 1810, soldiers were being moved off their holdings on the Perth estate and there was a certain amount of legal business, deciding whether the government could interfere between tenant and proprietor, or whether the soldiers did in fact have a right of tenure during their lifetime.[30] Tenacious as ever, some were still in possession in 1816. Eventually Strelitz was almost wholly hidden by plantations, the largest in the barony of Stobhall. Traces of Borelandbog, on the other hand, are very much in evidence. At least two of the soldiers' houses, extended and modernised, are inhabited, one very suitably by a noted Scottish historian. Another of the three left on the farm of Lower Borland stands in outline as it did in the mid-eighteenth century. In living memory, it was the home of farm workers and is now used by the local farmer for tools. And, while the upper part of Borland may have been badly laid out, the road through the sites of the lower rows of houses lies straight and not too narrow by the standards of the time, though the stoniness of the ground, complained of in 1763, is attested by its condition today. The fields behind the houses are also known by the names of some of their earlier cultivators.[31]

On Struan, there were three settlements, at Kinloch Rannoch, Georgetown, and Black Park. It will be remembered that Small, the Struan factor, refused to agree that he could find any land in 1763, but in 1764 he reported that the village was being built, as well as the bridge at Kinloch Rannoch.[32] Additional delay had arisen from the need to harvest the departing tenants' corn before beginning the new houses. Of the three, only Kinloch Rannoch has survived as a village. Black Park, by the burn Allt na Moire Buidhe, was shown as a few houses in the 1862 Ordnance Survey, and the foundations are still visible. Rannoch barracks occupied the site of Georgetown long before 1862.

Unless one accepts the title of New Tarbat, the areas chosen for colonies on the Cromartie estates were not given names. They figured only as 'stations' on the baronies of the estate. Like Benniebeg on Drummond Castle grounds, the houses built on the policies of New Tarbat house offended the eyes of the reinstated proprietor, and he seems to have begun to remove tenants from them immediately on his entry into his family estates. At New Tarbat in 1764 there had been thirty-two houses, and twelve spread around on Tullich and Kilmuir, the inhabitants including four weavers, two shoemakers and one tailor. On Strathpeffer, there were twenty-six King's Cottagers, four unmarried. These included two masons, one flax-dresser, three tailors, four weavers and two shoemakers. On the estate of Lovat, small numbers of soldiers were given holdings on various farms. In 1764, the factor could report that fifty-one soldiers and King's Cottagers had been provided for, including twenty on Barnyards, and ten on the Morass of Conon, which were the largest groups, with only two on Castle Downie, and one on Crochell, who happened to be a surveyor. None of these groups were apparently meant to develop into villages. In all, fifty-eight houses had been built, but two on Crochell were used as the school and schoolhouse, and two others had been given to a flax-dresser and a spinning mistress as the factor considered these necessary. The Lovat factor encountered a difficulty with settlers regarding their houses. These had been well enough built but, as the colonists thought the commissioners were to keep the houses in order, they were making no attempt to do so and some were even 'inclined to hurt them'. They had to be informed that the Board would spend no more on them.

While the trades practised by the soldiers make it obvious that the scheme had been effective to a degree in helping to bring craftsmen into the areas at the end of the Seven Years War, the origins of these men give rise to the suspicion that many might have found their way back in any case. The majority came from the northern counties of Scotland. On Lovat, two hailed from Fermanagh and one from Inniskillen; on Cromartie, there were a few 'foreigners', one from Armagh, one from Devon, another from Renfrew, but the greater number gave the place of their birth as Ross, Sutherland, Caithness and Inverness-shire.[33]

Like other landlords who built villages, the commissioners were anticipating economic growth, but initially on the annexed estates there was a drop in rental. The Struan rentals show a decrease of £16.14.11$\frac{8}{12}$ in Kinloch Rannoch until 1767, because the cottagers did not pay rent until Martinmas that year. The old rent had been £19.14.8$\frac{8}{12}$. In 1775, Georgetown had only eight cottagers, paying a total of £6, while in Wester Finart, in 1767 considered part of Georgetown, there were six tenants paying £20. By 1775, too, there were eleven crofters in Kinloch Rannoch, assessed at £24.18.0; rents were raised that year for improvements.[34]

In its conception, the plan of providing for disbanded soldiers and sailors, increasing the population of the Highlands and Islands, importing necessary trades, and building houses of a higher standard than was usual, all in one step, was a splendid one. In its implementation, little can be said in its favour. Haste was perhaps necessary at the end of the Seven Years War, but haste without accompanying caution and care led to the situation described. This was yet another occasion when the commissioners paid far too little attention to the full implications of their brainwaves, and certainly too little to the practical details of management. Equally, in this case, the Treasury could perhaps have exercised more control more profitably than on some other occasions, but no doubt, to the government, it must have seemed the ideal answer to the problem of what to do with the demobilised forces, trained in many cases only for fighting.

Though the commissioners fairly quickly gave up the idea of forming completely new towns, they continued the encouragement of settlement in towns that were already established, in Crieff and Callander particularly. When the Callander minister, Mr. Robertson, wrote about Perthshire agriculture, he remarked that several people could at that time, 1794, remember the town when it contained four families. The attainted Earl of Perth had begun to enlarge it and the commissioners continued his work, both by helping to establish small factories in the town, by obtaining an allowance of £200 to place craftsmen in Callander and Crieff and, as we have seen, by placing soldiers there. This last step is in some quarters given the credit for starting Callander's prosperity.[35]

Crieff was even more important in the commissioners' eyes, and industry and craftsmen as well as the hotel trade were all assisted. In 1762, the inhabitants complained of loss of the droving trade and of the assistance the late owner of the Perth estate had been wont to give them, but the town was so well placed in an eighteenth-century context that it was bound to, and indeed did, begin to thrive again. In 1768, Mr. Swinton studied the feus granted by the Earl of Findlater and decided that the Board could use the same formula for feuing the land they owned in Crieff. It was believed that many people settled there because of the good reputation of the school. In 1771, the factor wrote that the increase in the size of Callander had increased the rents by £30 yearly in rent and feu duties, which no doubt pleased the Board, but the local heritors in Crieff viewed increased number of feus there with mixed feelings. By 1775, the factor wrote that the number of poor in the parish had multiplied by so much that an assessment had had to be made, something that most parishes considered a step to be avoided. The tax was not large, at 5/6 in £100 rent, but in 1776 it was pointed out that, as the Board for the Annexed Estates had been responsible for bringing such large numbers into Crieff, it was to be hoped that they would help care for the poor. The new houses built were so much better than most Highland dwellings that in almost all of them rooms were let, one to a whole family. As the work these incomers were looking for was not always available, they became dependent on poor relief from the parish.[36]

Despite the help that the Board could bring to each of these towns, neither could claim the quick success of Grantown-on-Spey, where building only began in 1765. By 1780 it was said to be in a 'very thriving condition'.[37] Certainly Grantown could alone attract much of the local business of Badenoch, Rothiemurchus, Strathaven and Glenlivet, in a way neither Crieff nor Callander could perhaps manage. Also, Grantown was the brainchild of one proprietor, while the lack of a resident landlord in the Perthshire towns may have been a disadvantage. Among the soldiers' settlements, too, the comparative success of Strelitz, under the watchful eye of George Young, provides some evidence of the benefits of that particular oversight which the factors were unable, or perhaps unwilling, to provide.

Moved as ever by contemporary trends, the commissioners, towards the end of the annexation but too late for any positive steps to be taken under their creaking administration, glanced at the possibility of a spa. The mineral well at Strathpeffer had attracted favourable attention, as the doctor at New Tarbat, Dr. Alex. McKenzie, had reported to the Royal Society that it was equal to that at 'Harrowgate'. According to him, it created an appetite and helped the digestion. John Baxter the architect was sent to have a look at it but, despite the factor's suggestion that some of the Board members should come up to experience its benefits themselves and the further pleasures of good hunting,[38] nothing more came of the suggestion under the commissioners' aegis. One cannot help feeling that this was just as well for Strathpeffer.

It will be remembered that, in the parliamentary debates on the annexation, the foundation of coastal villages as well as inland towns was contemplated. The Lord Chancellor, too, suggested that fisheries established on the west coast would bring economic benefits to the whole country and, further, would help provide skilled manpower for the navy. In 1763, it was a superfluity of manpower from the navy that posed problems, but the principle of encouraging the fishing industry was the same. Concurrently with their plans to settle demobilised soldiers, therefore, the commissioners decided to cope with three national problems at one blow, in a similar fashion.[39] They thought that fishermen who had been pressed into the navy had been greatly missed in several ways. Firstly, their landlords lost their share of the catch; secondly, neighbouring inhabitants had been deprived of fish in their diet; thirdly, there had been general national loss as there had been no surplus of fresh and dried cod, which had previously been exported. It was declared, on no apparent concrete statistical grounds, that 1,000 men were required to replace them, and the Board proposed that 500 discharged sailors should be encouraged to settle as fishermen on the annexed estates, and another 500 would be given support on those of other proprietors.

An expensive and rather grandiose plan was put to the Crown for approval, by which 124 boats were to be provided at £15 each, half on the annexed estates, half on those of private landlords, where houses were to be built, or at least made available at a rental of £1 per annum, to be paid by the Board. It was assumed that not all the sailors would be married, and on that calculation only 375 houses were to be rented but each was to receive a bounty of £3. Once established, houses, gardens and boats were to be the responsibility of the tenants, and crews were expected to furnish sails, nets, oars and any other fishing tackle needed. The landlords' share was to be one-fifth of the fish caught, or the equivalent in money as rent or 'boat-dale'. On the annexed estates, the Board proposed to build fishing villages near the mouth of the Cromarty Firth on the estate of Cromartie, on Barrisdale, and on the side of Lochbroom, thereby accommodating yet another 500 men. The same number of boats and houses was reckoned necessary as on private estates, but the bounty was to be only £2.   The total cost was estimated at £6,610, and placed in conjunction with the Board's annual surplus of £4,500 in a good year, this might indicate a certain lack of realism among the commissioners. Admittedly, it was not the only one of their plans about which this accusation could be made but, in this case, they had some excuse, as the lack of expenditure on anything but fairly basic administration between 1755 and 1760 had left them a little in hand. Originally, too, they had some hope that private proprietors, who were to reap the benefit of the influx of fishermen, should provide the boats, and this would have cut down their capital outlay, but their final estimates included the price of all the boats required. At the end of three years the crews were to own the boats and to settle wherever they wished, while settlers on the annexed estates were to live in rent-free houses as long as they remained there. Difficulties immediately appeared in the spring of 1763 when the Lovat factor found that he could not procure boats for the sailors, but he was instructed to apply to the Banff boat-builders for such boats as were used on the Moray Firth or by Mr. Garden of Troup's crews.

The commissioners then went off on their usual summer adjournment, leaving the secretary to face what must have been in many respects for him a nightmare summer. Like the soldiers, the sailors appeared in considerable numbers at the Edinburgh office, where Mr. Barclay had to do something about them. The first group who applied were easy to deal with. Eleven Orcadians, fishermen bred, claimed the bounty, wanting to go home first, and then to settle near New Tarbat. There were neither houses, boats nor land ready, so Barclay gave them each £1 to travel home and then to New Tarbat by next Lammas. In fact, these men do not seem to have used the bounty in the way it was meant, as no natives of Orkney appear in the Cromartie factor's lists. Some other Orcadians also applied, but as they meant to live in Orkney they merely had their names recorded and were given instructions to apply for the bounty when they had settled. In an attempt to speed things up and at the same time to provide profitably for the sailors, he sent twenty-six more to New Tarbat, where as yet there had been no time to prepare for them, telling the factor to mark out the ground and then to set the sailors themselves to collecting material to build their houses, and also to throw up ditches round their portions of ground. They were to be paid the usual country rates, were to start collecting fuel for the winter and, whenever the houses were ready, the factor was to buy boats.

Fortunately it was realised that the idea of the Lochbroom settlement needed some further inquiries and Peter May, the surveyor, was sent there to make a proper survey. but, with an astonishing degree of insouciance, 117 sailors were sent off with a 'viaticum' and letter of introduction to some noblemen and gentlemen considered likely to welcome them, and to the magistrates of some seaside burghs, Campbeltown, Fort William, Aberdeen, Peterhead, Stonehaven and Montrose, and to those of the northern counties, Caithness, Orkney, Shetland and Cromarty. Two snags arose. Firstly, it was soon found that many of the sailors had never gone to the places assigned to them. The secretary stopped handing out travelling expenses at the office. If the wandering mariners arrived, the letters they carried told the addresses – factor, heritor or magistrates – how much to give them, promising repayment by the commissioners. Secondly, the secretary reported, in what would seem a slight understatement, that it had been found inconvenient to send off sailors, without the heritors having made any previous application for them, and he began to advertise for offers from landowners in the 'disarmed counties'. Some sailors who were already settled had applied, with certificates from 'Reputable persons', who asked the Board to forward the bounty.

The question of recommendations was one that also caused the secretary some worry. Sailors, unlike soldiers, did not get official discharges and none brought any references. He obviously felt the best thing was to get rid of them at once, but several never set off and others, who did reach their destination, refused to become fishermen. Another complication arose in Campbeltown where the boats went out only twice a year, in the spring for cod and in September for herring; the sailors had missed their opportunity there for immediate employment. Some of the group who arrived there must have been genuinely seeking work, for they travelled back to Edinburgh specially to report this, and those willing were sent to Lewis where Dr. John McKenzie had given houses and tackle for three boats. Because of his generosity the same bounty was allowed as on the annexed estates. Unfortunately, these models of virtue did not maintain such commendable behaviour, for, in January, 1765, Dr. McKenzie wrote asking for money to replace one of the boats which he had originally provided. The crew had deserted in the summer before, taking the boat with them. Earlier reports varied in their verdicts, a Mr. Silver being tolerably satisfied with the seven sailors and a marine whom he had settled at Johnshaven and provided with hired boats, clothing and lodgings. Lord Fyfe on the other hand wrote in some disgruntlement that he had given three sailors a guinea each to bring their families to settle but only one returned. Having built boats in expectation of being supplied by men from the Board, he was left with only one possible crew member. He had to be repaid by the Lovat factor.

The picture emerging was not a cheerful one and, by 1764, the commissioners had to admit, contrary to their views on the soldiers' settlements, that the scheme was not succeeding. They had to report that 154 of the 205 who accepted the bounty had deserted. Travelling charges had amounted to £124.14.2, house and boat-building to £429.19.7 $\frac{3}{12}$, with the bounty, the total was £758.13.9 $\frac{3}{12}$. Many sailors had applied, not realising that they must confine themselves to being fishermen, and withdrew their applications when the conditions were explained to them. However, the Board persisted with the scheme in outline. In 1764, they had expressed a hope that they might still establish fisheries for either discharged sailors or natives of the annexed estates, at Lochbroom near the Cromartie estates, or at Inverie on the estate of Barrisdale, and had suggested that £1,000 be allocated for this purpose. In 1765, they paid out bounty money to eighty-eight sailors settled on the coasts of the Highlands and paid their house rents for a year. They also paid £27 in bounty money on Barrisdale, built houses there, and provided three boats and tackle worth £60.10.0, a total for the year of £264.10.0.[40] Originally, tackle had been intended to be the crew's responsibility, but, by August, 1763, the factor on Lovat, Captain Forbes, had written that the sailors demanded nets before they could make a living. A week later, the Board accepted this, allowing £5 – £6 for nets, similar to those used in the Moray Firth, and for bladders and ropes.

Assistance to the fishing industry did not end with the failure of the original plans for settling sailors. Many of the optimistic economic theorists of the time considered the underdevelopment of the fishing industry by those living in or near the coasts in the north and west most reprehensible. Further, such neglect was totally incomprehensible, for it was considered that the potential food supply should have been an irresistible attraction to a population existing at subsistence level. It was beyond the understanding of writers and travellers like James Wilson that the people in most parts of Scotland would fish 'only on compulsion' whereas, by regular exploitation of the sea's harvest, they could 'add most materially to the comfort of their family'. What Wilson and many of his contemporaries did not see on a superficial survey of the situation, but what modern historians have illustrated only too well, was that the capital outlay on efficient equipment was beyond the means of most aspiring fishermen, while loans made from whatever source gave rise to interest charges that absorbed any financial gains. This was especially so where the landlord was the lender and had also a legal right to a sizeable share of the proceeds. Land in Shetland was let on condition that fish be delivered to the proprietor in exchange for goods at set prices.[41] Something else that received no sympathy at all, and was not wholly understood, was the innate distrust of the sea displayed by the landsmen, added to unfamiliarity with the skills needed for successful fishing on a commercial basis in deeper waters.

The sin of lack of comprehension cannot of course be laid at all doors, and can certainly not be attributed to the factors on the coastal estates. The writer of *The Highlands in 1750* pointed out that the country people had neither the ability nor the skill to fit out proper vessels to catch the plentiful herring in Loch Broom, while the gentlemen did not concern themselves with the trade. It is interesting to note in light of their energy in road-building activities, some of which we shall look at later, that the gentlemen of Argyllshire were among the few who had made quite a profit out of fishing in the year he was writing.[42] This was a harbinger of things to come when several of the landed gentry in the Highlands asked for assistance from the funds of the annexed estates to forward their fishery schemes. Pennant was another who realised the potentialities of fishing cod and ling near Canna, but he also understood that the inhabitants were too poor to be able to take full advantage of this wealth.[43]

Ninian Jeffrey and Henry Butter, both factors on remote estates with seacoasts, Coigach and Barrisdale, realised the need for capital expenditure, if the inhabitants' poverty was not to be an unconquerable obstacle. Jeffrey, when asked to prepare a plan for organising the fishing in his area, emphasised that experienced fishermen would be essential immigrants if any fishing was to succeed, as the natives were not used to such activity on a commercial scale. He had noted, in 1766, when there had been some herring shoals nearby, that ships subsidised by the bounty had caught fish when the local boats did not. His enquiries as to the reason for this had elicited the answer that the latter used inferior nets with too few ropes, and he suggested that the Board could help by supplying better nets. A few years later, in 1772, nothing had been done and, as a result, though the fishing generally had been good, the Coigach people had been unable to take any advantage because the shoals had not come north of Gairloch, and their equipment was only of use locally. He pointed out that fishing in Coigach must always be 'a precarious rent' as long as it depended on so many poor people unable to afford the better gear, which in the long run was so much more profitable. He and Butter, separately, also proposed schemes by which the Board could usefully give assistance in overcoming yet another impediment to profitable fishing in remote areas. This was the lack of a convenient supply of salt for the curing of the fish, and barrels for storage and transport. Jeffrey suggested that a storehouse should be provided and a cooper's business subsidised at a cost of about £500, while Butter, who must also be given credit for the idea of settling fishermen at Inverie, thought a cooper should be employed. In addition the latter was prepared to purchase salt and casks to deposit at suitable centres along the coast, where he would sell them to the local fishermen at cost price.[44]

As the commissioners had been receiving applications for similar help from several gentlemen with estates on the west coast, such as John Stewart of Fasnacloich, Daniel Campbell of Shawfield, and Donald Campbell of Mingary, they were disposed to listen to the factors, particularly to such a notion as Butter's which promised some immediate return on their outlay, and he was given permission to spend £500, rather less than the sums of £700 and £1,000 he had wanted for Barrisdale alone. Unfortunately, as the herring with their usual fickleness did not appear in such profusion during the following seasons, Butter came to rue his earlier enthusiasm. In February, 1767, the minutes record his report that the herring fishery had disappointed everyone concerned and that the salt and casks would have to wait until the following year to be used. He had been provided with £648.11.8 of supplies, and in his accounts for 1768 showed he had sold only £104.18.1 worth. He had also discovered that managing debenture salt at a distance was no sinecure, and said quite bluntly that had he realised all the inconveniences he would not have been very willing to engage in the business. One of his suppliers who had sold him casks had to write to the Board for payment of over £300, a year after the goods had been provided. As he said, it was 'a great hardship for a person in trade to lye out of his money'. The remaining casks were to be sold by public roup to retain some of the capital.[45] As a result, this experiment was not repeated.

Various proposals thereafter reached the commissioners from would-be entrepreneurs, such as John Woodhouse, a Liverpool merchant who wanted to smoke herring 'in the Yarmouth way' on Island Martin. Colin Mackenzie, the kelp merchant in Lochbroom, asked for a lease of a Coigach farm where he could follow not only the fishing but the kelp, rope and net-making industries. However, there were only two more large grants towards the fishing. One was to Daniel Campbell of Shawfield who wanted to build a boat, costing £200, and quays in Islay, where what he described as the ignorance of the people, the rapidity of the tides, and inadequate vessels prevented any advantage being taken of the rich banks of fish near the island.[46] The other was the sum of £250 towards the exotic cairban fishing.

The cairban is the sailfish or the basking shark, which was hunted only for its liver oil. About six to eight barrels of a pure sweet oil could be extracted from each one caught and this was bought by the tanners for up to £3 a barrel. Inspector Menzies described the oil as being reckoned superior to any other for 'currying leather'; it was also approved of by clothiers and he thought something might be made of this type of catch. Many of these somewhat sluggish fish were to be seen between June and October, sometimes in pairs, sometimes in shoals, and he thought their slow speed ensured that they could be easily harpooned. The adventurer who eventually benefited from the Board's largesse was Donald M'Leod, a tacksman on Canna, whose name was brought before them by Dr. Walker.[47] M'Leod was too young to be able to afford a boat large enough to stand up to the strength of the cairban or to follow it far enough. A wherry of fifteen to twenty tons was needed. £250 was duly spent on the project, which does not seem to have brought long-lasting benefits to either M'Leod or to the country. He 'tryd the kerban', catching seven in 1767 and eight in 1768, but his letters show that he was not happy with the arrangement. He complained that the vessel given him was too unwieldy for either cairban or cod and, at the end of 1768, he wished he had never had any connection with cairban, 'at least in a public way'. On the other hand, Pennant thought that 'the person they (the commissioners) confided in shamefully abused their goodness' and, when he visited the area, only private adventurers were 'trying the kerban'. The Board too instructed their inspector to make sure the boat was being properly used. Whether cairban fishing is in fact very practical seems doubtful. M'Leod claimed that it could not succeed without subsidies, and at least one twentieth-century attempt was unprofitable, as Gavin Maxwell described.[48]

All things considered, it may plausibly be argued that the greatest contribution the commissioners made to the fishing industry in the west was an indirect one. Leasing land to the Liverpool merchant, Woodhouse, for a lengthy period provided a market for local catches, and the appointment, jointly with the Board of Trustees, of justiciary bailies to maintain order in the fishing season must have been a boon to the local inhabitants at least. The fishing fleet was not the most peaceful of groups and the need for some sort of policing was perennial. In 1755, orders were sent to Lord Beauclerk, the Commander-in-Chief in Scotland, to send a party to Lochbroom and Coigach to prevent 'the usual abuses committed by the herring fishers'. The mutual misunderstandings of the crofters and the fishermen are illustrated by the description of the inconveniences suffered by the farmers of Lee and Skiarree, the only safe harbour in Loch Hourn, where the herring fishermen cured and salted their fish on the verge of the grassland and also walked over the fields in bodies, thus spoiling the grass for the cattle. They also cut wood indiscriminately, but they were not alone in that. In 1756, the baron bailie of Coigach was appointed a sheriff substitute to try to control the 'many disorders' resulting from the numbers of boats and people in Lochbroom during the season, and this was an annual problem the inhabitants had to face. In 1773, Archibald MacDonnell asked for powers to supervise the area between Loch Broom and Mull, as this area was rather far from the nearest official in Stornoway and Lewis. He claimed that the greatest herring fishery was in this area and in 1779 his son Coll joined him as a justiciary bailie. The bailies' performance did not always satisfy the Board and, indeed, on occasion there were suggestions that their salaries should be withheld or cut, but their presence in the area must have provided a useful tangible proof of the existence of authority, and the information they sent was clearly of use; the Board of Trustees borrowed John McIver's report in 1764.[49]

One final point may be made that not everyone was enthusiastic about the results of a thriving fishing industry. One can understand the hostility roused among farmers by the sort of behaviour they faced in Skiarree; those who thought the hope of the Highlands was the introduction of manufacturing industry found much to complain about in the seasonal attractions of the fishing. Mr. Robertson, the minister of Lochbroom, wrote to Captain Forbes protesting that industry would never thrive as long as a man and maidservant could be released from service to go to the fishing, 'he to fish and she to gut'. No servants could be got to work for any hire, 'no not a herd or little girl', because of this practice. He foretold the impoverishment of the tenants and the loss of cattle through lack of labour. Worse in his eyes, perhaps, when the fishing ended, the potential servant had become accustomed to drinking and idleness and, when the herring forsook the loch, they became beggars. Robertson, however, was swimming against a tide which was to flow strongly until the early twentieth century and which, it may be, brought more capital and comfort to the west than any of the abortive industrial schemes dreamed up by the eighteenth-century entrepreneurs.

It is unlikely that the members of the Board, any more than later landowners who transported their tenants to the coasts, had any idea of the magnitude of the financial and educational programme that would have been needed to produce, from a race imbued with attachment to the land, a community that was prepared to settle for a house and garden in a fishing town. Coming events cast their shadows before, however, in Jeffrey's plans for cod, ling and herring fisheries at Coigach; he proposed that families with too small farms, whom he castigated as 'just a nuisance upon every Highland estate' because they could not support their families, should be employed by the Board at 5/- to 20/- a year, provided with boat and tackle free, and lodged in a fishing town. This was the classic clearance programme, one the Board could not adopt, not on any moral or emotional grounds, but because of financial stringency. They would probably have considered the financial benefits expected to accrue to the tenants apology enough, and consistent with the philosophy of the annexation. But even had they been inclined to follow such a plan in its entirety, it is unlikely that government consent would have been won so soon after the fiasco of their recent foray into a similar field, the settlements for discharged soldiers and sailors.

COMMUNICATIONS

9
Road Building

ONE important area of Highland life in which the Board played an active part remains to be considered. This is the contribution made from annexed estates funds to the development of access to, and of communications within, the Highlands and Islands area. One's view of such developments are rarely objective, and the extremes that can be expressed are well illustrated, on one side by the dictum of A. J. Byrne that 'if they have no roads, they are savages',[1] and on the other by the sturdy refusal of Alexander Robertson of Struan to encourage the building of roads on his estate, on the grounds that lack of them had never yet prevented his friends from visiting him, and he saw no point in encouraging his enemies. In between, there is room for the idea that poor roads may merely indicate self-sufficiency in the local population or that roads encourage effeminacy. Eighteenth-century government attitudes towards Highland road- and bridge-building inclined towards the first of these extremes, and indeed General Wade is reputed to have carried on his building and labouring in the belief that civilisation went along roads and bridges. Wade was sent north in 1724 after George I had received Lord Lovat's memorial on the state of the Highlands, and by the end of the year, after describing the conditions he found, he went on to assert that the Highlands were 'still more impracticable for the want of roads and bridges'.[2] J.B. Salmond claims that this is the first mention of the question of Highland roads and bridges; it was not to be the last. On Wade's becoming Commander-in-Chief, he asked for supplies among other things for mending the roads between garrisons and barracks and, since that date, Highland communications may have been neglected or ill-planned for practical purposes but, from 1724 to the present day, they have rarely been ignored.

For the convenience both of local inhabitants and would-be visitors, either tourists or traders, it is difficult to counter the argument that too little has been achieved. The main traffic arteries exist, but they are not always flexible enough to cope with changing traffic demands, while cross-roads and side-roads, which might have been expected in more populated, more growth-oriented areas, have either not appeared or have not been developed. The route for example from Callander to Comrie, by the water of Keltie over the hills to the Water of Ruchill and down Glenartney, traversed an area which was then sufficiently populated for the Board of Commissoners for the Annexed Estates to consider it important to ease communications by building bridges at various points.[3] Now it serves a few farms only and has no through route for the ubiquitous combustion engine. In the middle of the twentieth century, there were still mainland communities, such as Applecross in Ross-shire, without any road access except for travellers by foot, horse or bicycle, and dependent on the sea for carriage of all goods they could not produce themselves, for medicine, and for burials.[4]

It cannot be said that the area has been completely overlooked, for there is a continuous, if not consistent, thread of attention to the problem running through two hundred and fifty years. First there was Wade, building military roads, then the Parliamentary roads, the British Fisheries Society, the Caledonian Canal Commission, Destitution Roads, Commissioners of Supply, the County Councils and, today, the Highlands and Islands Development Board, who must take the question of access into their calculations. It can unfortunately be pointed out that not all the efforts made by these bodies were well-directed from the point of view of Highland society and Highland economy. The military roads were an honest straightforward approach to a military problem, as it was then seen. Edward I may have carried out a punitive expeditition over an astonishing area of Scotland in a very short time,[5] but the army of the government in 1715 had discovered that Highland terrain was not suitable for speedy movement by troops in modern dress and equipment. The government's attempts to provide against such an eventuality in the future turned out to be useless, or at best not tailor-made, for commerce, and worse, in the 1745 rebellion, these military roads were more useful to the Pretender than to the Hanoverian troops. Obvious deficiencies such as lack of bridges over the Esk at Montrose hindered the government but not the rebellious guerilla-type forces.

Too little, too late, and in the wrong place, is not too unfair a description of government forays into communications in the north, whether directly or by official agencies, the building of the Caledonian Canal being the prime example of expenditure that was overtaken by unseen future development in the size and style of transport. Like so many aspects of Scottish life, roads had not been neglected by the legislature before the eighteenth century, but effecting what was intended was a different matter from passing a law, and while the Justices of the Peace had been given power to mend highways from market towns and sea ports in 1617 and, in 1669, to exact, in conjunction with the sheriff, six days' labour on the roads each year for man and horse, from tenants, cottars, and their servants, for three years, and four days annually thereafter,[6] the results obtained by these measures did not impress travellers throughout the eighteenth century. While soldiers were probably among the earliest to appreciate the practical need for roads, by the middle of the century the improvers like Grant of Monymusk were expressing some surprise at the long neglect. Grant's particular plea in 1754 was for roads for wheeled carriages and carts to save the husbandman's time, and his notion that time and carriage would be lessened by better roads is amply borne out by the information given to the poet, Southey, during his tour of Scotland in the early nineteenth century. The postmaster at Dalmally assured him that carts that could formerly carry only nine cubic feet of timber, on improved roads took twenty-one.[7]

In the somewhat doleful catalogue of road and bridge builders sponsored by the government, however, as opposed to the energetic action of landowners like the Marquis of Breadalbane, who is reputed to have built fifty bridges on his own estate,[8] the Commissioners for the Annexed Estates were among the least negligent, having done all and more than might have been expected of them with their limited resources. They were very ready to accept and act on the thesis expressed by Sir Alexander Mackenzie of Coul that 'the key to all improvements in the Highlands' was to make them accessible. Among their first queries to the factors concerning conditions on the estates were requests for information about the state of the roads and bridges, showing that the state of communications was an early matter of concern. Inquiries were also made about the number of changehouses and inns, an essential part of the communication system in the days of slower travelling, though in the context of the queries, this question was connected with the consumption of alcohol, for the number of stills and maltmakers was also wanted.

The factors' answers provided information about local needs as the factors saw them, but also the position of the individual baronies – estates were described barony by barony even in this respect – with reference to such main arteries as were then in existence.[9] The picture that emerged from the 1755 reports showed how far the military roads had affected communications in Scotland, and how well placed some of the annexed estates were in connection with these. The king's highway from Stirling to Inverness ran through Muthill parish where part of the estate of Perth lay; the Stirling-Fort William road served a large part of the western part of the same estate from Callander to just short of Killin, and also passed through Strathyre, the part of Arnprior not claimed by a subject superior. Further north, as far as Inverness, the Fort Augustus-Inverness road ran through the barony of Stratherrick, part of the Lovat estate. Monaltrie in Crathie parish held a strategic position at a Dee ferry, about halfway between Perth and Inverness, where the country road from Aberdeen met the king's road. It is just conceivable that such a favourable site had had some influence on the choice of Monaltrie for annexation, but no special instructions seem to have been issued to the commissioners on that account.

However, the king's highway stopped on the west at Fort William and on the north at Inverness, and outside these limits roads and bridges, if they ever existed, usually deteriorated rapidly where they did not actually disappear. In the estate of Barrisdale there were no roads of access at all; even at the end of the next decade the General Inspector had to hire a herring buss, the *Woodhall*, to get there. The factor in 1755 thought the commonalty were honest, but their isolation helped keep them poor, idle and superstitious. Conditions tended to deteriorate generally from east to west and from south to north, even in the same barony in the same estates. Campbell of Barcaldine, the Perth factor, could declare that in the barony of Auchterarder, almost diametrically opposite Barrisdale, the people were peaceable and honest, there were no bridges needed and the roads providing access were tolerably good. The factor on Lovat and Cromartie on the other hand provided answers that illustrated very clearly the lack of uniformity within estates and the tendency to north-west deterioration. The baronies of Beauly and Lovat were both better served to the east than to the west, Beauly having no public roads, but still tolerable 'ways' in the east part, while communication to the west with Glenstrathfarrar was very difficult. Lovat had 'tollerably good' roads between Inverness and Castle Downie for eight miles, but to the west the roads were extremely bad. Coigach he simply wrote off as having among the worst roads in the Highlands, mountainous, rocky and full of stones, with no bridges over the rivers, so that 'nothing but necessity makes strangers resort here and for a great part of the year it is almost inaccessible'. The area round New Tarbat house had very good roads and easy communications with Tain and other public places, while a few miles further west in Strathpeffer, there were very bad roads which were never repaired, with no bridges. Always excepting the fastness of Struan, however, it is a fairly safe generalisation to state that not only were the 'publick roads' or the 'king's highway' at a more developed stage in the south; so were private and public interest and activity in the building of roads and improvement of communications generally.

The inhabitants of Balquhidder were sufficiently interested in the convenience they presumably felt they gained from the Stirling-Fort William road's passage through the east end of their barony to try to bridge the deep ditch or gott that lay between their land and the road. This ditch and the morass on each side of it, which they attempted to solidify by filling in with stones, had been a considerable obstacle in wet weather. Their bridge was castigated as a very bad one, but at least they showed some initiative. So did the tenants of the estate of Perth in the barony of Kinbuck who, with their neighbours, had built a bridge over the river Allan at Kinbuck, in 1753, at their own expense, borrowing £25 to complete it. Roads in that area from Dunblane over towards Strathearn were all reasonable, even the cross-roads being described as tolerable. The Commissioners of Supply were also taking some action, in Perthshire at least, for the road on Lochearnside which, according to Barcaldine, had previously been so extremely bad as to be almost impassable, had been repaired by parish work from Balquhidder and Comrie, i.e. statute labour, and was now good enough for carriage traffic. The road was apparently neither complete nor particularly well made for, in 1765, the factor produced an estimate of £210 which was needed over and above the statute work to improve a length of it at the west end of Loch Earn, west of the wood of Ardvaich. This expenditure was approved on the grounds that the road opened up communication between the Lowland parts of Perthshire and the west Highlands.

Another line of new road, a comparatively large scheme, had been decided on by Colonel Watson, the military Supervisor of Roads in Scotland, who was also one of the original commissioners. After what James Small called 'a view of Rannoch', Watson had decided that more necessary than any other was a cross-country line from the Stirling to Fort-William road through Glenorchy, Rannoch, along the Tummel, crossing the Perth-Inverness highway, then over the hills of Stormont to the Perth-Braemar road by Glen Brerachan and thence down the Ardle valley to Alyth. This road was to open Rannoch both to trade and the civilisation to be gained from the marching of troops through the country. Watson apparently envisaged opening up an east-west highway from the sea, Alyth giving access to Strathmore, whence goods could reach Montrose. He had used his military manpower – a sergeant and twelve men – to encourage the locals, with some effect, for the six miles between Tummel Bridge and Kinloch Rannoch had been made, and work was now continuing along the south side of the loch, the king's side, Slisgarrow. East of Tummel Bridge, local labour was being applied, and it was expected that in three years this would reach Alyth. The making of such a road answered every demand of the annexation; it opened the country that had been a centre for thieves and stolen cattle, so helping prevent such misdemeanours, and also made the entrance of such civilised activities as manufactures easier and hence more likely, as well as increasing the possibilities of social intercourse with the Lowlands. As a result the commissioners gladly spent money on it each year, beginning with £65.7.3½ in 1755, even before the central government began to take an interest in their proceedings.[10]

The high road through Rannoch on the south side of the loch lay almost entirely in the estate of Struan, the area called Slisgarrow, twenty-four miles long and six miles broad; therefore any statute labour required was likely to be demanded from Struan tenants. As the road was only part of a larger scheme, the Board told Small to apply to the Justices of the Peace and Commissioners of Supply in May of 1756 for assistance in repairing the roads leading to and from and through Rannoch. Thereafter such aid and authorisation was forthcoming each year, though the Commissioners for the Annexed Estates provided tools and had them repaired, and the labour usually included a sergeant and twelve men. By 1758, the road was sixteen miles long but still needed three miles to Innercomrie where there was an army headquarters. The presence of the barracks there no doubt helped persuade the Commander-in -Chief to hire out men on this particular stretch of road, though in 1757 Lord George Beauclerk deferred permission until after the reviews, and in 1758 the order had come too late to be of any use. Small had found soldiers very useful both in directing and instructing the natives of the area and, indeed, he went so far as to say that, without them, the road could not be carried on. In 1757, he had been prepared to put up with an overseer if no military men were available, but overseers were expensive. In 1770, an overseer in Struan was paid £5.7.1 out of the total of £8.2.1 for road works and, in any case, gangs of soldiers, used to the work, were much more efficient than local labour.[11]

Tools too were an expense that had to be borne by the commissioners as the country people had nothing suitable. In 1756, the factor had had to pay £2.1.0 for spades and shovels, £1.5.8 $\frac{7}{12}$ for twelve pickaxes, 10/- to a wright for making shafts for picks and hammers, £2.2.10 to a smith at Kinloch Rannoch for making and mending tools, and 7/- for the carriage of wheelbarrows and pickaxes from the army stores at Blairgowrie. Though buying secondhand from the army was initially cheaper, it was not always an unmixed blessing, for replacements were needed more often.[12] The Justices of the Peace and the Commissioners of Supply could direct statute labour to certain undertakings, but the tools were not their concern. When the minister at Lochbroom had persuaded the Board to ask for statute labour for making a road to a limestone quarry, the factor had to be allowed £20 for tools and for paying an overseer. The commissioners were perhaps sometimes unrealistic about such matters as the reactions of the inhabitants, over whose lives they had so much control. In Barrisdale, the committee discussing the road funds proposed that the factor should buy tools and sell them to the tenants at prime cost, at the same time binding them to keep the tools in good order. Fortunately the Barrisdale factor must have been in Edinburgh at the time, and three days later that plan was scotched, on his pointing out that the people in Barrisdale thought it a grievance to be obliged to work on the roads at all; it was not to be expected that they could be brought to pay for the tools.[13]

As far as the Rannoch road was concerned, however, despite the fairly speedy and promising start on the route from Alyth to Glen Orchy, Watson's design was never finished, for the last nine miles from Rannoch to the head of Glen Orchy are still unmade. In 1755, the factor described this as mostly moss, not fit for horses. By the time the estates were returned to the old families in 1784, military interest in Highland roads was decreasing and there was insufficient demand from any other pressure lobby to complete this line. 1894 saw the opening of the railway line from Helensburgh to Fort William by Rannoch Moor, so the B846 makes its way west from the head of Loch Rannoch to Rannoch station and stops there. The traveller wanting to cross that piece of ground by any other means than on foot has to go by rail. The road from Kinloch Rannoch, however, along the south side of the loch through the Struan estate, passing the factor's farm at Carie, to the west end of the loch, engaged funds each year until 1784.[14]

One major project in road-making directly affected the annexed estates. Captain Forbes, the Lovat and Cromartie factor, suggested that one of the great contributions that could be made towards the 'civilising' of Coigach in Lochbroom parish was to have the road from Dingwall to Lochbroom made up for, without this, overland trade between the east and west coasts was impracticable. This line had already been surveyed on behalf of an official body, the Board of Trustees. Their surveyor, John Neilson, had pointed out that the expense of making such a road suitable for wheeled carriages was so great that it could not possibly be defrayed by the usual county methods.[15] Though there was a rocky foundation, statute labour would have been of little use, as eighteen of the twenty-four miles planned ran through uninhabited country. In 1757, the local heritors, led by Sir Alexander Mackenzie of Coul, approached the Board with suggestions as to how this problem could be overcome, but they received little encouragement other than the promise of a review of the situation if, after application to the Quarter Sessions, there was still a deficiency. The following year, after Mackenzie and another proprietor, Kenneth Mackenzie of Dundonnel, had reported on the results of that type of action, they were asked to provide estimates, which were to include a suggestion as to what proportion of the expenses they expected the Board to pay. This estimate lay before the Board in December of that year and contained the public-spirited offer by the Mackenzies that, if the Board would pay three-quarters, they would pay the rest of the total of £500 for a twelve-foot wide road of 48,000 yards, the cost including tools, a 'consideration' for an overseer, and necessary bridges, not always an integral part of road-planning. The normal division of costs would have been three-fifths by the proprietor of the Cromartie estate, one-fifth divided between the memorialists and the remaining fifth by the other heritors but, as this suggestion was made to avoid 'fractions and subdivisions', one is led to speculate that the Mackenzies may have been the only road-building

M

enthusiasts in the Lochbroom area.[16]

In the years before 1760, consideration of even such a generous offer had to be delayed, and it was 1763 before Sir Alexander reopened the subject. On this later occasion, he succeeded in obtaining assistance, and not only because of his economic argument that the combination of safe bays and harbours in West Ross-shire and a plentiful supply of herring and cod could be exploited fully only if there was access by a highway from Dingwall to Lochbroom. By then, he could also point to improvements made at each end of the proposed road by the local heritors while the Board was freed from the fetters of government inactivity. As a result, Mackenzie was asked if he would undertake to build the centre mileage, 'a desert with a steep at each end', which had defied improvements by local resources alone, on account of the lack of inhabitants. His figure of £5 per mile to make it 'rideable' was accepted and the Board proposed that in addition he should make three miles fit for wheeled traffic. Though the Lochbroom heritors spent £200 on the road, it was still unfinished two years later, and there was some unwillingness to give supplementary aid. However, the committee which dealt with roads stressed that there was none of more consequence and the factor on Lovat and Cromartie was authorised, in 1767, to buy tools, pay an overseer, and direct statute labour to the road. The Board were also persuaded to ask the Commander-in-Chief in Scotland for the help of a sergeant and twelve men used to road work to labour alongside the country people.[17]

It was not only the local terrain, the weather, and the lack of a convenient labour supply that handicapped road-making in such an area. The tools used by the local inhabitants were so poor that a supply had to be shipped to Coigach, thus adding considerably to the overall cost. In 1768 alone, the bill for tools and carriage of these tools was £25.12.9$\frac{1}{2}$ which, compared with 19/4$\frac{6}{12}$ d in the Struan accounts for the same item, illustrates only too well the difficulties faced in the north.[18] It is likely that without the existence of the Board for the Annexed Estates this particular stretch of road would have waited longer than it did to be made, for it is clear from correspondence that the heritors started the project in hopes of a contribution from the crown estates, in an underpopulated area where statute labour as a result was impracticable, while the presence of annexed lands at each end of the projected line made government help a reasonable expectation.

The roads in Caithness were also much needed, and John Knox later found nothing there that he was prepared to describe as a road on his tour. As A.R.B. Haldane points out, though the records are scanty, it is certain that almost all com-munication in the second half of the eighteenth century was primitive and inade-quate. Even after the initial making of the road, usually inefficient, the upkeep was a drag on resources that nobody at the time possessed. The road from Contin to Lochbroom, that the Board for the Annexed Estates had so highly approved and whose completion Sir Alexander Mackenzie of Coul had so actively pursued, had apparently disappeared by the time the British Fisheries Society began to establish Ullapool, for they decided to undertake the construction, not the repair, of a road from Contin to Ullapool. Seduced by urgent need for transport and employment in the area, and bullied by the government into accepting a cheap estimate, their road was finished in 1797 for £4,582 instead of £8,000 which an earlier surveyor had considered necessary. Economy in making any road tends to be false saving, nowhere perhaps more than in the Highlands, and twelve years later this stretch of road had to be remade once again by the Commission for Highland Roads and Bridges.[19]

Roads tend to beget roads for, once their convenience has been experienced, those in less-endowed areas begin to feel their own needs. The Dingwall-Lochbroom highway was soon followed by the logical continuation further north, the road from Ullapool to the Dornoch Firth through Glen 'Achell' – Oykell. The inhabitants of Easter Ross had made two miles of this before the Board was approached in 1768, and the Inspector, Archibald Menzies, was directed to consult Captain Ross of Balnagowan about the tools needed for continuing it for nine miles through the glen. Menzies saw Ross, who thought that an overseer would be needed and of course tools, for which Captain Ross was prepared to take the responsibility in case they were 'embezzled', returning them when the road was made. He had also applied to the county to be allowed to use all his tenants' statute labour on this road. The commissioners paid David Aitkin £13.13.2 to measure, survey and mark out the line of road, and also provided the overseer's wage of £3 per annum for three years from 1770, when Captain Ross claimed that one was necessary to speed the work and to be sure it was properly executed.[20]

It does not appear that the commissioners initially envisaged their duties as involving them in large-scale subsidisation of road-making. The factors were usually instructed to ask for county aid, and the Board were willing to pay for tools beyond the normal expense they would have incurred as heritors. But it was a prime interest, nevertheless. In 1763, Small reported that all extra money, 'overplus' as he called it, from the baron bailie court went on roads or similar projects. In Barrisdale, where it will be remembered that road access was lacking, by 1762 the factor had the Knoydart tenants at work on opening a road, which he represented as the shortest from the south through Lochaber to Skye and the Western Isles. This was not an easy task, for there were not many inhabitants, and the farms were scattered and at some distance from the roads wanted. In addition they had no tools so that progress had been slow. The commissioners had no hesitation in authorising him to buy tools, to employ a sergeant and twelve men and, in addition, a skilful man to direct the making of the said roads. The Commissioners of Supply had authorised this line along the north side of Loch Arkaig, through Glen Dessary to Inverie, where a bridge cost £89.4.0 in 1763. There was also a ready response to Inverness-shire requirements, over and above what could be provided by statute labour. To improve a difficult part of the main road from Inverness to the ferry at Beauly, the Commissioners of Supply had assessed the county at 10d in the £100 Scots of valued rent, but this had produced only £30, and a further £25 was necessary. On the factor's representing just how bad this particular stretch of road was and how many complaints travellers made about it, he was instructed to supply the extra £25 – but no more – once the sum raised by assessment was exhausted.

In Perthshire, the whole road system was somewhat more sophisticated than that existing further north. The main arteries leading from the south were made before 1745; and, as we have seen, some cross-roads aimed at joining these were either planned or already improved. Individual landowners were also more active; Lord Breadalbane for example had made the whole road along the north side of Loch Tay, including thirty-two bridges.[21] Later there seemed to be a change, and the Perthshire heritors would not accept assistance from the Commission for Highland Roads and Bridges, with the result that Southey describes an incident when a traveller's carriage came on what he called a 'devil's bowling green', but the driver was quite unconcerned and merely remarked 'Perthshire! We're in Perthshire, Sir'.[22] What the commissioners found themselves mainly concerned with in their Perthshire estates was improving or building lines of road that would benefit their own lands primarily. As well as aiming at such improvements in communications as would, for instance, allow timber to be transported more easily, or in opening access to lime quarries and kilns, which would enhance the value of their properties, they also did take steps to make life materially more comfortable for their tenants by improving roads and building bridges between the estates and main thoroughfares, as well as churches, schools and towns. Though undoubtedly beneficial, this policy was only partly altruistic, for better communications facilitated the inflow of Lowland habits and ideas into the Highlands, and that was one of the fundamental aims of the annexation.

One stretch of road, the improvement of which could be represented as fulfilling all these needs, was that west from Callander along Loch Venacher, through Strathgartney. This road would open up the Trossachs, which in 1755 had been almost inaccessible and a barrier to the upper part of the barony of Strathgartney, which could be reached only by boat over Loch Katrine. And the Strathgartney woods could be expected to become even more valuable than they already were. By 1763, six miles of good road had been built under Campbell of Barcaldine's supervision, by means of statute labour and a £20 subsidy from the Board. This work, incidentally, provided another example of Barcaldine's inefficient book-keeping and gave the Board some grounds for wondering about his integrity, as he could produce no vouchers, and the overseer employed by him was able to sustain his claim that he had been paid no wages between 1754 and 1760. The road went on, however, but only as far as the Trossachs, until the Inspector saw the possibilities of using gunpowder at a place called the Ladders, to blast away the rockface and provide a better base for a roadway, at the cost he thought of £40-£50. He was very critical of the layout of parts of the road, particularly at the Bridge of Turk. The commissioners looked even further and envisaged a continuation of the road to the barracks at Inversnaid.[23]

By 1770, Small was able to write enthusiastically of what had been achieved between Callander and Loch Katrine.[24] Horses could ride the whole road by that time and he expected that carts would be able to follow suit by the following year. At one point, the road level along the side of the loch had been raised by five to ten feet, and about a quarter of a mile had been cut out of whin rock which had been ten to twenty feet high. Giving full credit to the Inspector and the overseer, James Stewart in Edralednoch, Small remarked, with perhaps justifiable pride, that 'there was never a road of the kind undertaken in Scotland by a subject or by statute work' before this. The whole had cost £60, more than the Inspector's 1765 estimate, but Small maintained that the same amount of money spent on the previous line 'every year for 500' would never have made it so good. More was needed, of course, but such success had interested the local heritors. £15 was awarded to Captain Charles Stewart with other heritors in the area, when they asked for further help, on condition that they would finish the work. Once it was completed, the line was taken over by the Perthshire Quarter Sessions, and George Nicolson was perturbed, near the end of the annexation, by their suggestion that the road should be altered to the south side of Loch Achray, from Duncraggan. Apart from the expense the county would have incurred, as an additional bridge would have been required over the Black Water, the extra distance might have raised the carriage costs on the Strathgartney oak woods and affected their selling price. The commissioners may well have felt aggrieved if the county had made a change which had deleterious results for the annexed estates, when their initiative and funds had been responsible for the initial improvement to the road. The road still remains on the north side of the loch, however, and the continuation to Inversnaid was never made up. In 1818, one traveller, John Anderson, reported that even the footpath from the Trossachs to Inversnaid was wretchedly bad,[25] and today access by 'carriage-road' is still only through Aberfoyle.

Two other lines of road considered at different times by the commissioners were also abortive. Archibald Menzies was once again responsible for the idea of one, a direct road from Loch Rannoch to the head of Loch Tay. His motives on this occasion were purely for the internal good of the estates of Struan and Perth, for the relevant report, which was read in June 1767, made the point that, if this road was opened, then the Rannoch timber could be sent to the Perth estate, providing the tenants there with much better quality than that supplied from Drummond. It would also have benefited the tacksman at Carie sawmill who had not been able to sell his wood that year. Another road, the public road from Braemar to Atholl, had destroyed his market, carriage of other timber being easier and presumably cheaper than by the paths from Rannoch and the county road towards Pitlochry. The Inspector had persuaded the Commissioners of Supply to allow statute labour for work on the road proposed and he wanted some military help too.[26]

This scheme got as far as having some financial arrangements made but, unfortunately, despite the Board's allowance for tools both for this and for a road leading from Loch Tay to the Water of Lyon, government policy towards road-building in Scotland had already begun to be less generous, and the Marquis of Lorne, the Commander-in-Chief, refused the help of the military on the suggested Tay-Rannoch line. The government, he said, had resolved to begin no new roads in Scotland and had scarcely sufficient troops for those already undertaken. The Commissioners of Supply in Perthshire appointed a committee in 1769 to consider the petition but there cannot have been sufficient interest in the idea to press it. George Nicolson in 1783 still persevered in pointing out the benefits of such a highway for the sale of Rannoch wood, all the more likely to be of use as by then there was a road from Glenlyon to Breadalbane,[27] but this was too late for the

Board, and it was the 1960s before this line along the side of Ben Lawers was macadamised.

The idea of the other abortive line in Perthshire also emerged too late in the Board's lifespan to have any chance of completion under their auspices. It too was cross-country, from Callander to Glenartney, along the Water of Ruchill to Comrie and Crieff, and the conception of such a route rose from the Board's policy in providing access to lime quarries. Where lime was found, convenient for their tenants but without easy access, the commissioners were usually able to find money for a road. There were several examples of this, not only in the Perthshire area. In March, 1763, £20 was allowed for tools and an overseer's wage, for the country people to make a passable road to a quarry near Ardmair in Coigach; £10 was spent on the road to a limestone quarry at Finart. That to the quarry at Leny in contrast took some time to come to fruition. The charges there first attracted the Board's attention in 1757 and the factor was asked to see if statute labour could be used to make a cart road. The estimate was too expensive, so the matter was dropped until in 1762 Lord Kames brought it up again, and his plea for improvements was reinforced by 'some of the gentlemen in the neighbourhood of Callander of Menteith' in the following spring. An estimate by William Shields was simply ordered to be laid upon the table, but John Buchanan of Auchlessie, who had a tack of the quarry, offered to make the road for £60 if the Board would entrust him with the money through the factor.[28] This offer was accepted with alacrity as Shields' estimate had been for £173.

Any improving landlord was likely to look favourably on such constructions and, in 1755, William Cockburn had mentioned roads made from Lochearnside to lime quarries on the Perth estate. Buchanan also discovered lime on the farm of Lurgavie, two miles from Callander, and a road was commissioned towards this quarry, for which the factor in one year at least paid out £69.10.0 after the Board's order of July, 1781.[29] Having begun this route, it apparently occurred to the Board after considering Frend's journal and survey of the Perth estate that it would be a reasonable idea to join this up with the existing road along Glenartney, to Achinner, where the funds of the estates had already been used to build bridges. Estimates were drawn up in 1783 for the junction, $3\frac{1}{4}$ miles at £96.13.8, varying in price from 3d per ell, where there was hard bottom available, to 5d per ell on soft or mossy ground. But today's traveller who would cross there must still go on foot, or perhaps on horseback.

When the annexation officially began in 1752, military roads were still of importance, and the skill the troops gradually acquired in road-making was, as we have seen, often available for county or private use in making new lines and developing old ones. But the situation gradually changed, as the Highlands became more amenable to Lowland habits and discipline and Highland gentlemen who some years previously might have been likely supporters of a Stewart attempt on the throne had become loyal officers in George III's army. As a result there was less need for such large bodies of troops in the northern parts of Scotland. At the same time, the increasing demands of the Seven Years War withdrew forces from the Highlands. This reduced the number available for work on any roads that were not the direct responsibility of the army. Their expertise was no longer available for application to other lines of communication.

Indeed, according to Lieutenant-General Mackay, there were not enough men to keep the military roads in repair. In 1767, Lieutenant-Colonel Skene, who incidentally became a tenant on the annexed estates,[30] succeeded William Caulfield as Inspector of the Military Roads. Caulfield had been Inspector since 1732, and Dr. Salmond gives him credit for the burst of bridge-building that took place on these roads thereafter. When Skene succeeded him, there were 858 miles of highway made and 139 miles in the course of construction. But although this mileage of 997 had increased by 1784 to about 1,100, Mackay wrote to the Treasury that, not only were they in general in bad repair at that date, but that Skene had found them so on his appointment; and he had not been able to remedy the situation 'for want of troops to work upon them with which I could not supply him from the small numbers we have had'. Mackay also propounded that there was a case for public assumption of the burden of road-making where the wildness and barrenness of the country and the sparse population made this inevitable. He still supported the use of statute labour, of course, where it was practicable, but he thought the situation needed 'clarification' regarding the military participation, 'however proper and necessary the making of these roads may originally have been'. Clarification almost inevitably resulted in a decrease in military responsibility for roads that were no longer essential for policing, except occasionally for ensuring evictions. By 1799, only 599 miles of military roads were kept in repair and, in 1814, the Commissioners for Highland Roads and Bridges were made the responsible body. They proceeded to rationalise the system and maintain only roads that could be shown to be of public use.[31]

As the military authorities lost both the will and capacity to maintain roads, it was fortunate for the future of the Highland road system, however deficient it may still be, that others became willing to shoulder some of the burden. The heritors were foremost among those by whom 'the salutary effects of the great roads made by the government through the Highlands were sensibly felt'. It was they who would bear the greater part of the expense of road construction and who could influence the Commissioners of Supply. Without their appreciation of the benefits of better transport and their expenditure, which was beyond the calls of private interest, Highland communications would have deteriorated from even the eighteenth-century conditions. The Commissioners of Supply were able to achieve little in the northern counties with the limited financial resources and the inefficient labour at their disposal. Turnpikes were never highly developed in the Highlands; Inverness-shire had twelve miles and the other crofting counties none in 1855, when a commission inquired into the conditions of public roads in Scotland.[32]

So much depended on the heritors in individual districts. The writer of the account of Abernyte in the *Old Statistical Account* complained that the roads were bad because there were no resident heritors, while John Stewart, petitioning for aid for Ballachulish pier, claimed that the landed gentlemen and the inhabitants of the county were carrying on so much road-construction by subscription that no more could be expected from them.[33] The areas in which the annexed estates lay were fortunate for, with regard to communication, the commissioners, though absentee landlords, took a wide view of the subject and of their responsibilities, and were prepared to spend in this field to the limit of their resources. This was one aspect of their activities that almost always received prompt attention and approval from the central government. Initially, they acted as generous, far-sighted landlords did all over the country, and of course they had more of their income from the estates at their disposal than the normal landowner, who had to maintain his family and house in some degree of comfort. They supported the other local heritors when they showed any disposition to help themselves, as in Lochbroom and Rannoch. The factor in Arnprior was directed to take his due part with the other gentlemen in the area in making a road through Arnprior moss to Glasgow. Where more funds were needed than the county could reasonably supply, they gave subsidies whenever possible, the Trossachs road being the most dramatic example, and their assistance to bridge-building was a notable contribution, as we shall see later. They objected to any implicit assumption, however, that they would automatically underwrite expense; when the Committee for the Western District of roads in Perthshire forwarded a memorandum, asking that the Board order an estimate to be made of the gravelling of a road between Callander and Cardross Bridge and order their factor to advance this, there was an immediate and unexplained refusal.[34]

Until the 1770s, however, their activities were confined to cross-roads or local roads leading off completely new lines of made roads. Thereafter there is a widening of interest. This was, like most of their activities, an interest that was injected from outside. It is not improbable that the applications that appeared were inspired from outside, but the lack of hesitation on the part of the government in agreeing to the commissioners' suggestions may show an awareness of a deficiency which the annexed estates rents could usefully make good. Just how insufficient county funds were even when converted is illustrated in a letter from Henry Butter to the secretary of the commissioners, Barclay, in July 1778.[35] He wrote that in Argyllshire the county was now divided into administrative districts, and the statute labour was converted and commuted at 1/- per £1 sterling valued rent, payable by the heritors to the collector of the land tax. Four-fifths was to be applied within the district, one fifth was at the disposal of the general meeting of Justices of the Peace and Commissioners of Supply. In the Ardnamurchan district, the first great road proposed under this new administration was that from Strontian to Corran Ferry, through Ardnamurchan. Butter was involved through the part of Lochiel he managed in the area, valued at £75. He told the Board that, after deducting the county's statutory fifth and the clerk's salary, £25 was the most that could be raised annually in the district, with the result that only £250 could be borrowed towards building a road estimated as likely to cost about £600, excluding bridges, as there was so much impassable rock to cut. As the main heritors, who included the Duke of Argyll, the annexed estates commissioners and the trustees for MacLean of Ardgour were not at the relevant meeting, only conditional arrangements had been made, but the Board prepared to advance £75, or

£60 if the general meeting insisted on its legal rights to one fifth of the whole.

In such circumstances, it must have been a happy realisation in many areas that funds existed beyond the statutory provision, funds that were not precisely cornucopic but could certainly be tapped, and one of the earliest appeals came from Hugh Seton of Touch. He succeeded in persuading the Board to seek the king's approval to enable them to pay half the price of a road through Glencoe, to meet the military road from Fort William south to Stirling, by way of the King's House at Black Mount. Fifteen miles were to cost £1,000, but half had been obtained by subscription and the most expensive part went through the estate of Ardsheal. The existing road was so bad, over 'high almost perpendicular hills, often impassable even on horse, in winter', that even the inhabitants of Lochiel avoided it, using the Corran and Ballachulish ferries instead. As well as these particular advantages for the annexed estates, Seton could enumerate public benefits; the drovers bringing cattle from Ardnamurchan, Morvern, Sunart, and the islands could cross the ferry and then have immediate access to the military road, instead of taking the lengthy route round the head of Loch Eil; recently formed sheep farms in the area were handicapped, as things stood, because wool could not by law be transported by water.

These factors alone would have justified quite a large grant from annexed estates funds; added to Seton's financial blandishments, they were irresistible. He promised to make up any unforeseen financial deficiency, to build the five bridges necessary himself, and to finish the road in five years. It was also obvious that it was impossible to raise any more funds from the county, or from that thinly populated district, or from the Argyllshire heritors who had just subscribed £1,600 for a road in Kintyre. Seton's estimates regarding the time and money required were optimistic and, five years after his original application in December, 1776, the commissioners, somewhat restive, authorised one of their number, Lord Stonefield, to use the interest of the £500 set aside for the Glencoe road to help public road building generally in Argyllshire. However, in the following year, when the Argyllshire Commissioners of Supply put in a plea for payment, on the grounds that, though the road was unfinished, it was so expensive that they needed immediate help, Stonefield was allowed to hand over the capital sum.[36]

The Board had also given some assistance at an earlier date to the line that is today the continuation of the road through Glencoe, from Ballachulish ferry, now Ballachulish bridge, north to Fort William. Some parts of it were then impassable except at ebb-tide. The county did do a little apparently, but the most important contribution from annexed estates funds was the bridge over the Kiachnish, a few miles south of Fort William, which the factor thought necessary. Though this bridge is now by-passed, as the road lies nearer the lochside, it was at the time in a more reasonable position than many in Glenelg, built by the contractors on the road from Fort Augustus to Bernera barracks. There the contractor seems to have been sent on ahead and naturally chose places for bridges where he could build them most cheaply, without regard to the most suitable lines for roads.[37] A later request for help from the Inverness-shire Commissioners of Supply came too late, in 1783, for that year the Board's funds were allocated to combat the previous year's dearth, leaving little surplus for even such favoured activities as road building.

While the assistance given to the Glencoe road could be described without much stretch of the imagination as directly affecting the annexed estates of Lochiel and Ardsheal by improving access, further extensive aid to the Commissioners of Supply in Argyllshire must be considered as contributing to the wider aims of the Annexing Act, the development of the Highlands and Islands of Scotland generally. £300 to the Inveraray-Campbeltown post road, £250 to the proprietors in South Knapdale and Kilberry for a district road to join it, £300 to Kintyre and Knapdale, all between 1780 and 1782, absorbed a considerable part of the Board's income. While no doubt Lord Stonefield's interest must have been of significance, the Argyllshire heritors presented a very deserving case, for they invariably contributed generously themselves. The Duke of Argyll's share was certainly important, as can be seen when he donated £700 of the £1,700 collected, but the other heritors were not backward in committing themselves. They assessed themselves quite highly, as well as subscribing voluntarily to road and bridge building in the various districts in the county, and all the Board's grants were more than matched by local funds.[38]

One other county not directly connected with the annexed estates became conscious of the possibilities of obtaining help from the Board. Headed by Sir John Sinclair of Ulbster, the Caithness heritors asked for assistance, claiming that for some years they had made roads and bridges as well as could be expected with bad tools and unwilling workmen, which was all that anyone seemed to expect from statute labour. Like everyone else, they declared that the ground their roads traversed was the most difficult in Scotland, not only for making roads but for repair, in this area because of the high hills, precipices and deep mosses. The petitioners were not of course selfish. The roads they built were, as they claimed, the only ones leading to Strathnaver in Sutherlandshire, and towards Orkney and Shetland. Nor were they *too* boastful. They were 'not inclined to vaunt of aid' they had afforded the government, in furnishing a greater proportion of men for the forces than any other county in Scotland. They calculated their expenses at £20 a mile, and the total would amount to £2,640, with £500 for additional bridges. The Board allowed them £100 in 1779, but Sinclair was indefatigable and business-like. He had used the first allowance on the road from the Ord of Caithness to Wick, and the following year sent his vouchers to the secretary of the Board of Trustees showing that £50 out of the total had been spent on bridges on the road. His estimates for work proposed on the Caithness roads in the summer of 1780 totalled £525, including the cost of bridges. One interesting item was £100 for maintenance of the tenants working on the roads on account both of their poverty and 'their disinclination to roadmaking'. Another £100 was also to be spent on hiring labour. He had 800–900 men working and would have 1,000 more before he was done with them. The commissioners asked permission to grant a further £150.[39]

The Caithness freeholders did not restrict their appeals to the commissioners, but applied as well to the Treasury, only to have their petition handed on to the

Board for the Annexed Estates, though it would appear that this may have been on the applicants' suggestion. R.B. Sheridan was the Treasury officer responsible and the Board, replying to him, pointed out that they were restricted to spending £500 a year on roads, which was the reason for the application being made to the Treasury. The restriction was based on the idea that the greater part of the public roads in the Highlands were repaired from the General Military Fund,[40] an official notion which obscured the facts, if General Mackay was to be believed. While approving of improvements to the Caithness roads in general, in December 1783 the Board delayed consideration of the proposal until they had detailed plans and estimates, and this meant that it was too late for any further annexed estates rents to reach Caithness, though the Parliamentary Commission for Highland Roads and Bridges spent money there.[41]

Lord Kames used his influence on the Board to have one line of road repaired on the grounds that the Perth estate would benefit. According to the road overseers, David Gourlay, Colin McLenan and John Grinnock, it was carriages to the annexed estates which had done most of the damage to the road from Stirling, round the back of Stirling Castle, to the bridge at Drip. In 1772, the committee on roads suggested a contribution of £60, but the full Board delayed a decision until estimates were seen. These were duly provided and were satisfactory at the time, but in 1775 Kames reintroduced the subject as the work was costing more than the estimates. If the Board allowed £100, he undertook to make sure the work was properly done, but some years later, in 1782, the road was still unfinished, though Kames was reported as having received £100 towards it in 1776. This time, Kames suggested that some feu-duties owed by him to the Perth estate, which he had evaded for some years – a remarkable admission by a Board member who was also a judge – should be spent by his stepson, George Drummond, on finishing the 600 yards still unmade. Once the road was complete, coal and lime could be carried all winter, something that was impossible until the surface had been metalled with six or seven inches of hard whinstones, and only then would the Perth estate reap the full benefit from the new bridge at Drip Coble, to which the Board had also contributed.[42]

It must be noted that the road from Stirling past Drip is also the line towards Blair Drummond but, as there was no common law liability in Scotland on anyone to maintain the roads, it could only be considered fortunate when private interest and public convenience coincided. The commissioners, however, were usually able to be objective about their duties as landlords, and were prepared to pay their full share in any reasonable projects, such as the proposed road to Glasgow through Arnprior moss, where the factor James Fogo was empowered to collaborate with the other gentlemen in the neighbourhood.[43]

The commissioners' Journal, noting sums paid out daily from 1767–1784, shows £1,520 laid out from the Edinburgh office directly on roads but, in addition, it must be remembered that the factors were also carrying out the ordinary duties of landowners throughout the estates, providing tools and making sure that the tenants carried out their statutory labour on the roads. The detailed expenditure for each estate is shown throughout the factors' intromissions, and these accounts illustrate the difficulties and inefficiencies involved in using statute labour. The administrative costs incurred by the Board were a surprisingly high proportion of the whole. The factors had to spend time attending the county Quarter Sessions, as they needed warrants to carry on particular roads. On Struan this amounted to £2 to £4 each year. In 1756, £3.10.0 of the £11.9.0 $\frac{7}{12}$ spent on the Rannoch road was allocated to the factor's visit to Perth. Henry Butter, who was assiduous in carrying out road improvements, claimed £10 in two months in 1765 for his expenses in travelling round meeting the gentlemen of the county to arrange agreements as to how the statute labour should be organised. The Struan factor's expenses for similar duties and attendance at the Quarter Sessions in 1768 amounted to £8, while the overseer for the Rannoch road alone was paid £7.3.11, so that £15.3.11 was spent on administration out of a total for that year of £46.13.3 $\frac{6}{12}$ on roads and bridges.[44] At the other end of the administration scale, the Dunblane constable, James Edie, was paid 3/- for calling the people out to work on the roads through Kinbuck. The sums spent varied, depending on the plans of the Commissioners of Supply, the availability of money at the Board's disposal overall as well as in individual estates, and on the energy and interest of the factor concerned, just as in privately owned estates the inclination of the heritor was all-important. In 1767, for example, £71.2.10 was reported spent on Barrisdale roads, and in 1770 £108.4.6. The factor there was criticised, as his costs for road building were higher than in other estates but, considering the deficiencies of the area, the expenses were possibly excusable.[45]

The accounting methods used for the reports to the king and Treasury seem to have varied without much rhyme or reason, so that one year the figures for estates are given separately, another they are conjoined. Then the schedules included with the reports, supposedly detailed accounts of expenditure, on occasion presented merely a lump sum for roads and bridges, sometimes noting the number of bridges built, sometimes not. Despite having the same factor, Lovat and Cromartie are sometimes reported separately, sometimes together, even before 1774, when the Lovat estate was returned to the Fraser family. 1771 saw in 'Expenditure on roads' £35.12.5 on Cromartie; 1773 under a similar heading saw 'Lovat – roads and four bridges, £141.19.5'; in 1774, £54.0.5 was spent between Lovat and Cromartie.[46] But, however the figures were presented, they amount in all to quite an impressive picture of interest in improving the road system in the estates and the counties in which these lay. The benefits that arose were apparently so universally accepted that a memorandum on a petition from the Caithness heritors merely remarked, 'It is unnecessary to enter into general arguments that making good roads of communication is the best method of promoting industry and improvements in that part of the country'.[47]

A further practical form of assistance to improving the facilities for travellers can be seen in the financial aids given to map-makers. Andrew Skinner and George Taylor were provided with several subsidies towards their survey of the roads in Scotland, published in 1776; they were given £105 in July 1776, and £50 in July 1779, for which they were duly grateful. John Ainslie was also paid £98.15.0 in March, 1784, for his maps, and James Stobie, another of the cartographers of the era, sold the Board twenty-five copies of his coloured map of Perthshire for £52.10.0. Taylor and Skinner's road map, laid out in linear style, is of use only for travel along the roads they set out, but Ainslie's work is a pleasure to look at, however inaccurate it may be.[48] Then, in road work as in other aspects of improvements with which the Board concerned themselves, they were prepared to reward invention, and a Peter Fraser was paid 16/- in 1772 for making a machine with wheels for measuring distances.

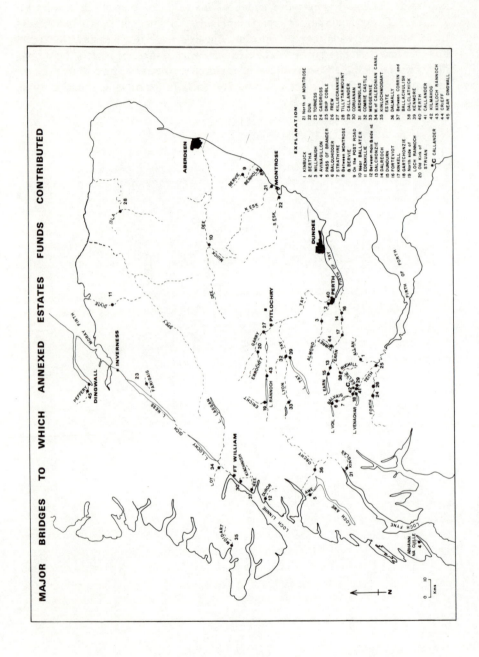

MAJOR BRIDGES TO WHICH ANNEXED ESTATES FUNDS CONTRIBUTED

EXPLANATION

1 KINBUCK
2 BERTHA
3 MILLHAUGH
4 AVINAGILLON
5 PASS OF BRANDER
6 BALQUHIDDER
7 STRATHYRE
8 Between MONTROSE
  & BERVIE
9 On the POST ROAD
10 Near BALLATER
11 EDENKILLIE
12 Between main B side rd.
13 DALCHONZIE
14 DALREOCH
15 DUNIRN
16 FORTEVIOT
17 KINKELL
18 GARTCHONZIE
19 North side of
  LOCH RANNOCH
20 Old Kirk of
  STRUAN

21 North of MONTROSE
22 DUN
23 TORNESS
24 CARDROSS
25 DRIP COBLE
26 PREW
27 KILLIECRANKIE
28 TILLYTARMOUNT
29 CALLANDER
30 CORGIANAN
31 ARDNINGLAS
32 COMRIE CASTLE
33 MEGGERNIE
34 W of CALEDONIAN CANAL
35 KINLOCHMOIDART
   ESTATE
36 DALMALLY
37 Between CORRIN and
   BALLACHULISH
38 DALCLATHICK
39 KENMORE
40 PERTH
41 CALLANDER
42 KILMAHOG
43 KINLOCH RANNOCH
44 CRIEFF
45 NEAR DINGWALL

10

Bridges and Inns

IN Scotland, the building of the roadway itself is only part of the provision of good communications and, had the Board restricted its contribution to that part, though the amount spent was a reasonable proportion of their income, their overall share in improving the road system would have merited little attention. In fact, all the elements essential for comfortable travel in the eighteenth century — bridges, inns, ferries, good harbours — shared in their largesse at one time or another during the annexation. A cursory glance at a map of the country, noticing the innumerable rivulets which cross almost every road, will convince one of the truth of Maurice Taylor's statement that 'Without bridges, in Scotland, roads are of no use'.[1] The Board's attitude to bridge building, constantly encouraging, demonstrated that they implicitly agreed with that dictum. Though it may seem self-evident today in a society that considers a shallow ford an adventure, even when it is traversed on four wheels, and a deepish burn an insuperable obstacle, such an approach was far from being generally accepted until fairly recently. The streams and rivers on the path of public roadways were not automatically bridged. Quite a substantial bridge over the river Lyon near the ruins of Comrie Castle, built as late as 1896, bears the inscription that it had replaced an older structure, and had been financed by public contributions organised by Egidia Charlotte Menzies of Menzies. The earlier bridge had also been built privately, though the commissioners had subsidised it to the tune of £200, paid eventually by the Barons of the Exchequer out of annexed estates funds, as it was not finished until after the estates were disannexed.[2]

There was a clear division between roads and bridges which is almost incomprehensible to the twentieth-century mind. Wade, for instance, claimed maintenance for 250 miles of roads and above forty stone bridges, two distinct categories which today would be intrinsically part of one concept.[3] Some very large projects, such as the Forth and Tay road bridges, may be prohibited or delayed, because of expense or lack of great urgency, but even a minor metalled road will include arches over the tiniest of burns as part of the initial expenditure. The method of funding county work also illustrated this idea of separate development, for the bridge fund was self-contained and quite inadequate. The situation in the eighteenth century was not improved by the fact that the funds available were not always applied correctly to bridge building. In 1754, the Commissioners of Supply for Perthshire found that the Bridge-money fund was always exhausted by the large sums paid yearly to the overseers and officers, who called out the county services for road and bridge repair, so that the fund could not in fact be used for its proper purpose.[4] It was proposed that these officers should in future be paid from funds obtained from commuting statute labour.

By the time that the Commission for Highland Roads and Bridges was in operation, one may trace signs of appreciation that a road without a bridge over a passage for water, whether always wet or not, is only a half a road, for they noted that they had built more than 1,100 bridges over rivers and streams.[5] They commented that in the Highlands the erection of bridges over unfordable rivers was of more urgent importance than even the formation of carriage roads for, while the latter did materially contribute to the promotion of commercial intercourse, the building of bridges added the removal of personal danger. Fatal accidents were common as Highland rivers were so liable to be swollen by mountain torrents. The very strong construction required to stand up to the weather and these swollen rivers constituted about one third of the cost of making Highland roads.[6] That factor alone helps explain the deficiencies of earlier days, given the limited resources.

Individual contributions from resident heritors played a very large part in remedying the deficiencies in county and government road funds. In their capacity as proprietors, the Board were expected to play their part, especially after 1770, on a large scale. We have seen Hugh Seton of Touch putting pressure on the commissioners to assist road-building schemes in which he was interested. He also shamed them into spending £90 on a bridge over the Duror on the estate of Ardsheal. He pointed out that it was the only bridge lacking on the coast road from Inveraray to Fort William; he himself had previously spent £150 on another bridge on that line and £600 generally on roads and bridges. The Board had given one grant of £60 but had refused another of the same amount, and he showed that he considered their refusal both miserly and unreasonable.[7] The area of land annexed in Perthshire was so large that the Perthshire Commissioners of Supply were bound to realise at an early date that the Board for the Annexed Estates would have to undertake at least the ordinary duties of heritors, and that this would be a considerable addition to the resources of the county. In 1756, one of their number promised to apply to the Board as well as to other gentlemen in the neighbourhood for aid towards a new bridge over the Earn at Comrie.[8] Another method of providing bridges beyond what the county funds would allow and the heritors contribute was to make 'judicious application of the vacant stipend which has fallen from time to time'.[9]

However, the Commissioners for the Annexed Estates seem to have been fully alive to the need for bridges in the Highlands generally and on their estates in particular. Information about the state of bridges was asked for from the factors in 1755 and was duly provided in some detail, with reference both to the internal convenience of tenants within the estates and to the general development of the road system. William Cockburn had also described the condition of roads and bridges in his survey of the estates.[10] Not surprisingly, where the roads were bad, the bridges, too, tended to be either poorly built or more likely non-existent. Strathpeffer barony, which had very bad roads, never repaired, had no bridges; and the road to Coigach had no bridges over the rivers, making it almost inaccessible for the greater part of the year.

In the report on Struan, the factor did not mention bridges at all, despite the current building of the road through Rannoch. Alexander Robertson's dislike of roads, however, did not apparently extend to bridges, for he not only provided the oak binding for the piers of Wade's bridge at Aberfeldy but composed a poem to celebrate its opening. Entitled 'Taybridge to the Passenger', it included sentiments so out of tune with Robertson's normal lifestyle that it is no wonder it is not a poetic gem:[11]

> Not less surprizing was the daring Scheme,
> That fix'd my station in this rapid stream,
> The North and South rejoice to see me stand,
> Uniting in my Function, Hand in Hand.
> Commerce and Concord, Life of every Land!

Even more surprising, coming from the rebel of 1689, 1715 and 1745, was the beginning of the third verse:

> Methinks the anxious Reader's at a stand,
> Not knowing, George for GEORGE (to bless the Land
> Averse t'Obedience) spoke the stern Command.

Robertson also built, or at least paid most of the cost of, one bridge for the convenience of his tenants, a timber structure over the Ericht, on the north side of Loch Rannoch. But by 1759 it was 'entirely ruinous and decayed', with the result that the high road from Perth to Lochaber by the north side of the loch was often closed, as the Water of Ericht was always rapid, and often impassable for days or weeks on end. Sir Robert Menzies of Weem approached both the Commissioners of Supply for Perthshire and the Board for the Annexed Estates for help in replacing it. He had been granted £20 out of county funds, the estimate being £51.18.4, and he hoped to be given timber from Struan, the only estates in the area with suitable woods, enough for the whole if a wooden bridge were built but, in case of stone being used, just sufficient for the cooms, the wooden centering or frame on which an arch or vault of stone rests during its construction. As the factor bore out Sir Robert's arguments on the need for the bridge, and the latter was prepared to contribute £10 and buy a boat costing £6 to transport necessary materials along the loch, the Board felt constrained to donate more than the timber and undertook the payment of any balance after other subscriptions were exhausted. Despite such favourable financial conditions the bridge was a long time building and it was 1770 before £30.10.0 was called for. A change of site had increased both the costs and the timespan.[12]

Even main roads were not always completely bridged and, on the recently made Lochearnside road, there were three or four 'very rough rapid waters' with no bridges provided by the county. The Perth factor thought that single arches only were necessary, and mentioned the plentiful supply of stone near, and the lime obtainable from, a neighbouring estate. Campbell of Barcaldine was very enthusiastic about the potentialities of Crieff, and he gave as an additional reason for having these bridges the increase in the town's trade from the Western Highlands.[13]

In one area, there were no complaints about the king's highway. The Stirling to

Fort William road went up the south side of Loch Lubnaig (William Monteath the factor spells it Lochludnick), and as it was recently made, it was in very good condition, with stone bridges at every place they were needed. A timber bridge serving local needs, however, required frequent repairs, and Monteath suggested that it should be replaced when next it gave way under force of spate water. The Barons of the Exchequer had repaired it fairly recently.[14]

The factors in their reports differentiated between bridges, saying about one that it would be very useful, while for others there was 'great occasion'. For yet another, the detailed local needs for a bridge were given. When Henry Butter replied to the Board's request for lists of bridges required, after they had been authorised to spend £500 on this type of construction, he remarked that he mentioned only those that were 'absolutely necessary', meaning locations where communications were interrupted whenever there was a small rise in the level of the water.[15]

One description of the consequences of the lack of a bridge of any kind, not even a rickety wooden structure, clearly and vividly illustrates the inconveniences. In the barony of Lix in Killin parish the factor wrote:

> There is a small water called Adlchromie that is in the way from this barony to the parish church the school and the miln they are obliged to bring their corns to be grinded and also betwixt them and the smiddie they go to with their labouring instruments. This water in the time of winter rises so high as to hinder their children from going to school, which is the only time of year their parents can spare them from their work and sometimes hinders the people from going to church.[16]

Absence from church and school might worry the factor, schoolmaster and minister, more than the children and the congregation, but regular transport of corn and agricultural implements for repair over an unbridged burn was no recipe for the greater speed and efficiency that Lowland society wished to graft on the Highland economy.

However willing the commissioners may have been in the first five years of office to remedy such deficiencies, large-scale bridge building was something they could only embark on with specific permission from the central government. They had early commented on the disadvantages of poor communications, the lack of bridges especially, including among those disadvantages the fact that parents accepted baptism for their children from the first pastor who came along, rather than have them unbaptised – and that pastor might well be a Roman Catholic priest. The commissioners advocated a positive policy, but it was only after the accession of George III that they were effectively in a position to carry out their ideas. By August, 1761, they had been authorised to spend £500 on bridges in the Highlands, wherever they thought it best, taking into consideration access to churches and markets and also easier intercourse among neighbours. A committee was appointed to decide on the most advantageous way of spending the money.[17]

The commissioners were very willing to act with neighbouring proprietors in the Highlands and with the Commissioners of Supply, but they were not prepared, even had they been able, to assume total financial responsibility for all the building needed. The factors often had to discover the extent of contributions likely to be obtained from other interested parties, particularly when suggested sites lay either outwith the annexed estates or on important highways through them. And even then estimates had to be as modest as possible. No other attitude was practical, for the first £500 allocated for this purpose built only small bridges needed on the Lochearn road, provided assistance of £200 for that over the Teith at Callander (the first public work in the area to which the Board devoted part of their funds), £50 towards the crossing of the Almond at Bertha on the Perth-Dunkeld road, and £103 for that over the Dee (now the E) at Garthbeg on the Lovat estate, leaving a small amount over for contingencies.

The remaining twenty-seven bridges on the factors' lists of those which they considered most useful and necessary included seven on the estates of Perth and Lochiel, three on Lovat, two on Cromartie, and one each on Struan, Arnprior, Monaltrie, Barrisdale, Kinlochmoidart and Ardsheal.[18] Some of these estates, of course, were still being managed by the Barons of the Exchequer, while the claims of the subject-superiors remained unsettled, but the commissioners were hopeful at the time that they would soon come under their control – mistakenly as we know. However, even a review of essential crossings, which was restricted to the estates annexed outright, revealed such clamant need that the committee considering bridge building proposed that the Board should request permission to spend a further £1,000. This was duly authorised, with the additional concession that the money might also be used for repairing any bridges in danger of falling down.

Apart from the very large capital sums of over £9,000 for the settlement of discharged soldiers and sailors and £1,200 for manufactures, already earmarked for maintaining the undertakings the Board of Trustees were abandoning, this was the largest amount the commissioners had to deal with on this occasion for a single purpose. There was room for manoeuvre too, for estimates varied considerably, depending on the width of the bridge. Butter's list in 1761 included ten bridges at a total cost of £270, but one over the River Pean running into Loch Arkaig he reckoned would cost £5, while a larger one over the Arkaig at Bunarkaig would require £130. The next dearest he estimated at £30, over the Kiachnish at Coruanan, two more at £20, three at £15 and two at £10. He had to admit later that the arch over the Kiag had cost more than the estimate, but he thought it an essential part of the Lochaber-Argyllshire road.[19] That at Coruanan turned out to be even more expensive, and the sum of £129.15.4 he claimed was initially struck off his accounts, as he produced no vouchers for it.

The commissioners' approach to the subject of bridge building was a nice blend of consideration of their wider duties to the Highlands and Islands as a whole and to their narrower duties as landlords. One of their earlier contributions to bridges in the north of Scotland was that over the Tummel at Kinloch Rannoch. Indeed, this was the most important for which they undertook total financial responsibility. James Small had suggested Kinloch Rannoch at the east end of Loch Rannoch as the most suitable place for a village, but he had not in 1755 mentioned access or the possibility of a bridge. However, by 1757 he was urging a bridge or ferry-boat at Kinloch, preferably a bridge, if only to enable children to go to school at Kinloch. He first gave estimates for a timber bridge at £40–£50, a timber bridge with stone pillars at £80, and an arched stone bridge at £200 but, when asked for a particular estimate for a stone bridge, he produced one of £194 with the curious statement, considering his previous opinion, that a timber bridge would not cost much less. Another economy the commissioners were disposed to consider was restricting the width over the parapets to fourteen feet,[20] possibly a shortsighted attitude as roads were supposed to be twenty feet wide, at least when approaching market towns.[21]

Though Small was allowed £5 for a ferry-boat in 1758, there was no likelihood of any such project being realised in the frustrating period before 1760, and it was only after the soldiers' settlements were set up, one at Kinloch Rannoch and one across the Tummel at Black Park, that the bridge became a pressing necessity, for the factor at least. He had great difficulty in finding a mason, once the Board did authorise the expenditure. Several at Dunkeld refused to put in an estimate and that of the only one who did, Donald MacEwan, was £470, a great increase on the earlier price proposed. Even at that, the hesitant tradesmen may have been wiser for, in 1765, MacEwan asked the Board, without success, for the considerable amount he had had to lay out over the estimate, £128.15.4.[22] Their refusal was based on the curious grounds that the mason had been several times employed by them on what they termed 'other profitable work'. His four-arched bridge still stands, bearing today's traffic and several inscriptions, announcing in English that it was erected in A.D. 1764 at the sole expense of His Majesty out of the annexed estates funds and then extensively repaired by Perthshire County Council in 1946 and again in the 1970s. The Latin inscription put up by the commissioners states *Pontem Hanc in Publicum Commodum Georgius III Rex Construi iussit.*

At the time, it was an essential part of the proposed road through Rannoch, and joined the country road on the north side of the Tummel to the continuation being built along the south side of Loch Rannoch under Small's supervision, with aid from annexed estate funds. The bridge was also of great benefit to the tenants on the south side of the loch but, in 1767, it was argued that it would be even more useful if the burn entering the Tummel about a mile east of Kinloch Rannoch were bridged at Innerhaddon, on the road joining the military highway from Aberfeldy to Tummel Bridge at White Bridge. The Board and the Quarter Sessions agreed, each allowing £20 and local subscriptions amounting to £15.[23]

Considering the plans in existence for the cross-country highway from Alyth, it seems surprising that the commissioners did not ask for county aid for the Kinloch Rannoch bridge and that, in addition, they undertook the whole expense of the four small arches on the county road along Lochearnside, three on annexed estates, and one over the Ogle at Fonab, belonging to a Major Campbell. This omission was probably politic. They had other plans in hand for which they would need county assistance, the crossing of the Teith at Callander and the Balvaig at Balquhidder. The heritors who would benefit from these were few and none was important, except the Earl of Moray, whose land lay across the Balvaig from the Crown's lands. The areas were also sparsely populated so that local resources were small. In the circumstances, Colin Campbell, son of the Perth factor, John Campbell of Barcaldine, advised the commissioners against prejudicing their case for help in these much more expensive schemes by tapping limited county funds for the smaller bridges, which were of most benefit to the Perth estate.[24] Some twenty years later, we find the factor paying £13 for the repair of Lochearnside bridges, and also building four small ones on the continuation of the same road, from Lochearnside to Crieff, at a cost of £37.18.0. Presumably these had not been considered necessary, even on a main road, in the middle of the century, or had been like so many more, precarious structures of timber.

In the first few years after 1760, most support was given to bridges that were either on the annexed estates or could be shown to be of undoubted direct value to them. £50 went to the £1,000 bridge over the Almond at Bertha on the Perth-Dunkeld road, a sum promised by the commissioners before 1760. A bridge there was so clearly useful, as the Commissioners of Supply recorded, to 'prevent many melancholy accidents' which befell travellers fording the river as well as being in the vicinity of some of the annexed estates, that the recommendation was made that the previous Board's promise should be made good. At least, it would be once the bridge was finished, for the committee which considered this said they had heard it had fallen down the autumn before. William Sandeman, the Perth merchant who had organised the subscription from the nobility and gentry and the town of Perth, was able to claim the money in 1763, however.[25]

£100 went towards the bridge over the Earn at Kinkell, and another £100 to that at Dalreoch, to replace a ferry whose high freight rates had roused complaints that were taken to the Quarter Sessions.[26] One was on the line of the main Glasgow-Perth road, the other on an important approach road thereto, and both could certainly be described as of some assistance to the tenants of the annexed estates in Auchterarder parish, but the main long-term benefit was to the long-distance travellers on the road. Today Dalreoch bridge provides only private access to a farm, Chapelbank, as the line of road has been altered, lying further west.

The bridge at Callander over the Teith, already mentioned, involved the commissioners in one of their larger outlays at this time. There had originally been a ford by the church and a ferry a little east of it[27] and later a timber bridge, but apparently not one that would take wheeled traffic. To hasten the construction of this particular bridge, the commissioners were prepared not only to allow £200 and another £15 towards any deficiency in carriage but to build a limestone kiln – the Leny quarry was nearby. Furthermore, when Barcaldine suggested that timber from Gartchonzie wood would be sufficiently good for brandering (*anglice* scaffolding), they agreed to sell at a very reasonable price. This and the use of other local timber, firs from the Mains of Callander, resulted in a saving in carriage costs. Instead of transporting all the necessary wood from Alloa, only ten extra large trees were needed as the bases for the cooms.[28] Despite the importance of Callander's position in the road system of the time, the Board might not have been persuaded to commit themselves so heavily had the area not been largely under their management.

The sums originally authorised for general bridge building and quickly extended to road repairs were soon either totally expended or committed for future use, despite careful supervision of costs. For instance, it was decided that the centering used in building the bridge over the Teith should be properly laid up and preserved for future use; an estimate from the Lovat factor of £103 for a thirty-foot arch was promptly compared to a Perth estimate of £27.10.1 for one of a similar size and Captain Forbes was told to take note. Tenants of Camaghouran had five per cent interest added to their rents on the advance of £50 for a bridge that was considered of more use to them, at the time, than to anyone else.[29]

The greater part of the programme of bridge building reflected the factors' priorities, and could be shown to be of most advantage either to the Board's administration, as for example when rivers disrupted communications between annexed estates, or to their own tenants. Where small new arches were purely for the benefit of the estate, then the commissioners bore the whole cost without any hesitation if there was money available. On the other hand, when the factor wanted three bridges on the main road from Dingwall to Inverness, he was told to apply to the gentlemen of the county before the commissioners would move. When the Board did allow £25 for three that required rebuilding, over the burn at Bunchrew and two others, even though these were on the estate of Lovat they did so only on condition that the Commissioners of Supply would make up the remainder, as these were on the Inverness-Dingwall thoroughfare, an important public road north. Economy in this area of the country was not the best answer, however, for in 1769 several had been carried off in floods, that at Bunchrew among them, and the factor was in a hurry to have them rebuilt as he thought the fords were more difficult to cross than before the bridges were built.[30]

Workmanship on bridge masonry was not always expert then and remained suspect for some time. Thomas Telford in the following century had difficulty in finding experienced bridge-builders, and even more in discovering any who could claim to have built large arches.[31] Techniques in stone bridge-building were not perfected even in the nineteenth century, as the Commissioners for Highland Roads and Bridges discovered, and we should perhaps not be over-critical of their predecessors in road and bridge construction. The speed of the short Scottish burn in spate posed a challenge that was not always properly met, one indeed that had not been fully faced in previous ages. Even footbridges of timber had needed regular and frequent repair and replacement, and quite a number of the stone arches financed in part at least by annexed estates rents needed renewal before the disannexation. Some the commissioners were prepared to deal with at once, like the three in Glenartney in a 'ruinous' condition in 1781, for which the factor's estimate of £11.15.0 was at once agreed to. But these were an essential part of the road planned from Comrie to Callander and had been looked on favourably in 1762, when the only thing that delayed the Board's approval of spending £150 on them was the absence of a reply to their last report to the king. Several on the Comrie-Dunblane road were described as having never been properly finished and £5, admittedly a very small sum, was at once allowed for these.[32]

It must have been more disconcerting when a newly built bridge fell down whenever the timber supports were removed, as happened to the fairly expensive structure over the river Ruchill near Comrie, half paid by the commissioners and half by the county. The Board's subscription was withheld until the work was completed and the builders had given an assurance that they would maintain it for seven years, not an unreasonable condition in the circumstances or an unusual one. A few years later they refused to compensate the two masons who built the bridge for their losses at this time, when they declared that a flood had carried away part of the structure. It is not surprising that the Perthshire Commissioners of Supply in 1774 expected the gentlemen concerned to be responsible to the public for 'upholding' bridges, allowing them to adjust prices with the builders accordingly.[33] Bad design or bad workmanship and the strength of Scottish flood waters were not the only hazards faced by bridge-builders, however; in 1772, it was reported that a madman had thrown down the ledges of an arch being built at Carie on the south side of Loch Rannoch, near the factor's house.[34]

One request for rebuilding got a very unfavourable reception from the Board. If they were to attain the Inspector's aim of a road from Rannoch to Loch Tay, the river Lyon had to be bridged and, in 1767, £200 was proposed for the purpose, one argument put forward in its favour being that it would raise the value of the fir woods in Struan. In February, 1780 William Jeans, the mason who carved some of the Board's memorial tablets, reported that the bridge was in very bad state, with water having made holes near the foundations; some of the stones covering the parapet were missing and the others so unevenly laid that water had leaked in and caused damage. Though immediate repair was ordered, it was too late. The masons sent by Robert Menzies, the Struan factor, to inspect it, came back to say that a great flood had carried away the whole bridge a few days before, and the water was still so high they could not even tell if any part of the pillars had remained. When neighbouring heritors asked the Board to have it rebuilt, the committee was not surprisingly somewhat peevish and refused, blaming the local people for not having done small repairs in time. However, they relented when a further petition with a list of subscribers appeared a few months later and promised £100 in two parts, £50 at the beginning of the work and £50 when it was finished, with a ten years' guarantee from the masons.[35]

When tenants on the estate wanted the Board to act by providing some additional funds towards particular bridges, they were in the habit of drawing attention to the particular needs of their districts,[36] and the commissioners always kept in mind that their first duty was to the inhabitants of the annexed estates. However, it was soon realised by other interested parties that the advantages arising from bridge building as well as roadmaking could usually be represented as spreading far beyond their immediate vicinity, and hence often to the estates in particular and the Highlands in general. The first of these large-scale plans brought to the notice of the Board was the decision of the Perthshire Justices of the Peace at the Quarter Sessions in May, 1763 to promote the building of a new bridge over the Tay at Perth. There had only been a ferry there since 1621, when flood water had carried away the structure built by John Mylne. According to tradition recounted in Pennant, this was regarded at the time as punishment for the town's iniquity in holding the Parliament of 1606, when bishops were restored to their old position in church and state.[37]

After considering the advantages that such a bridge would bring, according to the town and county of Perth, and discovering that the town alone would subscribe £1,000 towards a toll bridge or £2,000 to a free one, the Board suggested that, subject to Treasury approval, £4,000 should be granted from the annexed estates rents, in two instalments in 1765 and 1766. The commissioners' arguments for laying out such a large sum in this way interestingly demonstrate London's priorities. They first mentioned historical antecedents, abortive attempts by both Charles I and Charles II to rebuild there, the first by collecting subscriptions, the second at his own expense. Then they recalled that, in 1715 and 1745, government troops could not have crossed the river there but for ice on the first occasion and low water on the second. Finally, the general easing of communications was presented as a good reason for supporting the venture. By the time the warrant for paying £4,000 had arrived, the Board had had second thoughts about the first proposed method of paying, and informed the Perth writer, Peter or Patrick Miller, the agent for the group responsible for building the bridge, that they would pay over four years. Even with this precaution, the final £500 could be provided in 1769 only by delaying promised grants to the hemp factory at Inverness and the salt pans at Brora.[38]

Like so many estimates for construction work in the north, it was apparent by 1770 that Smeaton's first price of £9,723.11.1 had been wildly inaccurate. By 1772, Smeaton himself felt the need to comment that 'I have found in every work I have been concerned for in Scotland that though the work has been well executed, yet it has not been possible to get it done for the prices at which I executed similar works in England, and particularly in masonry and carpentry branches'. In later estimates for the commissioners, he remarked that the only thing he could be certain about was the quantities, for the final price depended on the type of labour and carriage; he allowed for one mile by land and five or six by water, but the price of Scottish labour he found impossible to forecast, except that it was always dearer than he expected.[39] However, in the case of the Perth bridge, other factors were responsible for the increase in costs. The engineer had been advised of the fourteen-foot difference in the levels of the Tay in summer and winter, and that the bed of the river was generally gravel. He took several careful preliminary borings at various points, deciding eventually on a site which resulted in one unfortunate, James Bissett, losing part of his garden. Ice did not collect there and shallower foundations would suffice than near the position of the previous bridge, where ruins of old buildings were found which would have necessitated digging deeper to come to solid material. Unfortunately, he had underestimated the weight of water brought down by the river, which was not too culpable in one who had never seen the Tay in full spate. The strengthening of both foundations and superstructure required as a result raised the estimate to £24,840.0.8¾.[40]

When faced with such a massive increase, those responsible for the bridge once more had recourse to the Annexed Estates Board. The Earl of Kinnoull used his influence with his fellow peers and other acquaintances, both outside and inside the Board, to gain further financial support.[41] Moved no doubt partly by such pressure and partly by their genuine belief that, so far, the work had been 'executed in a very perfect manner', and the improvements to communications between Highlands and Lowlands that the bridge would bring about 'quite conformed to the spirit and the intention of the Annexation', the commissioners decided on an internal economy to help to complete the bridge. They did not appoint a new General Inspector to replace Archibald Menzies, who had just resigned on becoming a Collector of Customs, and his salary plus another £300 per annum was devoted to this very different purpose. Their total contribution reached £13,800, which still did not cover the whole cost, but Kinnoull advanced the greater part remaining.[42] The keystone of the last of the nine arches was struck on Saturday, May 26, 1770 and in 1787 Smeaton reported that everything was in perfect order, except for the footpath which had become very worn. For this, he had not been allowed to use Aberdeen granite, presumably because of the cost, and the stone used had not been hard enough. As at the Kinloch Rannoch bridge, today's traffic still flows over the basic eighteenth-century structure, which has been widened twice to cope with changing and increasing demands, first in 1869, with more recent alterations completed in 1972.[43]

Other would-be bridge-builders were not slow to realise that there might be a ready supply of much needed money, after watching the success of the Perth builders in tapping the annexed estates funds. The next important contribution to communications through bridge building was the proposed North Esk bridge, on the Montrose-Aberdeen road. This was of interest to a great many eastern areas of the country, provosts and magistrates of Aberdeen and Montrose, as well as gentlemen and noblemen of Forfar and Kincardine, signing the memorial.[44] The commissioners were a little hesitant about giving any assistance to this project, as they thought it should probably be built out of the Ordnance Funds, but once again they discovered defence reasons, in that a bridge there would have been of importance to the army in the rebellions. Also, it would be of general assistance to the penetration of the Highlands by Lowland custom. The foundation stone was laid by the local M.P., the Hon. Mr. Lyon, attended by Montrose magistrates and various masonic lodges in their 'formalities'[45] and, by February 1772, the builders could request the second half of the £500 granted to them, so fast had building progressed. Smeaton was the designer of this bridge too, and his estimate was once again on the modest side; in 1776, another capital sum of £300 was granted.

Once the North Esk was bridged, it was logical to plan a span over the South Esk and, though there was a ferry boat at Dun, it was said not to be reliable. So, in 1784, a further petition from the area appeared before the Board, this time from the Montrose magistrates, presented by Sir David Carnegie. The commissioners at once agreed to a contribution of £500, an eighth of the total cost, but their promise had to be carried out by the Barons of the Exchequer after the disannexation.[46] The precedent of the aid to the crossing of the North Esk also made it a logical step that other crossings on the post roads in the area should receive assistance. £100 was allowed towards the rebuilding of an arch at Benholm in 1777, and £120 to a new structure over the Bervie on the Laurencekirk to Stonehaven road, the bridge of Mondynes. There the vacant stipend of Glenbervie was at this time directed towards bridging rivers, so saving lives rather than souls.[47]

The salt-pans at Brora had to suffer further delay in receiving the grant of £200 allocated to them when pressure was put on the commissioners, through the Earl of Findlater, to grant £100 to the Duke of Atholl's agent towards a bridge over the Garry near Killiecrankie. The Board had intended delaying their contribution to the bridge there until all their previous engagements were honoured, but such high-powered persuasion was too much for them, and the precepts already signed and waiting in the office for sufficient funds to accumulate were ignored. However, there was some urgency in this case. The Garry was rarely fordable from October to March, and in February, 1767 a ferry-boat with thirty passengers had been swept away with the loss of twenty-seven lives. The third accident in twelve months, though the first when there were fatalities, at what was the only point of access to the west in an area which the *Scots Magazine* described as 'very populous country', must have given impetus to local and national recognition of the need for a bridge.[48] Probably it was the exigencies of the Board's finances, rather than any unwillingness to contribute, which restricted their assistance to £100 instead of the £250 asked for by the Duke of Atholl, once the General Inspector had assured them of how useful it would be to the estate of Struan. The Commissioners of Supply also gave £50 towards it.[49]

It was certainly shortage of money that prevented any assistance being made available to help Lord Fortrose, Sir Alexander Mackenzie of Gairloch, Sir Alexander Mackenzie of Coul, and various other proprietors, to build a bridge over the river Orrin on the road from Beauly to Lochcarron, despite the fact that Mr. Menzies, the Inspector, had been held up for three days by this river. The factor agreed on the need for the bridge, though he considered the estimate of £199 too little, but in any case the Board could merely recommend that the gentlemen should apply to the Marquis of Lorne and Colonel Skene for aid from the military bridge fund. There was no help forthcoming from that source either, however, and when the Commissioners for Highland Roads and Bridges began their work, the Orrin was still unbridged. The Ross-shire proprietors, though they had assessed themselves at £75 in 1768, were not very cooperative in the first decades of the nineteenth century, and in 1827 there was still no Orrin bridge.[50]

From the late 1760s until the demise of the Board, requests for assistance flowed in. Some went unrewarded for reasons other than lack of funds. For instance, despite the note 'sent by Lord Kames' on the back of the petition from the heritors and freeholders of Berwickshire in 1780, wanting help for estimated expenditure of £1,860 for bridging the Whitwater, there was summary dismissal of the appeal. Berwickshire was too far from the Highland area. Nor was there any interest in a very generally phrased petition for aid for Argyllshire bridges.[51] The Board liked to know exactly how it was proposed that their money was to be spent.

The Kenmore bridge over the Tay was another expensive, if not the most important, addition to the road system. £1,000 was eventually paid out of the rents towards this. The original petition played up the great benefit it would be as an essential junction between the annexed estates, between Perth and Struan, Lochgarry and Cluny, completing the road to Lochiel, Callart, etc. To talk of completion showed some degree of poetic licence, but the Board were ready to be convinced. When an architect, Mr. John Baxter, approved by Mr. Clerk and General Oughton, had given an estimate, even though it was higher than that of £1,400 originally produced by the Earl of Breadalbane and his fellow heritors, it was immediately decided to ask for approval from the king for an allowance of £1,000 to be paid in three parts, in 1773, 1774 and 1775.[52] Mr. Clerk and General Oughton were also asked to inspect the foundations.

At this period in the life of the Board, it is possible to sense that the commissioners felt that their work was unappreciated. Certainly much of it was unacknowledged. Dislike of visiting the sins of the fathers on their children was to result in the return of the Lovat estates in 1774; there were few encomiums to be found for what the Board had accomplished, and more brickbats than bouquets. Even where they had made an important contribution of one kind or another, as in their financial aids to communications, this was not always known. The Tay bridge at Kenmore, for instance, was, according to one tourist in 1776, 'generally said to have been built at the sole expense of Lord Breadalbane, but some say the Government allowed him £700'. This it must be admitted was hard, in the year after the Board had just completed paying £1,000 for that very bridge.[53]

In 1773, the commissioners decided that some public notice should be taken of the very considerable sums that were being handed out all over the country on various types of construction, especially in the Highland areas, and they decided that, in future, inscriptions would be fixed on these, giving the sums contributed. Sir Adolphous Oughton composed these, and Mr. Baxter the architect was the first employed to inscribe them. On the bridges, these inscriptions included in English the amount that was granted by the king, and in Latin *Viator Totu Transeas, sis memor Regii Beneficii* or *Pontem Hanc in Publicum Commodum Georgius III Rex construi iussit.*[54] This decision to blazon abroad their good works could be construed as an act of defiance at that particular time, as rumblings of doubt about the effectiveness of annexation could be heard. There was no doubt about the bridges. There they stood – most of them! – and many still do today. Given the manner of financing bridge building at the time, many would certainly have made their appearance much later without funds from the annexed estates; more plans than that for bridging the Orrin would have lapsed.

Latterly, little or no pretence was made by petitioners that there would be any direct advantage to any of the annexed estates. Those interested in a bridge over the Dee at Tullich near Ballater in 1777 were quite blunt, saying that they had been encouraged to apply by the Board's attention to 'erecting bridges . . . as the first and best improvement on the face of all countries'. The bridge over the Awe, for which the Argyllshire Commissioners of Supply had managed to collect £400 from the Duke of Argyll, the Earl of Breadalbane, and the partners of the Lorn Furnace Company, among others, was represented mainly as being of assistance to the drovers. They normally made for fords, ferries, or crossings that the animals could swim across, but they found the Awe crossing at the east end of the Pass of Brander a difficult one.[55]

Once the Awe was bridged, it was not surprising that the active gentlemen of

Argyllshire quickly foresaw the economies that could be made by immediately building its neighbour over the Orchy, on the road to Tyndrum. The timber scaffolding, the cooms, and the machinery could be moved the few miles along the road at once, instead of having to purchase a completely new lot at some time in the future, and have carriage to Glen Orchy to pay in addition. Despite having collected £400 the year before towards the Awe bridge, they did not approach the Board until they had amassed almost half the sum estimated for the Orchy bridge. Unfortunately, the Awe bridge was another that came down during its construction, after three arches had been completed, and the Board ended by giving £300 to both the Awe and the Orchy bridges, £100 more than was originally decided on for the Awe.[56] The road line approaching the Awe has been altered, and a newer stone bridge now takes through traffic on the A85, though on the north-east the old line is still used for access to houses around. The south-west approach is almost overgrown. The Orchy bridge, however, still carries the B8077 over the river, though most traffic to the west keeps further south along the A85.

The Board's largesse where road and bridge building was concerned had the effect, on one or two occasions, of arousing some slight peevishness on the part of those who felt they had not had their fair share. One of those who complained was Mrs. Susanna MacDonald, daughter-in-law of Donald MacDonald of Kinlochmoidart, who wrote in 1779 that, whatever the commissioners might have done for other estates, not a shilling had hitherto been laid out on Kinlochmoidart, despite its being so remote. The public road from Strontian had boats at all the ferries except across the river Moidart, and she considered a bridge there absolutely necessary. A similar petition from her husband had been read in 1775, and in 1779 a contract was signed for £100 to an Oban mason, John Stevenson, allowing the tenants' services for carriage of rubble, stone flags, limestone and coal and for filling up the ends of the bridge, and timber from the Lochiel fir woods to make cooms and centers. Also necessary was a specially made landing stage.[57]

In 1775, another complaint came from the Earl of Aboyne and others, including Francis Farquharson previously of Monaltrie, who 'took the liberty of mentioning' that the seven Highland parishes in the Braes of Aberdeenshire had hitherto received no benefit from the annexed estates. They wanted help for a bridge near Tullich, about twelve miles below that on the Braemar-Fort George military road, as between that and Aberdeen there were forty miles of river with no bridges. They eventually got £300.[58] A petition in 1777 claimed that no public money had been spent in Monaltrie. Perhaps they did not count the few soldiers settled there as a benefit.

Events have overtaken the commissioners' work on bridges, in some cases only in the twentieth century under pressure from the combustion engine. Lines of road with a sharp turning to obtain access over a high-backed bridge were not impossible for horses and carriages, but are resented by motorists for the deceleration imposed on them, and have led to a supercession of many of the older constructions and the older lines of road by gentler curves on the road and by flatter bridges. The changes are not always aesthetic improvements. The slender arch over the Almond at Millhaugh, for which Lady Catherine Drummond of

Logiealmond was one of the petitioners in 1779,[59] does not have any competition in beauty from its modern metal replacement, squat and uninteresting, though no doubt safer.

On secondary lines, secondary that is by modern computation, the chances are that the old bridges still do the work they were built for if proper repairs have been continued, and there are several of these to be seen. Where eighteenth-century highways have become part of the modern arterial system, then most of the old bridges have gone. On the A9, the Almond at Bertha near Perth needs wider and sturdier structures to support today's traffic. The bridges, also on the A9, over burns on the south side of the Beauly Firth between Inverness and Dingwall had been washed away even before 1784, and there again far greater width and strength is now necessary than was ever provided in the eighteenth century. The bridge over the North Esk, however, still takes the main Dundee to Aberdeen coast road, the A92, right-angled approach and narrowness regardless.

Many are still standing, but sadly barricaded off like that over the Forth at Drip near Stirling, or are used only for private traffic as at Dalreoch. Of another, over the Frew at Wester Frew, nothing is left but some signs of mason work and the raised road on the south side, but this bridge was unfortunate from the first. The gentleman who was the chief promoter of a bridge at that spot died before the work had begun and, in 1768, Lord Kames thought that the others involved had lost interest. He proposed, therefore, that half the sum allocated towards its construction by the Board should instead be directed towards the expensive Drip Coble bridge, estimated at over £700. It was 1779 before the Frew project came alive again, and the Board gave £200 as the county services had made the road from Callander. Building it was not without incident, for the cooms at one point sank in the clay bottom of the river and the arch 'keyed itself', an explicit phrase. Then a spate brought down the main and the north arches.[60]

Despite such mishaps, the contribution to bridge building was a very positive one, the Journal from 1767 specifying the payment of £3,575.6.8 for particular bridges, excluding the payments towards the Tay bridge at Perth and the many smaller structures that the factors dealt with. The latter were included generally in lump sums towards 'Public Works' and can only be traced in their 'Accounts and Vouchers'. But this was only a beginning and the need was greater than the Board's resources, perhaps greater than any that have so far been tapped even today.[61] The Board's funds filled in many small gaps in main roads not provided for by the county or military funds. Other crossings were basically of local convenience to the tenants of the estates and their immediate neighbours, like the two over the Pean and the Dessary in the estate of Lochiel. Of course, had a road to the west by the side of Loch Arkaig been completed, that over the Dessary (Deshair in the factor's notes) would have helped communications to the west. In the expectation that it would, the river Cia-aig at the east end of the loch was also bridged.

When they had funds in hand, the commissioners were often prepared to spend small sums on timber bridges, which they knew must be temporary, to save their tenants and the inhabitants generally from the inconvenience of passing through streams rather than over them. It is arguable that these smaller structures may have made more difference to the quality of life of the inhabitants of the estates and were more appreciated by them than the larger spans, though the latter made a more dramatic impression on travel generally and on the commercial life of the time. The last bridge assisted by funds arising from the annexation should not be forgotten. In 1793, £1,000 was handed over to Mr. David Robertson, the treasurer for a bridge over the Pease at Cockburnspath.[62] This money came from the capital repayments by the returning heirs, a matter considered in Chapters 11 and 12.

It is clear that, from their first days in office, the commissioners accepted that a good communications system involved bridging the maximum number of streams and rivers that crossed roads; they were equally prompt in recognising the importance of good inns. When horse-power was indeed provided by horses and not by petrol, and journeys shortened today by the energy obtained from fossil fuel then involved an overnight stop or at least a change of beasts, accommodation where horses and humans could be fed, watered, and rested, was essential. The petrol pump has replaced inns in supplying energy to continue a journey, but in earlier days an additional public need was filled by these establishments. They were often the only building apart from the kirk that could contain large gatherings, including the baron courts, albeit conditions were not always ideal. At Killin, one end of the public house was also the jail, and at least one prisoner had access to the other end as often as he pleased.

Scottish inns or changehouses, however, had a poor reputation where their primary function was concerned. The gentry and nobility rarely deigned to use them, for on most routes they could find kith and kin, however distant, who would provide them with bed and board. Innkeepers, therefore, were for the most part catering for the poorer sort of traveller, for topers, or sometimes for members of the armed forces, all of whom were likely to be less than nice in their requirements. Miss Grant's description of one inn she and her family were acquainted with, in her youth, paints a picture that must have fitted many: '. . . no carpets on the floors, no cushions on the chairs, no curtains to the windows . . . the dinner itself was excellent; hotch-potch, salmon, fine mutton, grouse, scanty vegetables, bad bread, but good wine'. A few travellers found a kind word for them, John Wesley describing them as clean and comfortable but, as he had heard 'miserable accounts' of them, the reality may simply have been less unpleasant than his anticipation. Southey, too, was agreeably surprised to find books provided for the use of guests, an amenity he believed to be found also in Irish inns, but not common in England.[63] However, such mild praise was rare compared to the general reports of dirt, unpleasant food, and unwilling service, and Ramsay of Ochtertyre went so far as to say that in no capacity did the Highlander in particular make a worse figure than as an innkeeper, an ostler or a waiter. 'He too often ingrafts pride, sloth, and contempt of cleanliness, on the worst qualities of an English publican'.[64] The commissioners were conscious of the general need for such accommodation, as some of them in their legal duties travelled around the country and were at the mercy of local innkeepers. After receiving the factors' answers to their inquiries in 1755, they were aware equally of the deficiencies on the annexed estates and in the Highlands generally, if indeed they were not before. The strangers whom they wished to entice to the north would be less willing to enter some areas without assurance of being able to obtain reasonable food and shelter, but the picture of accommodation gained from the factors' reports was hardly encouraging and became less so as one looked further north and west.

On the estate of Barrisdale, though there were neither maltmakers nor stills, yet there was a 'multiplicity of whisky-houses' to which the factor attributed the inhabitants' poverty. He did not mention changehouses as such, which could hardly have been neeeded in that inaccessible land where there were only footpaths. The most northerly estate annexed outright in 1755, Cromartie, seemed to be almost equally empty of inns though it was not without roads. Lovat was fairly well supplied with public houses and stills in the two northern baronies, Beauly and Lovat, but in Stratherrick, there were only a few 'hutts where they sell whisky', except in Fort Augustus, and there the public houses were in the liberty of the garrison. Of the five changehouses on the Struan estate further south, the factor thought two scarcely deserved the name. On Monaltrie, the somewhat con-tradictory information was given that there was no changehouse, except two which were kept by the miller and the boatman, two occupations which the com-missioners later stated they considered unsuitable for innkeepers.

The situation on the widespread Perth estate varied from one district to another. One at the Mill of Kinbuck was described as better than the ordinary run of country changehouses, but few received the factor's approval. He could say of only one that it was very good; this was kept by James Cliphane in Crieff. Crieff was well provided numerically with small inns and ale-houses, but apart from Cli-phane's only one other was considered tolerable. In Callander, though he thought every house was a 'sort of changehouse', he could talk of only one 'tolerably good inn' kept by Donald McNab. The inhabitants of Muthill once again excelled themselves by being singled out unfavourably as sometimes having ale and whisky but sometimes not, in their very bad, small changehouses. For the rest, indifferent to bad would suffice as a general categorisation.

The Board had been faced at an early stage with requests for help in remedying these deficiencies. One such petitioner was Angus Symon, a smith to trade, who wanted a farm on Monaltrie. He claimed there was no smith on that estate and he also proposed providing accommodation for travellers. There was no inn on the part of the king's road where he hoped to get a farm, Concraig. The factor approved the general suggestion, though he slightly lowered Symon's estimate for improve-ments. In 1759, the Barons of the Exchequer directed the commissioners' atten-tion to the inn at Dalnacardoch, which was not strictly speaking their responsibility at that date. This house lay on Lochgarry estate, still managed by the Barons because of the legal difficulties arising from the position of the Duke of Atholl as subject superior. The Barons had already done something about its repair, but this was an important stage on the road north; so, when the factor brought to the Board's attention the fact that it was in great disrepair and unfit for receiving travellers, he was asked to obtain estimates, one merely for repairing, the other for considerable improvements. The first for what he described as 'habitable repair' was for £18.4.10, the second for 'commodious repair' arrived at the figure of £67.19.4, and it was the more expensive that was accepted.[65]

By 1763, the Board was prepared to ask for the large capital sum of £800, to be allocated for the construction of inns in suitable places, and towards buying a house on sale in Crieff, which would be cheaper than building. It was unfortunate for their idea of developing a chain of inns that, in the same year, the Seven Years War ended, and the absorbing interest of the factors and commissioners became the expensive and time-consuming plan to settle demobilised soldiers and sailors on the estates. The request for the authorisation of a capital sum for the general purpose of building inns was ignored by the Crown and never revived by the Board, though sums were allocated for specific inns throughout the annexation, the two on the Great North Road, at Dalwhinnie and Dalnacardoch, having most time, attention, and money devoted to them. Dalnacardoch was one of the shelters used originally by General Wade's men whence on occasion he sent letters with the heading 'From my Hutt at Dalnacardoch', and over forty miles of the road from Crieff to this point were constructed in 1730.[66]

The repairs to the exisiting inn there, though 'commodious', had been insufficient, and in 1765 the innkeeper, Donald Macdonald, appealed for still more largesse. He was prepared to spend £25 of his own money, but he wanted another £75, £50 of it to be used towards enclosing and improving his farm, particularly to raise hay, an essential part of an innkeeper's supplies. It is somewhat surprising to find the Board instructing the factor to ascertain how much he had already been allowed, for such information would have seemed more readily available at their central offices and from the Barons of the Exchequer, and this procedure delayed any response to Macdonald's request. Swamped by work involved in setting up the soldiers' settlements, James Small, the factor concerned, did not present his report until early in 1767. Uncomplimentary about the house itself, he did endorse the innkeeper's suggestions, and some repairs were once again authorised, though responsibility for any land was laid where it belonged, until 1770, on the shoulders of the Barons. Despite further expenditure, the building was in such a decrepit condition that, in 1773, Small had to prepare timber merely to 'support the inn' until the following year, when a new hostelry would be built and the old one converted to stables. Small then saw the chance of a bargain. The original innkeeper had died, and his widow was being courted by a very efficient, well-off mason, Peter McNaughton, an 'ingenious fellow', who had built the inn at Killin for Lord Breadalbane. Small felt that self-interest would persuade the man to make a good job of the new house at the estimated price. Lathed and plastered, with the principal rooms and staircases papered, by 1776, it was ready to be insured for £500. Two inscriptions were fixed above the front door and are still to be seen on the tall white house. One was similar to that placed on bridges, with the necessary change of *Hospitium hoc* for *Pontem hanc*, and the other was the welcoming Gaelic, *Gabhaif Fois car Tamuill Bhig*, inviting travellers to 'Rest a little while'.[67]

Some miles north of Dalnacardoch, the inn at Dalwhinnie, near the junction of the main road north to Inverness and the cross-country route to the Great Glen by Corrieyairack, was also the subject of extensive improvements, though it was not part of any annexed estate. In the 1760s, the inn and adjoining ground belonged to one, John MacPherson, who was not considered by the commissioners 'by any means qualified for the business of an innkeeper'. As Dalwhinnie was an essential stage on the highway to Inverness, the commissioners spent £540 on repairs and extensions and took a fifty-year lease of the property. This ensured that their money was not wasted and enabled them to install Peter Robertson as their choice as mine host, and he gave satisfaction until the disannexation. Even with backing from the Board, Robertson had his problems. High freight charges were one; Dalwhinnie, he claimed, was further from any seaport or market town than any other place in Scotland. Another was that the innkeeper's attempts to raise hay had been rendered ineffectual by the exposed situation and the severity of the climate. He was also unhappy about the arable ground he was offered from the nearest annexed estates, and about the grazing land near the inn, but a compromise was reached on that score. John Baxter, the architect, assessed Robertson's lack of skill as a farmer as having some bearing on these latter difficulties, but his trials in trying to improve the accommodation within the house were none of his making. The repairs to the roof, which the Board had paid for, had been very badly executed, with a suggestion of chicanery on the contractor's part; every third course of slates had been missed out and only a piece of slate inserted, so that the rain got in and the wind made a 'great noise'. The original 28,000 slates had to be taken off and replaced with an additional 10,000. In 1776, internal alterations had increased the accommodation available, but neither satisfactorily nor sufficiently. There was no 'common hall' for soldiers and, when they were lodged in rooms and beds intended for gentlemen, the results were broken furniture and disgruntled gentlemen guests thereafter. As for those who could not be lodged in beds, they were put in the hay loft and made the hay totally unfit for horses. Then his kitchen chimney smoked, despite new Carron stoves bought in 1771 and his use of a machine for preventing smoke.[68]

The Board took his complaints seriously and General Oughton, the Commander-in-Chief in Scotland, was deputed to look into all of them on his next trip north. Unfortunately for Robertson, Oughton became ill, went south instead of north, and died at Bath. As a result it was 1784 before the next round of improvements was carried out, and then only after a further petition from the innkeeper. And in 1784 both Mr and Mrs Robertson were tired and depressed. They blamed the climate, but they had been struggling against adverse conditions for over ten years, and had just suffered another blow, when 200 of their sheep were smothered in heavy snow. No wonder they were asking for a reduction in their rent. Despite these difficulties, however, the inn must have seemed a thriving concern to some, and the owner offered it to the Board outright for £1,000 in July, 1784, when their lease had still forty years to run. The Board refused the offer immediately and, after the estates were disannexed in the following month, first the Barons of the Exchequer and then the Highland Society became involved in managing the inn. The Society accepted responsibility for paying the rent until the end of the lease, on receiving funds from the balances of the estates. Robertson got into trouble with the Barons at one point for subsetting, and finally gave up his position in 1803.[69] At his best, he seems to have been an active and interested hotelier and, in the bleak country round Dalwhinnie, the knowledge of decent beds – despite the occasional presence of 'other ranks' – and reasonable food must have been cheering. Taking over the inn was a worthwhile venture, though the effects may not have been lasting for, in 1818, John Anderson's diary of his tour in Scotland describes it as an 'indifferent house'.[70]

Through the Crown's negligence in responding to the request for permission to buy one inn at Crieff when John Caw, an Edinburgh writer, put it up for sale, this particular opportunity was missed, but the Board had an interest in another in Crieff, kept by Charles Murray, a vintner, as they were his feudal superiors. He and his wife were competent managers for whom the Inspector had nothing but praise, both during Murray's lifetime and during his widow's continuing proprietorship. Indeed, he went so far as to say they deserved the protection of the Board more than any others he had met on the estates. They must have made him very comfortable. But certainly Murray was keen to keep his house in good repair and, after his death, Mrs Murray not only kept on the inn and the vintner's business but tried to obtain extra land to have butter, as well as the more usual hay and corn.[71] Good as the Murrays were, however, the Board considered assisting another would-be innkeeper in Crieff, for the growing town could support more than one. They certainly felt that a good inn was needed there at such a road junction, but they were not prepared to support a monopoly.

The commissioners did not restrict their attention to the inns needed on the main roads north. Before 1760 they had authorised the factor to have one built at Kinloch Rannoch, which was not to be either very large or very well endowed with land. This one was a long time on the way. In 1757, the factor was asked about the 'public house presently building' at Kinloch Rannoch, and gave estimates of £40 for a two-storey house of stone and lime with garrets, or £30 for a three-roomed house with a kitchen on a stone floor. Two years later, the keeper of the public house wrote piteously that for two years he and his family had lived in the house in great danger, for the roof was held up by trees. Not surprisingly, no stranger or passenger would stay a night in it. Despite the reluctance of travellers to put up at his house, he declared that he needed more land, presently held by one he described as a troublesome neighbour. As the factor bore out his statements, the neighbouring tenant was to be evicted; also it was resolved to build a new inn at an estimated cost of £38.12.3 excluding timber. The innkeeper's troubles were not over even when he was decently housed, however, for the soldiers settled in the area brought competition from the redoubtable wife of the storekeeper in the village, the spouse of Sergeant McIntyre. Contrary to the Board's orders, the sergeant kept alcohol for sale, and his wife was in the habit of going to the authorised public house in Kinloch Rannoch, where she beat up those who would not drink at her house.[72]

Callander was another centre where a good inn was a necessity, for it was the first stage between Stirling and Fort William. In 1755, the factor had reported that while all the houses in the village had claim to be some sort of changehouse, there was only one tolerable inn, kept by Donald NcNab. As the existence of changehouses was tied up with the availability of alcohol, the commissioners tried to control both. In 1762, Lord Stonefield wanted to limit the number and fix the situation of houses on the estate to 'prevent the debauchery, idleness and dissipation occasioned by having an unnecessary number of changehouses', and he also suggested that no officer employed by the Board should be allowed to keep any type of premises which sold wine, ale or spirituous liquors by retail. Later that year, the factor on Lovat and Cromartie was to inform tenants that none should retail alcohol without a licence on pain of eviction.[73] The threat of eviction had little effect in the north, for, in 1765, the factor complained that changehouses were being kept without licences, and that distilling had become universal and was likely to ruin the tenants. On other occasions, factors noted that the illicit nature of distilling caused tenants to make night journeys to sell their products, with the result that neither horses nor men were fit for work on the farms during the day.

As far as Callander was concerned, however, a John McDiarmid had by 1761 realised the possibilities of such a site. He spent between £200 and £300 on improving his inn, and wanted only meadow and arable ground near the village to augment his supply of corn and hay, most of which he had to buy. Granting him the land he wanted meant that another tenant, John MacArthur, had to give up his land, but this was considered a sacrifice that had to be made. Unfortunately for McDiarmid, his inn and all its contents were burnt to the ground through a servant's carelessness in April, 1763, and he had been insufficiently insured at £250. In 1763, he was allowed £60 towards refurnishing, the interest on this sum being converted into feu duty. He claimed that his was the only house that could accommodate a gentleman with a night's lodgings between Stirling and the head of Lochearn. McDiarmid did not rest on his laurels and he kept on adding to and improving the facilities in his inn, no doubt to his own benefit, as the village of Callander and the number of travellers on the road through were increasing. He received further financial assistance from the Board, £50 in 1773 and £20 in 1784, as his inn was described as inferior to others by regular travellers on the road, who had asked the Board to remedy the inconveniences; but the innkeeper was expected to spend his own money on improvements in addition to any subsidies.[74]

One other inn received fairly large-scale financial aid, one at Inverness. This was a local venture sponsored by local businessmen, including a merchant and a glazier, and it was clearly quite a large building, for one petition mentioned that £500 to £600 was still needed. In 1778, the Board allowed £200 towards this but, a few years later, when they reported awarding another £100, they were constrained to point out to the Lords of the Treasury and the King that in the past there had been no proper accommodation for the Judges of the Court of Justiciary during their circuit in the area, nor for the Commander-in-Chief at the review. The Lord Justice Clerk, Thomas Miller, had made the same point earlier when he forwarded a begging letter from one of the subscribers, accompanying it with the comment that it was as well entitled to Board's bounty as any one of the inns between Blair and Inverness. He added what would seem a statement of the obvious, except that it is only now apparently being taken to heart, that it was vain to bring travellers on to Inverness if they could not be accommodated there.[75] One wonders if Miller may not wholly have approved of the lavish assistance to the two inns at Dalnacardoch and Dalwhinnie, lying between Blair and Inverness.

Inns were so necessary that the Board were almost too willing to try to supplement deficiencies. Any innkeeper trying to improve the amenities of his establishment was likely to be able to draw on their funds, whether it was for better stabling or better housing or for improving his farm; the successful hotelier in these days had to be at least an adequate farmer, with sufficient ground allotted to his house to keep him adequately supplied with raw materials for food and fodder. This the commissioners fully understood, and the connection between grazing and efficient innkeeping was recognised in that much pasture was leased to the innkeeper only for the duration of his tenure of his inn.[76] On one ocasion, however, the Board overstepped itself. The existing inn at Lix was considerd too small for the Stirling to Fort William traffic and the factor in the area was instructed to set about looking for a new site, being informed in somewhat cavalier fashion that he need not pay much attention to what was already there. His response gave them pause, however, for he pointed out that the present house was not only on the best site, but the occupant, an old soldier, was doing quite well, managing a good stable, which was extremely important, with plenty of hay and corn in an area where these were usually hard to come by.[77]

Though most attention and money were devoted to those inns which would serve most travellers – those on the main roads – less obviously important routes were not wholly neglected. £100 was willingly spent on repairing a Coigach changehouse, for example,[78] and the pressing need of the factor and the members of the baron court for decent accommodation, when they visited the estate of Barrisdale, hastened the building of a changehouse at Inverie, at the estimated cost of about £30, though twice as much was in fact spent. The innkeeper there had to be removed however in 1766, having failed to convince the committee of the Board concerned of his competence. Among other misdemeanours he had 'squandered his funds'. One other innkeeper, who was also a sawmiller and drover, provided accommodation for the baron courts; this was Alexander Cumming in Carie, previously mentioned. He wanted more land, and the comment on the possession he had, of three and a half acres of arable, sowing about four bolls of oats and bear, with grazing for about twelve black cattle, four hill horses and two dozen sheep and goats, was that 'doubtless it was scarce enough for a publickhouse keeper', once again showing the Board's appreciation of logistic difficulties. At any rate he was given two extra farms, one belonging to a woman, Katherine McPhail, whose son had a bad character, and the other to a man who had not replied to complaints made against him. But at least Mrs McPhail was to be given another holding.[79]

Not surprisingly, there was refusal initially to build a new inn on the estate of Monaltrie. Only eight miles south from the proposed site, there was a 'commodious' public house at Castletown of Braemar, and five 'tippling houses', as the factor described them, between, with three of these on the estate itself. Considering its size – two and a half miles round – this seems an excessive number, and it is the more surprising that the Board retracted the following year when the factor suggested that one was in fact needed. There was even a suitable innkeeper at hand, Sergeant Low, a former sutler for the 87th Regiment of Foot, supplied with satisfactory references from two of his officers.

The Board improved the facilities for travellers in other ways too, giving timber for repair to the King's House on the Fort William to Tyndrum road from the woods at Ardsheal, Lochiel and Callart, and thirty tons of timber towards a new inn to be built halfway between Fort Augustus and Fort William, where previously there had been none. The military funds were to be drawn on there to the tune of £50–£60, with the Duke of Argyll's permission, provided the Board allowed timber. In the same area, later in the year, a lease was refused of the old glebe of Boleskine on the grounds that it would be unwise to tie up land that seemed a suitable, central place for an inn. Further north still, the factor had suggested in 1770 that the Board should buy a house in Miltown that rumour had it was for sale. The price, however, was 200 guineas, apparently too much, for in 1780 Sir John Gordon of Invergordon was empowered to purchase the house at not more than £100 and, when this offer did not succeed, Sir John suggested converting the Court House at New Tarbat. In 1782, however, there was still no tenant in the public house described as 'lately repaired'.[80]

The building of one changehouse gave rise to an odd exchange of information between the Board's servants, a neighbouring heritor, and themselves. Henry Butter, presenting his accounts, included a receipted bill by a Fort William wright, Peter Tarnish, for a pier and changehouse at Ballachulish ferry. James Morison, the surveyor, reported that on a visit he found only the walls of the house, a few couples set and no more, a few stones set on the beach for the pier, and no workmen around. Only eight months later, in August, 1782, James Stewart of Ballachulish wrote telling of the £250 inn he had built on the south side, and asking for £30 towards a quay there, similar to that built by the Board on the estate of Lochiel on the north.[81] Had Butter, having received a sharp query from the Board, harried his contractors into finishing the work, or had Morison stumbled on Corran Ferry, without the benefit of the twentieth-century notice that proved necessary before the building of the Ballachulish bridge – 'This is NOT Ballachulish Ferry'?

Even at that time, an improved ferry service with safer landing facilities was undoubtedly a sensible suggestion. Stewart thought it would remove what he called the 'only obstacle' on the new road through Glencoe, which it will be remembered was subsidised by estates funds. By 1782, having supplanted the military road to Fort William, it carried the mail and there was therefore a great incentive for the Edinburgh Board to assist here; improved communications would help accelerate the post to their outlying estates as well as to the north and west of the country generally.[82] The reference to Ballachulish pier and ferry leads us to consideration of yet another form of transport subsidised by the funds arising from the annexed estates. Last mentioned, it is certainly far from being least important, especially in the eighteenth century. This is of course the movement of people and goods by loch, river, and sea.

11
Travel by Water

IT was not to be expected that such men as the commissioners would overlook the then contemporary trends in transport, any more than any other aspect of the economic or intellectual life of their day. As well as showing a proper concern for existing ferries, by ensuring the proper maintenance of boats and the employment of efficient reliable ferrymen,[1] they were attracted by the canal mania and by the late eighteenth-century plans to deepen and enlarge harbours. Water was both a hindrance and a help to transport at the time – a hindrance where broad or fast rivers crossed highways, whether made or unmade, and a help where navigable stretches of loch or river provided facilities for travel or for carriage of heavy goods, which neither the existing road surfaces nor the vehicles using them could cope with. Boats were used on Loch Ranoch for taking provisions to the troops stationed at the west end, for example, and for carrying consignments of limestone from the source of supply at the west end of Loch Earn to customers in the east. Though the first example is taken from the beginning of the annexation and the second from near the end, by which time roads had been built along Lochearnside, at both dates a boat was more suitable for the transport of heavy goods.

Ferry services were legion. There was one at the west end of Loch Rannoch, for instance, for which the Board built a boat in 1759 to replace one that sounded extremely dangerous, and they then rented it to the ferryman. Boats needed regular replacements, that on Monaltrie seeming to give more trouble than most. It was renewed in 1761 and 1762, destroyed by ice brought down in a sudden thaw in 1768, and replaced again in 1779. After the incident in 1768 the factor implied that the boatman had been less than careful, and suggested that if he were bound to maintain the boat he would be more attentive to his vessel in future. Certainly thereafter the boat did seem to last a little longer.[2] Many of the crossings were connected to public houses, like those at Ballachulish and at Banavie ferry over the river Lochy, on the road from Fort William to Loch Arkaig and Lochiel. A ferryboat was built for the latter crossing in 1782 at a cost of £5.10.0, including 4d for 'whiskie at the launching', and in August, 1775, the Board decided to lease the farm and ferry of Banavie to the minister of Kilmallie, binding him to employ a proper boatman. However, this order was reversed in November and the factor, the previous tenant, was continued in the farm, though not the ferry; he was also charged with keeping the changehouse near the Kirk of Kilmallie in existence as a public house. The Board disapproved of the posts of ferryman and innkeeper being held by one man. Ferrymen of course could be quite badly effected by new roads and bridges. A change of the line of road or a new bridge deprived them of old custom, and both landlords and the Board were prepared to compensate them for loss of earnings.[3]

Only one major venture in ferrying was subsidised by the Board, a packet-boat to Mull. First brought to their attention in 1772, this scheme did not impress the commissioners favourably. It had been losing money during the year it had operated, and they asked for a detailed defence of the scheme, showing just how much advantage it would bring to the Highlands in general and the annexed estates in particular. The Campbeltown merchants who had originally financed the boat pointed out in their petition that they could hardly be expected to persevere in the trade, however useful to the public, if their private interest suffered. In 1773, it was agreed to allow £40 per annum for three years, the boat sailing weekly from Crinan to the Sound of Mull, though freight was just covering costs. In 1774, the balance-sheet presented by the owners James Shaw and Duncan MacKenzie showed a loss of £13, and it took a letter from the Duke of Argyll to persuade the commissioners to ask for permission for further aid in their report.[4]

When the Justices of the Peace and the Commissioners of Supply for Ross-shire represented to the Board how much mileage would be saved on the road north from Inverness, if carriages could go by Kessock Ferry and Inverbeakie, instead of round by Beauly and Dingwall, a subscription of £50, half the estimated cost of £100, was allowed, to make the Inverbreakie piers suitable for wheeled traffic. This aid was dependent on equal subscriptions from the county gentlemen, however, and the other half seems never to have been collected. Smeaton had been commissioned to estimate how much this would cost when he was in the area[5] but the ferry there was not extended until the early nineteenth century when, under the direction of the Commissioners for Highland Roads and Bridges, piers were built on both sides of the Cromarty Firth at Invergordon and Inverbreakie, 130 yards and 90 yards long respectively. The whole cost was £1,638, of which £616.18.11 was provided from the funds made available by the government under the Scottish Harbours Act.[6] A bridge there was not even dreamed of in either the eighteenth or nineteenth centuries, and only the demands of the oil industry and twentieth-century technology have made it a practicable proposition.

Petitioners for aid from the Board often used very far-fetched connections with the annexed estates to strengthen their pleas. In 1764, the Bailies of the Admiralty of Dunfermline and the Justices of the Peace of Fife contended that cattle from annexed estates were carried over the Forth at Queensferry, which may well have been the case. However, at this time the Board's resources were fully stretched, settling soldiers and sailors. Repairs to the harbours of both South and North Queensferry had to be carried out with only the help of £200 from local funds and £60 from the Convention of Royal Burghs. Eight years later the Fifers had a better reception for a much more expensive repair of these harbours, and for the erection of piers designed and estimated by Smeaton at £980. The commissioners were prepared to spend £400 on the crossing, part of a military road, as they declared Queensferry was the most frequented sea passage in Scotland. The grant was paid out in 1775 and, in the following year, on a favourable verbal report from Mr. Clerk on the progress being made, they awarded a further £100, informing Crown and Treasury that they had done so and were 'in hope of meeting with the

Royal approbation'. On a smaller scale, Colonsay pier benefited to the tune of £40, the petitioner Archibald MacNeil also laying out £20, 'to encourage manufactures'.[7]

The dramatic rise of Glasgow entrepot trade in the eighteenth century tends to obscure the growing prosperity of the east coast harbours. In fact, while Scottish trade generally was obtaining an increasing amount of British foreign markets, what statistics there are show that the east coasters were not sluggards,[8] even though the west coast obtained the lion's share of the tobacco trade. The increasing interest in the linen trade, despite the attempts to use home-grown flax, was bound to attract European trade, especially with Russia and the Baltic where the best supplies were obtained. The largest ports of Leith, Dundee, Aberdeen and, increasingly as the century progressed, Grangemouth, had the greatest share of import and export trade but, within Scotland, where mountain and stream made communications exceptionally arduous and the rivers were in the main too fast to be navigable, the coastal trade was an important and vital part of the country's economy. While the acceleration of both overseas and coastal trade was greater after 1780,[9] for those who had eyes to see the portents of things to come were visible before that date, and three towns had town councils or entrepreneurs sufficiently energetic and farseeing to raise funds themselves and then to approach the Board for the Annexed Estates. They thereby qualified for and deserved assistance, by the Board's standards of encouraging self-help. These were Cromarty and Peterhead on the east and Rothesay on the west coast.

Rothesay magistrates and town council were the latest to apply for aid in enlarging their harbour, in 1779, but theirs was also the least ambitious project and, by 1781, £425 had been paid towards it. Lord Stonefield and Mr. Oliphant, to whom a great many practical schemes were referred for their opinion, had suggested that the original estimate of £1,449 was excessive, and recommended that widening the piers to allow 'carriages' to load and unload would be sufficient. As Lord Bute was prepared to donate £100, the improvements would cost the town nothing in improving what they claimed was already the safest harbour in the Mulls of Kintyre and Galloway.[10]

It was the town council of Peterhead also who approached the commissioners for assistance, but they spoiled their case by stating that they had no town funds. The Board expressed approval of the extensions proposed, but a note was made on the back that the secretary was to inform those concerned that the Board did not feel it proper to give aid until subscriptions had been raised. There was no doubt about the utility of the plan, for Peterhead was well placed to offer shelter to both coastal and ocean-going vessels, as well as being in a good strategic position to act as a base, in time of war, against privateers. Unfortunately the pier on the south harbour – there were really two basins, north and south – had taken such a battering from the fierce south-east winds that it was in danger of collapse. The interested parties, however, raised £500 from the Royal Burghs, £300 from the Merchant Maidens Hospital in Edinburgh, who hoped for an increase in rents from the lands they owned near the town, and £1,000 on the harbour dues. They employed John Gwyn as engineer, and the merchants and shipmasters added their support to a petition to the Treasury. This was forwarded to the Board, who prepared to make the requested contribution of £3,500 in seven annual instalments, from 1779 to 1786. This was another undertaking by the Board which had to be completed after 1784 by the Barons of the Exchequer from the funds paid by the reinstated heirs. Gwyn's estimate of £6,891.3.6 was insufficient. However, the writer in the *Old Statistical Account* thought that had the extension cost three times that sum it should have been carried out, as £5,000 had only deepened the harbour and made two piers. There was no doubt that the extension to the piers was of great service to shipping but, as ships increased in size and more facilities were demanded, Peterhead, like so many other harbours, saw more improvements in the early nineteenth century, on the advice of Rennie and Telford.[11] Forfeited estates funds were again made available after 1806, through the agency of the Commissioners for Highland Roads and Bridges.

In the case of Cromarty, it was George Ross, the entrepreneur who was proprietor of the barony and town, who proposed improvements to the pier there in 1778. The commissioners must have been predisposed in favour of some sort of development of this kind in the area for, from an early date in the annexation, there had been awareness of the need for a proper landing place in the Bay of Cromarty. Their original interest sprang from their schemes to turn New Tarbat House into a factory; had this succeeded, easy access would have been needed for the delivery of materials and the export of goods. The want of a good pier or harbour was being increasingly felt, too, as agriculture began to produce a surplus in the lands around, notably on the south shores of the Moray Firth, on the estates of the Earl of Findlater. The Board had gone so far as to ask John Smeaton to draw up plans for a pier at Portleish, near Tarbat House. Unfortunately, shortage of funds at the time had made his estimate of £711.2.1 impossibly expensive and ensured that the plans were laid aside, however regretfully. As a result, they were all the more open to positive suggestions, particularly when Ross offered to make over his title to the ground and coast needed, besides making a financial contribution. Payment of a grant of £5,000 began, therefore, with three instalments of £500 in 1779, 1780 and 1781, and one of £700 in January 1782. Thereafter, despite speedy progress on the pier under Ross's management, he found himself out of pocket until August, 1783, when the Board at last found themselves able to honour their obligations with the next £700. He had to wait still longer for the final settlement, however, after disannexation had transferred responsibility for all such payments to the Barons of the Exchequer.[12]

One plea came too late for the Board to be of any assistance. Alexander McLeod wanted help towards roads and a pier in Harris, but his petition was read in July 1784, by which time the committee considering the correspondence had to tell him that all the Board's engagements had already been reported to the Treasury. The financial tidying-up that the disannexation involved had got under way, and they did not think they could enter upon any new undertakings. However, in the last ten years of the annexation, support for pier and harbour building, the subsidy to the Mull boat and, lastly, surveys for canals, had accounted for £5,883.19.7 of the Board's funds.

It would have been more surprising if the canal mania had bypassed the Board than it is to find that they commissioned James Watt to survey possible cuts from Perth through Strathmore and, later, a route for the Crinan canal, as his work on the former had impressed them. Watt had been only the fourth choice for the Strathmore survey, Smeaton, Brindley, and Robert Mackell having been originally recommended. Smeaton and Brindley were among the foremost civil engineers of the day, and Robert Mackell had been employed by some Glasgow merchants, first to try to find an alternative route to Smeaton's proposals for the Forth-Clyde canal which would not bypass Glasgow, and then with Watt to alter Smeaton's route so that it would finish nearer the Broomielaw.[13] When the Strathmore survey was mooted, however, Smeaton was too busy and the other two refused the commission. George Young, the merchant in Coupar Angus who acted for the Board on occasion, was asked to employ 'Mr. Watt of Glasgow'. James Watt was paid £216.4.4 for the survey, a copy of which is in the National Library. He apologised for the time he took in the field but defended this on the grounds of 'uneven country and unhospitable weather'. George Clerk-Maxwell's comment on his report was that he was happy to find a 'great share of genius in this performance and that he is particularly fortunate in arranging his thoughts, but am sorry to observe that he is not so good at stating his account'. It cannot be said that Watt was an enthusiastic advocate of this cut, but its building was aimed mostly at preventing depopulation, partly caused by difficulties in obtaining fuel in the area. He estimated that a level canal from Kinnoull to Coupar Angus would cost £27,214.0.4, while the expense of one with locks from Scone to Glamis would be £41,537.13.7.[14] The Strathmore cut was an abortive scheme, but the other canal surveyed by Watt at the Board's expense, Crinan, is still in use, though not built under their auspices or to his specifications.

Both Miss Lindsay and Dr. Haldane credit the annexed estates commissioners with having employed Watt to survey the route from Fort William to Inverness for an inland waterway, eventually the Caledonian canal, but in this case credit seems to be given where it is not due. There are no records in the Journal of any payments to Watt for canal surveys other than these two, the Crinan and the Strathmore, though Watt apparently did make a survey for the Caledonian canal for another employer.[15]

The only direct financial assistance made by the Board to the Crinan canal was in fact to pay Watt for his survey of the lines proposed by the Magistrates of Glasgow, when they approached the commissioners in 1771. All the Glaswegians wanted from the Board at that stage was in fact the cost of the survey, to see if it was a practicable proposition to make a canal from Loch Fyne west, either from Loch Gilp to Loch Crinan on the Sound of Jura, or from Easter to Wester Loch Tarbert. As the General Inspector's journal for 1768 could be quoted, mentioning the utility of such a canal at either place, the Board agreed to underwrite the cost. George Clerk-Maxwell thought that Watt preferred the Loch Gilp to Loch Crinan line, for which he presented estimates of £34,879.0.4 for a seven-foot deep canal and £48,405.5.3 for one ten feet deep. Clerk agreed with Watt's preference and also recommended the shallower cheaper estimate. Watt's account on this occasion was for £162.15.3.[16] There the connection of the Board for the Annexed Estates with the Crinan canal had to rest, but financial assistance from funds arising from the annexation was far from finished. There was a large amount of capital injected into Scottish communications, especially into building canals, harbours and piers, which arose from the return of the estates to the original families. Its use must now be considered, for it can hardly be divorced from the general effects of the annexation.

The repayment by the reinstated heirs of the money expended by Parliament in clearing their ancestors' debts amounted to a large sum.[17] The Disannexing Act allocated the money to specific Scottish projects, including the Forth-Clyde canal. The 'Great Canal', as it was called, had staggered on from one financial crisis to another during its construction, and it was perhaps not surprising that £50,000 was lent to the proprietors out of the funds. Like the Forth Road Bridge, this had been an idea in the mind of Scots for a long time before it was actually built, and it has been claimed that Charles I proposed such a waterway for strategic reasons.[18] In 1768, the *Scots Magazine* published the suggestions made in a pamphlet, generally believed to come from the hand of an Edinburgh merchant, George Chalmers, that the annexed estates should be sold and the proceeds used to realise this dream. His arguments for this course of action were that the estates did not yield $1\frac{1}{2}$ -2% of the sum they would realise if sold, and that the canal would make the western estates more accessible. He claimed that the great distance from the 'civilised trading part of Scotland' and the almost insuperable difficulties of access were the 'chief perhaps the only causes of the long unpolished rude state of the west Highlands and Islands'. Everyone knew, he said, that the estates were inaccessible by land from the east side for any purposes of trade or improvement, and he argued that, if his suggestion was accepted, it would contribute more to what he called the 'wise purpose' of the annexation in ten years than all the produce of the estates as 'we have hitherto seen them laid out' would do in a century. The next month's issue saw an objection from merchants to the proposal to tax vessels on the canal, on the grounds that the funds from such a sale would be sufficient with the addition of only a trifling toll.[19] Lord Elliock, Lord Advocate, and George Clerk-Maxwell, commissioners for the annexed estates, were also included among the proprietors of the canal;[20] their private interest would not prevent their considering the idea sympathetically, and at least the germ of the idea of using funds from the estates had been planted.

The canal was opened in July, 1790, but the financial arrangements made had caused a certain amount of acrimony between the proprietors and the Barons of the Exchequer, who acted as the government's agent in supervising the use of the loan and in receiving the interest, had that been forthcoming. Too often, officials of the Exchequer court had to press the directors of the canal company for the statutory abstracts of their accounts, only to find when these did appear that they were so generally framed as to be almost useless. James Loch and James Baird, the Deputy King's Remembrancer, were both vexed by their dealings with the company. On one occasion, they even threatened to have its books brought to court for inspection. This apparent negligence was really a symptom of the company's financial difficulties, which even the opening did not immediately relieve. Despite steadily increasing traffic, notably in the number of herring busses sailing from the west coast to fish in the Forth, it was 1800 before it was possible for any dividends to be paid and, by that time, the government no longer had a financial stake in the canal. In 1799, Parliament allowed the Forth-Clyde Navigation Proprietors to repay without interest the capital sum loaned by the government. Expenditure of the dividends on Highland roads and bridges, optimistically planned in 1784, had come to nothing.[21]

Any relief the Barons may have felt at being relieved of this unsatisfactory responsibility must have been shortlived, for they moved from dealing with one canal company to having to cope with another, plus a town council, neither of which proved to be a wholly satisfactory debtor. The repaid capital of £50,000 was immediately loaned out again: £25,000 to the Lord Provost and Magistrates of Edinburgh to complete the improvements to Leith harbour, and £25,000 to the Crinan Canal Company, John Seton Karr being the officially authorised recipient.

The Crinan Canal Company, like the Forth-Clyde, ran into financial difficulties at some points because of the failure of subscribers to pay up but, unlike those who reneged from the earlier project, proprietors in arrears were to be sued. As 1,378 of the original subscribers were English compared to 473 Scottish, perhaps distance lent disenchantment. John Rennie's plan for a fifteen-foot canal estimated at £107,512 was accepted. As £91,500 had been subscribed by February 1793, an act authorising the canal was obtained and the work began, with Rennie as chief engineer and Captain Joseph Huddart, a well-known marine surveyor, employed to pick the best harbour sites at each end of the canal.[22] The loan from the government came at an auspicious time, for the inflation due to the war had added to the costs, and a loan at 5%, even though the canal itself was mortgaged to the Barons, must have seemed to the proprietors preferable to the other possibility, that of abandoning the construction altogether. But the 5% interest on the capital was a pious hope; in 1806, the Barons wrote to the canal company pointing out that five and a half years' interest was due, amounting to £6,875, and begging that the same should be paid by 12th May next, a fortnight thence. A few days later, however, a letter from Henry Jardine, the Barons' agent, to Sir John Sinclair notes that, as the canal company had asked the Treasury to grant bygone interest, no legal steps would be taken as yet.[23]

Edinburgh Town Council had also run into difficulties of rising costs and, as the Lord Provost pointed out, there was no possibility of income from the harbour and hence no interest for the Barons until the first dock was completed. But the Exchequer Court very properly remarked that it was beyond their statutory powers to grant a deferment of interest payment, as the act 39-40 George III, C.57 directed an immediate application of the money. This 'immediate application' was, like the unforthcoming income from the Forth-Clyde canal, to have been spent on Highland roads and bridges. Both the Crinan canal and the Edinburgh docks needed additional state aid in 1806,[24] once more of £25,000 each. By 1817, the Edinburgh debt was paid and hence was available for use in the Highlands.

Growing consciousness of the need for good communications can of course be seen throughout the eighteenth century, and the special needs of the Highlands were not forgotten. In the nineteenth century, in 1803, the first major step taken towards improving the road system there was the appointment of the Commission for Highland Roads and Bridges, with a parliamentary grant of £20,000. It was expected that half the amount needed for any given road or bridge would be collected locally, after which the government commission would provide the other half. Improved communications being considered a sure step to increased profit for proprietors in the relevant areas, even landowners on entailed estates were to be allowed to join in contributing towards the expense. Three years later, the new Commission was given yet another task connected with Highland communications. The Scottish Harbours Act transferred to their control the balance of the sums which had been exacted from the returning heirs after 1784. The capital was to be applied by them in building railways, canals, harbour improvements, quays, or any other works of that sort which they considered would improve 'that part of the United Kingdom'.[25] The Royal Bank of Scotland had also a deposit of £15,125, held at 4%, to pay annuities for the servants of the Annexed Estates Board and the rent of the Dalwhinnie inn. £22,300 had already been granted for a variety of purposes and included £7,500 to the British Fisheries Society for building a harbour at Wick.[26]

The act also hopefully described as 'Balances' the two sums of £25,000 lent to the Crinan Canal Company and to Edinburgh Town Council. But the Crinan Canal capital was never repaid, nor the additional loans, the total amounting in all to £74,000. The Barons assigned their rights over it to the Commission for Highland Roads and Bridges in 1812, an empty gesture, except that it transferred the onus of pressing for repayment on to the latter body. The Caledonian Canal Commissioners took over the burden of management of Crinan in 1816, though any revenue was still at the command of Barons of the Exchequer to repay the first loan, but this unsatisfactory situation was remedied eventually in 1848, when the Crinan canal was vested in the Commissioners for the Caledonian Canal.[27] In 1919, the Ministry of Transport took over both, when the canal's income was still, as throughout its history, smaller than its running expenses. Despite the poor workmanship, restricted capacity and its totally unprofitable nature, an inquiry held by the Ministry in 1921 found unanimous agreement among witnesses as to the importance of the canal to the Hebrides. In the present century, though the number of commercial vessels using it has decreased steadily, this has been counterbalanced by the growing number of leisure craft, which avoid the long journey south round the Mull of Kintyre on the route to and from the western islands of Scotland. 1963 saw modern technology using the canal when a hovercraft passed along it from Loch Gilp to Crinan.[28]

The Commissioners for Highland Roads and Bridges expected the eventual receipt, through the Barons, of the interest and capital lent to the Crinan Canal Company and to Edinburgh Town Council. In 1807, however, they noted with resignation in their report to Parliament, 'we are not taught to expect speedy repayment of either of the large debts'.[29] Faced with the demands of Highland communications, which absorbed all the income they could lay their hands on, and though appreciative of the Barons' problems, they understandably felt they must keep asking for their legal dues. In response, the Barons wrote sharp letters to Edinburgh Town Council, who replied realistically that they were no better off than in 1807 and could repay no capital until the docks were completed. They did at least keep up interest payments, to the tune of £5,809.13.11, which was more than the canal company did, and in 1817 repaid the capital, by borrowing from a more complaisant lender in the post-war conditions, when money was slightly more easy to come by. Meanwhile, it must have been somewhat irritating for the Commissioners for Highland Roads to have the assignation of the Crinan canal debts, coming to a grand total of £48,781.0.1, described among 'Money aids by the Barons of the Exchequer to the Commission', as if it had been real money.[30]

Dr. A. R. B. Haldane, in his book *New Ways through the Glens,* has dealt with the work of the Commissioners for Highland Roads and Bridges as it was initially conceived in 1803; but the use to which they put the capital available from forfeited estates funds must be considered as much part of the total contribution to Scottish highways of all kinds, water and macadamised, from the conception of annexation, as that resulting from the work of the Annexed Estates Board.

The Commission had been at work since 1803, and had produced two reports by 1805 on their past progress and current programme in road-building.[31] They had found cause to complain incidentally about the inaccuracy of Ainslie's map and of the surveys drawn up for the Annexed Estates Board, though the restricted nature of the latter could hardly be faulted, as they were primarily intended for estate management. They had been very pleased to come upon Roy's map, drawn up like the original surveys of the annexed estates under the supervision of Lieutenant-Colonel Watson, and even better pleased to discover its comparative accuracy. Another mapmaker, Arrowsmith, was employed to copy it at the expense of £150. In 1807, however, their third report had to describe the new dimension added to their work, the added responsibility of administering the 'Funds Arising from the Forfeited Estates in Scotland' under the Scottish Harbours Act.

In the light of the increasing interest in harbour and dock development at the beginning of the nineteenth century, the number of applications they had received for assistance was surprisingly moderate. Eleven town councils or harbour proprietors (not necessarily the same) had put forward suggestions for improving their harbours by enlarging or deepening, or by lengthening or strengthening their piers: Ardrossan, Peterhead, Macduff and Banff, Oban, Portpatrick, Burghead, Kirkwall, East Anstruther, Culgower and, last, Islay and Colonsay, all wanted quays. Many of the applicants had not realised that loans could be made under the Harbours Act only under the same conditions as to road and bridge building, i.e. a 'moiety' (a half) of the proposed expense had to be provided by the petitioners; others had not specified amounts at all. In their third report, the commissioners decided to defer any proceedings until they had made some investigation into the comparative utility and urgency of the applications before them. This was for two reasons. First their funds were more limited than appeared on paper. As we have seen, £50,000 was tied up in Leith docks and the Crinan Canal, and only £12,931 had been received from the Barons. Secondly, the House of Commons Report on the bill had held out promise, or at least expectation, of assistance for several projects, including a canal from Loch Earn to Perth. Proposed expansion of Fraserburgh, Thurso, and Helensburgh harbours had brought what one might describe as anticipated expenditure to £13,800. It was only sensible for the commissioners to move warily.

By 1807, however, they had eliminated all but Burghead, Fraserburgh, Peterhead, Kirkwall and Culgower, as not being in conformity with the act of Parliament, and then they cut out Culgower because it was too small and too shallow. It was reckoned that without the financial assistance from the government through this agency, Burghead, Fraserburgh, and Kirkwall would have found it impossible to improve the facilities of their harbours. There were technical snags to be evened out in two of these cases. The usual rule adhered to in the case of assistance to roads and bridges was that it should not be retrospective but, as the proprietors of Burghead had carried out their improvements, relying on the act and on the circular letter sent out by the Commission itself in 1808, the commissioners thought that it would be inequitable to keep too strictly to the letter of the law. There was the further question of tolls, which both Burghead proprietors and Peterhead magistrates had intended using to reimburse their funds. This, however, was forbidden by the original act providing funds for the Highlands in 1803, and compromises had to be made.

Burghead proprietors had indeed increased their original expenditure to £9,000, so confident were they of obtaining aid. In the circumstances it was proposed that the revenue from the tolls should be counted as the local contribution, thus meeting the conditions of the act. The proprietors agreed to devote half the revenue to upkeep of the harbour, and a £2,000 subsidy was granted towards a nominal total of £8,000. The village sits on a promontory at the south entrance to the Moray Firth, admirably placed between Inverness and Peterhead. The promise of those involved to use any surplus from the grant of £2,000 to make roads in the neighbourhood of Burghead, added to the fact that between the two major ports only Cromarty could admit a vessel of 100 tons, must have encouraged this bending of the rules. Cromarty harbour, as we have seen, had been extended with the help of the Board for the Annexed Estates in the 1780s. Unfortunately, the plans used for Burghead led to later troubles. The work was completed in 1809 but, by the time the commissioners produced their report for 1810-1811, the disturbing factor had appeared that sand accumulated at the mouth of the harbour at an alarming rate, so that the port was not having such beneficial results as had been promised. Also, the walls were not watertight and constant labour was needed for repairs. The Burghead experience led to the refusal of extra assistance to Fraserburgh, where it was suggested that the south pier should be extended to enclose the area further, on the grounds that there were dangers in effecting too closed a space in the attempt to provide perfectly smooth water. That the funds were insufficient was an even more potent argument.

Despite the amount already spent on Peterhead, the harbour was said to be 'in great want of improvement' in 1809. The inhabitants there in the eighteenth century had shown that they were keen to improve their harbour, and their enthusiasm seemed not to have abated. When it was pointed out to them that their having procured an act authorising tolls in 1807 would disqualify them from obtaining aid from the funds available under the Scottish Harbours Act, they at once agreed to dispense with tolls and raise half the sum needed, £3,900. The magistrates also suggested that if they were given £400 more they would deepen the basin still more, but the commissioners were unsure that the benefits arising from this merited the extra expense. As it was, vessels drawing fourteen to sixteen feet of water could now, it was hoped, be accommodated in ordinary tides, and Rennie had inspected and certified the work done. In October, 1819, both Peterhead and Banff, which had already been recipients of the commissioners' funds, suffered extensive damage from a violent storm, which hit Banff on the 22nd and Peterhead on the 23rd and 24th of that month. The estimate of repairs at the latter was £3,000, which was shared by the commissioners and the town, and that at Banff was £2,000. In the latter case, it was decided to benefit by experience and provide a larger harbour of two Scottish acres with a better entrance; the largest merchant vessels of the time could then be accommodated if three-quarters loaded.

The urgent and immediate need for repair as a result of the 1819 storm had meant that money not definitely committed had had to be diverted to these two harbours, and Macduff was one that lost its chance of a grant thereby, for, in the ninth report, the commissioners were closing their harbour accounts. The Crinan Canal debt of £25,000 was still a paper one, but that and a claim on the Perth estate they had had to regard as 'of no convertible value'. Without these, the funds from the repayment of the annexed estates debts had realised £52,000, all of which had been applied to harbours, canals and piers, and had been almost doubled by contributions from individuals or from burgh funds. The amount of expense on individual schemes had varied greatly, from £30,000 on Peterhead to £130 for Keills Ferry Pier in Kintyre.

No railways appeared as a result of the 1806 act and the only canal built was that at Dingwall; the suggestion of one from Loch Earn to Perth never reappeared after the third report. The Dingwall canal was 2,000 yards long, and had enabled the town to have two basins with quays, one where the Great North Road crossed the Peffer, the other 600 yards east of the town, giving access at all times to vessels drawing nine feet of water and to larger vessels in the spring tides. Previously, cargoes had had to be discharged on a muddy shore a good mile from the town, then carried along a poor road. On this occasion, the other contributor had been a Mr. Davidson of Tulloch, who also undertook the contract totalling £4,000, £2,000 from the commissioners and £2,000 from the contractors.

Appendix Z in the ninth report showed how the money available had been spent at the date of the report. The details are given below, showing that £41,327.4.3 had been paid out and £8,893.17.4 remained of £52,640.16.0; some of the discrepancy was due to administrative costs, the salary paid to the commissioners' secretary, for example. The total unused for constructional purposes, as recorded in this appendix, amounts to only £2,419.14.5 for fifteen years' administration, which is not an extravagant sum in the circumstances. The use to which the remaining capital was to be applied was also noted, including the amount committed to finishing the landing pier 'of massive dimensions' at Ballintraid, spelled Ballintraed, for import of lime, coal, and other goods for use in Easter Ross, and for the export of timber and corn. The total due from the Commissioners for Highland Roads and Bridges, £638.15.9, had been paid, but in all £1,200 had to be contributed. The report described the Cromarty Firth as one of the best and most extensive harbours in Great Britain, but until recently it had lacked a pier.

It was hoped that under the Harbours Act some improvements to Nairn harbour costing less than £3,500 would be carried out, and also that a ferry pier at Channery (Chanonry) would be built with £500 from Mr. Mackenzie of Flowerburn and a like sum from the government funds. Here the report expressed some disapproval of the Ordnance Board's refusal to assist by building similarly on the other side of the Firth for the use of the garrison at Fort George. By the time of their next report on the roads, anticipated for 1822, the commissioners expected to be able to announce the completion of all these works. In fact, their tenth report did not appear until 1824, by which time apparently neither the commissioners were sufficiently interested to provide, nor the House of Commons to demand, details of the expenditure, and the final comment was as follows: 'Some of the harbours, piers and Ferry Piers will in future be maintained in repair by means of tolls authorised by the Road Repair Act of 4 George IV, c.56 parts 35, 36. Applications to this effect are not all of them in such form as can be complied with; but substantially the desired result will take place. A Bill is now pending in Parliament for due maintenance of the Dingwall Harbour and Canal which has hitherto been described as an object of solicitude to the Commissioners'. This marks the end of Parliamentary interest in the finance rising from the annexed estates; more general interest had died a long time before.

It will be seen from appendix Z in the ninth report that the greatest proportion of the money was directed to the east coast of Scotland from Gourdon to Portmahomack while, with the exception of Kirkwall, Portree and Kyle Rhea, the rest went to Argyllshire.[32] The weight given to the harbours on the Buchan and the Ross and Cromarty coasts was due largely to the awareness of the lack of shipping facilities of any kind in an area where an expanding agricultural economy was looking for outlets. Banff, for example, though a very bad harbour,[33] could, in the eighteenth century, have provided an outlet for any surplus produce from the lands of the improving Earl of Findlater and Seafield; later the Middleton brothers were growing wheat successfully in the Black Isle, and landlords and tenants were prospering all over the north-east. The proprietors of land in Ross, while grateful for help received and particularly for the canal at Dingwall, pointed out the need for more harbours, quoting the export of 10,000 bolls of wheat in 1816, whereas not long before this trading in corn had been unknown.

Harbours and piers in the west can by and large be seen to be connected to road building that the commissioners had subsidised or were interested in. In 1805, the roads that had been surveyed included 57 miles 670 yards from Kyle Rhea west to Stein on Loch Bay; 37 miles 990 yards from the Aird of Trotternish past Portree to Sconser; 16 miles 157 yards on Jura from the Ferry of Feoline to the Ferry of

Lagg, between which lay the Small Isles, where a pier was built; and 1 mile 528 yards from the quay at Keills to join a country road. Their assignment of funds to these harbours and piers was part of a consistent pattern of development.

In assessing therefore the effects of the annexation on Scottish transport and communications, the contribution from the repayment of debts by the reinstated heirs must be fairly highly weighted. The sum of over £50,000, as the Commissioners for Highland Roads and Bridges pointed out, was almost doubled by local contributions and, apart from any advantage to the economy of particular areas in the provision of better transport facilities, the injection of money wages to labourers must also have provided a welcome boost to local families and traders while the works were in progress.

Ninth Report, Appendix Z, showing the amounts spent from £52,640.16.0

Harbour, or Pier	Expenditure
Avoch	£527.17.0
Ballantraid (in part)	638.15.9
Banff in part	6,200.0.0
Burghead	2,000.0.0
St. Catherine's	83.10.0
Cullen	2,070.9.7
Dingwall Canal	1,904.2.2
Fortrose	2,007.13.3
Fraserburgh	5,277.17.7
Gourdon	994.18.8
Invergordon piers (in part)	616.18.11
Jura Small Isles Pier	373.10.0
Keills Pier	64.18.7
Kirkwall Harbour	1,972.2.0
Kyle Rhea	572.16.3
Peterhead, South Harbour	3,900.0.0
Peterhead, North harbour	7,880.4.0
Portmaholmack	1,584.9.2
Portree	338.1.2
Tarbet	863.11.9
Tobermory	1,455.5.4
Total	£41,327.4.3

The harbours themselves were not uniformly successful. The new basin at Banff in particular, destroyed in 1819 and then repaired with help from the Commission, was discovered to be unsafe, having vessels wrecked when moored inside it. Further, it was very quickly almost filled up with sand. The only advantage gained from the new pier was prevention of swell in the old harbour. By the time of the *New Statistical Account,* it was still of use for the live cattle trade and grain, though the herring fishery had declined, but obviously it had not fulfilled the expectations of the earlier years of the century. Others were longer-lasting in their benefits to the communities. In the middle of the century, Avoch still serviced sloops bringing coal and lime; steam vessels were able to make deliveries at Chanonry Point; and, though the minister of Tarbat might deplore the effects of the harbour at Portmahomack and of the herring fishery stimulated by its existence in bringing about a decline in morals in the parish, he had to admit that it was otherwise useful to the area's economy. Nairn harbour, like others on the south coast of the Moray Firth assisted by the Commissioners for Highland Roads and Bridges, had an accumulation of sand and in addition had to contend with river floods, so that it was of use only for fishing boats and small vessels. The Earl of Seafield got the whole credit for any improvements at Cullen, having in 1834 made an extra quay, but the Commissioners for Highland Roads and Bridges, as we have seen, did provide over £2,000. All the improvements were supposed to have cost Seafield personally £10,000. The Dingwall canal also received favourable mention in mid-century, but Fortrose was not mentioned.

In retrospect, it can be seen that the two basins most likely to succeed were in fact those of Fraserburgh and Peterhead, whether they received financial aid at this particular time or not. They were the largest, for one thing, and as transport systems have evolved, the tendency to increased growth in the size of cargo vessels has given the larger harbours and docks a built-in advantage, wherever hinterland conditions are favourable. More trade stimulated further improvements and both these ports refused to rest on early nineteenth-century improvements. The trustees for Peterhead began a pier to protect their north harbour almost as soon as it had been completed with the help granted under the Scottish Harbours Act. Fraserburgh was described by Robert Stevenson as being, with Burntisland, the best tidal harbour on the east coast in the first half of the eighteenth century, and investment in the two more northerly harbours continued in the nineteenth and twentieth centuries, to accommodate the herring fishery first and latterly the oil industry.[34]

However, from 1807 to 1821, the overall picture of the needs of transport and communications was very different from that of a very few years later, when the advent of railways affected both road and harbour traffic, and early nineteenth-century planners can hardly be criticised for lack of a crystal ball. Whether the sanding up of the Moray Firth harbours could have been anticipated then is doubtful, for even modern techniques used by hydrographers in constructing models simulating conditions expected in such constructions do not always foresee all the possible snags. The rising costs experienced in the period during which the Harbours Act mainly operated, one of the effects of the Napoleonic War, restricted its application, as did the delays in obtaining access to the capital, but taken all in all the building that took place as a result of the act must be considered a very real benefit arising from the 1752 annexation, even though an indirect one.

The large capital sum which became available for government use after disannexation, as the heirs repaid their forefathers' debts, was put to a variety of purposes, all of them Scottish, and these will be discussed in the final chapter, but by far the greatest proportion of it was devoted to improving water transport. Throughout the annexation, that and all other sections of eighteenth-century communications in Scotland shared in the profits of the estates and, of all the activities of the Board for the Annexed Estates, their work in supporting bridge, road, inn, and harbour construction was probably the most effective. Apart from H.M. Register House, which shared in both the small surplus from estates which were forfeited but not annexed and in the post-disannexation cash distribution, the Board's expenditure in these fields has left the most positive and lasting monuments of the annexation. The Loch Ericht Hotel at Dalwhinnie and the bridge at Kinloch Rannoch are only two of the mute witnesses that can be called for the defence of this case, and many more bridges particularly can be cited. Furthermore, the Board's ready encouragement of any improvements in the transport system once again demonstrated how very much they were in sympathy with contemporary attitudes and outlook. At least one petition was quite explicit as to this growth of interest; Sir Alexander Ramsay of Balmain, Sir James Nicolson of Glenbervie, and others excused their appeal for assistance for a bridge over the Bervie, which was not strictly speaking in the Board's territory, on the grounds that 'the building of bridges has now become much the object of public attention as being absolutely necessary for opening free intercourse of communication through the different parts of the country and consequently for advancing the progress of improvements in agriculture and manufactures'.[35] The Board's interest in all types of communication in use in the Highlands at the time followed the same course as that of the public at large. Starting off with financial assistance to roads, bridges, and inns, and maintaining that interest throughout their existence, the commissioners partook of the canal mania and latterly they gave considerable sums to aid harbour construction, just as interest developed in this nationally.[36]

Also, the commissioners did not work in isolation. We have seen that they sought the assistance of the Commissioners of Supply and in turn were appealed to by them. Large bridges were not built out of annexed estates funds alone, partly because funds were insufficient, but also because of the Board's philosophy of self-help; they would contribute only where local interest had resulted in practical effective steps being taken to amass at least part of the necessary capital outlay. So strong was this element in their allocation of their resources that, as we have seen, they argued against assisting the rebuilding of one bridge, that over the river Lyon, near Meggernie Castle, because the other heritors in the area had neglected it; and this despite the fact that the original reason for subsidising it had been to facilitate travel between the estates of Perth and Struan. That at Kinloch Rannoch was an exception, built solely from the Board's funds, because the Crown estates were so extensive in the area. It was also expected that the new settlement there would become a centre of communications to the west and north, a forecast that has a hollow ring today, but was not unreasonable in the 1750s and 1760s, with the prospect of a road across Rannoch Moor to King's House in Glencoe. The rapid pacification of the Highlands in the second half of the century helped to remove any sense of urgency in finishing such a line.

The general aims of the annexation once accepted, i.e. pacification of the Highlands, the introduction of industry, and the general assimilation of Highland into Lowland culture, then subsidisation of methods of transport became a logical course for the Board to adopt. The central government's ready and almost invariably immediate response to their requests for permission to be allowed to spend more money in this sphere contrasts vividly with reaction to, or ignoring of, some other of their activities, and shows the general appreciation of the importance of better communications. From the Lowland and London standpoint, defence of the realm loomed large throughout and alone would have been sufficient reason for much of the expenditure, particularly for spanning rivers, but overall expansion of communications was expected to bring far-reaching social and economic benefits. For instance, if the parish minister could move around more easily and make regular visits to his parishioners, there would be no need for them to seize on the services of the first priest who appeared to baptise their infants, as apparently they did, without regard to whether he was Roman Catholic or Protestant. It was also believed that increased contact with Lowland culture would soften the Highlanders' manners and quicken their industry, whereby they would shake off their 'sloth and indolence and improper means of supporting themselves'.

Nor did the commissioners ever forget their primary duty to promote the welfare of the annexed estates in particular; they extended as much sympathy and interest to the Callander minister's plea for a bridge to prevent his congregation being soaked on the way to church as they devoted to much larger structures. Captain Forbes' suggestion that they devote £150 per annum to the sole purpose of building bridges over 'little rivulets', especially those that led to churches and mills, was one that the Board would no doubt have willingly followed, had other demands not seemed more pressing in light of their resources. As it was, a considerable number of arches of both stone and timber that the Board did build and repair, without formal acceptance of any specific sum, must have added greatly to the comfort and convenience of their tenants.

The proportion of their expenditure devoted to communications shows the importance attributed to this aspect of Highland development, from the start of active involvement by the Board. In the Journal detailing sums paid out from August 1767, £3,675.6.8 was earmarked for bridges, excluding the large capital subsidy to the bridge over the Tay at Perth and the sums not specified in the amounts spent on 'Public Works' by the factors; £1,520 was allocated to roads and, in the last ten years, £5,883.19.7 to harbours, ferry piers, the Mull packet and Watt's surveys for the Strathmore and Crinan canals. The last sums are not even the total, for the Barons of the Exchequer had to discharge a proportion of the allowance on harbours after 1784.[37] Between 1761 and 1784, the Crown authorised £21,807 for road and bridge building. This was a far from derisory contribution towards the aims of annexation, assistance of industry and the integration of the population. But it was a slow process, many of the arches described as very necessary in 1755 and 1761 being built only ten or fifteen years later. It was 1780 before the inhabitants of Balquhidder and Strathyre had stone bridges over the Balvaig, assisted by a large contribution from the county.[38]

However, it must be admitted that the Board can be faulted on two points. First, they *initiated* few projects that actually materialised. They usually just waited for requests for help, though it can be argued that the annual expenditure they incurred from 1761 onwards on smaller local structures serving the estates was of major importance in proportion to their total income. Secondly, the concomitant of this lack of initiative is that most expenditure, on bridges particularly, was concentrated south of Loch Rannoch, as a glance at Map B will show. As heritors were thicker on the ground further south, there was more active interest in improvements, more money available, and hence more appeals for help. The theory of David Turnock, that differences between south-east and north-west have been intensified by all schemes to improve, is borne out here.[39]

Certainly it was logically necessary to open the roads further south before one could reach the more remote north but, despite pleas that work was held up for lack of money, most of the Lowland work might well have been accomplished with help from other sources, such as the Ordnance Fund. The large subsidy given to the Perth bridge, had it been spent on a number of less ambitious projects, would have achieved less spectacular results than Smeaton's graceful bridge, but would have built many small arches and improved many miles of road further north. Admittedly, statute labour was not the most efficient method of building roads, and the country people needed a great deal of expensive supervision, but the £700 a year granted to this expensive construction would have gone far. Even maintenance might have been improved, though this was an intractable problem, as the Commissioners for Highland Roads and Bridges discovered later. These later road-builders found that, despite initial enthusiasm for new roads and indeed for roads much superior in quality to what they considered justified or prudent in terms of expense, when the roads were left to the care of Highland gentlemen, they were allowed to fall into disrepair, through lack of co-operation and what the factor to the Duke of Hamilton, Robert Brown, called 'a shortsighted view of individual interests'. Brown had also worked for Clanranald and thus had some experience of such selfishness.[40]

Henry Butter was only one factor on the annexed estates who tried to impress on the Board the crying need for improvement in communications, and much of his correspondence shows how much thought he gave to the subject, as well as time and energy. In 1767, he claimed that he employed two to three thousand people on statute labour and made sure of the county services to make roads where there had formerly been 'only footpaths'.[41] Highland transport needed and still needs people with similar devotion, and it is a sad fact that, lacking either devotion or finance or both, many Highland roads are still 'only footpaths' by twentieth-century standards, though most streams are bridged. It is perhaps an even more pointed commentary that some bridges, built to eighteenth-century specifications and widths, are bearing the flow of twentieth-century traffic, without any change in their fundamental structure.

CONCLUSION

12

Conclusion

IN 1784 the experiment ended. At the beginning of August in that year, Henry Dundas, who was appointed to the Board in 1783, presented a bill to Parliament for a first reading which proposed returning the annexed estates to the former owners or to their heirs. Long before, in 1775, Dundas had argued for the return of the estates, expressing the view that 'it was to talk like children to talk of any danger of disaffection in the North'.[1] The bill passed quickly through all its stages and on 19th August the Royal Assent was given to an Act of Parliament revoking the annexation that in 1752 had been envisaged as 'unalienable'. The Board for the Annexed Estates, which can, not unreasonably, be called the first Highlands and Islands Development Board, was discontinued from Martinmas 1784.

Disannexation can hardly have come as a surprise. The writing had been on the wall for a long time, for the climate of opinion towards the Highlands in general and towards the forfeitures and the families affected in particular had been changing gradually over the previous quarter-century. As early as 1764, the Marischal, Panmure and Southesk estates, forfeited in 1715, had been bought back by the Earl Marischal, the Earl of Panmure, and Sir James Carnegie of Pitarrow, the heir-male of the family of Southesk, at the upset price. No-one had offered against them and, according to the *Scots Magazine,* 'the people in the galleries could scarce forbear expressing their joy by acclamation on seeing these estates return to the representatives of the ancient and illustrious families to which they had formerly belonged'.[2]

Ten years later the Lovat estates were returned to the Fraser family in the person of Major-General Simon Fraser. In 1748, it was possible for Baron Edlin to write that he was convinced 'they had better give young Lovat a Pension to ten times the value than reinstate him in his Paternal Estate',[3] but by 1774 the same 'young Lovat' was a high-ranking officer in the British army and, without being in formal possession of his paternal estates, had raised a regiment from them in defence of the dynasty that had beheaded his father. Other heirs of the forfeited persons were also officers in the army and of undoubted loyalty. Many were living on their ancestors' estates, fully accepted by their social equals who had not supported the Stewarts. Francis Farquharson was even offered the post of factor on his ancestral estate.[4] The Highlands themselves, 'formerly looked upon as a nuisance to these Islands', were, by the third quarter of the eighteenth century, valued for their scenic beauty, and their inhabitants as a vital source of supply for the armed forces. Even Gaelic culture was no longer so despised, MacPherson's 'Ossianic' poetry (1762–3) having had considerable effect. The avowed aim of the Highland Society of 1784, to assist this culture, would have been impossible and unacceptable in 1752.

There had never been wholehearted approval for the activities of the Annexed Estates Board. The views of one critic, George Chalmers, have already been quoted. Lord Kames had to admit that large amounts of money had been spent on the Highlands and on the annexed estates which had proved 'no better than water spilt on the ground',[5] and anyone who had cared to calculate the costs of the early support of the linen stations or of the soldiers' settlements must have felt constrained to agree. It was all very well for Thomas Pennant, who was appalled by the state in which he found one of the latter, to remark apologetically of the commissioners that: 'As these gentlemen with rare patriotism discharge their trust without salary, they might not be liable to censure like hireling placemen on every trifling failure'.[6] Others were likely to be less charitable and some of the failures after all were not so trifling. Southey's comment in the early nineteenth century is an illustration of the more critical view of the Board's administration. His phrase 'However much the money (i.e. the rents) may have been misapplied during a long series of years by those to whom it was entrusted . . .'[7] shows that he was clearly under the impression that it had been both inefficient and ineffective.

The management of the estates themselves came under fire during the debate on the Disannexing Act, when Lord Sydney declared that it was easy to distinguish the annexed estates because of the bad condition they were in compared to other men's estates and for the almost total neglect of their cultivation.[8] This was not just special pleading. As we have seen, little praise can be found from outside unprejudiced sources for the results of the Board's agricultural policies, however admirable they may have been in theory, and even one of the factors, Colin MacKenzie, on his appointment wrote of the estate of Cromartie: 'You will know how this estate has been harshly used since the forfeiture'. This was an opinion the family agreed with on their return.[9] The second Lord Melville, whose father, Henry Dundas, had bought an estate in Perthshire, had childhood memories of neighbours' severe strictures on the condition of the annexed estates in that county. There was, therefore, little opposition to disannexation and to the return of the estates to the families who had been rebels in 1745. Ardsheal, Callart, Cluny, Cromartie, Kinlochmoidart, Lochgarry and Lochiel were returned to the only or the eldest sons of the previous owners. Francis Farquharson received back his former estate, and Barrisdale was granted to the grandson of John MacDonnell of Glengarry, by whom the estate had been originally leased in wadset. Three of those attainted had no direct heirs, Drummond of Perth, Francis Buchanan of Arnprior, and Alexander Robertson of Struan. Some genealogical research was required before the Perth estates were awarded to the great-grandson of the first Earl of Melfort. For Arnprior, Francis Buchanan's sister, Jean, and another line of the family were held to be the due heirs, and Lieutenant-Colonel Alexander Robertson of Drumachine was the nearest male heir of Robertson of Struan.

Despite general approval for the measure, the new or returning proprietors were not to walk into their inheritance unscathed. It was considered only just that the public funds used to ascertain and settle their ancestors' debts should be reimbursed. The amount involved in paying creditors, purchasing the rights of superiorities, and in compounding claims made by subject superiors, was

£142,035.8.4 $\frac{7}{12}$ which with £808.1.6 Exchequer fees gave a total of £142,843.9.10 $\frac{7}{12}$. The actual debts totalled £90,124.12.5[10] The amount due from each proprietor was stipulated in the Disannexing Act, and the Dukes of Argyll and Atholl were also instructed to buy back for £3,248.2.4 the superiorities their families had previously possessed. The debts on the Struan estate were somewhat complicated by the fact that Alexander Robertson of Struan seemed to have paid none of his creditors since the estate was first forfeited in 1690, and in the Disannexing Act no attempt was made to calculate what was due. The Barons of the Exchequer, however, show £1,698.3.3 $\frac{2}{12}$ owing from before 1690 and £5,502.16.0 thereafter.[11]

Receipt and administration of the capital accruing from the repayment of debts by the proprietors and tidying up unfinished business of the annexation became the responsibility of the Barons of the Exchequer. This included such duties as arranging for the collection of rents and arrears due from before 1784, paying the pensions awarded to redundant officers of the Board for the Annexed Estates, and honouring any firm promises of financial aid still unpaid at the demise of the Board. Half the amount due from the new proprietors was to be paid by Martinmas, 1785, and was in fact by then in the Exchequer; the remaining moiety, due by Martinmas, 1788, was rather less punctual[12] and, as we have seen, the Commissioners for Highland Roads and Bridges had to accept that some of the debt due from the heirs to the Perth estate would never be collected. Simon Fraser had received much more generous treatment than those who regained their estates under the Disannexing Act. He was allowed ten years from 1774 to repay the capital of £20,983.0.1. with 3% interest charged, and then he had to be given twelve months' notice before having to produce the principal; the others were allowed only four years to find the capital, and paid 5% interest.

Our chief concern here is the use made of these not inconsiderable sums. Parliament might easily have allowed the money to disappear into anonymity in the Exchequer's maw. With what must be recognised as a continuation, conscious or not, of the principles under which the original annexation was planned, all the resulting capital was devoted to specifically Scottish, though not necessarily Highland projects. It was in the third reading of the bill for disannexing the estates that a clause was added awarding £50,000 towards the building of the Forth-Clyde canal, which had been languishing for lack of funds, and £15,000 toward completing a 'proper Repository for Records in Scotland'.

The question of the storage of Scottish Records had been a vexed one since the union of the two Parliaments. Duncan Forbes of Culloden had made a brave attempt at putting them in order, but he had not been able to solve the problem of finding a suitable place for depositing them once this had been done.[13] In 1765, the government authorised the expenditure of £12,000 from any free produce from the Forfeited Estates in Scotland that is, those not annexed to buy and construct a suitable building. The records had hitherto been kept mostly underground in a cellar in the Scottish Parliament House, where they had suffered from the damp so that 'some of the Records are thereby effaced, many of them rotting and all of them in imminent danger of being destroyed'. The foundation stone of the new repository was laid by the Lord Clerk Register, Lord Frederick Campbell, on 27 June, 1774 and it contained a hermetically sealed vase including one of each coin struck during George III's reign, as well as the gold medal struck at his coronation. H.M. Register House, as it was to be known, was designed by Robert Adam and is situated at the north end of the North Bridge in the extended Royalty of Edinburgh. It stood unfinished in 1784 for lack of funds, and it was hoped that the sum granted would be sufficient to complete the building.[14]

Once the Forth-Clyde proprietors repaid the £50,000 granted in 1784, the sums available began a financial roundabout, partly described in the previous chapter, assisting various schemes to develop and improve Scottish communications. Other awards were made as money became available and particular needs or worthy causes appeared. The award to the Society in Scotland for Propagating Christian Knowledge (SSPCK) was one such.[15] In 1786, £3,000 was allocated to the Highland Society founded in 1784, for any purposes its directors cared, as the society's general aims included the promotion of improvements, the establishment of towns and villages, making roads and building bridges, advancing agriculture, extending the fisheries and introducing useful trades and manufactures – the policy of annexation in a nutshell.[16]

From the time that the returning proprietors paid their initial instalments, the Forfeited Estates account maintained a credit balance in the Royal Bank, gaining interest but little else. All the previous grants, including £1,000 to build a jail at Inverness, had not exhausted the funds by the end of the century. In 1806, there was a balance of £22,329.18.4 unallocated, £15,125.0.0 at 4% to pay the annuities of the Annexed Estates Board's servants, and £9,000 proposed as a loan to Edinburgh to build new courts of justice. In 1806, three acts were passed to make more constructive use of this money, on the lines suggested by the Parliamentary Committee on the Funds Arising from the Forfeited Estates. First, £12,000 was awarded to replace the ruinous building which housed the Barons of the Exchequer. By another act passed shortly after this, the British Society for Extending the Fisheries was awarded £7,500 to make a harbour at Wick, where they had bought land but had no funds available to develop the site. By the same act, £2,000 was to be used to build a larger lunatic asylum at Edinburgh which had to cater for most of Scotland.[17] The Highland Society was awarded £800 per annum for ten years, but the first call on this sum was the payment of annuities to the officers of the Board. The total due under this head had now been reduced, through deaths, from over £800 to £460 a year, and in 1817, when the bequest to the Highland Society had run its course, those remaining were bought out for what at least one of those concerned thought a very fair sum.[18] Finally, the committee had suggested that public aid to harbour construction was of 'infinite consequence', and the resulting application of the balance remaining under the Scottish Harbours Act has been described in the previous chapter.

The use made by the government of the money repaid by the proprietors must be commended. It may not have been strictly applied to the benefit of the Highlands and Islands until the Scottish Harbours Act was passed, but Register House at least was a worthy object for any Scottish funds. The harbours built have been further extended, where there was a demand, as in Leith, Fraserburgh and Peterhead, and though other works, including the canals, have been overtaken by events, they merited the expenditure in contemporary eyes. Further, the influx of capital, providing employment and specie, can only have benefited the whole of the Scottish economy. Equally, the earlier inflow of money into the country from the capital authorised by Parliament to repay the debts of the forfeiting owners must have had a similar beneficial effect, but one so diffused as to be almost impossible to assess. It would involve the investigation of the personal expenditure of hundreds of individuals, humble as well as illustrious, many of whom will have left no written records other than their claims for repayment of the debts due them by the attainted rebels of 1745. How, one wonders, did Cosmo Gordon, a merchant in Inverness, spend the £60, capital and interest included, which the government paid him for the furniture he had supplied to the Earl of Cromartie more than twenty years previously? Did he invest it, spend it on riotous living, or simply use it to fend off creditors of his own? What must surely have been the case is that the grand total of these repayments would have some sort of cumulative effect, or at least would compensate in some measure for the financial embarrassment caused by the drastic stoppage of credit, when so many bondholders found that their security had disappeared, as their debtor was attainted and lost his estate.

It is perhaps worth noting, in connection with the return of the estates, that annexation made it more probable that the old families would resume ownership of their paternal estates. Not all were so fortunate as Oliphant of Gask, whose friends purchased the estate on his behalf, nor like the Marischal, Panmure and Southesk heirs of the 1715 rebels, who were able to regain theirs fifty years after. In the 1790s, some of those whose families had lost their possessions in 1715 formed a committee, largely at the instigation of Erskine of Mar, to plead for the return of the old titles; they accepted that it would be impossible to dislodge those who had legally become proprietors of forfeited estates.[19] Their campaign was not immediately successful, but the nineteenth century saw the revival of many peerages forfeited after both 1715 and 1745.

Assessment of the performance of the Board for the Annexed Estates must be more critical than Pennant's but less damning than Southey's. In retrospect, it is possible to see how heavily several circumstances weighed against complete success. Lack of time and lack of adequate funds were handicaps against which the commissioners found themselves struggling throughout, the latter affecting their activities from the earliest stages of annexation. It is not only historians who 'overestimate the incomes from large estates' and forget to calculate the running costs.[20] There can be little doubt that the whole concept of annexation was built on unrealistic contemporary calculations – if calculations there were: assumptions may be a more accurate word – of the financial resources that would be at the Board's command. Consider the income of £6,000 a year in the hands of the Board of Trustees for Manufactures and Fisheries in 1727, to encourage Scottish economic development in a limited range of industries; in 1753, £3,000 a year to the same body for nine years for the single purpose of encouraging industry in the Highlands. The SSPCK had an income of £1,500 for educational purposes only, and the annual income of £9,000 available in the second half of the eighteenth century to the Dukes of Argyll[21] was double the free produce of the estates annexed. The amount the Treasury disgorged in bounties to the Scottish whaling industry provides a still more startling comparison for, between 1750 and 1788, the total was £242,838, i.e. between £8,000 and £9,000 per annum, most of it directed to ships operating from the Forth. Even though these were not regular disbursements, amounting between 1753 and 1762 to over £8,000 each year, between 1778 and 1783 to less than £3,000 annually and after 1785 to over £13,000, the average was almost twice what was available from the annexed estates rent.[22] Compared to all of these, the Board's income was paltry. Certainly the expense of the maintenance of proprietors was removed, apart from widows' and dowagers' portions, which were not enormous, except on the estate of Perth, where the Dowager-Duchess occupied the greater part of the barony of Stobhall with a rental of £500. What was forgotten or incorrectly calculated or even more probably guessed, if remembered, was the amount that a centralised administration would cost. What never seemed to be realised was the large sums that were necessary, far beyond the resources of the estates, if some of the visionary schemes were to be sustained once they were beyond embryonic form.

At one point between 1755 and 1760, Gilbert Elliot of Minto, much troubled at the apparent melting away of resources, repeated the sums of the office in some disbelief.[23] Of £9,000, the surplus reckoned to be available over two years, fitting up the Edinburgh office cost £1,200, £1,865 worth of expenditure had already been allowed and plans made that would absorb £5,330 more, a total of £8,098. This was only a start and it was already clear that the purse was not bottomless. Unfortunately, this was a lesson the commissioners were slow to learn, and they sometimes showed what can only be described as arithmetical obtuseness where finance was concerned. Time and again, they approved schemes and proposed financial commitments, which the Treasury endorsed, for which no funds were available, either immediately or in the foreseeable future. 1775 saw them make the unusual statement that they would make no new proposals involving expenditure, as their resources were already totally committed, but the following year they returned to their usual habits, despite the good financial sense shown by Robert Oliphant of Rossie who had been examining the accounts.

The situation he found was as follows. The gross rent in 1760 was £7,679.0.1$\frac{8}{12}$; payment of feu duties and of the usual public burdens such as stipends, schoolmasters' salaries, etc. reduced this to £6,493.8.2$\frac{10}{12}$. After further deduction of managerial expenses and salaries to officers, the free rent had shrunk to £5,425.19.0$\frac{11}{12}$ in theory, but arrears amounted to £2,848.1.10$\frac{11}{12}$. That left £2,578.17.2. Set against this was the total expenditure authorised at that date, £9,225.7.11$\frac{6}{12}$, for which the Receiver General had cash in hand of £1,286.18.2. Very little of this cash was in any case available for new or authorised projects, for £925.16.0 was due in salaries and unavoidable incidental expenses, £200 was already committed for the inn at Dalnacardoch and £80 for seating Callander kirk. Delay in beginning even approved schemes was unavoidable.

Mr. Oliphant struck out as much as he could, an action that was in itself a criticism of the Board's financial administration, to which of course he was a party. He then made some sensible suggestions for the future, that no more engagements should be undertaken until the existing debts were paid, and that no order should be made for payment, even of firm undertakings, unless there was money actually in the Receiver General's hand. Little attention was paid to his strictures, however, for soon afterwards another £500 was allowed for bridges and roads on the grounds that the free rent was £3,663, and in 1783 £3,342 was promised against £873 in ready cash.[24] In their final report, £19,380.16.9 $\frac{6}{12}$ was the Board's calculation of the gross rent of the estates, but this figure included arrears from 1780 which had been collected, and from it current arrears of £5,646.14.2 $\frac{1}{12}$ had to be deducted. A few years earlier, an even less favourable picture emerged. The gross rent of £10,700.0.0 $\frac{7}{12}$ gave a net £6,542.14.2 $\frac{1}{12}$ with arrears of £3,098.3.6 $\frac{8}{12}$. Far more was needed to effect the desired radical transformation of the Highland people and economy than was ever at the disposal of the commissioners. It is doubtful if even the £10,000 Treasury loan recommended by one of the Board's gratuitous advisers would have been sufficient to accomplish the wide-reaching aims of the annexation. The Highlands have soaked up larger sums over the past two centuries and, whatever the aims of those responsible for such expenditure, whether private gain or public good, the results have rarely been commensurate with the relevant outlay of energy and money.

The passage of time has indeed been curiously kind to the commissioners, for their performance and achievements do bear comparison with the activities of most of those later would-be improvers and transformers of the Highlands. It is doubtful if the activities of the Congested Districts Board from 1897 to 1912, or those of Lord Leverhulme in the 1920s or, even more controversially, the Sutherland estate schemes of 1802–16,[25] showed any more results for the money spent than this first planned attempt at comprehensive development. What is somewhat depressing is that, throughout, there have been few new ideas as to how to improve the quality of life of the Highlanders. The latest policies of the Highlands and Islands Development Board set up in 1965 are in essence identical to those of the Board for the Annexed Estates, even to the building of hotels, and that, as an 'improvement', was actually proposed in the seventeenth century.[26]

The time available to the commissioners was, like their funds, limited, little though they realised this in 1755. Five years to 1760 lay fallow as far as their wider plans were concerned, though they immediately began agricultural change. It was 1770 before they gained control of the estates held of subject superiors, and only four years later that the beginning of the end could be discerned in the disannexation of the Lovat estate. Indeed, in 1775, the morale of the Board must have been at a low ebb. They had seen the failure of the linen stations, colonisation plans had gone sadly awry, and minor schemes, minor that is in the expense involved, such as encouraging craftsmen and settling day-labourers, had had only modified success. A few small firms were thriving with the help of subsidies but major industrial development had ceased. In agriculture, leases and security of tenure were the first aim of the commissioners and, in 1774, the Treasury suggested that no more long leases should be granted. The Treasury mind was plain: if one estate could be returned to a loyal army officer, so could others. Returning proprietors would be the less grateful if they found their paternal estates encumbered with long leases set at comparatively low rents, enforcing agricultural policies they might not wish to follow. At this point, an affronted Board dug in its heels and, declaring that such a policy would be 'fatal to industry', carried on making out leases of up to forty-one years in length to the end of the annexation.[27]

Only seven years later, however, in 1781, we find the Board refusing the prayer of the General Assembly to authorise their agent to carry on the process of a proposed new erection in Ardnamurchan parish, accepted in principle earlier. Their reason for this reversal of policy was that, having been 'some time ago discharged from exercising an ordinary act of management', unspecified, they were declining to enter into any matter of great importance 'especially such as tend to entail perpetual burthens upon the Estates under their management'. Here was another straw showing the way the wind was blowing, and an illustration of the reduced powers and therefore effectiveness of the Board.

Agricultural change in the Highlands, whatever the extent of manufacturing industry that might have been introduced, was bound to be the heart and core of the hoped-for transformation, involving as it did not only purely economic effects but basic social change. Such changes are by their very nature slow, unless they be of a drastic and revolutionary type like the forming of immense sheep-runs. It was the Board's misfortune that the annexation was revoked before the smaller tenants as a whole, not only on the annexed estates but in the whole of Scotland, were prepared to accept the need for change, or to realise that the new methods brought some benefits to themselves. Tenants desired the security of tenure that came with leases but were not prepared to slough off old habits. There had not been time to win them over, and the atmosphere of uncertainty that must have arisen after 1774 can have done nothing to persuade conservative farmers and the ignorant 'aukward, lazy inhabitants' to cooperate in altering practices which they fondly assumed would be resumed under the old families. George Nicolson wrote, not of tenants on the remote estates in the north and west, where recalcitrance could have been expected, but of some near Callander who, if they were sure 'the estates is to go away' immediately, would pull down a dike as fast as it was built 'over the Commissioners belly'.[28] This was in February 1784, so twenty-nine years of state control and attempts at organised improvements had not been enough to alter old attitudes.

In the next century, James Loch on reflection considered that the alterations on the Sutherland estates had been too rapid and had been carried 'farther than even the most active of the old tenants can undertake, understand or keep pace with', [29] The Commissioners for the Annexed Estates are unlikely to be accused of such a fault. The happiness of the inhabitants had to be considered and this involved their acquiescence and cooperation in no small degree. The aims of the annexation were not to be achieved by economic prosperity if that was combined with the alienation of the natives. Some of the servants of the Board felt that tenderness towards tenants was carried too far, as did other proprietors. The factors, however, did seem to appreciate the need to hasten slowly.

The most notable characteristic that may be attributed to members of the Board, both individually and collectively, is their modernity in eighteenth-century terms. 'Enlightenment Man' was forward-looking, far-sighted, excited by an interest in physical and mental experiment and change, and the commissioners and some of those who initiated the Annexing Act were typical of the best of their age. Every aspect of the policies proposed in the act and followed by the Board can be paralleled in the work of private landowners, and the commissioners' own estates reflect the beliefs, fashions, and preoccupations of the time. The century abounds with examples of model improving landowners, the building of new towns, and the attempted introduction of industry, where there was none before, by private individuals. Not least, proprietors at their own expense carried out improvements on the deficient transport system of the period.

Acting as a body within the confines of the statute of annexation and controlled in the last resort by the central government, it must however be admitted that the commissioners often displayed rather less wisdom, efficiency, and far-sightedness than their contemporaries generally, or themselves individually. It had been hoped that the annexed estates would be models for their neighbours, but the examples set by the commissioners in their private capacity must have made far more impression than similar policies carried out in the name of the Board. Lord Kames began the draining of Flanders Moss and carried it through with spectacular success; the failure of the attempt to drain Rannoch Moor was unlikely to inspire imitation. Lord Findlater and Lord Gardenstone built towns more successful at the time and after than Kinloch Rannoch, and the former's reputation as an agricultural improver did not arise from his position as a member of the Board for the Annexed Estates.

Far from praising the Board for far-sightedness, it is possible to criticise the commissioners for short-sightedness at various points. With the benefit of hindsight, we can say their acceptance of the responsibility for the Trustees' manufacturing stations was unwise; even at the time, it was hardly prescient to accept without question the Treasury's ignoring of their request for authority to spend more than the paltry £200 a year allowed for education. One earlier observer had seen that £5,000 was a more realistic figure.[30] While all praise is due for the decision to encourage craftsmanship by apprenticing boys and girls to various trades, there was little attempt to decide on any system of priorities as to where the greatest need lay, except perhaps as regards farm utensils. They totally discounted Factor Small's warnings on the nature of the type of settlers they proposed establishing all over the estates and, in arranging for these settlements to be built, showed a deplorable lack of practical sense, even allowing for the inevitable haste engendered by the end of the Seven Years War. The wholly meritorious encouragement of bridge, road, canal and harbour building was guided by no overall strategy but was awarded to individual projects, as first the factors gave their views on immediate essentials, and then as requests, recommendations, and petitions reached the Edinburgh office from outside sources. The response to the factors' lists was not particularly methodical.

Indeed, in the latter part of the annexation, it is possible to imagine a certain degree of despair in the wholehearted devotion of such a large proportion of the funds to the development of communications. By 1775, so many of the other types of activity aimed at transformation of the Highland scene had either failed, or had at most achieved doubtful success, that it is not wholly unreasonable to assume that the Board seized on the policy of encouraging bridge-building as a last resort in the face of possible disannexation. Bridges would at least stand as clear and visible proof that some of their work had not been in vain. This may be over-facile, however, and the more positive and charitable point of view is also tenable that they began to perceive, better late than never, that improved communications were the first and probably the most vital step in encompassing the Highlands in Lowland civilisation. The awareness of the need had been present from the early years of annexation, both in the questions sent to the factors and in the reports to the government, but it was in the second half of the Board's existence that the greater attention was paid to this aspect of their work. It is possible that the comments of Archibald Menzies too had their effect; he joined the Board as a commissioner in 1770. Whatever the reasons, there was explicit avowal of the Board's philosophy in a petition referring to the attention being paid to the erection of bridges as 'the first and best improvement on the face of all countries'.[31]

The importance attached to this and other policies was not always consistent, but the idea of agricultural improvements on the estates was ever-present and continued throughout the annexation, with different degrees of care and intensity on different estates. And here perhaps the greatest criticism of the commissioners must be made. There was a fundamental lack of balance in the care lavished on the various estates which, as David Turnock describes the process, 'compounded' instead of resolving the differences in culture and economy between the south-east and the north-west.[32] The most remote and most in need of change, if they were to be brought into the mainstream of Scottish economic and social life, were the least attended. Admittedly the length of time wasted in making the legal arrangements with subject superiors was one element in producing the situation. Map A shows that those estates that came under full annexation so late were just those furthest removed from 'civilisation', but even so, ten years later, Mrs Susanna MacDonald could complain that no public money had been spent on Kinlochmoidart.[33] Henry Butter was aware of unfulfilled needs on the estates under his management which were being catered for further south. Even in the building of bridges, Map B shows that most of these were in the south and east. The reason for this was that the Board demanded evidence of self-help from the inhabitants where major crossings were involved. Heritors in the south were wealthier and thicker on the ground than those in the northern parts of the country, and the commissioners did not take enough account of the fact that they themselves were the most influential landholders in so many areas.

Undoubtedly a defensible case can be made out, holding that the best way of ensuring the desired changes was to consolidate the government's control on the most southerly estates and those such as Struan, which straddled the centre of the country. James Small thought that if Struan could be kept honest, especially Rannoch, thieving would be wiped out;[34] by analogy, if Struan could be kept loyal, perhaps disloyalty too would disappear. It could have been argued that the most certain and effective way of securing peace, good government, industry, and agricultural improvement, not to mention the Protestant religion, was to form a sound base in the south and let the effects of this speak for itself. The fact that so few of the tenants in Perthshire could be persuaded to take part actively in the Forty-Five could have lent strength to this theory.[35] Unfortunately for the Board's reputation, there is no sign that such a definite case had been formulated. Inspector Menzies recommended the restriction of aid to industry and schools on the annexed estates, to facilitate the recognition of the results of the Board's activities. Such a restriction was never imposed and would probably have been contrary to the spirit and letter of the Annexing Act, which proposed devoting the rents to all the Highlands and Islands, with only special attention to the annexed estates. Accessibility to Edinburgh seems to have been of the greatest importance in influencing the Board, and factors of the more remote estates had least opportunity of pressing their points. There were fewer gentlemen of standing, too, in these wilder regions who could be on such terms with commissioners as the heritors and noblemen of Perthshire; the influence of the latter would be greater in wealth and numbers and presence, so that once again the south had the advantage.

The vulnerability of the Board to outside pressure was one reason too for the fact that so many of their decisions were *ad hoc* and that the same criticism can be made as Professor Adam makes of the plans for the Sutherland estates – there was regular under-estimation of practical difficulties and, equally important, a failure to coordinate the various developments.[36] The pressures were not exerted merely by private individuals; the paradoxical combination of close control and indifference emanating from the central government contributed in no small measure to this failure. In the first five years of the annexation, from 1755 to 1760, some attempt was made to draw up comprehensive plans of improvements on the lines drawn up in the Annexing Act and in the original instructions sent them. Thereafter, planning tended to be overtaken by events.

The greatest disadvantage that handicapped the Board for the Annexed Estates was that they were asked to operate a process of government with few precedents if any; their function was the equivalent of that of the governing board of today's public corporations or nationalised industries, but they were not provided with the essential, adequate administrative machinery which would have facilitated their work. Nor did the practice or the theory of the central government show any signs of developing, during the annexation, in a direction which would have enabled both Board and Treasury to cope more easily with the situation the legislature had created. Our greatest admiration must be reserved for those whose vaulting imagination conceived such an all-embracing social, economic, constitutional and political experiment in regional development, so far in advance of contemporary constitutional philosophy. The pity was that the creaking bureaucracy of the eighteenth century could not transform itself, or be transformed fast enough, to enable either the system to work automaticallly or those entrusted with its administration, competent as they undoubtedly were, to overcome the restrictions that it seemed so natural at the time to impose. Perhaps the most fitting epitaph on the work of the Board can be found in the words of their contemporary who remarked that '. . .it is not doubted (they) have acted as well as circumstances and the nature of their constitution could admit'.[37]

The annexation was of relevance to only about a quarter of all the estates involved in the process of forfeiture, but its wide aims and the astonishing variety and interest of the managing Board's activities must command far more attention than the fate of those which experienced simple escheat. The latter must not be ignored, however, in the final analysis. Financial profit was certainly not the main object of the operation, but the Barons of the Exchequer equally certainly were not expected to make a loss. The records of their financial transactions were sent at intervals to London and over the years presented a somewhat fluid picture, estimates of claims and valuations altering as new 'discoveries' of property and debts arrived at the Exchequer. The simplest and probably most conclusive statement can be found in information sent to the Treasury in 1780, by order of the House of Commons, after which date major change was unlikely.

The Barons then could report that as a result of the forfeitures, £84.14.6 $\frac{10}{12}$ in cash remained in the hands of the Receiver-General. They had sold twenty-one estates between 1751 and 1766 for £98,715.19.4 $\frac{6}{12}$. Under their management, which it will be remembered was largely one of care and maintenance, produce from these estates had amounted to £40,889.15.11 $\frac{9}{12}$, bringing into the state's, coffers £139,605.15.4 $\frac{3}{12}$ in all. This was not pure gain, however, as £122,428.1.6 $\frac{3}{12}$ had been paid out: over £97,558 to creditors, the surprisingly small amount of £2,873.3.5 $\frac{6}{12}$ on management, smaller sums on surveys and legal expenses in carrying cases to the Court of Session and the House of Lords, and £19,026.4.4 $\frac{7}{12}$ granted by the king, under the Royal Sign Manual, much of it to dependants of the forfeiting persons, but including £2,848.5.11 to the town of Dumfries, as compensation for damage suffered during the rebellion. A few creditors had not claimed the sums awarded to them; a negligible £135.0.1 $\frac{10}{12}$ had not been collected. The surplus of £17,042 has been committed to purposes unspecified in the statement but, of course, £12,000 had been awarded to the building of a repository for Scottish records. The percentage gain of about 12% on the total of £139,000, or 20% on the sale of the estates, is not derisory.[38]

Social, cultural, and political profit and loss is less easy to quantify under any circumstances, and it is well nigh impossible to separate the effects of the forfeitures and the annexation from the many forces impinging on Highland society during the eighteenth century. Government policy was only one of these and the forfeitures only part of that policy. Nor did these forces suddenly begin to operate after Culloden, and those who claim that the deterioration in the Highland economy and the drastic changes of the late eighteenth and early nineteenth centuries began in 1746 shut their eyes to historical fact. Increasing commercial intercourse between the Lowlands and the Highlands, assimilation of the Scottish aristocracy, both Highland and Lowland, with the English, the penetration of the Highlands by Protestantism through the agency of the SSPCK, all these were potent instruments of change long before the last Jacobite rebellion, as were a few chiefs with modern skills in modern estate management. Later, the defeat of the

Jacobites can hardly be said to have ensured the collapse of the black cattle market or the great increase in Highland population, which put such strains on the traditional system of land management as well as the whole economy.

The separation of the interests of clan chiefs from the ordinary Highlanders is sometimes attributed to the physical separation that the forfeitures brought about, but this can be exaggerated. The number of Jacobites or their heirs who were pardoned, tacitly allowed to live on their estates, or who managed actually to obtain possession of their lands through agents, is not negligible and, when it comes to the bit, was the chief who exploited his tenants by underpaying them for collecting and burning kelp very different from one who exported his clansmen to America as bondsmen? Culloden came between these two.

Neither forfeited nor annexed estates in the long run experienced a fate very different from that of the Highlands in general. This is hardly surprising in the case of these simply forfeited, where only a change of ownership was effected, but it is sad and perhaps portentous that annexation, this first experiment in regional development, left so few direct results, and was given neither time nor resources in sufficient measure.

Appendix A

Estate surveyed by order of the Barons of the Exchequer, by authority of the 'Vesting Act', 20 George II, c.41

	Estate	*Location (by Parish)*	*Attainted Person*
	Abernethy	Personal estate	Alexander Abernethy
	Abernethy	Banff	George Abernethy
a.	Aldie	Caputh, Fossoway, Kinross, Methven	Robert Mercer of Aldie
b.	Ardsheal	Lismore and Appin	Charles Stewart of Ardsheal
b.	Arnprior	Balquhidder, Callander, Kippen	Francis Buchanan of Arnprior
	Asleed	Monquhitter, New Deer	Adam Hay of Asleed
	Balmerino	Balmerino, South Leith, Coupar Angus	Arthur, Lord Balmerino
b.	Barrisdale	Glenelg	Archibald MacDonnell of Barrisdale
	Burnfoot	Newbattle	Andrew Porteous
b.	Callart	Kilmallie	Allan Cameron of Callart
a.	Clanranald	Ardnamurchan, Small Isles, South Uist	Donald MacDonald of Clanranald
b.	Cluny	Kingussie, Laggan	Ewan MacPherson of Cluny
b.	Cromartie	Fodderty, Kilmuir Easter, Kincardine Lochbroom, Logie Easter, Urquhart	George, Earl of Cromartie
a.	Dungallon	Ardnamurchan	Alexander Cameron of Dungallon
	Dunipace	Dunipace, Edinburgh	Archibald Primrose of Dunipace
a.	Dunmaglass	No papers in the F.E.P. 1745 collection	William McGillivary
	Elcho	Heritable Bond	David, Lord Elcho
	Gask	Gask, Madderty	Laurence Oliphant of Gask
	Glastullich	Fearn, Logie Easter	Roderick McCulloch of Glastullich
	Glenbucket	Fraserburgh, Kirkmichael	John Gordon of Glenbucket
	Glencarse	Kinfauns	Lord George Murray
a.	Glencoe	Lismore and Appin	Alexander MacDonald of Glencoe
	Gordon	Duffus	Lord Lewis Gordon
	Graden	Linton	Henry Kerr of Graden
	Hamilton	Huntly	John Hamilton
	Hay	South Leith	John Hay
a.	Henderson	Lochmaben	John Henderson
a. b.c.	Keppoch	Kilmonivaig	Alexander MacDonald of Keppoch
a.	Kilmarnock	Falkirk, Kilmarnock, Linlithgow Muiravonside, Slamannan	William, Earl of Kilmarnock

Estate	Location (by Parish)	Attainted Person
a. Kinloch	Mains	Alexander Kinloch
Kinloch and Nevay	Alyth, Coupar Angus, Eassie Nevay, Meigle	Sir James Kinloch of Kinloch
b. Kinlochmoidart	Ardnamurchan, Glenelg	Donald MacDonald of Kinlochmoidart
Lethendy	Lethendy, St. Martin's	Laurence Mercer of Lethendy
Lindsay	Personal estate	Patrick Lindsay
b. Lochgarry	Blair Atholl, Boleskine and Abertaff, Logierait	Donald MacDonnell of Lochgarry
b. Lochiel	Kilmallie	Donald Cameron of Lochiel
b. Lovat	Boleskine and Abertaff, Dores, Croy, Kiltarlity, Kilmorack, Kirkhill, Urray	Simon Fraser, Lord Lovat
McIntosh	Inverness	Lauchlan McIntosh
a. MacKinnon	Strath	John MacKinnon of MacKinnon
a. McLauchlan	Kilmorie	Lauchlan McLauchlan of McLauchlan
b. Monaltrie	Crathie	Francis Farquharson of Monaltrie
Nairn	Auchtergaven, Canongate, Kinclaven Moneydie, Redgorton	John Nairn, commonly called Lord Nairn
Nicolson	Leith	James Nicholson (sometimes 'of Trabroun')
Park	Marnoch, Ordiquhill	Sir William Gordon of Park
b. Perth	Auchterarder, Balquhidder, Callander Cargill, Comrie, Crieff, Dunblane, Killin, Muthill, Port of Menteith, Strowan	John Drummond, brother of James, the sixth earl, who died before the Act of Attainder took effect
a. Pitscandly	Rescobie	James Stormonth of Pitscandly
Pitsligo	Pitsligo, Tyrie	Alexander, Lord Forbes of Pitsligo
Redhouse	Gladsmuir	George Hamilton of Redhouse
Row	Personal estate	David Row
Strathallan	Blackford, Muthill, Trinity Gask	William, Viscount Strathallan
b. Struan	Blair Atholl, Strowan, Fortingall, Kenmore, Logierait	Alexander Robertson of Struan
Terpersie	Tullynessle	Charles Gordon of Terpersie
Watson	Arbroath	Thomas Watson

a. These estate were surveyed, having been assumed to be forfeited. For various reasons, some of them technical legal points, the forfeitures turned out not to be legally tenable and they were returned to the original owners.

b. Estates named in the 1752 Annexing Act, 25 George II, c.41.

c. Keppoch, although included in the Annexing Act, was found not to be legally forfeited, and so was returned to the family.

Appendix B

Members of the Board of Commissioners and Trustees for the Annexed Estates, 1755-1784.

The Lord President of the Court of Session, the Lord Chief Baron, the Lord Justice Clerk and, from 1755-1761, the Commander-in-Chief of H.M. Forces in Scotland, were *ex officio* members of the Board. Though the last official was ommitted from the general commission in 1761, two Commanders-in-Chief were personally appointed, Lord Beauclerk and Lord Sundridge, called the Marquis of Lorne. Major-General Oughton, Lorne's Lieutenant-General in Scotland, was also a member.

Ex Officio members

Lord Presidents of the Court of Session

1754-1760	Robert Craigie, Lord Glendoich
*1760-1788	Robert Dundas, Lord Arniston

*The SRO *List of Officers of State* gives Robert Dundas' date of death as 13th December, 1787. According to G. Brunton and D. Haig, *An Historical Account of the Senators of the College of Justice* (London, 1832), he died on 15th January, 1788.

Lord Chief Barons

1741-1755	John Idle
1755-1775	Robert Ord
1775-1801	James Montgomery of Stanhope, Lord Alexander

Lord Justice Clerks

1748-1763	Charles Erskine (or Areskine), Lord Tinwald
1763-1766	Sir Gilbert Elliot, Lord Minto
1766-1788	Thomas Miller, Lord Barskimming and Lord Glenlee

Commanders-in-Chief of H.M. Forces in Scotland

1753-1756	Lieutenant-General Humphrey Bland
1756-1767	Lord George Beauclerk

Ordinary Members

1755

	Archibald, 3rd Duke of Argyll, 1682-1761
1.	John Hay, 4th Marquis of Tweeddale, 1695-1762
1.	James Douglas, 14th Earl of Morton, c.1702-1768

1.3.	James Ogilvy, 5th Earl of Findlater and 2nd Earl of Seafield, c.1689-1764
1.	Hugh Hume, 3rd Earl of Marchmont, 1708-1794
1.5.	John Hope, 2nd Earl of Hopetoun, 1704-1781
1.3.4.	James Ogilvy, Lord Deskford, c.1714-1770
1.3.5.	Charles Shaw, 9th Lord Cathcart, 1721-1776
1.	James, Lord Somerville, 1697/8-1765
1.3.	Charles Hope Weir of Craigiehall, 1710-1791
1.3.	Andrew Fletcher, Lord Milton, 1692-1766
2.	Edward Edlin, d.1760
1.2.3.	John Maule of Inverkeilor, 1706-1781
1.	William Grant, Lord Prestongrange
3.6.	Robert Dundas, Lord Arniston, 1713-1787
1.	James Oswald of Dunnikier, 1715-1769
1.	Andrew Mitchell of Thainston, 1708-1771
1.	Gilbert Elliot of Minto, 1722-1777
3.	William Alexander, 1690-1761
1.3.	George Drummond, 1687-1766
3.	Lieutenant-Colonel David Watson, c.1713-1761
1.4.	Mansfeldt Cardonnel, 1697-1780
1.4.	Alexander Le Grand, 1682-1766
1.4.	Joseph Tudor, d.1774

New Appointments made by George III in 1761

	James Stuart MacKenzie, 1719-1800
3.	Henry Home, Lord Kames, 1696-1782
6.	Sir Gilbert Elliot, Lord Minto, 1693-1766
3.	Andrew Pringle of Haining, Lord Alemoor, d.1776
2.3.	William Mure of Caldwell, 1718-1776
2.	Sir George Allanson Winn, 1725-1798
3.6.	Thomas Miller, Lord Barskimming, then Lord Glenlee, 1717-1789
	Lord George Beauclerk, 1704-1768 (C-i-C, 1756-1767)
2.3.6.	James Montgomery, Lord Alexander, 1721-1803
3.	Francis Garden, Lord Gardenstone, 1721-1793
	Sir David Dalrymple, Lord Hailes, 1726-1792
3.	John Swinton, d.1799
3.	John Campbell, Lord Stonefield, d.1801

1764

2.3.	John Grant, formerly of Easter Elchies, d.1775
3.	Robert Oliphant of Rossie, d.1795
3.4.	George Clerk-Maxwell, 1715-1784

1767

3.	James Veitch, Lord Elliock, 1712-1793

In May, 1769, the Treasury requested a list of those comissioners who had died since 1755. Although there had been eleven deaths and further erosion of the complement of the Board as a few members moved into the *ex officio* class, only four new members had been appointed since 1761. New commissioners were named in the following year and at irregular intervals thereafter.

1770

5.   Charles Sholto Douglas, 15th Earl of Morton, 1732-1774
        John, Lord Sundridge, called Marquis of Lorne, 1723-1806 (C-i-C, 1767-1778)
5.   John Stewart, Lord Garlies, 1736-1806
        Major-General James Adolphus Oughton, 1720-1780 (Lorne's Lieutenant-General
            in Scotland, often acting for him)
5.   Thomas Dundas of Fingask, 1708-1786

1771

        Captain Archibald Grant, 1731-1796
        Major-General David Graeme, 1716-1797
4.   Archibald Menzies, Younger of Culdares, d.1777

1772

3.   Henry, Duke of Buccleuch, 1746-1812

1776

3.   David Ross, Lord Ankerville, 1727/8-1805
3.   Alexander Murray, Lord Henderland, 1736-1795

1777

        John, Baron Cardiff, commonly called Lord Mountstuart, 1744-1814
1783

3.   Henry Dundas, later Viscount Melville, 1742-1811
2.3.   Sir John Dalrymple, 1726-1810

1.   Re-appointed to the Board in 1761
2.   Baron of the Exchequer
3.   Member of the Board of Trustees for Manufactures and Fisheries
4.   Commissioner of Customs
5.   Commissioner of Police
6.   *Ex officio* members at a later date

Appendix C

Factors Serving on the Annexed Estates

Estate	Factor	Years of Service
† Ardsheal	* Henry Butter	1770-1784
Arnprior	* William Monteith	1755-1761
(Strathyre)	Walter Monteath	1762-1764
	John Campbell of Barcaldine	1765

From 1766, Strathyre was included for administrative convenience in the Highland Division of the estate of Perth (q.v.) under the same factors.

† Arnprior (other than Strathyre)	* James Fogo	1770-1784
Barrisdale	* Mungo Campbell	1755-1758
	Henry Butter	1759-1784
† Callart	* Henry Butter	1770-1784
† Cluny	* Henry Butter	1770-1784
Cromartie	* Captain John Forbes of New	1755-1774
	Hector MacKenzie	1774-1777
	Colin MacKenzie	1777-1784
	(appointed 1775, Treasury approval received only 1777)	

In 1764, the Barony of Coigach, the part of the estate of Cromartie lying farthest west, was sensibly placed under a separate factor. Access was hardly easy

Coigach	Ninian Jeffrey	1764-1773
	Hector MacKenzie	1773-1784
† Kinlochmoidart	* Henry Butter	1770-1784
† Lochgarry	* James Small	1770-1777
	Robert Menzies	1777-1784
† Lochiel	* Henry Butter	1770-1784
Lovat	* Captain John Forbes of New	1755-1774
Monaltrie	* James McDonald of Reneton	1755-1767
	Francis McDonald	1767-1772
	John Farquharson	1773-1777
	William Farquharson of Bruxie	1778-1784
Perth	* John Campbell of Barcaldine	1755-1765

From 1766, two factors were appointed to the estate of Perth, managing what were entitled the Highland and Lowland Divisions. The former also included the Barony of Strathyre and the other small parts of the estate of Arnprior not held of a subject superior

Estate	Factor	Years of Service
Perth, Highland Division	James Small	1766-1777
Perth, Highland Division	John Campbell of Lochend	1777-1780
Perth, Highland Division	James Goodlatt Campbell of Achlyne	1780-1784
Perth, Lowland Division	Thomas Keir	1766-1784
Struan	* James Small	1755-1777
	Robert Menzies	1777-1784

*   Factors who were employed by the Barons of the Exchequer on the same estate as that to which they were appointed by the Commissioners for the Annexed Estates in 1755 or shortly after.

†   Estates held of subject superiors which were managed by the Barons of the Exchequer until 1770.

Appendix D

The Disannexation

Estate	*Returning Proprietor*
Ardsheal	Duncan Stewart, son and heir of Charles the forfeited person.
Arnprior	Jean Buchanan, sister of the forfeited person, and John Buchanan of Auchlessie.
Barrisdale	Duncan MacDonnell of Glengarry, grandson of John MacDonnell who had granted a wadset of the estate.
Callart	John Cameron, son and heir of Allan Cameron the forfeited person.
Cluny	Lieutenant-Colonel Duncan MacPherson, son and heir of Ewan the forfeited person.
Cromartie	John MacKenzie, Lord MacLeod, eldest son and heir of George, Earl of Cromartie who forfeited the estate.
Kinlochmoidart	John MacDonald, son and heir of Colonel Alexander MacDonald, son and heir of Donald MacDonald who forfeited the estate.
Lochgarry	Colonel John MacDonnell, son and heir of Donald, the forfeited person.
Lochiel	Donald Cameron, grandson of Donald the forfeited person.
1 Lovat	Major-General Simon Fraser, eldest son and heir of Simon Fraser, Lord Lovat, the forfeited person.
Monaltrie	Francis Farquharson, the forfeited person.
2 Perth	James Drummond, great-grandson of John Drummond, first Earl of Melfort brother of the fourth Earl and first Duke of Perth.
3 Struan	Lieutenant-Colonel Alexander Robertson, son of Duncan Robertson of Drumachine.

1 The estate of Lovat was returned to the family by an Act of Parliament in 1774 (14 George III, c.22). All the others were returned by virtue of the Disannexing Act (24 George III, c.57).

2 The heir to the estate of Perth was unknown when the Disannexing Act was passed. Parliament passed an act allowing the heirs-male of John Drummond to be granted the estate by the Crown (24 George III, c.10) and, in 1785, the Court of Session found the above James Drummond to be the legal heir.

3 Struan having been forfeited in 1690, re-forfeited in 1715, and granted in 1723 to the sister of Alexander Robertson of Struan, she handed it over to trustees for her brother's benefit and in the event of his death without heirs, to Duncan, the son of Alexander Robertson of Drumachine. His son eventually received it in 1784.

Notes

Chapter 1 Forfeitures and Management by the Barons of the Exchequer

1. Audrey Cunningham, *The Loyal Clans* (Cambridge, 1932) 504.
2. Byron Jewell, *Legislation Relating to Scotland after the Forty-Five,* a D.Phil. thesis at the University of North Carolina, 1975, (Facsimile by University Microfilm International, 1978) deals with government attitudes at the time. To this work, and to Alexander Murdoch, *The People Above* (John Donald, 1980) I owe a very considerable debt for the light they have cast on aspects of the forfeitures and later the annexations, hitherto somewhat puzzling. They are cited hereafter as Jewell and Murdoch.
3. Jewell, 56.
4. 19 George II c.46.
5. 20 George II c.52.
6. 19 George II c.39.
7. Jewell, 163 ff.
8. 20 George II c.53.
9. Jewell, Chap. 4, 5, 6.
10. Athol L. Murray, 'Administration and Law' in T. I. Rae, ed., *The Union of 1707* (Blackie & Son, 1974), 43.
11. David Murray, *The York Buildings Company* (Bratton Publishing Limited, 1973), *passim.*
12. Jewell, 98ff.; NLS Ms 17528, 72-83, a 1747 elaboration of the idea of annexation in the Saltoun papers.
13. 25 George II c.41, hereafter the Annexing Act.
14. 20 George II c.41, hereafter the Vesting Act.
15. Jewell, 31, 32; Murdoch, 37.
16. Murdoch, 15.
17. 13 George I c.20.
18. I George I c.20, repealed in part 21 George II c.34.
19. E714/1/1,18,9,146.
20. E700/1.
21. E702/1, p.10
22. E702/1, p. 96.
23. *Scots Magazine,* 14, 398.
24. A. & A. MacDonald, *Clan Donald,* (Inverness, 1904) vol. iii, 234.
25. E701/2, p. 92.
26. Donald J. MacDonald, *Clan Donald,* (MacDonald Publishers, Loanhead, 1978), 395.
27. E710/12.
28. See Appendix A.
29. See the Inventory of Forfeited Estates Papers (1745) in S.R.O. 8.

30. E766/3.
31. E701/2, pp. 92–95.
32. E703/3/27.
33. E702/2, pp. 13–14.
34. E702/2, p. 202; E703/3/13.
35. E709/9, p. 3.
36. E710/1/10.
37. E702/2, p. 202.
38. See below, p. 21, 22, 45, 46, 225, 226.
39. E710/1/6.
40. E738/16.
41. E714/18, pp. 5, 6.
42. E702/1, 139; E702/2, pp. 174, 195–6; E714/15/1.
43. E703/2/16(1).
44. E702/2, p. 202.
45. E729/12/4.
46. E714/18, pp. 9–10.
47. E700/1, p. 202.
48. E700/1, 7.
49. E702/1, pp. 11, 15.
50. E701/1, 2–4.
51. E702/2, pp. 148, 149.
52. E705/2/1(1)13.
53. E702/2, pp. 235–6.
54. E729/2, pp. 52–53.
55. E700/1, p. 17.
56. E702/2, p. 222
57. E702/1, pp. 24–26.
58. E702/2, p. 223.
59. E714/14/2.
60. E708/3/1(1).
61. E708/5.
62. E707/7/4.
63. E700/1, p. 28.
64. E700/1, p. 31; E702/1, p. 30
65. E702/1, p. 123.
66. E700/2(19-2-1756).
67. E700/1, (20 Jan. 1764).
68. E700/1, p. 18
69. E702/1, p. 77.
70. NLS. Adv. Ms. 28.1.6. i. pp. 79–80.
71. E700/1, p. 91.
72. E702/2, p. 65.
73. E750/11, 17.
74. T. T. Kington Oliphant, *Jacobite Lairds of Gask*, Grampian Club (London, 1870), 269–277, 340–346.
75. NLS. Adv. Ms. 28.1.6., i, f.12.
76. E703/3/19, 20, 21, 22.
77. E701/1, p. 142.

78. E701/2, p. 125.
79. E701/2, p. 108.
80. E701/2 11-1-1754.
81. E702/1, p. 54.
82. E703/2/14.
83. E702/1, p. 100.
84. E701/2, 27 July, 1757.
85. E700/3, p. 13.
86. E702/1, p. 36.
87. E702/2, p. 3.
88. See p. 71, 229, 230.
89. E702/1, p. 103.
90. E702/3, p. 5.
91. E702/3, p. 61.
92. E702/3, p. 88.
93. E700/1, p. 27.
94. E700/4, p. 66.
95. E701/2, p. 171.
96. E700/2, p. 305; E779/1/4, p. 16.
97. E700/1, p. 63.
98. E701/1, p. 13.
99. E700/1, p. 195.
100. E758/1/2; E758/8/1, 2; E700/1, p. 247.
101. E776/18/2.
102. E700/2, p. 146.
103. E776/18/1, 4, 5.
104. E700/4, pp. 16, 78.
105. Sir James Balfour Paul, *The Scots Peerage* (Edinburgh, 1911) vol. 8, 508, 509, 513.
106. E749/5.
107. E735/1; E775/1.
108. E702/2, p. 46.
109. E703/3/31.
110. E700/2, p. 198.
111. E784/4.
112. E702/2, p. 146; E703/3/29.
113. E703/3/13.
114. E702/1, p. 80.
115. E702/2, p. 183, 186, 188.
116. Murdoch, 62–68.
117. E703/3/16.
118. 24 George III, c57, The Disannexing Act.

Chapter 2   The Annexing Act

1. In this chapter, I follow particularly Jewell, Chap. 2.
2. Bruce P. Lenman, *The Jacobite Risings in Britain, 1689–1746* (Eyre Methuen Ltd., London, 1980), 281.

3. Basil Williams, *The Whig Supremacy* (Oxford, 1939) 325.

4. Jewell, 217.

5. G. W. T. Omond, *Lord Advocates of Scotland* (Edinburgh, 1883), i, 342. Hereafter, Omond, *Advocates*; NLS. Ms. 17528, 72–83.

6. NLS. Ms. 98.

7. Jewell, 211.

8. Jewell, Appendix II.

9. E702/2, p. 253.

10. Omond, *Advocates*, ii, 49.

11. The debates can read more fully in *Scots Magazine*, 14, 417–27, and in Hansard, *Parliamentary History*, xiv, 1235–70.

12. See map A, p. 24, *Descriptive List of Plans in the Scottish Record Office*, iii, p. viii, fig. 1. This map is reproduced with the permission of the Controller of Her Majesty's Stationery Office.

13. See Murdoch, 73–82, for more detailed discussion of these points.

14. E721/1, p. 1.

15. A. H. Millar, ed., *A Selection of Forfeited Estates Papers, 1715–1745*, SHS (Edinburgh 1909). Hereafter Millar, FEP. Millar's introduction on p. xii includes the statement: 'The work of the Commissioners began in 1716 and the annexed states were restored in 1784.'

16. *Scots Magazine*, 18, 212.

17. 10 George III, c. 52.

18. Murdoch, 82.

19. Lenman, *Jacobite Risings*, 245.

20. Jewell, 235, 236.

21. E729/1, pp. 26–27. One factor talks of the wadsetters and lesser gentlemen who wanted to keep the people in ignorance and slavery.

22. E714/18/C.

23. E721/1, p. 48; E723/1, p. 48.

24. E721/6, pp. 301, 326; E723/2, p. 103; E721/7, pp. 22, 130, 151.

25. *Scots Magazine*, 22, 363; E721/6, p. 301; E723/2, p. 38.

26. E721/10, p. 148.

27. E723/2, p. 105; E727/43.

28. E721/6, p. 150; E777/327; E721/4, p. 173—'A pretty considerable part' of the augmented stipend had fallen on the Perth tenants.

29. E777/327, 1775–76.

30. E721/1, p. 7; E728/9.

31. See p. 93; Chapter 7.

32. Gordon Donaldson, *Scottish Historical Documents* (Edinburgh, 1970), 174. Hereafter Donaldson, *Documents*.

33. Donaldson, *Documents*, 178.

34. MacKinnon, Kenneth M., 'Education and Social Control; The Case of a gaelic Scotland', in *Scottish Educational Studies*, 4, No. 2, 128. Hereafter MacKinnon in *SES*.

35. Hew Scott, editor, *Fasti Ecclesiae Scoticanae* (Edinburgh, 1926), vi, 473, 474.

36. MacKinnon in *SES*, 129–131.

37. See Chapters 4, 5.

38. NLS. Adv. Ms. 19.1.35, ff. 22–24.

39. E728/36; E723/2, p. 224.

40. T. C. Smout, 'Lead Mining in Scotland, 1650–1850', in *Studies in Scottish Business History*, ed. P. Payne (London, 1967), 105. Hereafter Smout, *'Lead Mining'*.

41. Baron F. Duckham, *A History of the Scottish Coal Industry*, (Newton Abbot, 1970), i, 14. Hereafter, Duckham, *Coal*.

42. Ian Lindsay and M. Cosh, *Inveraray and the Dukes of Argyll*, (Edinburgh, 1973), 221. Hereafter, Lindsay, *Inveraray*.

43. E777/86/23(5).

44. E723/2, p. 238—£105 to Dr. Walker; E727/45; E721/7, p. 119; E727/46; E732/9, 28-2-1780.

45. Duckham, *Coal*, 11, 12.

46. E732/9, 13-5-1769, 5-3-1771; E732/9, 4-8-1777.

47. J. U. Nef, *The Rise of the British Coal Industry* (London, 1932), i, 52.

48. Andrew Wight, *Present State of Husbandry in Scotland* (Edinburgh, 1778–1784), iv, part ii, 302. Hereafter Wight, *Husbandry*.

49. Smout, *Lead Mining*, 103, 104.

50. E777/86/23(3).

51. 1774–5, £1.7/- to a farmer in Corriechrombie for the damage done to his land.

52. E777/86/23–27.

53. Smout, *Lead Mining*, 104. Greta Michie and Bruce Lenman, 'The Mines of Glenesk', in the *Scots Magazine*, 98, 104–113.

54. E727/47; NLS. Mss. 2507, 2508.

55. E729/1, p. 27.

56. E702/2, p. 191.

57. V. E. Durkacz, Language in Celtic Education (unpublished Ph.D. thesis, University of Dundee, 1980).

58. E702/1, p. 141; E702/2, pp. 158, 161, 190.

59. E783/84/1, p. 3.

60. This information on schools is extracted from the factors' reports, sent in reply to the commissioners' questionnaire. These are to be found printed in *Reports on the Annexed Estates*, ed. Virginia Wills (HMSO, 1973) as well as in the original manuscripts in SRO, reference numbers E729/1, 2; E777/244; E738/58; E783/84. Hereafter Wills, *Reports*.

61. E721/6, p. 12.

62. E729/8, p. 134.

63. John Mason, *A History of Scottish Experiments in Rural Education* (London, 1935), 75. Hereafter, Mason, *Rural Education*.

64. E786/33/1; E786/37/5.

65. E721/10, p. 172; E721/8, pp. 33, 55.

66. E737/19/2; E737/1/5.

67. E721/4, p. 224; E/721/7, p. 74; E721/8, pp. 33, 144; E777/326/6; E786/37/5.

68. E786/37/11; Irene F. M. Dean, *Scottish Spinning Schools* (London, 1930), 132. Hereafter Dean, *Spinning Schools*.

69. John Mason, *Schools on the Forfeited Estates* (typescript, SRO.216.08), 151.

70. E721/7, p. 181.

71. Dean, *Spinning Schools*, 132.

72. 26 George III c.27.

73. Schools mentioned were at Strelitz, Craigneich, Glenartney, Lochearnside on the estate of Perth, at Strathyre in Arnprior, on Lochgarry, at Kinloch Rannoch, Finart, Glenerochty and Camaghouran and Carie alternately on Struan, at Kinlocharkaig, Strathlochie and Mamore on Lochiel, on Cluny, in Coigach on the Cromartie estate and on South Uist.

74. Dean, *Spinning Schools*, 131, 135; BPP 1806 (221) ii, 307.

75. Mason, *Rural Education*, 56, 63.

76. See Chapters 7 and 8.

Chapter 3 Annexation and Administration

1. NLS, Ms. 10781. f.112.

2. Murdoch, 75.

3. A. & H. Tayler, *Jacobites of Aberdeenshire and Banffshire in the Forty-Five* (Aberdeen, 1928), 92–93.

4. E721/1–5.

5. Quoted by Murdoch, 15.

6. Murdoch, 76–77.

7. E721/1, p. 16.

8. Murdoch 77; E727/4/1(2).

9. E725/3/8, 12.

10. E721/6, p. 246; E725/3/11.

11. E727/3.

12. E721/2, p. 5; E732/1/4.

13. E721/11, p. 138; E728/5.

14. E732/1/4, 5, 6, 10.

15. E721/2, p. 107; E721/6, p. 292; E721/4, p. 43; E721/5, p. 32; E732/1/6.

16. Inglis, H. R. G., *The Early Maps of Scotland*, R.S.G.S. (Edinburgh, 1936), 12, 98. Hereafter Inglis, *Early Maps*.

17. E.g. E723/1, £62.5.0 paid to May, the balance for 1757–58; p. 57, £20 to John Leslie, £19.7.0 to Adam; p. 74, £167.7.6 for surveying; p. 85, £50 in 1760.

18. Ian H. Adams, ed., *Papers on Peter May, Land Surveyor, 1749–1793*, SHS, (Edinburgh, 1979), xxii, xxviii.

19. SRO, RH2/8-26. This is available through the courtesy of Colonel D. H. Cameron of Lochiel who allowed the SRO to photocopy the original. Most of the surveys and plans were given to the returning proprietors in 1784.

20. NLS. Adv. Ms. 28.1.6, f.428.

21. E777/84/2.

22. The Treasury warrants of approbation in E725/1-5 refer to the appointment of officials and to salaries.

23. E723/1, pp. 58–64.

24. Murdoch, 80.

25. Millar, *FEP*, xlvii.

26. SRO, FEP, 1745 Inventory, Introduction.

27. E721/10, p. 197; E721/11, p. 23.

28. NLS, Minto Papers, EFP 11035, f.23.

29. Murdoch, 4.

30. E721/6, p. 198.

31. E723/2, pp. 69, 75; E721/8, p. 72.

32. E723/2, p. 107.

33. E721/10, p. 104.

34. E723/2, p. 137.

35. NLS, Ms. 11035, ff.7-9.

36. 32 George II c.36; 10 George III c.52.

37. J. Gray, ed., *Clerk of Penicuik's Memoirs*, SHS (Edinburgh, 1892), 220.

38. SRO, GD87/1/77; E721/2, p. 14.

39. E721/4, pp. 158, 159, 160, 267.

40. E721/6, pp. 13, 17, 30.

41. Murdoch, 78.

42. *Caldwell Papers*, Maitland Club (Glasgow, 1854), Part II, i, 130.

43. Henry Hamilton, ed., *Monymusk Papers*, S.H.S. (Edinburgh, 1945), 98. Hereafter Hamilton, *Monymusk*.

44. *Scots Magazine*, 32, 630.

45. E721/4, p. 115.

46. E726/1, p. 49.

47. E729/8.

48. E732/22; E721/11, p. 211.

49. NLS, Adv. Ms. 19.1.35, ff.22–24.

50. E783/84/1, p. 13; E729/1, pp. 30, 31.

51. E726/1, pp. 82–83; E721/10, p. 72; E724/1, p. 14.

52. E701/2, p. 125.

53. E777/144/8; E788/11.

54. E741/38/2; E741/52; E721/8, p. 145.

55. E777/321—1772, 1775, 1776.

56. E721/7, pp. 183, 189; E721/8, p. 98.

57. E721/27, p. 38.

58. E786/33/20; E787/9/138, 147, 151.

59. E787/11/3.

60. E721/4, pp. 6, 223.

61. E721/9, p. 140.

62. E777/84/101; E777/87/29; E721/8, p. 82.

63. E721/9, p. 4.

64. E731/9/1, 2; E721/11, pp. 40, 42.

65. E746/99/1(2), 2(2); E727/9; E769/69.

66. E777/276/1, 2.

67. E777/87/25, 50.

Chapter 4 Landholding

1. E726/3; E701/1, p. 2; E746/78.

2. E726/1, pp. 7, 8.

3. See Wills, *Reports*, originals in SRO, E729/1-6 and in NLS. Adv. Ms. 17.1.6 and 17.1.7 wrongly dated in catalogue.

4. The inspector's reports are to be found in Wills, *Reports* and in E729/7-10, E741/40, E787/24.

5. M. Flanders and D. Swann, *'Design for Living'*. Song, 1957.

6. Malcolm Gray, *The Highland Economy*, (Edinburgh and London, 1957), 66. Hereafter, Gray, *Highland Economy*.

7. E777/72, 341.

8. E701/2, p. 28.

9. 14 George III, c.55.

10. E721/1, p. 64; E721/2, p. 127; E721/4, p. 67.

11. E738/40/1.

12. NLS. Ms. 11035 f.41.

13. E777/249/6.

14. E723/2, p. 25.

15. E723/2, p. 10; E721/4, p. 203; E730/32/2.

16. See Chapter 7.

17. E768/76; E738/60/14.

18. E721/6, p. 12; NLS. Ms. 11035, f.41.

19. E721/11, p. 24; E721/8, pp. 67, 68.

20. E783/85; E777/305(1), p. 101.

21. E777/280/3; E777/305(1), p. 101.

22. E777/244, p. 39. Duke of Argyll, *Scotland As it Was and As it Is*, (Edinburgh, 1887), 425. NLS. Ms. 1309, f.228.

23. E777/251/1.

24. E783/103/18. This was wrapped round the Struan factor's vouchers.

25. E721/7, p. 235.

26. E723/1, p. 24.

27. E777/258.

28. E746/78/2.

29. E777/305(1), p. 46; E777/251/1.

30. E741/38/2.

31. E783/58/23(1); E783/84/1 pp. 15, 16.

32. E721/6, pp. 249, 341.

33. E777/84/96.

34. E721/2, p. 127.

35. E746/75/21.

36. Gray, *Highland Economy*, 74 note.

37. John Walker, *An Economical History of the Hebrides and the Highlands of Scotland* (Edinburgh, 1808), i, 34, 55. Hereafter, Walker, *Economical History*.

38. Lang, *Highlands*, 147.

39. Hamilton, *Monymusk*, 148.

40. E721/11, p. 71.

41. See p. 60.

42. Wight, *Husbandry*, 1, 153.

43. E777/1-6, 70-80.

44. Wight, *Husbandry*, iv, pt. 1, 140.

45. The Cromartie rentals are to be found in E746/72/1-12.

46. E723/2, p. 227.

47. E777/3, 5-2-1747.

48. E721/4, p. 234; E721/5, p. 22; E723/2, p. 81.

49. Ian D. Grant, Landlords and Land Management in North-Eastern Scotland, 1750–1850 (unpublished Ph.D thesis, University of Edinburgh, 1979), i, 57.

50. E787/9/121, 138, 145.

51. E777/340/9.

52. E788/8.

53. J. A. Symon, *Scottish Farming Past and Present* (Edinburgh & London, 1959), 91. Hereafter, Symon, *Farming*.

54. E708/3, p. 4; E721/6, p. 86; E741/19, Crop 1755.

55. E777/3, pp. 27 ff.

56. E777/298/1(26).

57. Robertson, *Southern Perthshire*, 120.

58. E721/4, p. 125; Symon, *Farming*, 45.

59. E721/7, p. 27; E721/8, pp. 92, 97; E721/25, p. 314.

60. Court of Session Register of Deeds, 1775, Durie 233 f. 473 clause 10. Hereafter Durie 233; E738/60/1; Adv. Ms. 31.1.2, p. 49; E721/6, p. 311; 39 George III, c.55.

61. E777/305(1) 24-9-1780.

62. Dr. Johnson, *A Journey to the Western Isles* in *'A Tour to the Hebrides'*, ed. R. W. Chapman, 1944, 52–53.

63. SRO. R/11 28, p. 13; E741/20/7.

64. NLS. Ms. 11035 f.9.

65. E714/18/w.

66. *OSA*, xi, 183; *OSA*, xiii, 539.

Chapter 5 Divisions, Enclosures and Stocking

1. Virginia Wills, 'The Gentleman Farmer and the Annexed Estates', in *Lairds and Improvement in the Scotland of the Enlightenment,* ed. T. M. Devine (*Proceedings of the Tenth Scottish History Conference, 1978,* published 1979), 39.

2. E723/2, p. 187; E746/72.

3. E721/6, p. 217.

4. Wills, *Reports*, Introduction, p. xii.

5. E700/3, p. 197.

6. Wight, *Husbandry*, iv, part i, 151.

7. E777/280/3.

8. E729/8, p. 25; E777/252; E777/305(1), p. 58, March 1781.

9. E721/8, p. 19.

10. E777/84/90(1).

11. *OSA*, xi, 183.

12. E786/37/2, 5, 11; E777/263/3, 12.

13. E777/263/8(1).

14. E729/1, p. 69.

15. E721/, p. 30; E783/58/28(1); E783/84/14.

16. E721/6, p. 251; E769/110.

17. E746/160; E769/108; E783/82.

18. E777/111, 112, 179-82.

19. E777/308; E732/2, p. 109 ff.

20. E777/94/17, 18, 20, 24. See also p. 9.

21. E769/95/4.

22. E777/94/9(1), 20.

23. E777/86/21; E788/13/3.

24. J. Robertson, *General View of the Agriculture in the County of Perth,* (Perth, 1799), 326. Hereafter, Robertson, *Perth*.

25. E783/84/1.

26. E721/6, p. 319.

27. Durie, 233, f.473 Clause 10.

28. E721/22, p. 3; E783/84/1, p. 8; Robertson, *Southern Perthshire*, 69.

29. Adv. Ms. 31.1.2. p. 53; Adv. Ms. 17.1.6, *passim.*

30. E769/106.

31. E729/1, pp. 10, 30.

32. E783/97.

33. E783/84/1, pp. 6, 7.

34. E730/5.

35. E777/287; E777/326/1. £12 awarded for the best stallion, £6 for the second best.

36. E746/75/11(1).

37. E729/8, p. 94.

38. E777/255/3, 5.

39. E787/24, pp. 8, 10.

40. E729/3.

41. E746/75/51, 52; E721/8, p. 227.

42. Breadalbane Papers. Letter from the factor at Achmore, 27.1.1791. I am indebted to Mr. Malcolm Gray for this reference.

43. *Scots Magazine*, 36, 523 ff.

44. Sir G. S. Mackenzie, *General View of the Agriculture of the Counties of Ross and Cromarty* (London, 1813), 130. Hereafter, Mackenzie, *Ross.*

45. I. F. Grant, *Everyday Life on an Old Highland Farm* (London, 1924), 114.

Chapter 6 Arable Farming

1. M. Gray, *Highland Economy*, A. J. Symon, *Scottish Farming*, J. Handley, *Scottish Farming in the Eighteenth Century*, and others, are examples of writers presenting the earlier picture.

2. Ian Whyte, *Agriculture and Society in Seventeenth Century Scotland* (Edinburgh, 1979); B. P. Lenman, *Economic History of Modern Scotland* (London, 1977); T. C. Smout and A. Fenton, 'Scottish Agriculture Before the Improvers—an Exploration', in *Ag. H. R.* 13, 1965.

3. Lang, *Highlands*, xxxvii.

4. E746/78.

5. E721/4, p. 123.

6. E721/6, p. 147.

7. Letter to all factors, 15.1.1783.

8. E741/40, p. 6.

9. NLS. Ms. 2508, f.142.

10. E727/25-27; E730/17; E732/9, 26-1-1768.

11. Robertson, *Southern Perthshire*, 38.

12. Captain John Henderson, *General View of the Agriculture in the County of Sutherland* (London, 1812), 207. Hereafter, Henderson, *Sutherland.*

13. Robertson, *Southern Perthshire*, 24, 45, 47, 48.

14. E721/10, p. 133; E721/24, p. 11.

15. E777/157/12; E777/162/7.

16. E721/18, p. 18.

17. E721/7, pp. 6, 58; E721/10, p. 133.

18. E773/68; E783/104, *passim.* See also E777/259.

19. E723/2, pp. 41, 150; E723/2, p. 150; E724/1, p. 15; E783/93, 104, *passim* to 1778.

20. Robertson, *Perth*, 33; W. Marshall, *General View of the Agriculture in the Central Highlands of Scotland*, (London, 1794), 37. Hereafter, Marshall, *Central*.

21. E783/104/2 – £42.0.9½d. in 1764.

22. E746/113, 1st folder; E746/75/6.

23. E721/8, pp. 200, 201; E721/10, p. 6.

24. E737/27.

25. E741/23, 10.2.1768.

26. W. R. Scott, *Report of the Board of Agriculture for Scotland, on Home Industries*, 9.

27. Wight, *Husbandry, passim*; Frend's Journals, E777/305 & 252; *Reports to Board of Agriculture* (1794); Robertson, *Southern Perthshire*, 46 ff; Walker, *Economical History*, i, 3.

28. Wight, *Husbandry*, i, 272.

29. E729/8, pp. 9, 36, 47, 48.

30. E721/6, p. 286.

31. E721/27, p. 15.

32. E730/47.

33. E729/1, p. 68.

34. E721/6, p. 332.

35. Walker, *Economical History*, i, 121, 124.

36. Wight, *Husbandry*, i, 3, 67.

37. Sir John Sinclair, *General View of the Agriculture of the Northern Counties and Islands of Scotland* (London, 1795), 22. Hereafter, Sinclair, *Northern Counties*; E729/8, p. 95.

38. J. P. Day, *Public Administration of the Highlands and Islands* (London, 1918), 304 ff. Hereafter, Day, *Administration*.

39. E746/78.

40. E721/9, p. 85.

41. E787/24, p. 13.

42. E721/8, p. 23; E777/76.

43. E741/46, p. 4.

44. E777/324, 325; E721/16, p. 14.

45. E721/8, p. 24; E729/8, p. 30.

46. E738/64/1.

47. E777/252, *passim*; E777/244.

48. Sinclair, *Northern Counties*, p. 50.

49. James Robertson, *General View of the Agriculture in the County of Inverness*, (London, 1808), 56. Hereafter, Robertson, *Inverness*.

50. Wight, *Husbandry*, iv, Part 1, 151.

51. R. Heron, *General View of the Hebrides* (Edinburgh, 1794), 10. Hereafter, Heron, *Hebrides*. For full title see Bibliography.

52. E721/9, p. 85.

53. E721/6, p. 215; E729/8, p. 108.

54. E721/1, p. 27.

55. E777/269/1; E721/10, pp. 201, 202; E723/2, p. 91—£40 for Robert Menzies.

56. E721/7, p. 68.

57. See Chapter 7.

58. E721/11, p. 38; E730/9.

59. E721/7, p. 10; E783/84/9.

60. *N.S.A.*, x, 534.

61. Rosalind K. Marshall, *The Days of Duchess Anne* (London, 1973), 57; Hamilton, *Monymusk, passim.*

62. E729/8, pp. 152-153.

63. Wills, *Reports*. If one consults the index, one finds that trees and woods are mentioned throughout.

64. E784/84/1, p. 8; Robertson, *Perth*, 235.

65. E726/1.

66. E777/84/85; E721/4, p. 171.

67. E721/6, p. 66; E723/2, p. 171; E721/7, p. 246.

68. E721/7, p. 79; E721/24; p. 105.

69. E721/4, p. 189; E783/58; E777/340/7.

70. E737/19; E723/1, p. 18.

71. Wight, *Husbandry*, iv, part i, 216.

72. E729/8, 9, 10 *passim.*

73. E721/11, p. 114.

74. Wight, *Husbandry*, i, Preface, ix, xii.

75. E777/269/2.

76. Wight, *Husbandry*, i, 21.

77. Wight, *Husbandry*, i, 60 ff., 87, 114, 131, 140, 143, 154.

78. Wight, *Husbandry*, i, 160 ff.

79. Wight, *Husbandry*, iv, part i, 256.

80. E746/70-198; E787/9-41.

81. Wight, *Husbandry*, iv, part i, 212, 215-6, 226; E729/8, pp. 108, 109.

82. A. J. Youngson, *After the Forty-Five* (Edinburgh, 1973), 41. Hereafter, Youngson, *Post Forty-Five.*

83. See Chapter 10.

84. E777/252, 305(1).

85. E777/280/6.

86. Heron, *Hebrides*, 10.

87. Robertson, Marshall, Sinclair, etc. in their *Reports* to the Board of Agriculture.

88. N.L.S. Ms. 2508, f. 149.

89. E730/47.

90. Wight, *Husbandry*, iii, part i, 344-5.

91. E768/76; E745/57; E764/32; E767/44; E743/22; E737/27.

92. E737/19/2.

93. E733/42.

94. V. Wills, 'The Gentleman Farmer and the Annexed Estates', in *Lairds and Improvement in the Scotland of the Enlightenment*, ed. T. Devine (Proceedings of the Scottish History Conference, 1978), 39-40.

95. E746/72/9, 11, 171; Fraser, *Cromartie*, 1, cclvii.

96. Gray, *Highland Economy*, 78.

97. NLS. Adv. Ms. 31.1.2, p. 50.

98. E730/45/2; NLS. Ms. 1259.

99. E727/60/2.

100. E721/5, p. 7; E721/9, p. 134.

101. E777/280/5.

102. R. J. Adam, ed., *Sutherland Estate Management, 1802–1816*, SHS (Edinburgh, 1972). Hereafter, Adam, *Sutherland*.

103. Cf. Chapter 2.
104. E702/2, p.197.

Chapter 7 Aid to Industrial Development

1. Dean, *Spinning Schools*, 9; J.R. Elder, *Royal Fishery Companies of the Seventeenth Century* (1912).
2. T. Wodrow, *Analecta*, iii, 319.
3. William Marshall, *Historic Scenes in Perthshire* (Edinburgh, 1880), 291. E777/213.
4. SRO NG. 1/7, iv, p.43; Mason, *Rural Education*, 19.
5. See the factors' reports, E729/1-3 and Wills, *Reports* for the following information.
6. E721/2, p.42; E729/3.
7. E777/203/4.
8. E721/6, p.92.
9. E723/1, pp.58-64.
10. E746/77/13; *O.S.A.*, vi, 187.
11. *APS*, viii, 348, 598.
12. H. Hamilton, *The Industrial Revolution in Scotland* (Oxford 1932), 79. Hereafter Hamilton, *Revolution*.
13. 13 George I, c. 26.
14. Dean, *Spinning Schools*, 16.
15. A. J. Warden, *The Linen Trade, Ancient and Modern* (London, 1864), 445. Hereafter, Warden, *Linen*.
16. Quoted in Hamilton, *Revolution*, 80.
17. E729/8, pp.126, 127; Warden, *Linen*, 435, 448-9.
18. SRO N.G. 1/7, i, p.234.
19. Mason, *Rural Education*, 3.
20. It is sometimes said, by Professor H. Hamilton among others, that this money came from the Forfeited Estates rents but the act itself (26 George II c. 20) mentions only 'unallocated funds'. The rents of the estates annexed were tied up by 26 George II c. 41.
21. SRO N.G. 1/7, iv, p.205.
22. E730/15; E729/8, p.58; E777/289/2(1); E777/200/10(1).
23. E721/7, p.89.
24. E727/20/2(1); E721/9, pp.120, 121.
25. E721/7, p.250; E730/16.
26. E728/15/1-3.
27. E728/15/2.
28. E769/87/1(1,2).
29. E728/15/16.
30. E727/27/1(1).
31. SRO N.G. 1/7, iv, pp.41, 47.
32. E787/24, pp.8, 9; T. Pennant, *A Tour in Scotland in 1769* (Warrington, 1774), 198. Hereafter, Pennant, *1769*.
33. J. Cameron Lees, *History of the County of Inverness* (Edinburgh, London, 1897), 212. Hereafter, Lees, *Inverness*.
34. E746/111/1.

35. Durie, *Scottish Linen Industry*, 90.

36. E746/138/11.

37. E732/9, 26-1-1768; E727/21/7; E746/94/7, 8.

38. E746/94/1, 4.

39. E727/26; E728/16.

40. Durie, *Scottish Linen*, 91.

41. E729/8, pp.118-127.

42. E721/10, p.28.

43. E730/15; E787/11/2.

44. E723/1, p.47; E721/6, p.10; E730/13.

45. E721/6, pp.198, 262.

46. E730/27; E721/7, p.192.

46. E721/7, p.203; E721/7, p.192.

47. E721/7, p.203; E783/103/7.

48. E777/127.

49. *Scots Magazine*, 13, p.418.

50. E728/27/1(1).

51. E730/19/3.

52. David Loch, *Essays on the Trade, Commerce, Manufactures and Fisheries of Scotland*, (Edinburgh, 1778), Preface, xii; i. pp.136-137. Hereafter, Loch, *Essays*. Hamilton, *Revolution*, 144, 145.

53. E727/20/2(1); O.S.A., ix, 617.

54. E787/24, pp.12-13; E729/10/2; O.S.A., ix, 617; Loch, *Essays*, ii, 108. E728/28/3(2).

55. E777/124/6, 7(2, 6); E730/15; E777/289/2(2).

56. Loch, *Essays*, i, Chap. 3, Section 1; Dr. James Anderson also advocated encouraging the woollen industry in his essay, *Observations on the Means of Exciting a Spirit of National Industry*, (Edinburgh, 1777).

57. E721/24, p.212; E777/289/2; E777/124.

58. E787/24, p.8.

59. A. W. Kerr, *History of Banking in Scotland* (Glasgow, 1884), 60.

60. E730/15.

61. E727/60/1, 2.

62. John Butt, *The Industrial Archaeology of Scotland* (Newton Abbot, 1967), 53. Loch, *Essays*, ii, 104, 108, 112. O.S.A., viii, 440-441.

63. E721/6, p.76; E723/2, p.16.

64. E728/25/1, 2.

65. E721/6, p.325.

66. E727/31/1.

67. O.S.A., ix, 618; Joseph Mitchell, *Reminiscences of My Life in the Highlands* (David and Charles reprint, 1971), i, 50.

68. E714/18/0; E723/3, p.60; E777/47/1(4); E777/201/6.

69. E728/26.

70. E727/33/2, 3, 4.

71. Alistair G. Thomson, *The Paper Industry in Scotland 1590-1861* (Edinburgh, 1974), 1; D. Bremner, *The Industries of Scotland* (Edinburgh, 1869), 322; O.S.A., ix, 593; E723/2, p.137; E777/201/4.

72. E777/329, 332.

73. E777/124/3.

74. E730/50/1, 2.

75. E783/103/4; E788/21/1.

76. Mason, *Rural Education*, 21, 26. *Scots Magazine* 22, p.98; E728/17/3(1). Donald Grant, a weaver, claimed that the Countess of Sutherland had 'educated' him.

77. E723/1, p.60; E721/6, p.9; E725/1, p.8.

78. E777/140/1(2); E721/6, p.14; E723/2, p.237; E721/8, p.56.

79. E721/6, pp.192, 193; E721/8, p.56.

80. E777/140/1.

81. E746/90/7; E746/123/9(2); E721/10, p.38; E721/15, p.23.

82. E746/75/6, 11.

83. E721/6, p.213.

84. E721/15, p.3; E732/2/19; E721/11, p.20; E728/10/6.

85. E721/15, pp.5, 13, 15.

86. E746/90/1-8.

87. E746/92.

88. E721/15, pp.19-22; E746/173.

89. Millar, *FEP*, 109.

90. E723/3, pp.40, 57; E721/15, July, 1784; E746/91/2, 3.

91. E746/123/8.

92. *Scots Magazine*, 28, p.110.

93. E723/2, p.11; E746/75/22; J. Dunlop, *British Fisheries Society*, 53.

94. E783/65/10, 13, 14; E721/27, p.21; E768/63/5.

95. E728/15/5; E783/65/3.

96. E768/63/1-4.

97. E783/65/4, 13.

98. E721/8, p.72; E723/2, pp.15, 89.

99. E721/2, p.101.

100. E723/2, pp.91, 149; E730/15; E727/23.

101. E728/20/2(1).

102. E777/330/7; E777/287.

103. E769/130; E786/33/9; E786/37/4.

104. E777/24/1(1).

105. H. D. Gribbon, 'The Irish Linen Board, 1711-1828', in L. M. Cullen and T. C. Smout (eds.), *Comparative Aspects of Scottish and Irish Economic and Social History, 1600-1800* (Edinburgh, 1977), 83; E729/8, p.121.

106. *O.S.A.*, viii, 440; *O.S.A.*, xi, 604, 182; *O.S.A.*, ii, 460; *O.S.A.*, ix, 592.

107. E777/326.

108. Knox, *Tour*, cxx.

109. E729/8, pp.133, 134.

110. A. R. B. Haldane, *New Ways through the Glens* (Newton Abbot, 1973), Chapter 2; see Chapters 9-11.

Chapter 8 New Towns by Land and Sea; Fishing

1. T. C. Smout, 'The Landowner and the Planned Village in Scotland', in *Scotland in the Age of Improvement*, ed. N. Phillipson and R. Mitchison (Edinburgh, 1970), 73-106; J. D. Wood, 'Regulating the Settler and Establishing Industry in Planning Intentions for a Nineteenth Century Scottish Estate Village', *Scottish Studies*, 15, part 1, 50.

2. NLS. Adv. Ms. 19.1.35.

3. E723/1, p.46; E721/2, p.19; E725/2, p.9; Cosmo Innes, *Origines Parochiales*, Bannatyne Club (Edinburgh 1851), ii, part 2, 5-7.

4. J. M. Houston, 'Village Planning in Scotland', in *Advancement of Science*, v, 18, 1948-9, 130.

5. 3 George III c.8.

6. D. G. Lockhart, The Evolution of the Planned Villages in North-east Scotland, Unpublished Ph.D. thesis, University of Dundee, 1974, Vol. 2, 130-131. Hereafter Lockhart.

7. E721/4; E777/84/66.

8. E721/7, p.138; E746/75/22; E723/2, pp.46 ff.

9. Quoted by William MacGill, *Old Ross-shire and Scotland* (Inverness, 1909), 214, 215.

10. James Wilson, *A Voyage round the Coasts of Scotland* (Edinburgh, 1842), i, 311. Hereafter Wilson, *Voyage*.

11. E721/4, p.76; E721/7, p.106; E721/14, p.38.

12. E721/8, p.194; E721/14, pp.52, 77, 88.

13. E721/14, pp.6ff.

14. Lockhart, i, 226.

15. E721/7, p.145; E723/2, pp.53, 74, 75.

16. E777/84/15, 16; E721/7, pp.31, 59; E721/14, p.25; E729/8, p.58.

17. E721/14, pp.34, 115; E721/10, p.187.

18. E746/75/3; E721/7, pp.218, 240; E729/8, P.38; E721/14, p.74.

19. E729/8, p.55; E721/9, p.92; E721/8, p.190; E777/119.

20. NLS. Adv. Ms. 28.1.6 Vol.2, p.58; E777/84/238.

21. E746/75/11(1), 18; E721/14, pp.45, 56.

22. E702/4; E777/32/8, 14.

23. E783/58/23; E721/8, p.156.

24. E721/14, p.86; E721/24, p.8; E721/15, p.116; E721/27, p.62.

25. E777/305/1, pp.4-5, 67, 78, 85; E723/2, insert between pp. 46-47; E777/128, 252.

26. T. Pennant, *Tour in Scotland and Voyage to the Hebrides in 1772* (London 1776), ii, 91. Hereafter Pennant, *Tour*; *NSA*, x, 314.

27. RHP. 3477; E721/8, p.16; NLS. Ms. 213. George Douglas, Advocate, *Tour to the Hebrides*, in his autograph; *O.S.A.*, iv, 43.

28. Wight, *Husbandry*, i, 17, 118; E777/252.

29. *NSA*. x, p.1171; William Marshall, *Historic Scenes in Perthshire*, (Edinburgh, 1880), 245.

30. T. Hunter, *Woods, Forests and Estates of Perthshire* (Perth, 1883), 351; Wight, *Husbandry*, 1, 114; E777/32.

31. I have to thank Mrs Kirk of Lower Borland Farm for this information. Note the modern spelling.

32. E721/8, p.22.

33. Sir William Fraser, *The Earls of Cromartie* (Edinburgh, 1876), 1, cclviii. Hereafter, Fraser, *Cromartie*; E787/28/1-5, E721/14, p.8.

34. E783/42, 43.

35. James Robertson, *General View of the Agriculture of the Southern Districts of the County of Perth*, (London, 1794), 65. Hereafter, Robertson, *Southern Perthshire*; Francis Groome, *Ordnance Gazetteer of Scotland*, (Edinburgh, 1882), i, 222. Hereafter, Groome, *Gazetteer*.

36. E721/6, p.175; E721/11, p.23; E729/8, p.84; E777/301; E777/87/86, 87.

37. SRO. GD. 248/25/2/8.

38. E746/106; E746/110/6.

39. E723/2, p.39 ff.

40. E723/2, pp. 52, 53, 86.

41. Wilson, *Voyage*, i, 198, 199; M. Gray, 'Crofting and Fishing in the North-West Highlands, 1890-1914', in *Northern Scotland*, i, No. 1, 89-114; *Caledonian Mercury*, 25 August, 1784.

42. A. Lang, *The Highlands of Scotland in 1750*, (Edinburgh and London, 1898), 34, 45; see Chapter 9.

43. E721/14, p.36; E727/60/1; E728/13/2; Pennant, *Tour*, i, 313.

44. E721/7, p.27; E741/38/2; E746/75/4,20; E786/22/2.

45. E721/9, p.145; E721/10, p.33. 2.2.1767; E786/51; E721/17, pp.2, 6.

46. E727/60/1; E723/2, 1777; E746/127.

47. J. Knox, *A Tour through the Highlands of Scotland and the Hebrides Islands in 1786*, (London, 1787), 36-38; E729/9; E721/8, p.74.

48. E727/16; E721/17, p.1; E728/13/4; Pennant, *Tour*, ii, 194; Gavin Maxwell, *Harpoon at a Venture*, (London, 1964).

49. NLS. Ms. 305/130; E729/1, 70; E746/93/2; E702/2, p.228; E727/18, 19; E728/14/1(1, 2).

Chapter 9 Road Building

1. Quoted as a chapter heading by J. W. Gregory, *Story of the Road*, (London,1931), 131.

2. E783/84/1, p.10; J. B. Salmond, *Wade in Scotland*, (London, 1938), pp.26, 48. Hereafter, Salmond, *Wade*.

3. See Map B, p. 182.

4. Magnus Magnusson, 'Highland Administration', in *The Future of the Highlands*, (London, 1968), ed. D. Thomson and I. Grimble, 277.

5. G. S. Barrow, *Robert Bruce*, (London, 1968), 98. Map of invasion of 1296.

6. *APS*, 1617, c.8; *APS*, 1669, c.16.

7. Hamilton, *Monymusk*, 161; R. Southey, *Journal of a Tour in Scotland, 1819*, (London, 1929), 237. Hereafter, Southey, *Tour*.

8. NLS. Ms. 1021, f.23.

9. For these queries and answers, see Wills, *Reports* and the original Mss. E729/1-6 *passim*.

10. E783/84/1, pp.4, 10-11; E783/102.

11. E721/2-4; E783/104.

12. E721/4, p.202; E783/102, 1756.

13. E721/6, p.327; E721/7, p.78; E721/9, pp.135, 145.

14. H. A. Vallance, *The Highland Railway*, (London, 1971), 49; E783/84/1, p.11; E783/102-106.

15. SRO. NG. 1/7, iv, p.47.

16. E721/4; E746/87.

17. E721/7, 8, 10, 11.

18. E746/195/5; E783/104/6.

19. A. R. B. Haldane, *New Ways Through the Glens*, (London, 1962), 12-14. Hereafter, Haldane, *New Ways*.

20. E721/11, p.10, 11; E721/19, p.19.

21. Pennant, *Tour*, ii, 104.

22. Southey, *Tour*, 25–26.

23. E721/7, p.74; E721/8, p.218; E721/9, pp.95, 152; E729/8, p.65; E777/269/1.

24. E777/249/7.

25. NLS. Ms. 2509, f. 13.

26. E729/8, pp.150-151; E721/10, p.130.

27. E727/35/9; E731/11/6; E788/22/4; PLA 2/1/1, p.66.

28. E721/2, p.43; E721/27, p.70; E721/6, p.239; E777/259; E721/7, pp.51, 78, 114.

29. E777/321.

30. E777/165; E777/305(1).

31. Salmond, *Wade*, 298-302.

32. *Report of the Commissioners for Inquiring into Matters Relating to Public Roads in Scotland*, (Edinburgh, 1859). BPP. 1860 (2596) xxxviii, 1; 1860 (2596-1) xxxviii. 301.

33. *O.S.A.*, ix, 149; E728/31/3.

34. E721/16, p.15; E721/25, p.174.

35. E768/59/11.

36. E728/30/1, 8; E721/11, 12, 18.

37. E786/33/1; *O.S.A.*, xvi, 274; E721/12.

38. E728/30/6; E721/11; E723/3; E727/35/1.

39. E728/30/2, 3; E727/35/6, 8.

40. E728/30/12.

41. Haldane, *New Ways*, 139.

42. E721/11.

43. E721/16, p.15.

44. E721/8, p.145; E783/104/6.

45. E723/2, p.147; E732/7; E721/17, p.6.

46. E723/2, pp.188, 211, 223.

47. E728/30/12(1).

48. E728/53; E732/9; CHRB, 2, p.271.

Chapter 10 Bridges and Inns

1. M. Taylor, *Stone Bridges in Scotland*. Neale Prizewinner, 1947, Royal Institute of British Architects. I am grateful to Mr. Taylor for having allowed me to read this essay.

2. E728/29/34; E714/18, p.18.

3. Salmond, *Wade*, 150.

4. PLA, 14/1/2, f. 18.

5. CHRB, 8, p.5; CHRB, 5, p.21.

6. CHRB, 8, p.6.

7. E737/21; E786/33/7.

8. PLA, 14/1/2, f.42.

9. *O.S.A.*, x, 126.

10. E777/243, *passim*.

11. Salmond, *Wade*, 21, 22, 234.

12. E721/4, 5, 6; E783/62; PLA, 14/1/2, f. 102.

13. E777/244, pp.30, 56-57.

14. E738/58/1, p.7.

15. E786/33/1.
16. E777/244, p.2.
17. E723/1, pp.48, 81; E721/6, pp.10, 22.
18. E721/6, pp.22, 112; E786/33/1.
19. E786/33/1; Cia-aig at the east of Loch Arkaig.
20. E721/2, pp.74, 124.
21. *APS*, 1617, c. 8.
22. E783/71/2; E721/8, p.159.
23. PLA, 2/1/1, p.82; E721/10, p.119; E721/27, p.2.
24. E777/84/74.
25. PLA, 14/1/2, f. 109; E721/7, p.16.
26. PLA, 14/1/2, ff. 100, 126.
27. *Macfarlane's Collections,* 1. 134
28. E721/6, pp.110, 183, 217; E777/84/8.
29. E730/20/3.
30. E721/9, pp.122, 189; E721/18, p.32.
31. Haldane, *New Ways,* 120.
32. E721/25, pp.284, 216.
33. PLA, 1/1/2, pp.119, 194, 195; E721/26, p.7.
34. E732/16.
35. E729/28/24; E721/11, pp.211, 216; E732/2, p.141; E727/34/18; E728/29/26.
36. E768/68/1, 2; E777/512; E788/14.
37. J. Smeaton, *Reports of the late Mr. John Smeaton, FRS,* (London, 1797), i, 174-5. Hereafter, Smeaton, *Reports*; Pennant, *Tour,* ii, 114.
38. E728/29/6.
39. Smeaton, *Reports,* i, 177; E730/22/16; *Scots Magazine,* 34, 397.
40. Smeaton, *Reports,* 1, 184; E728/29/6.
41. NLS. Ms. 1021, f. 28; SRO. GD. 248/2308/6. I am grateful to Dr. Ian Grant who directed my attention to a relevant letter from Kinnoull to the Earl of Findlater.
42. E727/34/13.
43. *Scots Magazine,* 31, 340; Smeaton, *Reports,* i, 190.
44. E728/29/7(1); E721/11, p.31.
45. *Scots Magazine,* 32, p.728.
46. E721/12, p.27; E728/29/36; E713/14; E714/18/o.
47. E721/11, p.170. 186; Map showing postal routes in A. R. B. Haldane, *Three Centuries of Scottish Posts,* (Edinburgh, 1971); E728/29/22.
48. E727/34/4; *Macfarlane's Collections,* i, 221; *Scots Magazine,* 29, 166.
49. E721/11, p.17, 18; PLA, 2/1/1, p.79.
50. E728/29/4; E721/18, pp. 14, 45; Haldane, *New Ways,* 120-1, 140.
51. E728/29/25; E721/11, pp.181, 215.
52. E728/29/9; E721/11, pp.75, 76, 79.
53. NLS. Ms.1021, f. 22.
54. E721/11, pp.113, 114, 141; E730/46.
55. E728/29/16; E729/28/18; A. R. B. Haldane, *The Drove Roads of Scotland,* (Edinburgh, 1971), 88-89.
56. E721/11, p.184; E728/29/20.
57. E764/31, 3, 4; E764/33.
58. E728/29/15; E728/29/18.
59. E728/29/23.

60. E721/11, pp.17, 204; E728/29/33; E721/12, p.23.

61. A more detailed description of the Board's contribution to bridge building than can be given in this volume can be found in the author's thesis, 'The Forfeited Annexed Estates', Ph.D., University of St. Andrews, 1975, Appendix G.

62. E713/12/1, 2; 29 George III c.42.

63. Elizabeth Grant of Rothiemurchus, *Memoirs of a Highland Lady*, ed. Angus Davidson, (London, 1950), 114; W. L. Mathieson, *Church and Reform in Scotland*, (Glasgow, 1916), 46; Southey, *Tour*, 90.

64. J. Ramsay of Ochtertyre, *Scotland and Scotsmen in the Eighteenth Century*, (Edinburgh, 1888), ii, 402. Hereafter, Ramsay, *Scotland*.

65. E721/4, p. 232.

66. Salmond, *Wade*, 130, 136.

67. E767/12; E767/32; E788/13.

68. E728/34/1-17.

69. E713/19; 26 George III, c. 28; E702/4, pp.193, 201.

70. NLS. Ms. 2509, f. 66.

71. E721/6, p.354; E721/24, p.77; E729/8, pp.85-86, 139.

72. E721/2, pp.66, 104; E721/4, pp.199, 244; E729/8, p.38.

73. E721/6, pp.173, 278.

74. E777/164, 233, 257.

75. E727/40; E728/35; E721/11, p.88.

76. E721/2, p.42; E721/11, p.124; E721/6, p.180.

77. E721/6, pp.337, 353.

78. E746/75/14.

79. E741/52; E786/37/8.

80. E721/11, p.93; E721/18, pp.60, 83, 132, 177, 180; E721/22, p.5.

81. E723/31/3.

82. E728/31/3.

Chapter 11 Travel by Water

1. There are accounts and receipts for ferry boats being built and repaired in all the estate papers.

2. E721/6, pp.24, 237; E721/23, p.1, 5, 9, 15.

3. E768/82; E721/22, pp.5, 18, 20.

4. E727/59; E728/49.

5. E728/31; E730/22, 45.

6. CHRB, 9, pp.49, 108; 46 George III, c. 155

7. E721/11, pp.92, 188; E723/3; E728/31/1.

8. T. C. Smout, *A History of the Scottish People, 1560-1830*, (London, 1969), 245.

9. H. Hamilton, *An Economic History of Scotland in the Eighteenth Century*, (Oxford, 1963), 286.

10. E728/33/4; (1-4).

11. Gibb, Sir Alexander, *Story of Telford*, (London, 1935), 65, 152-3; *O.S.A.*, xvi, 598-600; E728/33/2, 3.

12. E730/22; E728/33/3; E732/9; E721/11, pp.188, 192; E714/18/o.

13. Jean Lindsay, *The Canals of Scotland*, (Newton Abbot, 1965), 16. Hereafter, Lindsay, *Canals*.

14. NLS. Ms. 3164; E726/2, 1772; E727/37.

15. Lindsay, *Canals*, 142; Haldane, *New Ways*, 78n.; Samuel Smiles, *Lives of Boulton and Watt*, (London, 1865), 157, 197.

16. E728/31; E730/21/2, 3.

17. E714/18/m. See Chapter 12.

18. R. S. Fittis, *Illustrations of the History and Antiquities of Perthshire*, (Perth, 1874), 293.

19. *Scots Magazine*, 30. 289, 290, 294.

20. NLS. Ms. 1497, f. 131.

21. Lindsay, *Canals*, 34, 35; 39 George III, c.71.

22. Lindsay, *Canals*, 116, ff.; 39-40 George III, c. 57.

23. E702/4, pp. 209, 210.

24. 46 George III, c. 156.

25. 43 George III, c. 80; 46 George III, c. 155.

26. 46 George III, c.156. See Chapter 12.

27. Lindsay, *Canals*, 133; E713/25/7; 56 George III, c. 135.

28. Lindsay, *Canals*, 140, 141.

29. CHRB, 3, p.33.

30. E704/12/3, 4; Haldane, *New Ways*, 117; E702/4; E713/25/7.

31. The eleven reports (1803-1825) of the Commissioners for Highland Roads and Bridges are published as British Parliamentary Papers, and it is from these that most of the information in the next few pages has been gleaned.

32. See T. Telford, *Life Written by Himself*, ed. J. Rickman (London, 1838), Appendix L.18.

33. Pennant, *1769*, 133.

34. H. Hamilton, ed. *The County of Aberdeen*, (Glasgow, 1960), 228, 328. This is a volume in the *Third Statistical Account of Scotland*. For nineteenth-century comment on these harbours, see the entries for the relevant parishes in *NSA*, xii, xiii, xiv.

35. E728/29/22.

36. B. Lenman, *From Esk to Tweed*, (Glasgow and London, 1975), Chapter 2.

37. E714/18/o.

38. PLA, 2/1/1, p.201.

39. David Turnock, *Patterns of Highland Development*, (London, 1970), *passim*. Hereafter, Turnock, *Patterns*.

40. CHRB, 9, p.14; CHRB, 6, p.35.

41. E786/33/1, 2.

Chapter 12 Conclusion

1. C. R. Fay, *Adam Smith and the Scotland of his Day*, (Cambridge, 1956), 12-13.

2. *Scots Magazine*, 26. 108-9.

3. Adv. Ms. 19.1.35, f. 26.

4. E768/61/4(1); E773/42; E777/146/2.

5. Ramsay, *Scotland*, i, 198.

6. T. Pennant, *Tour*, ii, 91.

7. R. Southey, *Tout*, 88.

8. *Parliamentary History of England*, (London, 1815), xxiv, 1372-3.

9. E746/88/10(2); Fraser, *Cromartie*, ii, cclvii.

10. E714/18/m; BPP. 1806 (221) ii, 307.

11. E714/18/j, k.

12. E700/5, p.13; E702/4, pp.102-103.

13. G. Menary, *The Life and Letters of Duncan Forbes of Culloden*, (London, 1936), 174-181.

14. E770/3, p.322; E727/71/1; *Scots Magazine*, 36, 333.

15. See Chapter 3.

16. 26 George III, c.28; *Scots Magazine*, 46, 697.

17. BPP. 1806 (221), ii, 305; 46 George III, c. 154; 46 George III, c. 156.

18. E702/4, 6 December 1817.

19. NLS. Ms. 5209, ff. 13-44.

20. Review by J. Kenyon of Roy A. Kelch, *Newcastle, A Duke without Money*, in the *Observer*, 31.3.1974.

21. Lindsay, *Inverary*, 238.

22. I am very much indebted to Professor S. G. E. Lythe and to Dr. Gordon Jackson of Strathclyde University for these figures, which they obtained from the Customs House papers (PRO. Board of Trade 6/230 f.92).

23. NLS. Minto EFP 35.

24. E731/11.

25. Adam, *Sutherland*, i, Introduction.

26. Donaldson, *Documents*, 172.

27. E727/65; E721/20, p.20.

28. E777/136/19.

29. Adam, *Sutherland*, 1, xcvii.

30. Lang, *Highlands*, 159.

31. E728/28/18.

32. Turnock, *Patterns*, 16.

33. E764/31/4.

34. E783/84/1, p.14.

35. Lang, *Highlands*, 130.

36. Adam, *Sutherland*, 1, xxxv.

37. *Scots Magazine*, 30, 294.

38. E714/17/1; E714/18, pp.9, 10.

Select Bibliography

Manuscript Sources

Scottish Record Office, Edinburgh

Abercairny Papers
Forfeited Estates Papers, 1715 and 1745
Records of the Board of Trustees for Manufactures and Fisheries
Records of the Society in Scotland for Propagating Christian Knowledge

Sandeman Library, Perth

Minutes of Perthshire County Commissioners of Supply and the Justices of the Peace

National Library of Scotland, Edinburgh

Minto Papers

Ms. 98 (xviii)	*Information anent the Highlands*
Ms. 213	*Tour in the Hebrides, 1800* – autograph of George Lewis Augustus Douglas
Ms. 293 (xxxi)	*Accompt of all the Forfeited Estates in Scotland*
Ms. 298 (x)	*Abbreviat of surveys made on the Forfeited Estates* from Mss. in the Signet Library
Ms. 301	*The highland man's observation on the alteration of the times*
Ms. 642 (1)	*Memorial relating to ash-burning for bleaching,* Ebenezer McCulloch, 1782
Ms. 1021	*Journal of a Tour in Scotland* (21 May to 11 June, 1776), 'Mr. Parker and myself'
Ms. 1080	*Journal of a Tour in Scotland in 1789* (J. Deighton)
Ms. 1259	*Letters of Captain Lawrence Day*
Ms. 1309	*Letters of the Macdonalds of Sleat*
Ms. 1497	*On the Forth-Clyde Canal*
Ms. 2507, 2508	James Robertson's *Journals of his Travels in Scotland, 1767–1771*
Ms. 2509	*Sketch of a ramble through the Highlands of Scotland in 1818,* John Anderson
Ms. 2911	*Tour of William Burrell in 1758* (later Sir Willliam)
Ms. 2970 (x)	Forbes Papers, *Manufactures and Revenues*
Ms. 3164	*Report on a Canal into Strathmore in 1771,* James Watt
Ms. 5209	*Letters regarding forfeitures after 1715*

Advocates' Library (within N.L.S.), Edinburgh

Ms. 17.1.6; 17.1.7	*Factors reports on the Annexed Estates, 1755,* (wrongly dated in Summary Catalogue as c.1745)
Ms. 19.1.35	*Miscellaneous*
Ms. 25.7.18, 19	*Lists of the Faculty of Advocates and the Senators of the College of Justice*
Ms. 28.1.6	*Letters* (under the Bookplate of Baron Maule)
Ms. 31.1.2	*History of Monievaird and Strowan,* by James Porteous
Ms. 81.1.5	*Memorandum on the state of the Highlands*
Ms. 82.1.5	*Gask Letters*

Parliamentary Papers and Official Publications

Reports of the C.H.R.B., 1803 to 1825

Survey and Report on the Coasts and Central Highlands of Scotland, 1802, (London, 1803), Thomas Telford

Report of the Select Committee on Mr. Telford's Survey

Report to the Board of Agriculture of Scotland on Home Industries in the Highlands and Islands, 1914 (by Mr. W. R. Scott)

Report of the Parliamentary Committee on the Balances Arising from the Forfeited Estates in Scotland, 1806

Report of the Commissioners for Inquiring into Matters Relating to Public Roads in Scotland (in two volumes, published, 1859)

Reports on the Annexed Estates, 1755–1769 (H.M.S.O., Edinburgh, 1973), Wills, Virginia (ed.)

Statistics of the Annexed Estates, (H.M.S.O., Edinburgh, 1973)

Periodicals Consulted

Advancement of Science
Annals of Science
Caledonian Mercury
Edinburgh Evening Courant
Gentleman's Magazine
Northern Scotland
Scottish Educational Studies
Scottish Geographical Magazine
Scottish Historical Review
Scottish Studies
Scots Magazine
Strathspey and Badenoch Herald, 1971 (articles by Geo. A. Dixon on the founding of Kingussie)

General Works of Reference

Burke's Peerage
Burke's Landed Gentry
Fasti Ecclesiae Scoticanae, ed. Hew Scott (New edition, Edinburgh, 1915–1928)
Dictionary of National Biography

Dictionary of the Older Scottish Tongue
Ordnance Gazetteer of Scotland, ed. Francis Groome (Edinburgh, 1884–85)
Ordnance Gazetteer of Scotland (New edition, Edinburgh, 1901)
Origines Parochiales, ed. Cosmo Innes. Bannatyne Club (Edinburgh, 1851)
Parliamentary History of England (London, 1815)
The Scots Peerage, ed. Sir James Balfour Paul (Edinburgh, 1904–14)
The Scottish National Dictionary
The Statistical Accounts of Scotland (Old, New and Third)

Some Secondary Sources

Adam, R. J. (ed.)	*Sutherland Estate Management, 1802–1816,* (SHS, Edinburgh 1972)
Adams, Ian H.	*Peter May, Land Surveyor, 1749–1793* (SHS, Edinburgh, 1979)
Adams, Ian H.	*The Making of Urban Scotland* (London, 1978)
Argyll, Duke of	*Scotland as it was and as it is* (Edinburgh, 1887)
Barclay, Hugh	*Law of Highways in Scotland* (Edinburgh, 1863)
Beatson, Robert	*General View of the Agriculture of the county of Fife* (Edinburgh, 1794)
Bremner, David	*The Industries of Scotland,* ed. J. Butt and I. L. Donnachie (Newton Abbot, 1969)
Brunton, G. and Haig, D.	*An Historical Account of the Senators of the College of Justice* (London, 1832)
Buchan, Alex. R.	*The Port of Peterhead* (P. Scrogie Limited, Peterhead, 1980)
Butt, J.	*The Industrial Archaeology of Scotland* (Newton Abbot, 1967)
Cameron, A. D.	*The Caledonian Canal* (Lavenham, 1972)
Campbell, R. H.	*Scotland since 1707* (Oxford, 1971)
Cunningham, A.	*The Loyal Clans* (Cambridge, 1932)
Day, J. P.	*Public Administration in the Highlands and Islands of Scotland* (London, 1918)
Dean, I. F. M.	*Scottish Spinning Schools* (London, 1930)
Devine, T. M. (ed.)	*Lairds and Improvement in the Scotland of the Enlightenment* (Proceedings of the Ninth Scottish Historical Conference, 1978)
Duckham, Baron F.	*A History of the Scottish Coal Industry* (Newton Abbot, 1970)
Dunlop, Jean	*The British Fisheries Society, 1786–1893* (Edinburgh, 1978)
Durie, Alexander	*The Scottish Linen Industry in the Eighteenth Century* (Edinburgh, 1979)
Fay, C. R.	*Adam Smith and the Scotland of his Day* (Cambridge, 1956)
Ferguson, William	*Scotland, 1689 to the Present* (Edinburgh and London, 1968)
Fittis, Robert Scott	*Illustrations of the History and Archaeology of Perthshire* (Perth, 1874)
Fraser, A. Campbell	*The Book of Barcaldine* (London, 1936)
Fraser, William	*The Chiefs of Grant* (Edinburgh, 1883)
Fraser, William	*The Earls of Cromartie* (Edinburgh, 1876)
Gibb, Sir Alexander	*The Story of Telford* (London, 1935)
Grant, Elizabeth, of Rothiemurchus	*Memoirs of a Highland Lady,* revised and ed. by Angus Davidson (London, 1950)
Grant, I. F.	*Everyday Life on an Old Highland Farm* (London, 1924)
Gray, J. (ed.)	*Clerk of Penicuik's Memoirs* (SHS, Edinburgh, 1892)

Gray, Malcolm	*The Highland Economy, 1750–1850* (Edinburgh and London, 1957)
Haldane, A. R. B.	*New Ways through the Glens* (London, 1962)
Haldane, A. R. B.	*The Drove Roads of Scotland* (Edinburgh, 1971)
Haldane, A. R. B.	*Three Centuries of Scottish Posts* (Edinburgh, 1971)
Hamilton, Henry	*An Economic History of Scotland in the Eighteenth Century* (Oxford, 1963)
Hamilton, Henry	*The Industrial Revolution in Scotland* (Oxford, 1932)
Hamilton, Henry (ed.)	*Monymusk Papers* (SHS, Edinburgh, 1945)
Henderson, Captain John	*General View of the Agriculture of the County of Sutherland* (London, 1812)
Heron, R.	*General View of the Natural Circumstances of those Isles adjacent to the North West Coast of Scotland which are distinguished by the Common Name of Hebudae or Hebrides* (Edinburgh, 1794)
Hunter, T.	*Woods, Forests and Estates of Perthshire* (Perth, 1883)
Inglis, H. R. G. (ed.)	*The Early Maps of Scotland* (RSGS, Edinburgh, 1936)
Jewell, Byron F.	The Legislation Relating to Scotland after the Forty-Five (University of North Carolina D.Phil. 1975. Facsimile by University Microfilm International, 1978)
Johnson, S. and Boswell, James	*A Tour to the Hebrides,* ed. R. W. Chapman (London, 1944)
Kemp, Daniel William (ed.)	*Tours in Scotland, 1747, 1750, 1764 by Richard Pococke* (SHS, Edinburgh, 1887)
Kermack, W. R.	*The Scottish Highlands* (Edinburgh, 1967)
Knox, John	*A Tour through the Highlands of Scotland and the Hebride Isles in 1786* (London, 1787)
Knox, John	*A View of the British Empire, especially Scotland* (London, 1785)
Lang, A. (ed.)	*The Highlands of Scotland in 1750* (Edinburgh and London, 1898)
Lees, J. C.	*History of the County of Inverness* (Edinburgh and London, 1897)
Lenman, B. P.	*Economic History of Modern Scotland* (London, 1977)
Lenman, B. P.	*From Esk to Tweed (London and Glasgow, 1975)*
Lenman, B. P.	*The Jacobite Risings in Britain, 1689–1746* (London, 1980)
Lindsay, Ian G. and Cosh, Mary	*Inveraray and the Dukes of Argyll* (Edinburgh, 1973)
Lindsay, Jean	*The Canals of Scotland* (Newton Abbot, 1968)
Loch, David	*Essays on the Trade, Commerce, Manufactures and Fisheries of Scotland in Three Volumes* (Edinburgh, 1778)
McArthur, M. M. (ed.)	*Survey of Lochtayside, 1769* (SHS, Edinburgh, 1936)
McGill, William	*Old Ross-shire and Scotland as seen in the Tain and Balnagowan Documents* (Inverness, 1909–1911)
Mackenzie, Sir George Stewart	*General View of the Agriculture of the Counties of Ross and Cromarty* (London, 1813)
Marshall, William	*General View of the Agriculture in the Central Highlands of Scotland* (London, 1794)

Marshall, William   *Historic Scenes in Perthshire* (Edinburgh, 1880)

Mason, John   *A History of Scottish Experiments in Rural Education* (London, 1935)

Mason, John   Schools on the Forfeited Estates (Typescript, SRO)

Maxwell, Gavin   *Harpoon at a Venture* (London, 1964)

Menary, G.   *The Life and Letters of Duncan Forbes of Culloden* (London, 1936)

Millar, A. H. (ed.)   *A Selection of Forfeited Estates Papers, 1715; 1745* (SHS, Edinburgh, 1909)

Mitchell, Sir Arthur (ed.) *Macfarlane's Geographical Collections* (SHS, Edinburgh, 1907)

Mitchison, Rosalind   *Agricultural Sir John* (London, 1962)

Moir, D. G. (ed.)   *Early Maps of Scotland* (RSGS, Edinburgh, 1974)

Munro, Neil   *History of the Royal Bank of Scotland* (Edinburgh, 1928)

Murdoch, Alexander   *'The People Above': Policies and Administration in Mid-Eighteenth Century Scotland* (Edinburgh, 1980)

Nef, J. U.   *The Rise of the British Coal Industry* (London, 1932)

Omond, G. W. T.   *The Lord Advocates of Scotland from the Fifteenth Century to 1832* (Edinburgh, 1883)

Payne, P. (ed.)   *Studies in Scottish Business History* (London, 1967)

Pennant, T.   *A Tour in Scotland in 1769* (Warrington, 1774)

Pennant, T.   *Tour in Scotland and Voyage to the Hebrides, 1772* (London, 1776)

Phillipson, N. T. and Mitchison, Rosalind   *Scotland in the Age of Improvement* (Edinburgh, 1970)

Ramsay, J. of Ochtertyre   *Scotland and Scotsmen in the Eighteenth century*, ed. A. Allardyce (Edinburgh, 1888)

Robertson, James   *General View of the Agriculture in the County of Perth* (Perth, 1799)

Robertson, James   *General View of the Agriculture in the County of Inverness* (London, 1808)

Robertson, James   *General View of the Agriculture in the Southern Districts in the County of Perth* (London, 1794)

Robertson, James   *General View of the Agriculture of Argyll and the Western parts of Inverness-shire* (London, 1794)

Ross, Ian Simpson   *Lord Kames and the Scotland of his Day* (Oxford, 1972)

Salaman, R. N.   *The History and Social Influence of the Potato* (Cambridge, 1949)

Salmond, J. B.   *Wade in Scotland* (London, 1938)

Scott, W. R.   *The Constitution and Finance of English, Scottish and Irish Joint-Stock Companies in 1720* (Cambridge, 1910-1912)

Sinclair, Sir John   *General View of the Agriculture of the Northern Counties and Islands of Scotland* (London, 1798)

Smeaton, John   *Reports of the late Mr. John Smeaton* (London, 1797)

Smiles, Samuel   *Lives of Boulton and Watt* (London, 1965)

Smith, Annette M.   'Annexed Estates in the eighteenth-century Highlands', in *Northern Scotland*, 3, 1

Smith, Annette M.   'State aid to industry – an eighteenth century example', in *Lairds and Improvement in the Scotland of the Enlightenment*, T. M. Devine (ed.) (proceedings of the ninth Scottish History

	Conference, 1978, obtainable from Dr. I. B. Cowan, Dept. of Scottish history, Glasgow University)
Smith, Annette M.	'The administration of the Forfeited Annexed Estates, 1752–1784', in G. W. S. Barrow (ed.) *The Scottish Tradition* (Edinburgh, 1974)
Smith, Annette M.	'Two Highland Inns', in *SHR*, LVI
Smout, T. C.	*A History of the Scottish People, 1560–1830* (London, 1969)
Southey, R.	*Journal of a Tour in Scotland, 1819* (London, 1929)
Symon, J. A.	*Scottish Farming, Past and Present* (Edinburgh and London, 1959)
Tayler, A. and H.	*Jacobites of Aberdeenshire and Banffshire in the Forty-Five* (Aberdeen, 1928)
Tayler, A. and H.	*1745 and After* (London, 1938)
Taylor, Maurice E.	Stone Bridges in Scotland (Neale Bursary, Royal Institute of British Architects, 1947)
Telford, Thomas	*Life written by Himself*, ed. J. Rickman (London, 1838)
Thomson, Derick S. and Grimble, Ian	*The Future of the Highlands* (London, 1968)
Turnock, David	*Patterns of Highland Development* (London, 1970)
Walker, John	*An Economical History of the Hebrides and the Highlands of Scotland* (Edinburgh, 1808)
Warden, A. J.	*The Linen Trade, Ancient and Modern* (London, 1864)
Whyte, Ian	*Agriculture and Society in Seventeenth Century Scotland* (Edinburgh, 1979)
Wight, Andrew	*Present State of Husbandry in Scotland* (Edinburgh, 1778–1784)
Wilson, James	*A Voyage round the Coasts of Scotland and the isles* (Edinburgh, 1842)
Youngson, A. J.	*After the Forty-Five* (Edinburgh, 1973)

Index

DATE DUE

APR 2 7 2000			